GERARD MANLEY HOPKINS
Selected Letters

Edited by
CATHERINE PHILLIPS

CLARENDON PRESS · OXFORD
1990

Oxford University Press, Walton Street, Oxford OX2 6DP
Oxford New York Toronto
Delhi Bombay Calcutta Madras Karachi
Petaling Jaya Singapore Hong Kong Tokyo
Nairobi Dar es Salaam Cape Town
Melbourne Auckland
and associated companies in
Berlin Ibadan

Oxford is a trade mark of Oxford University Press

Published in the United States
by Oxford University Press, New York

British Library Cataloguing in Publication Data
Hopkins, Gerard Manley Hopkins 1844–1889
Gerard Manley Hopkins: selected letters.
1. Poetry in English. Hopkins, Gerard Manley, 1844–1889.
Biographies
I. Title II. Phillips, Catherine
821'.8
ISBN 0-19-818582-0

Library of Congress Cataloging in Publication Data
Hopkins, Gerard Manley, 1844–1889.
[Correspondence. Selections]
Gerard Manley Hopkins : selected letters / edited by Catherine Phillips.
p. cm.
Includes index.
1. Hopkins, Gerard Manley. 1844–1889—Correspondence. 2. Poets, English—19th century—Correspondence. I. Phillips, Catherine.
II. Title.
PR4803.H44Z48 1990
821'.8—dc20
[B] 89-15955
ISBN 0-19-818582-0

Set by CentraCet, Cambridge
Printed and bound in
Great Britain by Biddles Ltd,
Guildford and King's Lynn

CONTENTS

INTRODUCTION

GERARD MANLEY HOPKINS has long been recognized as an excellent letter-writer for the vividness with which he expressed opinions on a wide range of subjects and conveyed the warmth yet rugged honesty of his personality. The letters in this selection are drawn from the three volumes edited by C. C. Abbott with the addition of eight of the letters found subsequently and published in the *Hopkins Research Bulletin.* The selection ranges in date from 1861, when Hopkins was still a boarder at Highgage, to May 1889, a month before his death. The first letter, full of questions about Goethe's *Faust,* was sent to Dr Müncke, who taught German to Gerard's brother Cyril. The questions show his awareness already of issues that were subsequently to become much more personally urgent to him. For example, Hopkins asked Dr Müncke why Mephistopheles should not have tempted Faust to choose earthly rather than eternal life by exposing him to 'the subtle charms of poetry, music, and art . . . the beauties of nature, and the sweets of a fuller knowledge than Faust had been able to obtain'. In his later desire to dedicate his life to God, Hopkins was to experience the potency of such temptations to the full.

Just how attractive he found the arts and the beauties of nature is clear in the letters to his schoolfriends Charles Luxmore and Ernest Coleridge, grandson of the poet. These abound with enthusiastic discussion of classical and contemporary writers and artists and with the friends' own creative projects. Hopkins's artistic sensibility shows itself too in his experiments with handwriting and the decorated salutations in the style of illuminated manuscripts. In these Hopkins, like other members of his family, adapts the sort of drawings 'Swain' made to illustrate articles on the seasons in *Once a Week* so that, for example, in place of the traditional ivy, he imaginatively festoons 'D' with thistles and oakleaves.

The letter to Dr Müncke also casts light on Hopkins's life at Highgate. To Luxmore and much later to Dixon, Hopkins expressed his dislike of school. The part played in this unhappiness by the headmaster, Dr Dyne, has been known for a long time; the letter to Dr Müncke suggests the contribution Hopkins's own personality may have made. He appears to have been far from meek, an intelligent pupil whose respect had to be thoroughly earned. To a teacher he did not admire, the letter suggests he could have given obedience in a way which showed his true opinion.

At Oxford, by contrast, Hopkins described himself to his mother as 'almost too happy', adding, 'I hope you will not consider it unkind to say how happy I am, but in fact there are so many companions of my own age and so much liberty to see and do so much, that it ought not to make you think it unkind' (4th May 1863). Among the friends Hopkins made at Oxford, two feature prominently in later parts of this volume. The first of these was Alexander William Mowbray Baillie, a Scot who had entered Balliol with an exhibition the year before Hopkins. They became close friends, Hopkins describing Baillie as 'my sole congenial thinker on art' (10 July 1863) and valuing him still more for the tactful reticence he defined as gentlemanliness. And Baillie wrote of Hopkins after his death that 'all my intellectual growth and a very large proportion of the happiness of those Oxford days, I owe to his companionship'. Unlike many of Hopkins's university friendships, this one survived subsequent differences in experience and religious belief. In fact, Baillie's letters were probably most important for Hopkins during the final few years of his life, when their shared interest in etymology spurred him to speculate about the influence of Egypt on the Greek language. In the example of these letters chosen here Hopkins explains one reason for his enthusiasm: 'it is a great help to me to have someone interested in something (that will answer my letters), and it supplies some sort of intellectual stimulus. I sadly need that and a general stimulus to being, so dull and yet harassed is my life' (29 Mar. 1886). It was not the first time that Hopkins had made wistful comments to Baillie about his situation.

The second of the Oxford friends, and recipient of the largest number of Hopkins's letters still extant, was Robert Bridges. On Hopkins's death, Bridges' letters were returned to him and, along with much of his other correspondence, probably destroyed.[1] Some of the content of these letters can of course be deduced from Hopkins's responses although this has not always been done as carefully as necessary—Hopkins's speculations as to Bridges's actions or motives are at times as wrong as they are confidently and memorably expressed. Bridges came from a landed family in Kent and had attended Eton. When he entered Oxford he was, like Hopkins, a High Anglican. Both were nominated for the Brotherhood of the Holy Trinity, one of the centres of High Anglicanism in the university at the time, but Hopkins decided against joining. They seem to have been little more than acquaintances until 1866 and much of the later friendship was carried on by letter. Hopkins's Journal shows that on two occasions in 1865 when he spent the evening with Bridges he afterwards had regrets about not working or being gossipy. It seems that Bridges' own outspokenness led Hopkins to speak his mind too openly. The letters suggest that it was Bridges who later called from him the widest range of response and to whom he expressed his moods most freely.

The major event of Hopkins's Oxford days was of course his conversion to the Roman Catholic Church in October 1866. The letters of 28 August–7 November 1866 mention this, showing the wide range of emotion it stirred in him. To Bridges he commented that 'the happiness it has been the means of bringing me I cd. not have conceived' (22 Sept. 1866). To his father Hopkins wrote coldly,

> You are so kind as not to forbid me your house, to which I have no claim, on condition, if I understand, that I promise not to try to convert my brothers and sisters. Before I can promise this I must get permission, wh. I have no doubt will be given. Of course this promise will not apply after they come of age. Whether after my reception you will still speak as you do now I cannot tell (16 Oct. 1866).

It is a pity that the letter to which GMH was responding is not extant. But, whatever may have been in it, one can understand the anguish of his father on receiving this declaration with its almost certainly unfair aspersions, its obvious

[1] The two letters and a card from Bridges to Hopkins that escaped destruction can be read in vol. i of *The Selected Letters of Robert Bridges*, ed. Donald Stanford (1983).

youthfulness and suggestion of an excited state of mind far from the cool rationality in which the taking of momentous decisions seems most safe. And yet, despite his father's fears,[2] there is no evidence that Hopkins ever regretted his conversion.

But this did not stop him from disliking some of the mundane aspects of his life. The pattern of complaint was established even before he joined the Society of Jesus in 1868. From the Oratory in Birmingham, where he taught briefly at the boys' school, Hopkins wrote to Baillie of missing companions with whom he could discuss art and literature, and of finding that teaching left him without energy for creativity. And yet, typically spreading his reserves still more thinly, he told his friend that he had started to learn the violin (12 Feb. 1868). This particular, musical project was soon dropped but Hopkins became increasingly interested in composition. C. C. Abbott suggests that, had he survived the attack of typhoid he contracted in 1889, Hopkins would have given to music rather than poetry whatever spare energy he possessed. (LI, p. xxxiii).

Before entering the Jesuit novitiate in London, Hopkins sent Bridges some corrected copies of his early poems, explaining that others had been destroyed because 'I saw they wd. interfere with my state and vocation' (7 Aug. 1868). Nevertheless, the letter ends with mention of his development of a 'peculiar beat'—later to grow into sprung rhythm—suggesting that with this symbolic destruction he was repressing something that still deeply interested him. He was to find the loss of artistic companionship—that exchange of ideas with people of similar interests—as much of a privation as restricted time and energy for composition. It is poignantly ironic that his expression of the resulting loneliness and frustration should have drawn so many modern minds to his.

Hopkins submitted himself to the ideals and discipline of his order with the complete dedication of which he was capable. So rigorous a submission called for a new state of mind. It even appears in a letter to his mother describing

[2] Manley Hopkins's reply to GMH's letter can be found in LIII, pp. 95–7. His note to Liddon asking him to try to persuade Gerard to change his mind is also worth reading (LIII, pp. 434–5).

Roehampton. In contrast with the parallel descriptions of Oxford in 1863 with their joy of liberty, in this ideas of permission invade in such phrases as '*must* keep our names', 'I *may* remark', 'you *can* of course tell me how you liked them' (10 Sept. 1868), making the tone a bit stiff. But his parents became reconciled to his decisions in what he called a 'kind and contented way' and there are no letters extant suggesting that he continued to try to convert them.

The same, however, was not true of his friends Edward Urquhart and Bridges. Urquhart, although he wavered, remained an Anglican priest and Bridges became an unorthodox Christian. The letter of 13 June 1868 to Urquhart shows clearly the sort of pressure Hopkins was capable of exerting and it seems probable that Bridges was subjected to something similar (and perhaps to criticism of his political views) during his visit to Hopkins in October 1869. The result was eighteen months' silence from Bridges followed by a letter in which he seems to have joked about Hopkins's bad opinion of him, perhaps using the political terms of the Paris Commune that dominated the papers of the day. Hopkins, encountering widespread urban poverty for the first time, expressed in his reply, the 'Red' letter (2 Aug. 1871), his sense of the injustice with which the poor had been treated. In his sympathy, he remarked that he could understand their destroying monuments of a society they had enriched by their labour but which denied them education and profit. Bridges did not reply. But Hopkins's suggestion that this was because of 'a greater keenness about politics than is common' (22 Jan. 1874)—essentially intolerant conservatism—was not entirely fair. Bridges certainly was more conservative and less tolerant than Hopkins but he was also a medical student at a charity hospital doing his level best to ease the physical suffering of the poor. Of this practical aid Hopkins makes no acknowledgement.

The 'Red' letter by itself also does not give a balanced picture of Hopkins's political views. He remained keenly aware of the injustice done to the poor and of their misery but he was not a socialist revolutionary. The letter of 1 December 1881 to Dixon shows more of the constant elements of his position. It lacks the true revolutionary's conviction that change is possible and shows a slight suggestion of the Victorian tendency to idealize a rural and feudal past. It also relates to Hopkins's expression elsewhere of his priestly disgust with Man's sinfulness:

> My Liverpool and Glasgow experience laid upon my mind a conviction, a truly crushing conviction, of the misery of town life to the poor and more than to the poor, of the misery of the poor in general, of the degradation even of our race, of the hollowness of this century's civilisation: it made even life a burden to me to have daily thrust upon me the things I saw.

What revived the correspondence with Bridges was Hopkins's letter of April 1877 in which he criticized Bridges's *Carmen Elegiacum*, a Latin poem about St Bartholomew's Hospital where he worked, and *The Growth of Love*, a collection of twenty-four sonnets. Hopkins's comments are succinct, praise and fault-finding dispatched with vigour: 'the italic introductory verses are the smoothest, the last the hardest and worst. I don't know when I remember to have read so much good Latin verse together, still I look upon such a performance as a waste of time and money (a pretty penny it must have cost you printing)' (3 Apr. 1877). Such competent and bluff comment was irresistible to Bridges and letters soon flowed between them filled with reciprocal queries, criticism, and explanations of their poems.

In 1878 Hopkins began a second correspondence that was to be an outlet for his interest in literature and the writing of poetry. This was with Richard Watson Dixon, who had been friendly with Morris, Rossetti, and Burne-Jones at Oxford and had subsequently taught Hopkins briefly at Highgate. When Hopkins wrote to him, Dixon was curate at Hayton, Carlisle. Noting the neglect of Dixon's verse, which he had long admired, Hopkins sent him in charitable compensation a letter full of praise. Its sensitive, kindly tone was to prevail throughout the correspondence because Dixon was himself kindly and modest and Hopkins was especially careful of his feelings. Since Hopkins and Dixon respected each other's religious commitment, none of the defensiveness nor irritation over 'untenable' positions entered here as it did at times in the correspondence with Bridges. Conversely, the letters to Dixon reveal rather less of Hopkins's personality.

A lot of the letters in which Hopkins expressed opinions of literature have been included in this selection because his pithy remarks frequently isolate aspects that are worth consideration; examples include his criticism of the prose style of Newman and Patmore for being too conversational (20 Oct. 1887) and a number of striking and surprisingly astute comments on drama (4th Nov. 1882, 17 May 1885). From his basic tenet that writers should always be in earnest springs advice, given to Bridges and Dixon, that they avoid obsolete diction because it prompts a reader to question the writer's sincerity. At other times his opinions are more important for what they reveal about him, as for instance, his 'Victorian' objection that Coventry Patmore's *Angel in the House* does not uphold women's subjugation to their husbands (24 Sept. 1883).

Hopkins was always interested in the writers of his day. Although his life was a short one, his contemporaries included not only such figures of the Victorian age as Carlyle, Browning, and Tennyson but a transitional writer like Thomas Hardy and a Modernist, W. B. Yeats, whom he met in Dublin (see letter of 7 Nov. 1886). Of all these he had acute and sometimes amusing things to say. Although the comments are less frequent Hopkins also retained an interest in contemporary artists such as Frederick Walker and architects such as William Butterfield. A letter, previously published in the *Hopkins Research Bulletin*, thanking Butterfield for sending a partial list of his buildings is included here because it shows that Hopkins's architectural interest was still active as late as 1877.

As well as contemporary art and literature, Hopkins wrote about the politics of the time, especially after he had moved to Dublin in 1884, when it affected his daily life. In addition to the well-known letters to Bridges (17 Feb., 30 July 1887) and Baillie (20 Feb. 1887), this volume includes one written to an Irishman, Dr Michael Cox. To his English friends Hopkins expressed his conviction that Ireland must be granted Home Rule and he urged them to realize that a crisis was imminent. To Dr Cox, on the other hand, Hopkins was scrupulously fair in analysing one of the simmering complaints of the day—that England had deliberately damaged the Irish wool trade. The detailed knowledge in the letter and the concern with which he urges the need for calm and balanced judgements show a far more practical response to the crisis than might otherwise be suspected.

Many of Hopkins's traits are visible or deducible from his poetry: his interest in language, in art and music, his religious fervour and patriotism, his loneliness. For these things the letters provide a fuller context and a more detailed picture of his personality. But the letters also show one characteristic that might not be guessed from the poems: that Hopkins had a sense of humour sparkling with his intelligence and originality. This took many forms from witty comments (12 Oct. 1881, for instance) to puns and 'cod Irish' (9 Dec. 1884) and an almost dead-pan humour (24 Dec. 1875).

It has sometimes been the omission of some example of this liveliness that I have regretted in deciding that more letters simply could not be fitted into this selection. Inevitably some readers accustomed to C. C. Abbott's three excellent volumes will find things missing here. I hope that the sample will prompt others, unacquainted with Hopkins's letters, to explore the fuller collections. The criteria for inclusion in this volume differ from those I used for the Oxford Authors edition where annotation of the poems clearly had to have priority. Since those passages are published with the poems, I have given more space here to letters with biographical or general historical or literary interest. The layout of the letters has been standardized. Hopkins's absent-minded repetition of words has been silently corrected and only occasional changes in wording noted where they suggest the modification or clarification of an idea. His spelling is retained without comment.

I am most grateful to the Society of Jesus for giving me permission to print copyright material and to Thomas, Lord Bridges for generously allowing me to use Hopkins's manuscript letters to Bridges and Dixon. I have also much appreciated the kind assistance of Mr. L. Handley-Derry, and Professor Peter Wiseman, who made time in a busy schedule to help me with the classical translations. I am indebted to St John's College, Oxford for a most pleasant and fruitful Visiting Scholarship, and to the University of Exeter for supporting my research. Warm thanks are also due to the obliging and competent staff who helped me in the Bodleian Library, Oxford, and the University Libraries of Cambridge and Exeter.

Abbreviations

GMH Gerard Manley Hopkins

LI *The Letters of Gerard Manley Hopkins to Robert Bridges*, ed. C. C. Abbott (2nd rev. imp., London, 1955).

LII *The Correspondence of Gerard Manley Hopkins and Richard Watson Dixon*, ed. C. C. Abbott (2nd rev. imp., London, 1955).

LIII *Further Letters of Gerard Manley Hopkins*, ed. C. C. Abbott (2nd edn., rev. and enlarged, London, 1956).

J *The Journals and Papers of Gerard Manley Hopkins*, ed. Humphry House, completed by Graham Storey (2nd edn., London, 1959).

OAH *Gerard Manley Hopkins*, ed. Catherine Phillips, Oxford Authors series (Oxford, 1986).

LIST OF LETTERS

Correspondent

CHRONOLOGY

1844 Born at Stratford, Essex (28 July). Gerard was the first of eight children. His father, Manley Hopkins, was a marine adjuster and ambassador for Hawaii in London.

1854–62 Gerard attends Highgate School. He does well academically, winning five prizes, among them the School Poetry Prize for 'The Escorial' (1860), the Governors' Gold Medal for Latin Verse, and a school exhibition.

1862 Wins an exhibition to Balliol College, Oxford.

1863 Enters Balliol (April).

1866 Decides to join Catholic Church (July). Received by Newman into the Catholic communion (21 October).

1867 Graduates with first-class degree (June). Teaches at the Oratory, Birmingham (September–April 1868).

1868 Decides to become a priest although unsure whether to join the Benedictines or Jesuits (2 May). Burns copies of his poems, indicating his new, vocational goal (11 May). Walking holiday in Switzerland with Edward Bond (3 July–1 August). Enters the Jesuit novitiate at Manresa House, Roehampton (London) (7 September).

1870 Begins three years of philosophy at St Mary's Hall, Stonyhurst, Lancashire (9 September).

1872 Reads the *Oxford Commentary* of Duns Scotus on the *Sentences* of Peter Lombard.

1873 From September teaches rhetoric at Roehampton.

1874 Begins three years of theology at St Beuno's, Wales (August).

1875 Begins to write 'The Wreck of the Deutschland' (December).

1876 Writes 'Silver Jubilee', 'Ad Episcopum', 'Cywydd', 'Penmaen Pool'.

1877 Writes 'God's Grandeur'. 'The Starlight Night', 'As kingfishers catch fire', 'Spring', 'The Sea and the Skylark', 'In the Valley of the Elwy', 'The Windhover', 'Pied Beauty', 'Hurrahing in Harvest', 'The Lantern out of Doors' (February–September). Ordained (23 September). Sent to Mount St Mary's College, Chesterfield, where a classical scholar was required as teacher (October).

1878 Moved to Stonyhurst to prepare students for the University of London examinations. (April). 'The Loss of the Eurydice' and 'The May Magnificat' written here. Acting curate at Mount Street, London (July–November). Becomes curate at St Aloysius's church, Oxford (December).

1879 Writes nine complete poems ('Duns Scotus's Oxford', 'Binsey Poplars', 'Henry Purcell', 'The Candle Indoors', 'The Handsome heart', 'The Bugler's First Communion', 'Andromeda', 'Morning, Midday, and Evening Sacrifice', and 'Peace') and a number of fragments, and begins to compose music (February–October). Curate at St Joseph's, Bedford Leigh, where he writes 'At the Wedding March' (October–December). Becomes Select Preacher at St Francis Xavier's, Liverpool (30 December).

1880 Writes 'Felix Randal' and 'Spring and Fall'.

1881 Becomes assistant in Glasgow. Visits Loch Lomond and there writes 'Inversnaid' (September). Starts tertianship at Roehampton (October); composes no poetry during the year but writes notes towards a commentary on the *Spiritual Exercises*.

1882 Sent to Stonyhurst College to teach classics (September). There he completes 'The Leaden Echo and the Golden Echo' and writes 'Ribblesdale'.

1883 RB begins his second collection of Hopkins's poems (MS *B*). Hopkins writes 'The Blessed Virgin compared to the Air we Breathe'. Meets Coventry Patmore (August).

1884 Moves to Dublin as fellow in Classics and Professor of Greek and Latin Literature at the newly formed University College (February). His duties at first were as examiner in Greek. Writes most of the extant passages of *St Winefred's Well* (October–April 1885).

1885 May well have written most of the poems called 'The Sonnets of Desolation' as well as 'The times are nightfall', 'To what serves Mortal Beauty', 'The Soldier', and 'To his Watch'.

1886 Meets RB while on holiday in England (May). Completes 'Spelt from Sibyl's Leaves', writes 'On the Portrait of Two Beautiful Young People', translates 'Songs from Shakespeare'.

1887 Holiday in England (August). Writes 'Harry Ploughman', 'Tom's Garland', and, perhaps, 'Ashboughs'.

1888 Begins 'Epithalamion', writes 'That Nature is a Heraclitean Fire . . .', 'What shall I do for the land that bred me', and 'St Alphonsus Rodriguez'. Holiday in Scotland (August).

1889 Retreat at Tullabeg (January). Writes 'Thou art indeed just, Lord', 'The shepherd's brow', and 'To R.B.'. Dies of typhoid (8 June); buried at Glasnevin, Dublin.

BIOGRAPHICAL REGISTER OF CORRESPONDENTS AND PERSONS FREQUENTLY CITED

Addis, William (1844–1917). One of Hopkins's closest friends at Oxford, he became a Catholic about a fortnight before GMH. In 1868 he joined the Oratory in London. In 1888, when he renounced Catholicism, married, and moved to Australia, GMH was much upset (see letter of 19 Oct. 1888). Addis returned to England and the Anglican Church in 1901, later becoming vicar of All Saints, Ennismore Gardens, in 1910.

Baillie, Alexander William Mowbray (1843–1921). Born in Edinburgh, where he attended Edinburgh Academy before winning a scholarship to Balliol College, Oxford. There he was one of Hopkins's closest friends. After obtaining a 1st, Baillie studied law and was called to the Bar. In the 1870s he suffered a severe lung haemorrhage and was advised to spend the winter in Egypt. He recovered and, after spending the following winter in Algeria and Greece, had no further trouble. He never married but lived in London with his mother and aunt. His wide knowledge of languages led to correspondence with Hopkins over the influence of Egypt on Greek etymology, an intellectual exchange that Hopkins greatly appreciated during his final years in Dublin.

Beechey, Katherine Hannah. Aunt Katie. Eldest daughter of Rear-admiral F. W. Beechey. She married the Revd Thomas Marsland Hopkins, Manley's youngest brother, and lived near Paddington Station. Later, after she was widowed, she moved with her three children to Oxford, where GMH visited them while he was attached to St Aloysius'.

Bond, Edward (1844–1920). Eldest son of Edward Bond who owned a furnishing business. Between 1854 and 1862 the family lived near Manley Hopkins at Hampstead and became friendly. Edward attended Merchant Taylors' School and St John's College, Oxford, obtaining a 1st in Greats in 1866. He accompanied GMH on a walking tour in the Swiss Alps in 1868. After teaching briefly at Radley he became a barrister and, spending most of the rest of his life at Hampstead, was active in the running of local charities and schools. He also participated in politics, representing Hampstead on the London County Council 1895–1901 and East Nottinghamshire in Parliament 1895–1905.

Bridges, Robert (1844–1930). Born in Kent and attended Eton and Corpus Christi, obtaining a 2nd in Greats in 1867. He then travelled in the Middle East with Lionel Muirhead and spent eight months in Dresden learning German before enrolling as a medical student at the charity hospital, St Bartholomew's, in London. Bridges's interest in medicine was in part the result of his having lost his father and two closest brothers to disease. However, medical knowledge was expanding rapidly and Bridges found that his memory was ill-adapted to its exacting requirements, although he was conscientious and made himself a good doctor. He fell seriously ill with pneumonia in 1881 and retired from medicine the following year. In 1884 he married Mary Monica Waterhouse, elder daughter of the architect, who shared his interest in music and calligraphy. The couple had three children. Bridges was devoted to his family and was frequently worried by their ill-health. He worked hard at a variety of literary, musical, and artistic projects, among them the editing of the poetry of Dixon, Dolben, and Hopkins. He was made Poet Laureate in 1913 and awarded the Order of Merit in 1929.

Challis, William Henry (1841–98). Read Maths at Oxford and was amongst the best of the finalists in 1863. He belonged to the Brotherhood of the Holy Trinity and seceded to Rome in July 1866. After teaching at the Oratory for a short time, he went to London and became joint editor of the *Westminister Review*. He left the Catholic Church in 1872 and became a barrister, writing a substantial part of the important *Law of Real Property* (1885).

Clarke, Marcus Andrew Hislop (1846–81). Son of a barrister. His mother died when he was young and his father when he was 17. At Highgate he was friendly with both GMH and Cyril and corresponded with the latter after emigrating to Australia. There he held a variety of jobs and wrote numerous sketches, stories, and three novels largely about Australia but frequently including characters modelled on Cyril and Gerard. He fell into debt and became terminally ill when he was only 35.

Coleridge, Ernest Hartley (1846–1920). Grandson of Samuel Taylor Coleridge and a close friend of GMH's at Highgate and Balliol, although they seem to have had little contact after this. He made a living as a private tutor 1872–93, then as private secretary to his cousin, the Lord Chief Justice. After that he devoted himself to editing his grandfather's works and those of Byron. He also published a volume of his own poetry.

Dixon, Richard Watson (1833–1900). Canon. He was a contemporary at Oxford of Burne-Jones and William Morris and later became vicar of Hayton (Humberside) and then of Warkworth (Northumberland). He published several volumes of poetry and a chronicle history of the Church of England in six volumes.

DOLBEN, DIGBY MACKWORTH (1848–67). Distant cousin of Robert Bridges, who knew him well at Eton. When Dolben later visited Bridges at Oxford he introduced him to GMH, who soon discovered their common interest in writing poetry and in religion. In March 1867 Dolben decided to become a Roman Catholic but, at his family's request, agreed to defer his reception. In May, he fainted while taking the Oxford entrance exam (his health was frail), thereby failing it. He returned to his private tutor's home but drowned in a swimming accident shortly afterwards. GMH was undoubtedly attracted to him but they do not appear to have met after Dolben's visit to Bridges and they exchanged few letters. In 1911 Bridges published a selection of his poems accompanied by an affectionate memoir.

GARRETT, ALFRED WILLIAM (1844–1929). Grew up in Tasmania. He was a member of Balliol 1863–7 and belonged to the Brotherhood of the Holy Trinity. GMH thought his own conversion influenced Garrett, who joined the Roman Church in October 1866. He served in the Indian Education Service 1868–84 before returning to Tasmania, where he entered the Education Department. Although their correspondence was infrequent, GMH and Garrett were still in touch in 1882.

GELDART, MARTIN (1844–85). A contemporary and friend of GMH's at Balliol. After teaching briefly at his old school, Manchester Grammar, illness caused him to move to Athens, where he married a German, Charlotte Andler. He was ordained in the Church of England and became a curate in Manchester (1869), then Liverpool, where he joined the Unitarian Church. In 1877 he moved to Croydon, where he was a minister in the Free Christian Church until early in 1885, when he was forced to resign because of his socialist opinions. He disappeared on the night-crossing to Dieppe a few months later. GMH thought it was suicide. See letter of 24 Apr. 1885 for his comments on this and on Geldart's autobiography, *A Son of Belial* (1882).

GURNEY, FREDERICK (1841–98). As an undergraduate GMH was friendly with Frederick and his brother Alfred. Frederick was a member of Balliol 1860–4 and belonged to both Hexameron and the Brotherhood of the Holy Trinity, for which he nominated GMH. He was ordained in 1865 and very happily but briefly married. His wife died in 1868 at the age of 24 (see LIII, p. 50). GMH visited the couple at Torquay in 1865 and 1867. After being curate at Bovey Tracey (1868–75), Gurney became vicar at Plymouth, then Prestbury (Glos.) 1884–90.

HARDY, the Hon. ALFRED ERSKINE GATHORNE- (1845–1918). Third son of the first Earl of Cranbrook. He attended Eton and Balliol, where he belonged to the High Church group. He spent part of August 1864 on a reading party in Wales with GMH and Edward Bond. He later became a barrister and MP.

HOPKINS, ANN (née MANLEY) (1785–1875) Grandmamma. GMH's paternal grandmother came from an old Devonshire farming family. She married Martin Edward Hopkins in 1814 and was widowed in 1836. Manley provided a home for her when he married in 1843 and she later moved to London, living with her daughter Ann.

HOPKINS, ANN ELEANOR (1815–87). Aunt Annie. She was the only sister of Manley Hopkins and lived with his family except from 1856 to 1875, when she lived with her mother.

HOPKINS, ARTHUR (1847–1930). Attended Lancing and then joined his father's firm before winning a gold medal at the Royal Academy. He then studied at the Academy and Heatherley's and became a professional artist, supporting himself largely through doing illustrations for journals. He was influenced by Du Maurier, Frederick Walker, and Millais.

HOPKINS, CYRIL (1846–1932). Like GMH he attended Highgate. He then joined their father's firm, in which he eventually became a partner. He married Harriet Isabella Bockett in 1872 but they had no children.

HOPKINS, EVERARD (1860–1928). Attended Charterhouse and the Slade school of Art, where he worked under Legros and held the Slade Scholarship for all three years of his training. He was an illustrator for a number of the journals of the day, including the *Illustrated London News* and *Punch*. He also regularly exhibited paintings in water-colour and pastel.

HOPKINS, GRACE (1857–1945). Hopkin's youngest sister, who was musical and set accompaniments to GMH's tunes for Bridges' and Dixon's poems. She was engaged in 1882 but, after the death of her fiancé, never married.

HOPKINS, KATE, sen. (1821–1920). Mamma. She was the eldest of the eight children of Dr John Simm Smith. Fond of music and literature, she encouraged the creativity of her children. She was also a devout Anglican.

HOPKINS, KATE, jun. (1856–1933). GMH's second sister. She had a keen sense of humour and a gift for drawing. She remained unmarried and, after her mother's death, lived on at the family home with her brother Lionel and sister Grace.

HOPKINS, LIONEL CHARLES (1854–1952). GMH's youngest brother went to Winchester where his talent for languages became clear. In 1874 he joined the British Consular Service in China as student Interpreter and eventually became Consul-General in Tientsin in 1901. His numerous articles on ancient Chinese language won him an international reputation. Although he was deeply attached to GMH, he was unsympathetic to his religious views and in time became an agnostic. Lionel was seldom able to visit England and the brothers, despite regretting the fact, met and corresponded only infrequently.

HOPKINS, MANLEY (1818–97). Papa. He left school before he was 16 and after working in an insurance broker's and an average adjuster's went on to found in 1844 his own firm of average adjusters. He wrote several manuals relating to marine insurance. In 1856 he became Consul-General in London for Hawaii. He was financial adviser to St John's, Hampstead, and taught in its Sunday Schools. He was interested in music and literature and published several volumes of poetry. A novel was rejected for publication.

LIDDON, HENRY PARRY (1829–90). Attended King's College School in London and Christ Church, Oxford; BA 1850; ordained 1853. He joined Pusey and Keble in the latter stages of the Oxford Movement; he was vice-principal of Bishop Wilberforce's Theological College, Cuddesdon, 1854–9, and then vice-principal of St Edmund Hall, Oxford; BD, DD, and DCL 1870; Ireland Professor of Exegesis 1870–82. His Bampton lectures of 1866 were very popular. While Hopkins was at Oxford, he attended both Hexameron, Liddon's Essay Club for undergraduates, and his Sunday evening discussion group. Liddon became canon of St Paul's Cathedral in 1870 and its chancellor in 1886, and attracted large audiences for his sermons, most of which were published, as was his *Life of Pusey* (3 vols.).

LUXMOORE, CHARLES NOBLE (1844–1936). Son of the Revd Henry Luxmoore of Barnstaple, Devon. He attended Highgate 1858–61. He was wealthy and studied art under GMH's brother Arthur, buying a number of his pictures and remaining his close friend. He lived at Torquay with his wife and two sons.

MACFARLANE, WILLIAM ALEXANDER COMYN (1842–1917). Born in Edinburgh, the son of a retired naval surgeon. He was a devout

Presbyterian attracted by the Oxford Movement. During his first year at Balliol he won a classical scholarship to St John's but owing to a breakdown only achieved an *aegrotat* in Greats. He was ordained in 1866 but, inheriting his uncle's estates in 1891, relinquished his orders and retired to Cambridge, where he engaged in agriculture and forestry.

Newman, John Henry (1801–90). BA Trinity College Oxford, 1820; fellow of Oriel College, Oxford, 1822; tutor of Oriel College 1826; vicar of St Mary's, Oxford, 1828. After a disagreement with the provost of Oriel he resigned his tutorship and travelled in the Mediterranean with Hurrell Froude 1832–3. During the trip he wrote most of the *Lyra apostolica*, including 'Lead kindly light'. On returning to England he joined William Palmer, Hurrell Froude, Arthur Philip Percival, and Hugh James Rose to support apostolical succession and the integrity of the Prayer Book. They were soon joined by Edward Pusey. Newman started giving popular four o'clock sermons at St Mary's and issuing Tracts for the Times, both important contributions to what became known as the Oxford Movement. However, in 1839 he began to wonder whether in breaking away from the Church of Rome the Church of England had left the true church. In 1841 his Tract XC pointed out the similarities between the Thirty-nine Articles basic to Anglicanism and Roman Catholic doctrine. The Tract caused a storm of controversy and Newman withdrew to Littlemore, near Oxford, to spend the next four years in seclusion and meditation. In 1843 he formally retracted his published criticisms of Roman Catholicism and in 1845 he joined that church. He was ordained priest in Rome in October 1846. When he returned to England the following year he established the Oratory at Birmingham. In 1854 he was made provost of the ill-fated Dublin Catholic University, to a revival of which Hopkins was later appointed Professor of Greek and Latin Literature. Newman returned to Birmingham in 1858 to found the Catholic boys' school attached to the Oratory where Hopkins taught when he left Oxford. Newman's *Apologia pro vita sua*, written to answer a slur on his integrity, won him widespread admiration. He was made cardinal in 1879 and spent most of the rest of his life in Birmingham.

Patmore, Coventry (1823–96). Worked as an assistant in the Printed Books Room of the British Museum and was well known for his volumes of poetry. He became a Catholic in 1864. GMH met him in 1883 and corresponded with him for the rest of his life.

Urquhart, Edward William (1839–1916). Eldest son of Adam Urquhart, advocate and sheriff of Wigton. At Oxford he belonged to the Brotherhood of the Holy Trinity and Hexameron. He obtained a 1st in Law and History in 1861 and for a while was a private tutor at Oxford. He was ordained in 1862, serving as curate in Bristol, Oxford, and then Bovey Tracey, where he married. At much the same time as Hopkins, he wondered about joining the Roman Catholic communion but decided to remain an Anglican, eventually becoming Licensed Preacher at Exeter.

WOOD, ALEXANDER (1845–1912). A Scot, he came from a strict Presbyterian family. GMH's conversion precipitated his own and he was confirmed by Manning with GMH and Addis on 4 November 1866. After living in Rome and America, he married and settled in Sussex (1874), then Hampstead, publishing a number of historical and ecclesiastical pamphlets. He visited GMH at Roehampton in August 1874.

WOOLDRIDGE, HARRY ELLIS (1845–1917). A close friend of Bridges. He was very knowledgeable about Renaissance art and was elected to the Slade Chair of Fine Art at Oxford three times. He was a painter and musician, and wrote the first two volumes of the *Oxford History of Music*. Bridges shared a house with him in London during part of his medical training. Wooldridge sent GMH advice on writing counterpoint and, at Bridges' request, painted Hopkins's portrait from a photograph and description sent by GMH.

To Dr. Müncke°

Elgin House.° May 8th. [1861]

Sir,

I take a great and unwarrantable liberty in thus addressing you, and one which I should be very unwilling to take, were it not that my brother Cyril enjoys the honour of your acquaintance and instruction. I have not had the advantage of reading Faust, the master work of the great Göthe, in the original tongue, but I have been much interested in reviews and translations of parts of that drama which I have seen, particularly in the critical analysis of the whole work by Lewis° in his 'Life and Works of Göthe'. Some difficulties which have suggested themselves to me in the moral of the play have emboldened me to seek for an explanation from one who must be deeply imbued with the thoughts and words of Göthe. The chief difficulty, then, I experience is the following. The contract between Faust and Mephistopheles is signed on the terms that if the philosopher shall ever, under the guidance of his demon-servant, be enabled to say to the passing moment 'Stay: thou art fair', he will through those words have condemned himself to be the slave of Mephistopheles in a future world, supposing, which he scarcely believes, such a world can exist. Why is it then, Sir, that it being so clearly the interest of the demon to supply Faust with all the delights which this life can afford, in order that the latter may pronounce involuntarily the fatal words, how is it, I say, that he nevertheless during the action of the play introduces the philosopher to only one of the pleasures which are able to attract the higher order of intellects? For surely the drunken revels of Auerbach's wine-cellar and the ghastly orgies of the Bloksberg cannot be supposed to be scenes very attractive to Faust. Indeed Mephistopheles exhibits the drinking boors as a specimen of what pleasures can enslave the grosser mind of the vulgar than as anything to entice the admiration of Faust. His real endeavours to fill with delight the senses of the discontented philosopher are visible in his inspiring Faust with the love of Margaret. Besides this, one would have supposed that he would have introduced Faust to the pleasures of power, to the subtle charms of poetry, music, and art, to the beauties of nature, and the sweets of a fuller knowledge than Faust had been able to obtain. Why do we see nothing of this, why is the love of Margaret the only real pleasure tried upon Faust? And lastly what are [we] to infer as the end of the contract, does Mephistopheles overcome the indifference of Faust, and why is a veil drawn over the conclusion? It is not to be expected that without having read the very words of the great Poet and without having deeply considered the design of the Play I should be able to solve Metaphysical difficulties out of my own internal consciousness, but should have sought an explanation from one skilled in the literature of both Deutchland [*sic*] and my own nation. Under the hope that you will not resent this liberty, which arises from a sincere wish to comprehend the great ideas of Göthe, permit me to conclude, Sir, and to subscribe myself.

Yours very respectfully Gerard M. Hopkins.

P.S. I have not written in French, because I should not have been able to express my difficulties in that language, and should have been unwilling to submit my imperfect sentences to the critical eye of Dr Münke.

To Charles Noble Luxmoore

Oak Hill.° Hampstead. N.W. May 7./62.

Dear Luxmoore,—

In the first place many thanks for your long and refreshing letter, for which I am not ungrateful though I may have delayed or rather been unable to answer it. Before proceeding to other matters I must endeavour to dispossess your mind of an extraordinary but firmly-seated idea that I wish to give you the cut which appears to have been smouldering on for a long time, and occasionally breaks out in your letters to Karslake° and to me. If I could shew you the first page of one of your letters to me, written immediately after you left, I think you would see that all your misconceptions are of your own making, this said page being a tissue of curious contradictions. I will not send you 'a long and really untenable defence', as you advise,—I do not need one . . . you ask whether I am 'still cock of the walk at Elgin'. Why no. I am not longer an Elginite—I am a dayboarder. Fancy that of me! But it arose thus. Last quarter while working for the Exhibition I petitioned Dyne° for a private room to work in, representing to him the great disadvantage I was at compared with my rivals and indeed the whole sixth, (for even the Grove-Bankites have their quiet sixth-form room to hold three), in this respect. I alone in fact was forced to work for the exhibition and keep order etc. at once, and in a noisy room. He quite readily and ungrudgingly (though to be sure Mrs Rich pays him for her rooms, and he has no right to do what he likes with them) granted me one of her rooms—the sitting room, but Mrs Chapple exchanged it for the bedroom. Dyne added unasked that I might have a fire every evening; so I was really quiet and comfortable for a little time. So far so good, but shortly afterwards I got nearly expelled, deprived of the testimonial which enables one to try for the ex. and degraded to the bottom of the prefects for the most trifling ludicrous little thing which I cannot relate at present and actually was turned out of the room and had to make 6 apologies to avoid the other punishments being inflicted. Dyne and I had a terrific altercation. I was driven out of patience and cheeked him wildly, and he blazed into me with his riding-whip. However Nesfield° and Mrs C. soon gave me back my room on their own responsibility, repenting, I believe, of their shares in my punishment. Shortly after this Bord's° cards were discovered but happily in that matter I was found irreproachable, but not so in the next case, when like a fool I seized one of the upstairs candles on Sunday night when they had taken ours away too soon and my room was denied me for a week. Nesfield presently offered it me back as a favour, but in such a way that I could not take it. Before, however, it was time for me to resume possession I was in a worse row than ever about absolutely nothing, with the chill off, and an accident. Clarke, my co-victim, was flogged, struck off the confirmation list and fined £1; I was deprived of my room for ever, sent to bed at half past nine till further orders, and ordered to work *only* in the school room, not even in the school library and might not sit on a window sill on the staircase to read. Dyne had repeatedly said he hoped I might not be at the top of the school after the exam., so you may suppose, when he took these last measures, I drew my own conclusions. Next—was late on Sunday; I was exemplary on other days but took Sunday as a 'day of rest' too literally, consequently the fifth time, Dyne having heard, sent me to bed at nine and for the third time this quarter threatened expulsion, deprivation

[*Here the first sheet ends, with no stop at 'deprivation'; what follows fills a separate leaf.*]

The last blow was this. I extract the account from my journal. 'April 13.' (Sunday). * * 'After prayers Alexander Strachey° came up to the bedroom at my request to have a last talk at the end of the quarter. I had found out from Clarke who had walked to Finchley with him the day before that on Clarke making some mention of me as 'your friend Skin', he said, 'He is not my friend'. 'O yes he is' said Clarke, and afterwards asked why he went no walks with me. 'Because he never asks me' said Strachey. Not wishing to compromise Clarke, I first asked him the same question, to which he gave at once the same ungrateful answer. Being thus master of the situation, I told him I had not expected so ungrateful an answer. He knew, I said, the reason; at least he might have appreciated the sacrifice; that he had not spoken except on the most trivial subjects and on some days not even that, that he had taken no notice of me, and that I had been wretched every time I saw or thought of it, was only what I had bargained for, I sowed what I now reaped; but after this sacrifice to be told he did not walk with me because I never asked him was too much. I put a parallel case to him; I told him he might find many friends more liberal than I had been but few indeed who would make the same sacrifice I had; but I could not get him to see it: after I had said all, the others came up to bed. I asked him if he had anything to say. He objected that the others had come up to interrupt it. 'But should you have had anything if they had not?' I asked. 'No, I don't think so' he said with a cool smile, and I left him. Perhaps in my next friendship I may be wiser.' When I got the exhibition my mother thought I might in civility write to him. He did not answer however, and, with the exception of a cold 'How do you do?', we have not spoken this quarter. Yet it is still my misfortune to be fond of and yet despised by him. If ever hereafter you should have any intercourse with him *experto crede* [believe one who knows] and do not believe in his unselfishness, his sincerity, or his gratitude, for he has little of either. Now you know my case.

How is it that Nesfield has so suddenly become a paragon in your eyes? In your old letters you used very different expressions. He seemed very pleased at your message, told me to thank you very gratefully, and said vaguely something about accepting your kind offer when he could. As to the 6th form ever getting up a subscription for him, it is at present the most remote idea from our thoughts in the world, for there has been a great political struggle between us and him, *re* construing aloud etc., and, I am sorry to say, the Dr sided with him and theoretically crushed our old privilege. (Of course we construe still.) . . . How could your Father think I took a day over that candle? It was certainly not more than five minutes. It is very kind of you to offer to draw me a picture, and a most acceptable offer considering how I value the adornment of my room. I will send a copy soon if you can really undertake it, as you ask.

Believe me, dear Luxmoore, | Yours very sincerely

Gerard M. Hopkins.

To Ernest Hartley Coleridge

Sept. 3rd. 1862. Oak Hill, Hampstead.

Dear Poet,

I have deliberated whether to go down to Brompton, call on the Lanes of Thurloe Square,° my cousins, with whom I think you are a little acquainted, and get one of them to do the pictures in the Exhibition with me, or to devote the afternoon to a letter to you. You see the result; not wholly due to friendship but partly to a stupid book which I read at dinner and went on reading after dinner. This extraordinary paper ought to speak for itself, and if so it would suggest that I would write on more usual material but that I am all alone in the house and can get no better. All my family are at Epsom and Croydon and I have been now some time alone. Your letter arrived precisely a week ago (after Wednesday home dinner, of my own ordering) and was read luxuriously in the garden—your letters being always great treats, to be taken deliberately (*vide* Wordsworth on Nutting.) I must then congratulate you on your promotion: if however you had stayed at Sir Rogers° you would have been in the 6th and the Dr's good graces long before now, I beg to say. Is your Sherborne° standard high? And what do you do in the way of classics? Do you ever read Theocritus and Moschus? If not, you *must*; they are lovely: read Theocritus' *Thalusia* and *Hylas* and Moschus' *Elegy for Bion*, and say if there is anything so lovely in the classics. I believe I have said this before but I cannot say it too often. I have been reading in the holidays the *Prometheus Bound*. It is immensely superior to anything else of Æschylus' I have read; indeed what stilted nonsense Greek tragedy usually is. It is really full of splendid poetry; when you read it, read with it Shelley's *Prometheus Unbound* which is as fine or finer, perhaps a little too fantastic though. Of course you know the celebrated phrase ἀνήριθμον γέλασμα° [countless smiles] in it; I have transla-[ted] the soliloquy in which it occurs as well as some beautiful lyric passages of which I give a specimen.°

What was that echo caught anigh me,
That scent from breezes breathing by me,
Sped of gods, or mortal sign,
Or half-human half-divine?
To the world's end, to the last hill
Comes one to gaze upon my ill;
Be this thy quest or other, see
A god enchain'd of Destiny,
Foe of Zeus and foe of all
That wont to throng Zeus' banquet-hall,
Sith I loved and loved too well

The race of man; and hence I fell.
Woe is me, what do I hear?
Fledgèd things do rustle near;
Whispers of the mid-air stirring
With light pulse of pinions skirring,
And all that comes is fraught to me with fear.

With regard to 'the Vision of Sin',° I confess that is very mysterious, not so much so though as your grandfather's poems. I do not profess to understand it entirely but will explain it as well as I can. The vision opens 'when the night was late'; a youth, the hero of the story comes riding to a palace gate; not to seek for too close parallels, we may consider that his riding 'a horse with wings that would have flown, but that his heavy rider kept him down' represents that his naturally sublimer part is clogged by the sensual; the palace is the abode of sin; the day of reckoning is near. The youth, now beautiful, is led in by 'a child of sin', he finds a company in the pleasures of indolent carousal, which presently give way to madder vices, not so hideous under the influence of the music and the coloured fountain as they really are. The youth partakes of them of course to the full. Meanwhile 'an awful rose of dawn' is in the sky, that is the ominous redness of the dreadful morning which must soon break has appeared as a warning, and 'a vapour heavy, hueless, formless cold' is 'floating on for many a month and year' towards the palace; at last it falls and the curled youth has shrivelled into 'a gray and gap-tooth'd man as lean as death', who also seeks for an hour of carousal, but a very different one from that of the youth at the palace-gate. We then perceive the frightful change in him, his self contempt, his bitterness. This vision fades and by 'the mystic mountain-range' we hear voices discussing the end of the hero of the vision: one thinks that the sensual crimes of youth were atoned for by the terrible reaction when sense is worn out and has no more pleasure in it: another says that so far from being atoned for, the crime of sense in youth has changed into the no less hateful crime of malice in age: a third says that he was not wholly bad, 'a little grain of conscience made him sour' who otherwise would have been utterly hard: a fourth asks 'Is there any hope?' but the answer to this is not told us: meanwhile the judgment is at hand . . .

I *have* seen Lord Dundreary.° It is truly admirable. I wish you could have seen it . . .

You ask do I admire *St. Simeon Stylites*.° Admire! Ha! Of course I do. If you have never heard it spoken of, either you have not attended to conversation or else so much the worse for those who don't speak about it. It is indeed magnificent.

I would gladly send you a picture if I could but have not a moment of time to spend on it. Indeed this letter is too long.

To the first then of my last two points. First I have been writing a good many poetical snatches lately. . . .The best thing I have done lately is *Il Mystico*° in imitation of *Il Penseroso*, of which I send you some extracts. It is not finished yet; write back whether you approve.° . . . Which to pure souls alone may be.

etc. etc.

The description at the beginning is founded on Milton's 'The cherub Contemplation'.° . . . I have no time for more. I have been writing numbers of descriptions of sunrises, sunsets, sunlight in the trees, flowers, windy skies etc. etc. I have begun the story of the Corinthian capital; of course you know it; I think we spoke of it before. I have done two thirds of 'Linnington Water, an Idyll', and am planning 'Fause Joan' a ballad in the old style.° All these things are done in scraps of time. Say what you think of what I have sent.

Secondly I must tell you that Clarke writes very good poetry. He and I compare notes and ideas. I think I shewed you his 'Lady of Lynn'. I suppose you do not mind; I told him about your writing and two of your ideas, the 'abyss of green' and 'the indescence of those hues' etc.; also since there was nothing private I read him your last letter. He would like to write to you, but does not know if you would like it. However, dear P., whatever you do, MIND YOU SEND ME SOME POETRY IN YOUR NEXT. Believe me, my very dear friend, Yours

most sincerely Gerard.

Finished on Saturday. What a monstrous letter! . . .

P.S. Do not read this till you have finished the letter. In 'Il Mystico' I had formerly instead of the lines resembling them which I have put in the enclosed copy, 'And when the silent heights were won, Alone in air to face the sun'. Now is that or is it not a plagiarism from Tennyson's *Eagle*,° 'Close to the sun in lonely lands,' (see the poem)? I am in that state that I want an unprejudiced decision.

To Ernest Hartley Coleridge

March 22nd. [1863]

Dear Coleridge,—

I am ashamed of not thanking you before for yr. kind congratulations,° received *per* favour of Mr Frodsham.° I go up to reside on the 10th April I think: I wish you would come up as soon as possible—to C.C.C. or Ch. Ch.° or Balliol—Balliol of course I should like best. The probability is I shall not see you for an age, unless we can manage to meet in the Long° (far from Cyril and other pomps and vanities of this wicked world). As usual I have loads to say and no time to say it. The Patriarch° of the Old Dispensation at Highgate has the insolence to force me to go in for the Easter exam. in which I have of course nothing whatever to gain, but my *prestige* to lose. Palmer,° my future tutor, examines, which makes matters worse.

I have been writing a good deal, in poetry I mean, lately, which things we will put off to a more convenient time. An old *Once a Week* with 'Winter with the Gulf Stream',° signed G. M. H, in it, if you should see, will—I have no time to think how I could finish this sentence. At any rate, if you come across it, read it, as by your affectionate friend, Gerard M. Hopkins.

P.S. My dear fellow, please forgive my not writing my thanks sooner. By the way, I wish you would not talk nonsense about 'Small Beer' etc.

Poor Clarke° is on the voyage out to Australia, his father having met with a paralysis of the brain. G. M. H.

Oak Hill, Hampstead. N.W.

To Kate Hopkins, sen.

April 22, 1863. Ball: Coll.

Dearest Mamma.—

First I must thank Papa for the P.O., which I have not changed yet however. I am afraid though that I shall have to spend a good deal just at first; there are still many things I want. Yesterday I subscribed to the Union,° whence I shall generally send my letters, as more convenient than any other place. And while I am 'in this connection' I may ask you to send me my Highgate School Exhibition Certificates, which you forgot; also a little square thin book, of the Oxford Pocket Classics Edition, in a chocolate-coloured cloth cover, with *Æschines and Demosthenes* or *Æschines et Demosthenes* on the back, to be found in the Little Room bookcase. It happens that this contains two speeches on the same cause, the prosecution and defence; but as I had all Demosthenes' works in three volumes, of course containing this defence, and as Æschines is not often read in comparison with Demosthenes, I did not think it worth while to bring the book up. Of course however directly I come, I find Mr Palmer lecturing on it.

My rooms are, I suppose you know, in the roof, which slopes up to the middle of the cieling. Running up and down between lectures is exhausting. However from four of my six windows I have the best views in Balliol, and my staircase has the best scout in the college, Henry. My rooms are three, bedroom, sitting-room and cellar. I have no scout's hole, and no oak to sport° when necessary. Southby° was horrified at them, whereas Darent Harrison° considers them not very bad for the first term. At night however they are comfortable enough, and though I want to change I like them pretty well. You may only change rooms once, and therefore if I really should find no rooms suitable next term I had better wait up here instead of committing myself irrecoverably. At one end of my landing used to be Cresswell,° but he has just taken a Trinity scholarship and gone, and Nash° the junior exhibitioner has come up (in two senses) today. At the other end, in I believe what is called, from its shape, the Trunk, is Secker,°

who has been endeavouring to persuade me to join the Oxford Rifle Corps.° Finding himself unsuccessful he promised he would send Bethell° and somebody else to try their powers on me but has not done so. Secker is said to dispute for the palm of ugliness with Geldart,° but his is only a fat, grotesque Chinese look, whereas Geldart—but I must describe him. Secker is Blundell scholar—a suggestive name, the Blundell scholarship being something from Tiverton school I believe, and by no means conferring honour with it. Would you believe that that dreadful and ghastly man I used to describe at the scholarshp exam., and whom you never managed to see, is absolutely Geldart? His grey goggle eyes, scared suspicious look as though someone were about to hit him from behind, shuddering gait or shuffle, pinched face, in fact his full haggard hideousness, are even now only breaking on me . . . The other scholar Barrett° looks commonplace, as indeed do most clever men here except Ilbert.° Ilbert lives on the staircase below me; he is the cleverest man in Balliol, that is in the University, or in the University, that is in Balliol, whichever you like. Besides having been one of the Marlborough Balliol scholars, he has taken the Hertford and Ireland. He is also handsome and in fact is an admirable Crichton. Papa has perhaps told you that on Sunday last, as I was going up stairs, he called up to me, asking whether I felt inclined for a walk. Of course I was only too much honoured, and we had a pleasant walk to some heights that overlook Oxford and past Aunt Katie's° Bagley Wood.° On the landing below Ilbert are Palmer and Grandmamma's° friend Owen.° Owen is amusing and talks well; I met him at breakfast at Palmer's last Sunday, but he takes no part in tuition beyond having been last term's Catechetical lecturer here, for he takes his fellowship from Tiverton School. Catechetical questions are on this wise: on Sunday afternoon, instead of a sermon, which I believe is never preached in our chapel—at all events there is no pulpit—after the second lesson, a lecture is delivered, on recondite metaphysical subjects. Questions are then set arising from the lecture, answers to which are shewn up to the Bursar on Tuesday morning. In fact the object is to see if we have been good and attended to the clergyman's sermon. This is the programme of my day—7.15, get up, dress; 8, chapel; 8.30, breakfast; 10, lecture; 11, second ditto; 12, sometimes third ditto; 1–2, buttery open for lunch; afternoon, boating or walking and following your own devices; 5, evening chapel, which I have never yet attended; 5.30, hall; 6, the Union; 7 to bedtime, tea and preparing lectures. On Sunday, University sermon at 10.30, evening chapel at 4.30. Last Sunday I thought evening chapel was at 5 and of course missed; I hope my catechecs., as they are called, may not betray me. . . .On the evening of Sunday I wined with Browne,° a man who went in for the exhibition and was matriculated with me. He is twenty-one and is more a modern than a classical scholar, and speaks several languages. The next evening I wined with Strachan Davidson,° who, if I understand his history, took the Greaves Scholarship or Exhib. when I went in for *the* scholarship, then took the Warner exhib. at the time I succeeded and gave up the Greaves. I like him very much. Yesterday afternoon he and I went boating on the upper river. We took a sailing boat, skulled up and sailed down. We then took canoes. I know nothing so luxuriously delicious as a canoe. It is a long light covered boat, the same shape both ways, with an opening in the middle where you recline, with your feet against one board, your back against a cushion on another. You look, contrary of course to ordinary boats, in the direction in which you are going, and move with a single paddle—a rod with a broad round blade at either end which you dip alternately on either side. The motion is Elysian. Strachan Davidson's canoe being low in the water and the wind being very high and making waves, he shipped much water, till he said that it was more pleasant than safe, and had to get to shore and bale out the water, which had nearly sunk him. I rejoicing in the security of a boat high in the water and given me because large and safe, was meanwhile washed onto the opposite lee shore where I was comfortable but embarrassed, and could not get off for some time. Altogether it was Paradisaical. A canoe in the Cherwel must be the summit of human happiness. On Saturday morning I breakfasted with Palmer, on Sunday Papa and I with Bond, on Tuesday I with Jowett. Jowett is my tutor; when you can get him to talk he is amusing, but when the opposite, it is terribly embar[r]assing. . . .Among the other tutors are Riddell° . . . he lectures on Æschylus and Homer; he and his lectures are much thought of and popular; Woolcomb,° or 'Woolx', a pinch-faced old man, whom everybody likes as much as they yawn over his divinity lectures: and Oily Smith,° the mathematical master, who has given me a paper in Algebra to try my powers. Palmer's lectures in Æschines and Virgil shew a height of scholarship which makes me awestruck. When he lectures, he does not hesitate, as in private, but reads long passages into the most beautiful fluent English. Jowett lectures in Thucydides. Each lecture lasts an hour. Besides preparing these, the catachecs., and mathematics, we have an essay a week, alternately Latin and English, but none this week. When I called on Jowett, he advised me to take great pains with this, as on it would depend my success more than on anything else, (which by the way was not a Highgatian theory), and to be careful to have no debts beyond at latest the end of the term. This afternoon I walked with Addis to Littlemore Church which Newman's mother built, and where was Newman's last sermon before the exodus. It is quite dark when you enter, but the eye soon becomes accustomed to it. Every window is of the richest stained glass; the east end, east window, altar and reredos are exquisite; the decorations being on a small scale, but most elaborate and perfect. It is a pity Margaret St. Church could not have borrowed something from it. I can not go on describing all Oxford, its inhabitants and its neighbourhood, but to be short, everything is delightful, I have met with much attention and am perfectly comfortable. Balliol is the friendliest and snuggest of colleges, our inner quad is delicious and has a grove of fine trees and lawns where bowls are the order of the evening. Sunk below the level of the quad, from which it is separated by a pretty stone parapet, is the Fellows' garden, kept very trim, and abutting on it our graceful chapel, which cost only one fourth as much as Exeter and did *not*, as that did, run us into debt. We have no choir, organ or music of any kind, but then the chapel is beautiful and two of our windows contain the finest old glass in Oxford.

The Bursar is going to receive the money for the valuation of my rooms, and may come immediately for it; so will Papa please write a cheque as before for £19 to the Revd. H. Wall,° Bursar of Balliol, as soon as possible, please. Whatever this is over the amount will be returned to me of course.

About the lamp, I can manage it without the spring; but it was not for want of attention that I broke it, but because, do what I would, I could not get it on in the way I was shewn.

Give my best love to Papa, and believe me, dearest Mamma,

ever your loving son, Gerard M. Hopkins.

In case the words may be indistinct—Revd. H. Wall, Bursar of Balliol, £19

To Kate Hopkins, sen.

Oxford Union Society [4 May 1863]

Dearest Mamma.—

I have not much time but I must write a few lines (The handwriting will shew you I am using Union pens.)

At the present rate it appears likely I shall know all Oxford in six weeks. I have not breakfasted in my own rooms for 10 days I think; (*ten* days: I am afraid you will consider the numerals vulgar.) I have just been wining with Jebb,° Warman's° friend. A few days ago I had a walk with him. This morning I breakfasted with Reiss.° Yesterday I commonized for breakfast with Hardy. Commonizing is drawing your own commons at another man's rooms, and is very pleasant, as it enables you to enjoy a quiet meal with him and at the same time feel independance. Hardy is the son of the M.P. for Leominster, of Hempsstead Hall, Staplehurst, in Kent, one of Lord Derby's government. We are great friends. But to continue. As we were frigh[t]fully late that morning, I had to go to S. Mary's Church for the morning service which, I think you know, takes place *after* the Varsity Sermon. The V.S. is at present the Bampton Lecture, delivered by Hannah, whose son is at this coll.° After the Litany the congregation went partly into the Choir for the Holy Eucharist, partly out of church. I did the latter, and after lunch had a walk with Brown: then back to evening chapel to hear Wall lecture and see Jowett laugh. . . .I shall have to go to a 'perpendicular,' i.e. A 'wall-flower' evening at the Master's this term: opinions differ: some call it intensely stiff, others say every kindness is shewn you. But let us return to our muttons. After lecture and chapel, Hall; after Hall, wine at Gurney's. Gurney, Addis, Hardy, Amcotts,° Jenkyns° and some others, (among them I humbly hope to be enrolled), represent the High Church section at Balliol . . . Then Gurney and several others went to Liddon's lecture (one of a series on the first epistle to the Corinthians) delivered at S. Edmund's Hall. Gurney took me. The lecture, I need scarcely say, was admirable. Liddon, perhaps you do not know, is Pusey's great *protégé* and is immensely thought of. After lecture, tea and coffee, while Liddon goes round chatting. Gurney introduced me, and I shall now go every Sunday evening. Is not that 'exceeding one's most sanguine expectations'? . . .

One thing I want to know what you think about, and that is the Long. It is invariably the time for reading, which is done as you know in the country. Hardy wants me to read with him; that is to say, at the same place, not of course the same books. I have promised to ask whether any such thing can be arranged, but have not of course promised anything farther. You will not suppose from this that you will not see much of me in the Long (which consists of three months) I hope.

This afternoon I have been seeing the cricket match between Exeter and ours; the latter was before, and has shewn itself again, the best eleven in the University, and, what is more, we have great hopes that our boat may do brilliantly. Hopes, but hardly expectations, for one of our men who was also in the Varsity eight has seriously injured himself, and cannot row.

Except for much work and that I can never keep my hands cool, I am almost too happy. This morning Grandmamma's friend Owen called on me. The other day I walked with Hardy to Radley which is a pretty place. I do not mean that these things in particular have any great connexion with my happiness more than others, but they occurred to me to mention at that moment.

My letter has after all extended to three sheets, or an hour and a half and more. I will write to Cyril soon. Best love to everyone. Believe me, dearest Mamma, ever your loving son,

Gerard M. H.

P.S. I hope you will not consider it unkind to say how happy I am, but in fact there are so many companions of my own age and so much liberty to see and do so much, that it ought not to make you think it unkind. G.M.H. . . .

To Alexander William Mowbray Baillie

July 10, 1863.

Dear Baillie,

Yes. You are a Fool.

I can shew it syllogistically, by an Epimenidiculum or paradoxling. For you will allow that he who lies is a fool in the long run, and that he who lies without any object to gain thereby is immediately and directly a fool. Now you are not a fool. But you say you are a fool. Therefore you lie. Syllogistically then.

MAJOR PREMISS.

He who lies without an object to gain is a fool.

MINOR PREMISS.

You have lied without an object to gain.

CONCLUSION.

Therefore you are a fool

Epimenidicularly proved. . . .

We all got through Smalls.° Hardy after the seizure of his *testamur* became light-headed, light-hearted, light-heeled. He, Brown and I proceeded to booze at the Mitre, and I forgot to pay my share, but I believe Hardy meant to feast us, in his delight.

For the first week of the Long I read the Georgics with

Bond, taming him *en passant*, but he takes longer to tame than you. Now I am with all our tribe at Shanklin. In the mornings I read the Histories of Tacitus. I must say they are very hard, and the *cruces* have a hopelessness about them which I do not think I find any where else in the classics. I have Tacitus and Cicero's Philippics to read (enough certainly) alone, for would you believe it? I have no Greek lexicon of any kind here. Shanklin is a delightful place. If you were here you would have soon

—forgot the clouded Forth,°
The gloom that saddens heaven and earth,
The biting East, the misty summer
And grey metropolis of the North,

where I do not envy you. The sea is brilliantly coloured and always calm, bathing delightful, horses and boats to be obtained, walks wild and beautiful, sketches charming, walking tours and excursions, poetic downs, the lovely Chine, fine cliffs, everything (except odious Fashionables.) My brothers and cousin catch us shrimps, prawns and lobsters, and keep aquariums. Ah and I will tell you a Pöpehenic° anecdote. I thought it would look strikingly graceful etc to wear sea-anemones round my forehead. (Mermaids do it, you know. Fragment from an unpublished?°) So I put a large one on in the middle, and it fixed itself correctly. Now one has heard of their stinging, but I had handled them so often unharmed, and who could have imagined a creature stinging with its—base, you call it in sea-anemones? But it did, loudly, and when the pain had ceased a mark remained, which is now a large red scar.

About Millais' Eve of S. Agnes, you ought to have known me well enough to be sure I should like it. Of course I do intensely—not wholly perhaps as Keats' Madeline but as the conception of her by a genius. I think over this picture, which I could only unhappily see once, and it, or the memory of it, grows upon me. Those three pictures by Millais° in this year's Academy have opened my eyes. I see that he is the greatest English painter, one of the greatest of the world. Eddis,° the painter, said to me that he thought some of its best men—he instanced Millais—were leaving the school. Very unfairly, as you will see. If Millais drops his mannerisms and becomes only so far prominent from others' styles as high excellence stands out from mediocrity, then how unfair to say he is leaving his school, when that school, represented in the greatest perfection by him, passing through stage after stage, is at last arriving at Nature's self, which is of no school—inasmuch as different schools represent Nature in their own more or less truthful different ways, Nature meanwhile having only one way. . . .

I am sketching (in pencil chiefly) a good deal. I venture to hope you will approve of some of the sketches in a Ruskinese point of view:—if you do not, who will, my sole congenial thinker on art? There are the most deliciously graceful Giottesque ashes (should one say *ashs*?) here—I do not mean Giottesque though, Peruginesque, Fra-Angelical(!), in Raphael's earlier manner. I think I have told you that I have particular periods of admiration for particular things in Nature; for a certain time I am astonished at the beauty of a tree, shape, effect etc, then when the passion, so to speak, has subsided, it is consigned to my treasury of explored beauty, and acknowledged with admiration and interest ever after, while something new takes its place in my enthusiasm. The present fury is the ash, and perhaps barley and two shapes of growth in leaves and one in tree boughs and also a conformation of fine-weather cloud. You remember the sketch that you would not criticize: I had continued it to my satisfaction, when an insane fury induced me to ravage it—

None, I think but an idiot could,—with a sky. It is now spoilt.

I will write again, and so please do you. | Believe me, dear Baillie, yours very sincerely, Gerard M. Hopkins.

Manor Farm, Shanklin, Isle of Wight. July 13.

I think I could save my life by swimming on the river now. . . .

To Ernest Hartley Coleridge

[Incomplete letter]

Oxford Union Society. [1 June 1864]

that young thing.

But to turn from that. I hope you will come up soon, for one reason because you do not appear to me very Catholic, and I think you could no longer be in that state of mind when you are come to the head and fount of Catholicism° in England and the heart of our Church. Beware of doing what I once thought I could do, *adopt an enlightened Christianity*, I may say, horrible as it is, *be a credit to religion*. This fatal state of mind leads to infidelity, if consistently and logically developed. The great aid to belief and object of belief is the doctrine of the Real Presence in the Blessed Sacrament of the Altar. Religion without that is sombre, dangerous, illogical, with that it is—not to speak of its grand consistency and certainty—*loveable*. Hold that and you will gain all Catholic truth.

Yours affectionately, Gerard M. Hopkins.

June 1, 1864.

To Alexander William Mowbray Baillie

{ July 20. 1864.
{ August 14.

Dear Baillie,—

I write solely, understand me, solely, because I know you are feeling in your bones that I shall not write. I have no time to write, I shall now lose my second, but let that pass; I will prove there is no truth in osteomancy if I die for it. . . . I am going to Wales, Maentwrog, Merionethshire, on the 1st of August I think, not the Lakes. If you hear nothing to the contrary direct to Miss Roberts, Pen-y-lan, Maentwrog, Merionethshire, North Wales, after that day. I am adscribed third into Alfred Erskine° and Bond . . .

I went yesterday to the Junior Water Colours and the British Institution (Old Masters.) The latter were charming. I had a silent gush before a Gainsborough; *ἀπ᾽ ὀμμάτων ἔσταξα πηγὰς* [from my eyes poured welling tears] of admiration. There was a portrait of a handsome young gentleman by Leonardo (it is most knowing of all to write it Lionardo), a Baptism of Our Lord by Luini, exquisite grace refined almost into effeminacy. There were numbers of Gainsboroughs, Sir Joshuas and Romneys. Romney is like them. Five Velasquezes, a Murillo, a Zurbaran, many Canalettos, which I have now unbared; you cannot deceive yourself when you see 'the Rotunda, Ranelagh' or Westminster Bridge whatever you may do in Venetian pictures. But I have *invented* a Canaletto with genius. His name is Guardi. If you see any of his things do not pass them by. The colouring is no warmer than Canaletto's, but the difference is vasty. There were also Carlo Dolces, a Sasso Ferrato, Correggios, Rembrandt's Mill, Vandycks, Wouvermans, Tenierses, Hobbimas, a charming Cuyp, Holbeins, and a fine early landscape painter we have, Crome of Norwich. There was a landscape by Sir Joshua Reynolds, curiously. Also Sir Thomas Lawrences, Sir Peter Lelys, and Sir A. W. Calcotts.

Nothing that I could see at the Junior Water Colours worth seeing, excepting Jopling's 'Fluffy' and a view in the East by Telbin which is the most intense effect of colour I ever saw in water colours. But I must not bore you with pictures.

I went to call on Mrs. Cunliffe;° she was not in, but sent me a note asking me to lunch with them next day. I went, and was introduced to Miss Lyall and her future husband, Bradley Alford, brother of the Dean of Canterbury. She is said to have every accomplishment, except singing and drawing, that civilization has yet devised for several and separate ladies. To be brief, she is a fair monster. She can repeat a whole canto of Dante which she has read once through the day before.

Her eyes and stockings are of heavenly blue,
Brown are her tresses and her studies too . . .

From the top of this page has been written at

Pen-y-lan, Maen-twrog Merionethshire, where I arrived

last Monday, August 1st. I have had adventures. I was lost in storms of rain on the mountains between Bala and Ffestiniog. It really happened what is related in novels and allegories, 'the dry beds of the morning were now turned into the channels of swollen torrents', etc. At last a river ran across the road and cut me off entirely. I took refuge in a shepherd's hut and slept amongst the Corinthians. They, I mean the shepherd and family, gorged me with eggs and bacon and oaten cake and curds and whey. Thus I did what old gentlemen tell you with a sort of selfish satisfaction that you must learn to do,

ROUGHED IT;

I believe it means irritating the skin on sharp-textured blankets. These old gentlemen have always had to do it when they were your age.

Your P. F. has a hard time of it to resist contamination from the bawdy jokes and allusions of Bond and Hardy.

We have four Miss Storys° staying in the house, girls from Reading. This is a great advantage—but not to reading.

I have been reading Sophocles with Herrmann's [Hermann] notes which are laborious beyond everything, but a great clue to scholarship I find. I am in misery about my first.

I have written a lot of my *Pilate*° I am thinking of a *Judas*,° but such a subject is beyond me at present. I have added several stanzas to *Floris in Italy*° but it gets on very slowly. I have nearly finished an answer to Miss Rossetti's *Convent Threshold*, to be called *A voice from the world*,° or something like that, with which I am at present in the fatal condition of satisfaction. I have written three religious poems° which however you would not at all enter into, they being of a very Catholic character. Also *The Lover's Stars*° (a trifle in something like Coventry Patmore's style), and a thing which I hope you will like, a soliloquy of one of the spies left in the wilderness,° and the beginning of a story to be called *Richard*,° and some other fragments. So, though I finish nothing, I am not idle. I am thinking, on account of the nobility of the subject,° of writing for the Latin Verse after Mods,° but not of course wth a view to success. It came to pass very happily for me that I shewed several things to Bond; used though I am to conceal what I write except from you, for what he said, though he gave no especial praise, was of such a kind that I have had great confidence since, such as I never felt at all before. I hope, dear Baillie, you will not think me too egotistical in speaking thus at length and thus freely about myself and my hopes. I have now a more rational hope than before of doing something—in poetry and painting. About the first I have said all there is to say in a letter; about the latter I have no more room to speak, but when next I see you I have great things to tell. I have been introduced to Miss and Miss Christina Rossetti.° I met them and Holman Hunt and George Macdonald° and Peter Cun[n]ingham° and Jenny Lind at the Gurneys'.

Hardy wishes you would look sharp and answer his letter, and sends his love.

Believe me, my dear friend, yours affectionately,

Gerard M. Hopkins.

P.S. 'Nothing so true as what you once let fall',° life is a preparation for Mods. Bond sends his love.

To Alexander William Mowbray Baillie

Sept. 10. 1864.

Dear Baillie,—

Your letter has been sent to me from Hampstead. It has just come, and I do a rare thing with me, begin at once on an answer. I have just finished *The Philippics* of Cicero and an hour remains before bedtime; no one except Wharton would begin a new book at that time of night, so I was reading *Henry IV*, when your letter was brought in—a great enjoyment.

The letter-writer on principle does not make his letter only an *answer*; it is a work embodying perhaps answers to questions put by his correspondent but that is not its main motive. Therefore it is as a rule not well to write with a received letter fresh on you. I suppose the right way is to let it sink into you, and reply after a day or two. I do not know why I have said all this.

Do you know, a horrible thing has happened to me. I have begun to *doubt* Tennyson. (Baillejus ap. Hopk.) It is a great *argumentum*, a great clue, that our minds jump together even if it be a leap into the dark. I cannot tell you how amused and I must say pleased and comforted by this coincidence I am. A little explanation first. You know I do not mistrust my judgment as soon as you do; I say it to the praise of your modesty. Therefore I do not think myself 'getting into my dotage' for that, and I will shew why. I think (I am assuming a great deal in saying this I fear) I may shew, judging from my own mind, how far we are both of us right in this, and on what, if I may use the word, more *enlightened* ground we may set our admiration of Tennyson. I have been thinking about this on and off since I read *Enoch Arden*° and the other new poems, so that my judgment is more digested than if the ideas had only struck me while answering you. I was shaken too you know by Addis, which makes a good deal of difference.

I am meditating an essay, perhaps for the *Hexameron*,° on some points of poetical criticism, and it is with reference to this a little that I have composed my thoughts on Tennyson. I think then the language of verse may be divided into three kinds. The first and highest is poetry proper, the language of inspiration. The word inspiration need cause no difficulty. I mean by it a mood of great, abnormal in fact, mental acuteness, either energetic or receptive, according as the thoughts which arise in it seem generated by a stress and action of the brain, or to strike into it unasked. This mood arises from various causes, physical generally, as good health or state of the air or, prosaic as it is, length of time after a meal. But I need not go into this; all that it is needful to mark is, that the poetry of inspiration can only be written in this mood of mind, even if it only last a minute, by poets themselves. Everybody of course has like moods, but not being poets what they then produce is not poetry. The second kind I call *Parnassian*. It can only be spoken by poets, but it is not in the highest sense poetry. It does not require the mood of mind in which the poetry of inspiration is written. It is spoken *on and from the level* of a poet's mind, not, as in the other case, when the inspiration which is the gift of genius, raises him above himself. For I think it is the case with genius that it is not when quiescent so very much above mediocrity as the difference between the two might lead us to think, but that it has the power and privilege of rising from that level to a height utterly far from mediocrity: in other words that its greatness is *that it can be* so great. You will understand. *Parnassian* then is that language which genius speaks as fitted to its exaltation, and place among other genius, but does not sing (I have been betrayed into the whole hog of a metaphor) in its flights. Great men, poets I mean, have each their own dialect as it were of Parnassian, formed generally as they go on writing, and at last,—this is the point to be marked,—they can see things in this Parnassian way and describe them in this Parnassian tongue, without further effort of inspiration. In a poet's particular kind of Parnassian lies most of his style, of his manner, of his mannerism if you like. But I must not go farther without giving you instances of Parnassian. I shall take one from Tennyson, and from *Enoch Arden*, from a passage much quoted already and which will be no doubt often quoted, the description of Enoch's tropical island.

The mountain wooded to the peak, the lawns
And winding glades high up like ways to Heaven,
The slender coco's drooping crown of plumes,
The lightning flash of insect and of bird,
The lustre of the long convolvuluses
That coil'd around the stately stems, and ran
Ev'n to the limit of the land, the glows
And glories of the broad belt of the world,
All these he saw. [ll. 572–80]

Now it is a mark of Parnassian that one could conceive oneself writing it if one were the poet. Do not say that *if* you were Shakespear you can imagine yourself writing Hamlet, because that is just what I think you can*not* conceive. In a fine piece of inspiration every beauty takes you as it were by surprise, not of course that you did not think the writer could be so great, for that is not it,—indeed I think it is a mistake to speak of people admiring Shakespear more and more as they live, for when the judgment is ripe and you have read a good deal of any writer including his best things, and carefully, then, I think, however high the place you give him, that you must have rated him equally with his merits however great they be; so that all after admiration cannot increase but keep alive this estimate, make his greatness stare into your eyes and din it into your ears, as it were, but not make it greater,—but to go on with the broken sentence, every fresh beauty could not in any way be predicted or accounted for by what one has already read. But in Parnassian pieces you feel that if you were the poet you could have gone on as he has done, you see yourself doing it, only with the difference that if you actually try you find you cannot write his Parnassian. Well now to turn to the piece above. The glades being 'like ways to Heaven' is, I think, a new thought, it is an inspiration. Not so the next line, that is pure Parnassian. If you examine it the words are choice and the description is beautful and unexceptionable, but it does not *touch* you. The next is more Parnassian still. In the next lines I think the picture of the convolvuluses does touch; but only the picture: the words are Parnassian. It is a very good instance, for the lines are undoubtedly beautiful, but yet I could scarcely point anywhere to anything more idiomatically Parnassian, to anything which I more clearly see myself writing *qua* Tennyson, than the words

The glows
And glories of the broad belt of the world.

What Parnassian is you will now understand, but I must make some more remarks on it. I believe that when a poet palls on us it is because of his Parnassian. We seem to have found out his secret. Now in fact we have not found out more than this, that when he is not inspired and in his flights, his poetry does run in an intelligibly laid down path. Well, it is notorious that Shakespear does not pall, and this is because he uses, I believe, so little Parnassian. He does use some, but little. Now judging from my own experience I should say no author palls so much as Wordsworth; this is because he writes such an 'intolerable deal of' Parnassian.

If with a critical eye and in a critical appreciative mood you read a poem by an unknown author or an anonymous poem by a known, but not at once recognizable, author, and he is a real poet, then you will pronounce him so at once, and the poem will seem truly inspired, though afterwards, when you know the author, you will be able to distinguish his inspirations from his Parnassian, and will perhaps think the very piece which struck you so much at first mere Parnassian. You know well how deadened, as it were, the critical faculties become at times, when all good poëtry alike loses its clear ring and its charm; while in other moods they are so enlivened that things that have long lost their freshness strike you with their original definiteness and piquant beauty.

I think one had got into the way of thinking, or had not got out of the way of thinking, that Tennyson was always new, *touching*, beyond other poets, not pressed with human ailments, never using Parnassian. So at least I used to think. Now one sees he uses Parnassian; he is, one must see it, what we used to call Tennysonian. But the discovery of this must not make too much difference. When puzzled by one's doubts it is well to turn to a passage like this. Surely your maturest judgment will never be fooled out of saying that this is divine, terribly beautiful—the stanza of *In Memoriam*° beginning with the quatrain

O Hesper o'er the buried sun,
And ready thou to die with him,
Thou watchest all things ever dim
And dimmer, and a glory done.

[st. CXXI]

I quote from memory. Inconsequent conclusion: Shakespear is and must be utterly the greatest of poets.

Just to end what I was saying about poetry. There is a higher sort of Parnassian which I call *Castalian*, or it may be thought the lowest kind of inspiration. Beautiful poems may be written wholly in it. Its peculiarity is that though you can hardly conceive yourself having written in it, if in the poet's place, yet it is too characteristic of the poet, too so-and-so-all-over-ish, to be quite inspiration. E.g.

Yet despair
Touches me not, though pensive as a bird
Whose vernal coverts winter hath laid bare.

This is from Wordsworth,° beautiful, but rather too essentially Wordsworthian, too persistently his way of looking at things. The third kind is merely the language of verse as distinct from that of prose, Delphic, the tongue of the Sacred *Plain*, I may call it, used in common by poet and poetaster. Poetry when spoken is spoken in it, but to speak it is not necessarily to speak poetry. I may add there is also *Olympian*. This is the language of strange masculine genius which suddenly, as it were, forces its way into the domain of poetry, without naturally having a right there. Milman's poetry is of this kind I think, and Rossetti's *Blessèd Damozel*. But unusual poetry has a tendency to seem so at first.

There is much in what you say about moderate men. With regard to Stanley° I have always been sorry for the cry, almost the scream, against him from Catholics. He is a man who *means well* or he is nothing, emphatically he means well. It is however I think easy to see why the kind of moderation visible in him is unsuccessful and distasteful. As to Macaulay it is not because he is a moderate man and an enemy that Addis etc dislike him more than an extreme enemy like Carlyle, but from individual qualities of his; an irritating assumption e.g. that Catholicism or Christianity or whatever it may be is now at last agreed on by thinking men to be an old woman's fable, which is far worse than to be bellowed at in the fiercest way. Now I hate one sort of extreme men as much to the full as you do. I assure you it fills me with humiliation, almost with despair, to see the excesses of such men as are represented by *The Church Times*, for unfortunately the letters in that paper shew that its conductors have their likes and peers. I say to you what I would not say to all heterodox, its pettiness, irreverance, vulgarity, injustice, ignorance, cant, may well make one suspect one's party. And when I think this, more and more I reverence the balance, the heartiness, the sincerity, the *greatness*, of Addis and men like him wherever they are. I assure you Dr. Newman, the extremest of the extreme, so extreme that he went beyond the extremes of that standard and took a large faction of his side with him, is a MODERATE MAN. So is Dr. Pusey, nay, you think he is, I am sure, yourself.

Read if you can a paper on *The ethics of friendship*° in the September *Cornhill*. It is good and worth reading. Do you read *The Mutual Friend*? The reviews will most likely be unkindly severe on it. Dickens' literary history is melancholy to me, yet to take that view of him which is taken or will be by some people is not just or balanced. You must also read, if you have not done so, Matthew Arnold on *The literary influence of Academies* in the August *Cornill*. Much that he says is worth attention, but, as is so often the case, in censuring bad taste he falls into two flagrant pieces of bad taste himself. I am coming to think much of taste myself, good taste and moderation, I who have sinned against them so much. But there is a prestige about them which is indescribable.

What do you think? It occurred to me that the story of *Floris in Italy*° is dramatic, and all of a sudden I began to turn it into a play. It is a great experiment. I shall alter the plot to suit requirements a little. I fancy there is a fascination about the dramatic form. Beside this I have done very little since I wrote last, except three verses, a fragment, being a description of Io° (transformed into a heifer.) It sounds odd.

I have been reading the twelve first (which is it? The first twelve then) books of the *Odyssey*, and have begun to receive Homer in earnest. How great his dramatic power is! Do you know, I am going, not at once of course, to reach Petronius Arbiter. I am though.

You must be tired of Parnassian by this time. I must however add a few words left out. A great deal of Parnassian lowers a poet's average, and more than anything else lowers his fame I fear. This is in the main what is meant by artificial poetry; it is all Parnassian. When one reads Pope's Homer with a critical eye one sees, artificial as it is, in every couplet that he was a great man, but no doubt to an uncritical humour and an uncritical flippant modernist it does offer a great handle.

I am ashamed to say I cannot make out the meaning of *The Voyage* in the new volume of Tennyson, though I have tried hard. Can you? After all, by the bye, perhaps his *Flower* is the best defence of him that could be written. *The Grandmother* and *Northern Farmer* are to my mind the best things in the book. They shew a knowledge of human nature which is less common in him than I could wish. *Boadicea* improves as one knows it; it is a grand thing, but I have (perhaps your cautions in criticism are here useful) doubts about the metre. Do you notice that the first syllable is always accented, which is not the case in the Latin? I like *The Sailor Boy* much.

You know, I did not say you were 'not such a pleasant critic to keep as Bond'. On the contrary Bond would be, was in fact, much more severe; but he has not your great reticence, and blames and praises boldly, so that one knows what he means.

The vasty length this has oozed to forbids my telling you about the swells at Gurney's.

Why, you goose, did you say at the end of your first letter, that you thought there was nothing in it I could possibly misunderstand? Of course *that* was very possible to misunderstand, and also made it more easy to find something to misunderstand in the rest of the letter.

In a week or so I shall be at Hampstead I suppose, but now I am at Blunt House, Croydon—my grandfather's.

And now at last goodbye. Believe me, my dear friend,
yours affectionately, Gerard Manley Hopkins.

Sept. 11. Blunt House, Croydon. S.

P.S. Here is a piece of antiquarianism for you. I believe New Inn Hall to be a blunder, a solecism. It should be Newing Hall. I argue this from the consideration of Stoke Newington, that is *(the) wood (at the) new town*, and the *Newingate* of some town I read of, I forget what. This is called indifferently the New Gate and Newingate. *Newing* is an old participle meaning *new*, from a verb to *new* (we have *renew*, unless that is from *renovare*), and = Medieval Latin *novans*, as in *Troja Novans*, Troy-novant, the legendary name for London. Besides New *Inn* Hall is improbable in itself. What do you think?

To the Revd Edward William Urquhart

Epiphany [6 January]. 1865.

Dear Urquhart,—

Thanks for your many letters which I have left so long unanswered . . .

Today (Tuesday, Jan. 10) I have been up till now in bed with a severe cold, and there I have finished *Romola* and made myself wretched over the fall of Savonarola. I did not know much about the latter events of his life except that the *Arrabiati* and Pope Borgia overthrew and burned him, and in especial nothing about his confession. I must tell you he is the only person in history (except perhaps Origen) about whom I have a real feeling, and I feel such an enthusiasm about Savonarola that I can conceive what it must have been to have been of his followers. I feel this the more because he was followed by the painters, architects and other artists of his day, and is the prophet of Christian art, and it is easy to imagine oneself a painter of his following. The author of *Romola*° from being pagan, clever as she is, does not understand him. Villari° whose mind is not poetical does not appreciate the poetical and picturesque character of his mind, but there is an excellent sketch of him, which naturally brings this out, in Rio's *History of Christian Art.*° How strangely different is the fate of two reformers, Savonarola and Luther! The one martyred in the Church, the other successful and the admired author of worldwide heresy in schism. But I must no longer bother you with historical commonplaces.

Why does not Colenso's trial° go on? I always become so ignorant of Church matters in the Vac. O and I have something to tell you. A circular has appeared in our church, issuing from Hugh Macneile, beginning '"Your fathers, where are they?" WILLIAM HALDANE STEWART, WILLIAM MARSH.' Beginning with this tasteful twaddle, it goes on in the same style, recommending recommendations and suggesting suggestions and exhorting exhortations. It says 'the growth of the sacramentarian and sacerdotal elements within the church was never more alarming' and that the great Evangelical party was never more strictly rubrical. An honest and manly opposition must at least inspire respect, but I cannot tell you the plaintive twaddle of this thing, which makes one feel what is the intellectual position of such a man's school. At Hampstead lives almost the only learned Evangelical going, Mr. Birks.

Goodbye. Believe me, dear Urquhart, yours affectionately,

Gerard Hopkins.

Oak Hill. Hampstead.

To Robert Bridges

Elm Cottage, Torquay. [28 August 1865]

Dear Bridges,—

I left Manchester more than a month ago and after a month on the borders of Dartmoor at Chagford am now writing, as you may see, fr. Gurney's house at Torquay wh. place I leave in a few minutes for Hampstead. Else nothing cd. have been so delightful as to meet you and Coles° and Dolben. Mr Geldart° is secretary of the Manchester City Mission and his office is in what they have the face to call Piccadilly, if I remember right. It is nearly opposite a big public building and is in the middle of the place. They live at Bowdon, eight miles off. Tell Coles it is safer to address Oak Hill, Hampstead. Give my love to him and Dolben. I have written letters without end to the latter without a whiff of answer.

Believe me yr. sincere friend, Gerard Hopkins.

Aug. 28, 1865. I write to you by Coles' direction. I wish you or Coles—but he was not there then, I suppose—wd. have written so that I might have heard while in Manchester, and seen you.

Forgive Mrs. Gurney her blotting paper.

To Ernest Hartley Coleridge.

[Balliol College, Oxford, 22 January 1866]

Dear Coleridge,—

I never wrote to congratulate you on your best essay wh. I meant to do. I was sincerely proud of you, and I had half thought beforehand it might be so.

I have thought often since you were here of what you said about the particular shape in wh. the doctrine of eternal punishment presented itself with offence to you. You said you know yr. repugnance was to view the issues of eternity as depending on anything so trivial and inadequate as life is. I do understand the point of view. But I think the answer wh. I gave then comes at once—that in fact the argument tells the other way, because it is incredible and intolerable if there is nothing wh. is the reverse of trivial and will correct and avenge the triviality of this life. To myself all this trivialness is one of the strongest reasons for the opposite belief and is always in action more or less. Of course it is plain too that the belief in the future of theology destroys the triviality in proportion to its intensity. I think certainly that strong beliefs make ordinary goings on look more ridiculously trivial than they wd. otherwise, but then the trivialness is one to wh. oneself does not belong and fr. wh. one longs to bring other people. However this is to the same effect as what I said before; but I have thought of something wh. will weigh perhaps more as not being merely a reversal of yr. argument. I think that the trivialness of life is, and personally to each one, ought to be seen to be, done away with by the Incarnation—or, I shd. say the difficulty wh. the trivialness of life presents ought to be. It is one adorable point of the incredible condescension of the Incarnation (the greatness of which no saint can have ever hoped to realise) that our Lord submitted not only to the pains of life, the fasting, scourging, crucifixion etc. or the insults, as the mocking, blindfolding, spitting etc, but also to the mean and trivial accidents of humanity. It leads one naturally to rhetorical antithesis to think for instance that after making the world He shd. consent to be taught carpentering, and, being the eternal Reason, to be catechised in the theology of the Rabbins. It seems therefore that if the Incarnation cd. *versari inter* [pass one's time among, be involved with] trivial men and trivial things it is not surprising that our reception or non-reception of its benefits shd. be also amidst trivialities. . . .

Believe me always yr. affectionate friend,

Gerard Hopkins.

Jan. 22, 1866.

To William Alexander Comyn Macfarlane

[10 July 1866]

Dear Macfarlane,—

It seems to me you not only never got my telegram but missed the letter also I sent after it. In that I gave the details about Lavington, in the telegram I just said it had good churches and beautiful country. I do not know who it is tells you the country is dreary and the neighbourhood uninteresting: the country is exceptionally beautiful—both woods and fine downs: so people who know it, e.g. Street the architect,° tell me. The place itself has modern interest at all events—the Bp's. palace, Mr. Cobden's country house and tomb, Manning's church, and another built by Butterfield. Chichester Cathedral is in the neighbourhood and what equivalent is as near Horsham? But I do not now urge you to go there; a higher and nobler selfishness makes me intend to have it all to myself and let nobody see a corner of it. Have your own wilful way and go to Horsham (not Cuckfield). If you will do so, I will come on Thursday evening. I shall send my box to the station before me and go to Haslemere on the S.W. line, walk to Lavington, see it, and walk over later to Petworth, fr. wh. I shall start by the 7.20 p.m. train and get to Horsham in half an hour or so I suppose. I shall thus gratify several passions and be able to settle the question of the charms of Lavington and Horsham. Oh Macfarlane, to think that a rag of popery—for that 'stately' service at Horsham means vestments of course—shd. be leading you and Garrett so palpably by the nose. Some people (and Garrett is one) try to keep up their thermometer of orthodoxy by an unbending line of talk or action with regard to almuces,° buskins, and apparels, and such anise and cummin. I am very much concerned (parenthetically, the last sentence reflects on your name, if aimed more directly at Garrett, I see) to find that I did not notice till so late yr. direction to write at once. If it is not too late, go to Horsham; if it is, stay at St. Leonard's, and I shall go to Shanklin with my people and later perhaps to Lavington alone. But whatever you do do not, I beg, go to these palatial residences: my purse, my patience, my principles alike will not stand it.

Yours as you use me, Gerard Hopkins.

Oak Hill, Hampstead. July 10 [1866]
P.S. In default of another means of knowing where you are I must ask you to leave your address at Horsham station.

To William Alexander Comyn Macfarlane

King's Head Hotel. | Horsham. | July 15, 1866

Dear Macfarlane,—

We do not think that you will be very well satisfied with our quarters but you must please be content to think them the best that cd. be got. It is such labour writing with the inn pens that I will do no more than tell you the ἀναγκαιᾶ [essentials]. The place is at Mr. Ings', Whiting's Farm, Horsham and Nuthurst: one addresses I believe like that because it is in two parishes. The church is a great one, very handsome, but you will not like anything else about it. There is another church rather more catholic and also there is Nuthurst church rather nearer than Horsham. Garrett shd. have come over by the appointed train, but I doubt if anything cd. have much bettered us. However the country is pretty, the services convenient (two celebrations a Sunday at St. Mary's and daily service and perhaps something of the same sort at the small church St. Mark's), and the terms not those of Eversfield Place—that is 30s a week for lodging, cooking, etc. and to board ourselves. I do not wish to say anything about the Lavingtons now. You will perhaps not object to Garrett and me planning out our time and work and you will of course make what alteration you wish: you remember it is absolutely necessary for me to read hard and for Garrett too. Will you kindly carve? He is going to cater and I shall take the Hours and give you copies of the responses for some wh. we might perhaps say at the beginning of the week. Come, if you can manage it, tomorrow, but as we cannot tell yr. train it will not be possible for us to meet you, but there are flies opposite. But yr. most economical plan most likely will be to come on Tuesday early, in wh. case we cd. hear by return of post and meet you, either with the spring-cart or else have that sent afterwards for the things. But do not linger behind—Yrs. ever, Gerard M. Hopkins.

To Robert Bridges

[4 August 1866]

Dear Bridges,—

I got your letter the day before we left Horsham. Thank you very much for the kind proposal you make. I should like nothing so much as to stay at Rochdale,° more especially (if one can say that) when you hold out the possibility of Dolben being there. You are kind enough to speak of reading: it would be impossible for me now to take any more holidays, my work is in such a state, yet I am afraid it sounds very odd to propose to read on a visit. We shall go home to Hampstead in three weeks fr. this time. After that all my time is my own to the end of the Long. I fear I find no news to tell you in return for yours. Challis did know Dr. Pusey I remember; he did not confess to him I think though. He never had much belief in the Church of England, and his going over in itself wd. prove as little as any conversion could ever do against it since he never used the same strictness in practices (such as fasting) as most of our acquaintance would, but on the other hand if its effect is to make him a strict catholic and to destroy his whimsies, that would say something . . . With many thanks, believe me, dear Bridges, very sincerely yours,

Gerard Hopkins.

Aug. 4, 1866.—Cintra, Shanklin, Isle of Wight.

To Robert Bridges

[26 August 1866]

Dear Bridges,—

Your letter has been forwarded. I am most happy to come any day in the first week of September which you like to name. We go home to Hampstead tomorrow. I hope you are better than when you wrote.

Believe me affectionately yours, Gerard M. Hopkins.

Cintra, Shanklin, Isle of Wight. Aug. 26. [1866]

To Robert Bridges

[28 August 1866]

Dear Bridges,—

Will Saturday suit for me to come? I would come earlier, on Wednesday, but I have some things which I must do first in town, as we only got home yesterday. If Saturday would suit you, I shd. leave home on Friday and sleep at Birmingham where I have some business° I must manage to do at some time while I am in the north, most conveniently I think then. If not Saturday, by the same rule I shd. have to come on this day week. Will you be so kind as to let me know if Saturday will do? Do not think about meeting me, thank you, as this going to Birmingham throws out the trains, and as I should come in good time on Saturday I shd. find little difficulty I suppose in getting to Dr. Molesworth's.

Believe me yr. affectionate friend, Gerard Hopkins.

Oak Hill, Hampstead, N.W.—(put N.W.—it may save a post).—

Aug. 28, Tuesday. [1866]

To the Revd John Henry Newman

[28 August 1866]

Reverend Sir,—

I address you with great hesitation knowing that you are in the midst of yr. own engagements and because you must be much exposed to applications from all sides. I am anxious to become a Catholic, and I thought that you might possibly be able to see me for a short time when I pass through Birmingham in a few days, I believe on Friday. But I feel most strongly the injustice of intruding on yr. engagements or convenience and therefore, if that is the case, I shall think it a favour if you will kindly let me know that you are unable to see me. I do not want to be helped to any conclusions of belief, for I am thankful to say my mind is made up, but the necessity of becoming a Catholic (although I had long foreseen where the only consistent position wd. lie) coming upon me suddenly has put me into painful confusion of mind about my immediate duty in my circumstances. I wished also to know what it wd. be morally my duty to hold on certain formally open points, because the same reasoning which makes the Tractarian ground contradictory wd. almost lead one also to shrink from what Mr. Oakley° calls a minimising Catholicism.° I say this much to take fr. you any hesitation in not allowing me to come to Birmingham if duties shd. stand in the way: you will understand that by God's mercy I am clear as to the sole authority of the Church of Rome. While much in doubt therefore as to my right to trouble you by this application, I wd. not deny at the same time that I shd. feel it the greatest privilege to see you. If it were so, I shd. hope not to detain you long. I may perhaps in some way introduce myself by reminding you of an intimate college friend of mine, William Addis, who once had the pleasure of spending an hour with you at the Oratory; I think also he has written to you since: I have little doubt that in not a very long time he will become a Catholic. If I shd. be so happy as to hear before Friday that you cd. spare time to see me, I shd. hope to be at Birmingham that day and sleep there, or if you had any convenient time in the two or three weeks after that I shd. like to come over fr. Rochdale where I shall be staying at Dr. Molesworth's. But in ending I wd. again say that I beg you will have no hesitation, as I have no doubt you will not, in declining to see me if you think best.

Believe me, Reverend Sir, your obedient servant.

Gerard M. Hopkins.

Oak Hill, Hampstead, N.W. Aug. 28, 1866.

To the Revd. Edward Willim Urquhart

[20 September 1866]

Dear Urquhart,—

Thanks for your letter. Do you know, my father and mother are at Dinan or have just left it. Perhaps you have seen them.

You say that neither Challis nor I nor anyone else that you have met can solve difficulties satisfactorily, but that he comprehends your position better than I do. By this I conjecture that you did not take my letter in the way I meant. I fear when I explain you may perhaps think me dishonest. I thought what I said led but to one result, but you perhaps were prevented fr. seeing by thinking of me as an unusually exacting Anglican, and not, what by the mercy of God I am, a penitent waiting for admission to the Catholic Church. It was right for me to be silent when I wrote that letter, though I did not refrain—perhaps I ought to have—fr. pressing what seemed to me to follow immediately fr. the things you have been kind enough to tell me. Now I may speak plainly: I have been for about two months a convert to the Church of Christ and am hoping to be received early in next term: I most earnestly hope you will delay no longer. There is nothing I need say in the way of argument, and I wish too not to say anything. It wd. be presumptuous of me to say more than this—that I am hoping for your conversion and expecting it and of course I do not omit to pray for it. I have today seen Dr. Newman, whose advice I wanted about my immediate duty: on one point I can reassure you fr. his mouth—an Anglican is at full liberty to believe in his Orders, for that re-ordination is not defined as conditional proves nothing; baptism was not defined as conditional in the case of the conversion of heretics till after hundreds of years. When I see you I will say more but not in this letter: I hope to see you a Catholic. Believe me, dear Urquhart,

your affectionate friend, Gerard M. Hopkins.

Please tell no one of my conversion till I am received.

Remember me kindly to Morris.° My brother desires to be remembered and is glad you are enjoying yourself.

Vigil of St. Matthew: your letter must be dated wrongly: tomorrow, the 21st, is St. Matthew. September, 1866.

St. Matthew.—I first heard of Mr. Riddell's death fr. Dr Newman. One ought no doubt to feel nothing but joy for himself, being so good a man, to have gone where *lux perpetua illucet ei* [the eternal light shines upon him], but it is a dreadful blow for the college.

To Robert Bridges

[22 September 1866]

Dear Bridges,—

I had not forgotten about Mr. Street.° I called there today, but he was out: you shall hear however as soon as possible. At Mayer's too I was unsuccessful, for they had, it seemed to me, not much of the altar service of any kind and no bottles at all, only cruets, which were not to the purpose! I am not sure now where to apply but I will try and find out and, unless you want the bottle ordered or got more immediately than I can be sure of doing it, it will give me pleasure to go about it. Am I to design the stopper? if you still wish it and it shd. turn out after all that my design wd. cost too much I cd. always fall back on the Maltese cross, wh. has no objection, I suppose, except that it is so common.

Dr. Newman was most kind, I mean in the very best sense, for his manner is not that of solicitous kindness but genial and almost, so to speak, unserious. And if I may say so, he was so sensible. He asked questions which made it clear for me how to act; I will tell you presently what that is: he made sure I was acting deliberately and wished to hear my arguments; when I had given them and said I cd. see no way out of them, he laughed and said 'Nor can I': and he told me I must come to the church to accept and believe—as I hope I do. He thought there appeared no reason, if it had not been for matters at home of course, why I shd. not be received at once, but in no way did he urge me on, rather the other way. More than once when I offered to go he was good enough to make me stay talking. Amongst other things he said that he always answered those who thought the learned had no excuse in invincible ignorance, that on the contrary they had that excuse the most of all people. It is needless to say he spoke with interest and kindness and appreciation of all that Tractarians reverence. This much pleased me, namely a bird's-eye view of Oxford in his room the frame of which he had had lettered *Fili hominis, putasne vivent ossa ista? Domine Deus, tu nosti.*° This speaks for itself. He told me what books to get and then left me at lunch-time to Mr. John Walford°—discovered at football. Mr. Walford gave me lunch in the refectory and shewed all the school and the oratory, then walked back and took me to St. Chad's cathedral. He told me to remember him very kindly indeed to you and to say how glad he shd. be to see you on yr. way to Oxford, if you liked it. You have much common interest fr. Eton etc, and of course he wd. avoid all religious subjects, I am sure.

I am to go over fr. Oxford to the Oratory for my reception next term—early in the term I must make it, and since a Retreat is advisable for a convert, Dr. Newman was so very good as to offer me to come there at Xtmas, which wd. be the earliest opportunity for it. He thought it both expedient and likely that I shd. finish my time at Oxford, and next term at all events I shall be there, since I shall announce my conversion to my parents by letter at the time of my reception. And now I have even almost ceased to feel anxiety.—Sept. 22.

You were surprised and sorry, you said, and possibly hurt that I wd. not tell you of my conversion till my going to Birmingham made it impossible any longer to conceal it. I was never sorry for one minute: it wd. have been culpably dishonourable and ungrateful, as I said before, not to have done one's best to conceal it: but I do not mean that, but this—the happiness it has been the means of bringing me I cd. not have conceived: I can never thank you enough for yr. kindness at that time. Notwithstanding my anxiety, which on the day we filled the aquarium was very great indeed, it gives me more delight to think of the time at Rochdale than any other time whatever that I can remember. I did not see Mrs. Molesworth at the last: will you give her for me my very greatest thanks for her kindness? Dr. Molesworth I did say Goodbye to. I am most distressed to think that the news of my conversion, if they hear it, may give them pain and alarm for you, but you must remember that when I came to Rochdale I did not look upon my reception as to be so soon as it really was to be. You see the point of what was on my mind at the Vicarage was chiefly this, that my wishes about you cd. not be gained except at your own and their trouble and grief. This will make it plain how I feel that wherever I go I must either do no good or else harm.

Walford believed that Dolben had been mobbed in Birmingham. He went in his habit without sandals, barefoot. I do not know whether it is more funny or affecting to think of.

My father and mother are still abroad and are or will soon be at Dinan in Brittany, where it happens that Urquhart now is, coaching Morris. I hope they will meet: My mother, my brother says, has some prejudice about Urquhart, I conceive because he is looked upon as leading me over to Rome.

I heard first fr. Dr. Newman of Mr. Riddell's death. He was always most kind to me. He was so good that one scarcely can regret his loss, but for our college it is very sad and disastrous.

I did leave something behind, my sponge. Wd. you be so

kind as to bring it if you can, though I am afraid I cd. not ask for anything more inconvenient.

I am now going to see Mr Street and I can find out fr. him, you know, any detail about the bottle. You shall hear this evening, if I have seen him.

Believe me, dear Bridges, with the utmost gratitude

your very affectionate friend, Gerard Hopkins.

Oak Hill, Hampstead, Sept. 24, 1866.

To Robert Bridges

24 September [1866]

Dear Bridges—

Mr. Street° was again not in this morning. He was to be in in the afternoon but I found I cd. not go then, and now he will not be home till Friday or Saturday. On Saturday however I hope to catch him. Hart's, if I remember is the place for all sorts of ecclesiastical furniture and I will go there soon.

Do you know Bradley? Yesterday at St. Alban's I saw him serving in some way in choir, and I saw too another Oxford man, whose name I do not know, with a delightful face (not handsome), altogether aquiline features, a sanguine complexion, rather tall, slight, and eager-looking: I did not know he was one of the faithful before. His face was fascinating me last term: I generally have one fascination or another on. Sometimes I dislike the faces wh. fascinate me but sometimes much the reverse, as is the present case. G.M.H.

Hampstead. Sept. 24. [1866]

To the Revd. Edward William Urquhart

[24 September 1866]

Dear Urquhart,—

I will copy out a notice of Mr. Riddell which has been shewn me in the *Guardian*—

'The Revd. James Riddell, M.A., Fellow and Tutor of Balliol College, who died at Tunbridge Wells on Friday last, at the early age of forty-three, was the elder son of the Revd. James Riddell, M.A., of the same college, sometime vicar of Hanbury, Staffordshire, and long resident at Leamington, and a member of the noble Scottish Border family of Riddell, now represented by Sir Walter Riddell, Bart. His mother was Dorothea, daughter and co-heiress of John Foster, Esq., of Leicester Grange. He was born at the end of 1822 or early in 1823, and was educated at Shrewsbury School, where he was one of the favourite pupils of Dr. Kennedy, and whence he was elected to a Scholarship at Balliol College in November, 1841, his colleague in the election being Mr. Matthew Arnold. As an undergraduate he was a great favourite both with his seniors and his immediate contemporaries, to whom the sweetness of his temper and his uniform kindness and courtesy particularly endeared him; while the authorities of his college always regarded him as one of the best and most promising scholars that ever entered the college. He took his B.A. degree in 1845, obtaining a first class in the Classical Schools, and was elected to a Fellowship in the same year. Shortly afterwards he was appointed one of the Tutors, and in this position he was much beloved and respected by his numerous pupils. He acted as one of the Public Examiners in *Lit. Human.* in 1858, and was one of the contributors to Mr Linwood's *Anthologia Oxoniensis.* He was also last year one of the Whitehall Preachers, to wh. office he was nominated by the Bp. of London. His name stands in the Oxford Calendar for this year as one of the Examiners for Moderations, and in May last, on the retirement of Professor Hansell, he was elected to a seat in the Hebdomadal Council. Mr. Riddell left Oxford at the beginning of the Long Vacation in his usual health, and, after paying a visit at Sherborne, in Dorsetshire, joined his family at Tunbridge Wells, where he suffered fr. an attack of quinsey. Fr. this, however, he appeared to recover; but it was succeeded by symptoms of heart-disease, wh. caused great uneasiness to his friends, and a fainting fit, after a carriage-drive, on the 7th, seriously alarmed them. After that day he did not leave the house again, and peacefully and painlessly, at an early hour on Friday morning last, he was taken to his rest. His old friend and colleague, the Revd. Edwin Palmer, was staying with him at the time, and was present to the last by his bed-side. His loss will be much felt, not only among old Shrewsbury and Balliol men, but throughout the University, and also at Leamington, where he and his family had long resided. It matters little now to add that he enjoyed the reputation of being one of the best—some wd. go so far as to say the best—Greek scholar of his standing in Oxford; but it is a melancholy pleasure to his old friends to recall the fact of his singular goodness, innocence, and purity; and many of his former pupils will bear testimony to the loving industry and patience wh. he brought to bear upon his college labours for nearly twenty years. It is not a little singular that the last production of his pen shd. have been a Latin verse translation, published in the August number of the *Gentleman's Magazine*, of the well-known lines of Watts—

Death, like a narrow sea, divides
That blessed land from ours.

Mr. Riddell was buried yesterday, in the cemetery at Tunbridge Wells. *Requiescat in pace*'

I think Mr. Edward Walford will have written this. The Friday must be the 14th of this month. I have not seen or heard fr. anyone who knew him but I shall call on Mr. Walford, who may have some particulars wh. he has not put down.

My parents did not go to Dinan so soon as we expected. We last heard that they were to be there either on the 22nd or else, if they waited for a *fête* at Avranches on that day, today I believe. So you may still see them, as I hope you will. As we write to the post-office we do not know where they will be staying.

I did not know Challis had written a pamphlet.° If I cd. remember his address I wd. write to him, or if I had time to go about I shd. like to see him.

You are the only friend whom I have deliberately told of my conversion, though I let Macfarlane and Garrett, with whom I was staying at the time, know it through my incaution. Fr. Bridges I hid it with difficulty while I stayed at Rochdale, till my going to Birmingham made concealment useless. His kindness at that time when he did not know what was the matter with me I perpetually thank God for. One of my brothers knows it; he forced it from me by questions. Dr. Newman of course and one or two other Catholics know, but no one else: Addis does not. I shd. have told him but I did not want by introducing a train of thoughts and difficulties about himself to break up his pleasure at Birchington, which he was enjoying when he wrote, he said, most deeply. But now I shall let one friend after another hear till the time of my reception. I hope the painful time of yr. hesitation may be short: one is sure in these cases that one is not alone but then if ever the saints and one's guardian angel are praying for one. If it is a relief possibly to write I shall be so glad to be hearing fr. you. But I am so sanguine, that I can scarcely believe your next letter will not put all doubt at an end and explain *Magnificavit Dominus facere nobiscum: facti sumus laetantes.*° I wd. write more if I were your friend in the same way that Challis or Gurney are, but I hope that I can sympathise as much as Challis will, for Gurney of course we cannot bring in here.

Believe me yr. affectionate friend, Gerard Hopkins.

P.S. I am so glad, do you know, that my conversion is surprising to you (though I am sorry that you shd. have had a shock from it), because although my actual conversion was two months ago yet the silent conviction that I was to become a Catholic has been present to me for a year perhaps, as strongly, in spite of my resistance to it when it formed itself into words, as if I had already determined it.

I hope this is not overweight. Kind remembrances to Morris.

Hampstead. Sept. 24. [1866]

To the Revd. John Henry Newman

[15 October 1866]

Very reverend Father,—

I have been up at Oxford just long enough to have heard fr. my father and mother in return for my letter announcing my conversion. Their answers are terrible: I cannot read them twice. If you will pray for them and me just now I shall be deeply thankful. But what I am writing for is this—they urge me with the utmost entreaties to wait till I have taken my degree—more than half a year. Of course it is impossible, and since it is impossible to wait as long as they wish it seems to me useless to wait at all. Wd. you therefore wish me to come to Birmingham at once, on Thursday, Friday, or Saturday? You will understand why I have any hesitation at all, namely because if immediately after their letters urging a long delay I am received without any, it will be another blow and look like intentional cruelty. I did not know till last night the rule about *communicatio in sacris*°—at least as binding catechumens, but I now see the alternative thrown open, either to live without Church and sacraments or else, in order to avoid the Catholic Church, to have to attend constantly the services of that very Church. This brings the matter to an absurdity and makes me think that any delay, whatever relief it may be to my parents, is impossible. I am asking you then whether I shall at all costs be received at once.

Strange to say of four conversions mine is the earliest and yet my reception will be last. I think I said that my friend William Garrett was converted and received shortly after hearing of my conversion; just before term began another friend, Alexander Wood, wrote to me in perplexity, and when I wrote back to his surprise telling him I was a convert he made up his own mind the next morning and is being received today; by a strange chance he met Addis in town and Addis, who had put off all thought of change for a year, was by God's mercy at once determined to see a priest and was received at Bayswater the same evening—Saturday. All our minds you see were ready to go at a touch and it cannot but be that the same is the case with many here. Addis' loss will be deep grief to Dr. Pusey I think: he has known him so long and stayed with him at Chale in a retreat.

I shall ask F. William Neville to open and answer this in your absence.

Monsignor Eyre° seemed to say that I ought not to make my confession by means of a paper as I have been used to do. Will you kindly say whether you wd. prefer it so or not?

Believe me, dear Father, your affectionate son in Christ,

Gerard M. Hopkins.

18 New Inn Hall Street, Oxford.—St. Theresa [15 October], 1866

P.S. And if you shd. bid me be received at once will you kindly name the day? The liberality of the college authorities will throw no hindrance in the way.

To Manley Hopkins

Oct. 16. [1866]

My dear Father,—

I must begin with a practical immediate point. The Church strictly forbids all communion in sacred things with non-Catholics. I have only just learnt this, but it prevents me going to chapel, and so yesterday I had to inform the Dean of Chapel. Today the Master° sent for me and said he cd. not grant me leave of absence without an application from you. As the College last term passed a resolution admitting Catholics and took a Catholic into residence it has no right to alter its principle in my case. I wish you therefore not to give yourself the pain of making this application, even if you were willing: I am of age moreover, and am alone concerned. If you refuse to make the application, the Master explains that he shall lay my case before the common-room. In this case there is very little doubt indeed that the Fellows wd. take the reasonable course and give me leave of absence fr. chapel, and if not, I am quite contented: but in fact I am satisfied as to the course our Fellows will take and the Master will at the last hesitate to lay the matter before them perhaps even. I want you therefore to write at once, if you will,—not to the Master who has no right to ask what he does, but to me, with a refusal: no harm will follow.

The following is the position of things with me. You ask me to suspend my judgment for a long time, or at the very least more than half a year, in other words to stand still for a time. Now to stand still is not possible, thus: I must either obey the Church or disobey. If I disobey, I am not suspending judgment but deciding namely to take backward steps fr. the grounds I have already come to. To stand still if it were possible might be justifiable, but to go back nothing can justify. I must therefore obey the Church by ceasing to attend any service of the Church of England. If I am to wait then I must either be altogether without services and sacraments, which you will of course know is impossible, or else I must attend the services of the Church—still being unreceived. But what can be more contradictory than, in order to avoid joining the Church, attending the services of that very Church? Three of my friends, whose conversions were later than mine, Garrett, Addis, and Wood, have already been received, but this is by the way. Only one thing remains to be done: I cannot fight against God Who calls me to His Church: if I were to delay and die in the meantime I shd. have no plea why my soul was not forfeit. I have no power in fact to stir a finger: it is God Who makes the decision and not I.

But you do not understand what is involved in asking me to delay and how little good you wd. get from it. I shall hold as a Catholic what I have long held as an Anglican, that literal truth of our Lord's words by which I learn that the least fragment of the consecrated elements in the Blessed Sacrament of the Altar is the whole Body of Christ born of the Blessed Virgin, before which the whole host of saints and angels as it lies on the altar trembles with adoration. This belief once got is the life of the soul and when I doubted it I shd. become an atheist the next day. But, as Monsignor Eyre says, it is a gross superstition unless guaranteed by infallibility. I cannot hold this doctrine confessedly except as a Tractarian or a Catholic: the Tractarian ground I have seen broken to pieces under my feet. What end then can be served by a delay in wh. I shd. go on believing this doctrine as long as I believed in God and shd. be by the fact of my belief drawn by a lasting strain towards the Catholic Church?

About my hastiness I wish to say this. If the question which is the Church of Christ? cd. only be settled by laborious search, a year and ten years and a lifetime are too little, when the vastness of the subject of theology is taken into account. But God must have made his Church such as to attract and convince the poor and unlearned as well as the learned. And surely it is true, though it will sound pride to say it, that the judgment of one who has seen both sides for a week is better than his who has seen only one for a lifetime. I am surprised you shd. say fancy and aesthetic tastes have led me to my present state of mind: these wd. be better satisfied in the Church of England, for bad taste is always meeting one in the accessories of Catholicism. My conversion is due to the following reasons mainly (I have put them down without order)—(i) simple and strictly drawn arguments partly my own, partly others', (ii) common-sense, (iii) reading the Bible, especially the Holy Gospels, where texts like 'Thou art Peter' (the evasions proposed for this alone are enough to make one a Catholic) and the manifest position of St. Peter among the Apostles so pursued me that at one time I thought it best to stop thinking of them, (iv) an increasing knowledge of the Catholic system (at first under the form of Tractarianism, later in its genuine place°), which only wants to be known in order to be loved—its consolations, its marvellous ideal of holiness, the faith and devotion of its children, its multiplicity, its array of saints and martyrs, its consistency and unity, its glowing prayers, the daring majesty of its claims, etc etc. You speak of the claims of the Church of England, but it is to me the strange thing that the Church of England makes no claims: it is true that Tractarians make them for her and find them faintly or only in a few instances° borne out for them by her liturgy, and are strongly assailed for their extravagances while they do it. Then about applying to Mr. Liddon and the Bp. of Oxford. Mr. Liddon writes begging me to pause: it wd. take too long to explain how I did not apply to him at first and why it wd. have been useless. If Dr. Pusey° is in Oxford tomorrow I will see him, if it is any satisfaction to you. The

Bishop is too much engaged to listen to individual difficulties and those who do not apply to him may get such answers as young Mr. Lane Fox did, who gave up £30,000 a year just lately to become a Catholic. He wrote back about a cob which he wanted to sell to the Dean of some place and wh. Lane Fox was to put his own price on and ride over for the Bishop to the place of sale. In fact Dr. Pusey and Mr. Liddon were the only two men in the world who cd. avail to detain me: the fact that they were Anglicans kept me one, for arguments for the Church of England I had long ago felt there were none that wd. hold water, and when that influence gave way everything was gone.

You are so kind as not to forbid me your house, to which I have no claim, on condition, if I understand, that I promise not to try to convert my brothers and sisters. Before I can promise this I must get permission, wh. I have no doubt will be given. Of course this promise will not apply after they come of age. Whether after my reception you will still speak as you do now I cannot tell.

You ask me if I have had no thought of the estrangement. I have had months to think of everything. Our Lord's last care on the cross was to commend His mother to His Church and His Church to His mother in the person of St. John. If even now you wd. put yourselves into that position wh. Christ so unmistakeably gives us and ask the Mother of Sorrows to remember her three hours' compassion at the cross, the piercing of the sword prophecied by Simeon, and her seven dolours, and her spouse Joseph, the lily of chastity, to remember the flight into Egypt, the searching for his Foster-Son at twelve years old, and his last ecstacy with Christ at his death-bed, the prayers of this Holy Family wd. in a few days put an end to estrangements for ever. If you shrink fr. doing this, though the Gospels cry aloud to you to do it, at least for once—if you like, only once—approach Christ in a new way in which you will at all events feel that you are exactly in unison with me, that is, not vaguely, but casting yourselves into His sacred broken Heart and His five adorable Wounds. Those who do not pray to Him in His Passion pray to God but scarcely to Christ. I have the right to propose this, for I have tried both ways, and if you will not give one trial to this way you will see you are prolonging the estrangement and not I.

After saying this I feel light-hearted, though I still can by no means make my pen write what I shd. wish.

I am your loving son, Gerard M. Hopkins.

23 New Inn Hall Street. Oct. 17, 1866.

P.S. I am most anxious that you shd. not think of my future. It is likely that the positions you wd. like to see me in wd. have no attraction for me, and surely the happiness of my prospects depends on the happiness to me and not on intrinsic advantages. It is possible even to be very sad and very happy at once and the time that I was with Bridges, when my anxiety came to its height, was I believe the happiest fortnight of my life. My only strong wish is to be independent.

If you are really willing to make the application to the Master, well and good; but I do not want you to put yourself to pain. I have written a remonstrance to him.

Many thanks to Arthur for his letter.

To Kate Hopkins, sen.

Oxford Union Society [20 October 1866]

My dearest Mother,—

Dr. Pusey has not been in Oxford till today, so I cd. not go to see him.° My friend Coles wrote to him begging him to come up: he answered 'I have seen only too much of that seeing Dr. P. for the satisfaction of friends: it means listening patiently to arguments for an hour or two hours as the case may be with a formed intention not to be convinced.' Mr. Liddon wrote, and then again before he got my answer, thinking his first letter had been misdirected, and on getting it a third time at length. All the influence therefore that he has on me has been brought to bear.

My father seems to think that I am off my head. If I am excited now (though I do not think I am) it is the effect and not the cause: at Horsham where I made my decision and since then my mind was quite cool. You on the contrary took my letter as hard and cold. It cd. scarcely then be excited.

I can hardly think that what is said about private judgment

can have been meant as an argument, but about Dr. Pusey and Mr. Liddon I am hit very hard. All people are inconsistent except those who are all right and those who are all wrong, and those who are most right are most inconsistent if they are a little wrong. If I think Mr. Liddon right in everything but in not being a Catholic I must of course think him inconsistent—intellectually inconsistent, that is. Dr. Pusey I revere most of all men in the world, but being pressed to explain how with all his learning and genius he did not become a Catholic I said he had a confusion of mind which in talk (I shd. not have said it in writing) I called 'puzzle-headed' (not 'muddle-headed', which is a worse word). It has been said by friendly people of his Eirenicon and one who was wholly devoted to Dr. Pusey said the same thing and more strongly. It is a thing which I am not ashamed to have said, though Cyril or Arthur was unwise to repeat it. Neither learning, genius, nor holiness nor all three together can bring anyone to the Church and it is as impossible to tell why some are led and not others as why some have any advantage which others have not, some die early and others old, etc.

There are some misconceptions which I shd. have thought my letters wd. have prevented. You seem to think that my doubts of the English Church occurred to me on three occasions only after I had been told to resist them and on the third of these I gave in. So far is this fr. the truth that the doubts or the conviction which remained when the doubts were forcibly not listened to were for ever present, sometimes they kept occurring for days, and I left off struggling (omitting trifling occasions) three times, in two of which I looked forward and saw what was inevitable, the third time I considered the thing itself and was converted. The subject has had years to bring its points before me, in fact I had long had the premises and had at arm's length kept off the plain conclusion. Surely too if I had not enough grounds to act upon, you cannot think you have much more. Your not being a Catholic is, I suppose, on conviction that the Church of Rome is wrong; my conversion is on conviction that it is right; I do not think you can have much examined the question: do you for instance know—to take a thing wh. is usually a stumbling-block—what the Church says in explanation of

Indulgences or in fact do you know what they mean? Strong persuasion is nothing when you do not know what is really said by the other side.

Then again I prayed for light before my conversion: to pray for light after I had got it or to consult Anglicans wd. have been resisting God. Dr. Newman did not advise me to wait, he advised me to do what I am doing: what he said was that he hoped I shd. be able to take my degree at Oxford.

About communicating you are also mistaken. The last time I communicated was at Todmorden:° I ought to have stopped at once, but for the very reason you give, namely that I needed grace, I did not do so. Strictly I owed no duty whatever to the Church of England, because it is not what it claims to be, a lawful church, but I did pay a provisional loyalty and even to the extent of keeping its fasts, until you induced me to give them up, which I said I wd. do for a little time: I cd. not otherwise have obeyed you.

You do not seem to realise how irrevocable my determination was fr. July—the day of my conversion. My mind is not more made up now than it was then.

It was perhaps unreasonable to make the first request I did, though it was natural to me: I still think you might do the second: it cannot be actual harm, it may be so much good.

These things I have wished to explain but they are not so important, but this is. I was never going to be received without warning you, though I was going to give you the warning only at the last. In this I have no doubt I was wrong. In not warning you of my state of mind long ago I strongly think I was perfectly right. But if I was wrong in both cases, I of course thought only of the way wh. I believed wd. give you the least pain: indeed if you can think I did otherwise it wd. be useless of me to assure you of it.

I am to be received into the church tomorrow at Birmingham by Dr. Newman. It is quite the best that any hopes should be ended quickly, since otherwise they wd. only have made the pain longer. Until then the comforts you take are delusive, after it they will be real. And even for me it is almost a matter of necessity, for every new letter I get breaks me down afresh, and this cd. not go on. Your letters, wh. shew the utmost fondness, suppose none on my part and the more you think me hard and cold and that I repel and throw you off the more I am helpless not to write as if [it] were true. In this way I have no relief. You might believe that I suffer too.

I am your very loving son, Gerard M. Hopkins.

Oct. 20, 1866

To the Revd. Henry Parry Liddon

[7 November 1866]

Dear Mr. Liddon,—

It may seem useless returning to what is quite past but there is one thing I wanted to say before and ought, to have done any good, to have said before which I shall say now. The two last letters you wrote and also a note from Dr. Pusey I got on Saturday night, in time to stop the last step if anything could, but my mind was made up. I wish to thank you for your kindness and even for the trouble you took to prevent my reception, for of course to you it was the right thing to do.

It wd. be most unreasonable to wish to put my conversion in such a light to you as to make it seem a justifiable thing, but I do want to prevent its being rationalised (as while an Anglican one always rationalised particular conversions) in such a way as to empty it of any influence it might have on any of my acquaintance, and therefore I am sorry I did not write before. You think I lay claim to a personal illumination which dispenses with the need of thought or knowledge on the points at issue. I have never been so unwise as to think of such a claim. There is a distinction to be made: in the sense that every case of taking truth instead of error is an illumination of course I have been illuminated, but I have never said anything to the effect that a wide subject involving history and theology or any turning-point question in it has been thrown into light for me by a supernatural or even unusual access of grace. If you will not think it an irreverent way of speaking, I can hardly believe anyone ever became a Catholic because two and two make four more fully than I have. I certainly said my conversion was sudden when it came, though the conviction which I wd. not acknowledge to myself was not sudden but old and always present, but this was quite natural: I had thought it my duty to resist the doubts of the English Church wh. were always assailing me, and this resistance was in the form of refusing to answer certain plain questions which I cd. not but be aware of or of answering them perversely. When at last I consented to listen to them it was not surprising that one minute shd. be enough to answer such questions as these—If there are Catholics who are not Roman Catholics, can the Church of Rome hold such people under sentence of loss of their souls and yet remain part of the Catholic Church? formally they are under this sentence, as is clearly expressed e.g. in the form of reconciling converts—or this: a Church° committing itself to heresy falls out of the Catholic Church: can a Church enjoin sin and not fall out? for the Church is the guardian of faith and morals both: but the Church of Rome enjoins sin by enjoining submission under terrible penalties and this submission is *ex hypothesi* schism: to say schism is not a deadly sin as Dr. Pusey does is useless, for a true Church cannot command any sin however small. There was also the obvious question Can the one Church be three Churches at war (two out of the three claiming each to be the whole meanwhile)? The latter is a point of common-sense, but as common-sense is open to discussion I will speak only of the others, which are direct reasoning. Where the issues are so simple you must permit me to say that to search the Fathers or Church history for parallels is to throw reason overboard and to prefer confusion. Now there is only one thing which can suspend the free use of reason (though in fact you have not told me it was my duty to suspend it) and that is the infallible authority of the Church. Of course if the infallible Church says there are three Churches, the Roman, Eastern, and Anglican, *causa finita est* [the case is closed], it is sin to have a doubt, and indeed it is meaningless to talk of a question to be examined at all unless we are also going to examine the question with the Calvinists or even Mormons. But not only has the collective church never said this but the theory has not been known even to individual Churches in it before how long a time? Not at the time of the separation of East and West certainly, for both East and West claim to be the whole Church. Not fr. the Reformation, for Anglican divines (you will know whether all do or do not; many at all events do) regarded the Lutheran, etc bodies as helping to make up the Church. Not even fr. the Tractarian movement, for Dr. Newman cd. at one time without being out of harmony speak of the Church of Rome as a Church insane. Has then the view that the whole infallible Church is made up of these three Churches, singly fallible but as yet orthodox, been believed by a body of men in the whole Church for more than 20 years? Of course as the view of individuals I do not know its age or history but individual views do not concern the Church; it is only with some sort of collective voice or consent that Churches begin to be compromised. I must have decided as I have done if I had waited till after my Degree for a leisure time of thought, but since the only claim the Church of England made on my allegiance was by a theory of 20 years prevalence among a minority of her clergy, it is not wonderful that the claims of the Catholic Church broke down my efforts to wait that time many months beforehand.

The above questions had not perhaps all the definiteness then with which I put them now but still they were quite clear.

Should you therefore ever again be speaking of our conversions I hope I may ask you as far as I am concerned (and the others wd. say the same) not to lay them to any belief in a personal illumination of the kind you spoke of, for I have had no such belief. My conversion was only sudden or quick because at last I consented to answer simple questions wh. I had refused to answer before and of which in fact I had for months known the answers. It is right for me to say this and I ought to have said it before. I hope I have not said anything more hardly than the truth needed.

Believe me, dear Mr. Liddon, always gratefully and affectionately yours, Gerard M. Hopkins.

Do not trouble yourself to write again: this needs no answer and I know how precious your time is.

Nov. 7, 1866.—23 New Inn Hall Street.

P.S. The Papal Supremacy on wh. you lay so much stress I did not of course believe as an Anglican and do of course believe as a Catholic, but it was one of the things I took up in the change of the position and was no element in my decision.

To the Revd. Edward William Urquhart

[16 January 1867]

Dear Urquhart,—

. . . I will send shortly a copy of *Barnfloor and Winepress.*°

About the other thing many thanks for your criticisms and to Lord Neaves for his and for the trouble he has taken. I think them both just (except the flattering opinion you have of *Barnfloor and Winepress*) and am quite satisfied, for I have ceased to care for *Beyond the Cloister*° being put into a magazine. Too many licences are taken for a beginner, but the objection is on the score of morality rather than of art, and as the licences in themselves I still think justifiable I need not alter what I cannot publish. (By the way *pérdurable* is the right accent: Shakspere has a line in *Measure for Measure*

Be perdurably fined. Oh Isabel!)°

I think you wd. find in the history of Art that licences and eccentricities are to [be] found fully as often in beginners as in those who have established themselves and can afford them; those in Milton, Turner, and Beethoven are at the end, those in Shakspere, Keats, Millais, and Tennyson at the beginning. I did send this piece first to *Macmillan's* wh. is always having things of Miss Rossetti. Part of it was written two years and a half ago and though that does not sound much one changes very fast at my age and I shd. write better now, I hope.

Believe me yr. affectionate friend, Gerard M. Hopkins.

I am going to Birmingham to the Oratory° tomorrow for the last week.

Jan. 16, 1867.—Oak Hill, Hampstead.

I want to make some slight corrections in *Barnfloor and Winepress* wh. I have not time to do now, and I want you to get the book at once, so I will send a copy shortly.

To Robert Bridges

[30 August 1867]

Dear Bridges,—

I heard of Dolben's death° the day I returned fr. Paris° by a letter fr. Coles wh. had been a week waiting for me. Edgell° has since written me a few more particulars. I have kept the beginning of a letter to you a long time by me but to no purpose so far as being more ready to write goes. There is very little I have to say. I looked forward to meeting Dolben and his being a Catholic more than to anything. At the same time from never having met him but once I find it difficult to realise his death or feel as if it were anything to me. You know there can very seldom have happened the loss of so much beauty° (in body and mind and life) and of the promise of still more as there has been in his case—seldom I mean, in the whole world, for the conditions wd. not easily come together. At the same time he had gone on in a way wh. was wholly and unhappily irrational. I want to know whether his family think of gathering and publishing, or at least printing, his poetry.° Perhaps you will like to hear what Dr. Newman says. 'Yes, we heard all about Dolben. The account was very pleasant. He had not given up the idea of being a Catholic, but he thought he had lived on excitement, and felt he must give himself time before he could know whether he was in earnest or not. This does not seem to me a wrong frame of mind. He was up to his death careful in his devotional exercises. I never saw him.' Some day I hope to see Finedon and the place where he was drowned too. Can you tell me where he was buried?—at Finedon,° was it not? If you have letters from him will you let me see them some day?

Many thanks about Rochdale. It is, as you say, impossible that I shd. see you this vacation. I may be in Oxford next term for a day or less, when of course I shall come to you. I am now staying with Urquhart, who desires to be remembered. On the 10th of next month I shall go to Edgbaston; on the 17th their school begins. I shall address this to Rochdale for you may very well have left Newmarket.

I hope your reading is going on well. So far as time allows will you write again please? I suppose your music is in abeyance but I hope it will on no account be stopped permanently. When you write let me hear everything you have to tell. Believe me always your affectionate friend,

Gerard M. Hopkins.

Aug. 30, '67—at Urquhart's, Bovey Tracy, Newton Abbot, in Devon.

P.S. Thanks for Miss Dolben's letter, wh. I enclose.

To the Revd. Edward William Urquhart

[30 September 1867]

Dear Urquhart,—

How badly you must think I have remembered my promise to write soon. If I had only done so the first week I was here it wd. have been well: ever since then I have scarcely had a minute of leisure.

First I must tell you that I had a wild tear to catch the train and there was a pain in my back for many days after it. At Exeter station I saw Tracy of Ch. Ch. and Mr. Oxenham° of Torquay together; the latter had on a remarkable cap like an ancient helmet with *bucculae*,° if you know what they were.

My box came all right. I went, the day before the boys came back, to Oxford to get my things and there Wharton° entertained me very kindly. I had to borrow one of Mrs. Ridley's boxes. For the first week I was in the Oratory as a guest: now I am in the house where Walford was and do not see anything of the Oratory. Fancy me getting up at a quarter past six: it is however done with a melancholy punctuality nearly every morning. The boys' mass is at seven; then what they call Preparation fr. 7.45 to 8.30; then breakfast in Hall, so to speak; at 9.30 school till 12; dinner in Hall at 1; school fr. 2 to 3; then the boys and sometimes I go to their field, which they call Bosco, for a game, just now hockey but soon football; at 6 tea in Hall; from 6.30 to 8.30 school. My class is the fifth but besides this my work includes two private pupils who come to me fr. 8.45 to 10 on all nights but Saturday and fr. 5 to 6 on the half-holidays Tuesday, Thursday, and Saturday. With reading the class books and looking over exercises (which takes a long time) I find all my time occupied. Today however is Sunday and the boys are playing fives like good ones: I wish they wd. play all the other numbers on the clock all the other days of the week. The fifth, the head class, has only five boys: thus I have seven. I feel as if they were all my children, a notion encouraged by their innocence and backwardness. They never swear beyond Confound you, you young fool, and that only one of them. The masters' table appears to be the dregs of Great Britain, indeed one of us is a Dutchman but I cannot spell his name: when I say dregs I only mean that they come fr. all quarters indiscriminately and I include myself: it is sweepings, not dregs I mean. They are nice souls and one of them, a very young man, I like particularly. I see no papers: if democracy shd. be established or Mr. Disraeli take that title I was mentioning of Earl Mount Horeb, Baron Bashan, will you let me hear of it? I get no letters, which may depend upon or merely synchronise with my not writing any. I see I have not given you a proper notion altogether of my employment, for I have my private pupils oftener. But F. Ambrose is going to make an arrangement by which I shall get some time for private reading. Today I have been hearing a quartet on violins and violincello by the music master, one of my p.p.s, one of my fifth form boys, and Dr Newman. The country round is really very good for so near Birmingham. I wonder if there is anything I cd. do, though the income were less, wh. wd. give me more time, for I feel the want of that most of all.—All but the last few words of this were written on Michaelmas day: it is now Monday. Last night I saw Mr. Thomas Pope, until this term one of the masters here, received into the congregation of the Oratory and we have had a half-holiday for it today.

Now goodbye. Many thanks for my pleasant stay at Bovey. You may yet, I hope, be a Catholic. You know what my specific is, if you wd. only make up yr. mind to apply it.

Believe me yr. affectionate friend, Gerard M. Hopkins.

I hope for reasons of my own that Mrs. and Miss Urquhart are not gone, and will you remember me very kindly to them?

The Oratory, or 22 Plough and Harrow Road, Edgbaston, Birmingham.

Sept. 30, is it not? '67. . . .

To Robert Bridges

12 Nov. [1867]

Dearest Bridges,—

Thanks for your photograph. It is like—so most photographs are—but I mean it has an expression of yours, and photographs often miss expression altogether. Though not the best that could be done I must say I like it.

With regard to the invitation very many thanks for your kindness. But I think I will, if you will let me, refuse it. I cannot feel at my ease with regard to Dr. and Mrs. Molesworth, but beyond that too I am very unwilling, I cannot exactly explain why, to come to Rochdale. Instead of the excuses I might have given I have put it in what I am afraid you may call the rudest way. But the very pleasure I had in my stay last year is part of the reason why I do not wish to make another, if you can understand. I do not know what you will think of all this.

After what you tell me about the Doctor are you not beginning to think more particularly about what you are going to be? I want to hear about this.

I had heard nothing at all about O'Hanlon's death° but what you told me till yesterday, when Challis spoke of it. In coming here he had spent two hours at Oxford and heard of it fr. Hood of Brasenose. I must tell you that Challis is now staying at the Oratory and I hope will be here permanently.

I own I felt a good deal of satisfaction that you liked the

pattern for the cruet.° I thought before that it had very likely come out badly in the execution—a natural thing with an amateur's designs—and in any case that the people at Thorndon did not like it, or else you wd. have said they did.

I wish I knew exactly when you are in the schools.° A 2nd is the class I have always imagined you wd. get: mind it is a good one.

Believe me yr. very affectionate friend, Gerard Hopkins.

Do not again address me with that alphabet of initials, please.

Nov. 12 [1867]

To Alexander William Mowbray Baillie

The Oratory | 12 Feb. 1868

My dear Baillie,—

Though my unwillingness to write letters, important or unimportant, now amounts to a specific craze I see quite fixedly that not to do so is virtually to see and hear no more of you. But even now that I have just begun I seem suddenly to have everything to say and an impatience to do little else than to communicate myself εἰς ἄπειρον [endlessly]. I am very much obliged to you for your letters for many reasons, and you must remember that I normally need the spur. I will answer yr. questions before anything else. About *Ecce Homo*,° I am ashamed to be in the position I am but the truth is I have not read it: somehow the very kind of notoriety it had made me not care and it was also the case that I had no time hardly for anything but schools reading when it came out. I see that I ought to have and I will when I can. About Garrett I also keep saying why does he not write? I sent a letter begging him to let me hear from him to his agents some time ago. Fr. the nature of things one cannot lay one's finger on him in the way that one can on other people. Is it certain that he has not left England? By this time you must have been in for that B.N.C.° fellowship but I see papers so brokenly and seldom here that I cannot tell whether you have it or not. I wish, do you know, that you would get one (if you have not). I was much disappointed about Poutiatine: I failed to write to his address at Mr. Popove's in Welbeck Street and I have not heard from Paris yet. I have not read Ruskin's new book:° the title is perhaps vulgar. Ruskin is full of follies but I get more and more sympathetic with 'the true men' as agst. the Sophistik (observe I say K—it is not the same thing as sophistical), Philistine, Doctrinaire, Utilitarian, Positive, and on the whole Negative (as Carlyle wd. put it) side, and prefer to err with Plato. This reminds me to say that I find myself in an even prostrate admiration of Aristotle and am of the way of thinking, so far as I know him or know about him, that he is the end-all and be-all of philosophy. But I shd. be sorry to bore you with philosophy, of which you no doubt have had enough what with reading for fellowships: with me on the contrary an interest in philosophy is almost the only one I can feel myself quite free to indulge in still.

I have begun learning the violin: I am glad I have.

I must say that I am very anxious to get away from this place. I have become very weak in health and do not seem to recover myself here or likely to do so. Teaching is very burdensome, especially when you have much of it: I have. I have not much time and almost no energy—for I am always tired—to do anything on my own account. I put aside that one sees and hears nothing and nobody here. Very happily Challis of Merton is now here; else the place were without reservation 'damned, shepherd'.° (This is not swearing.) I ought to make the exception that the boys are very nice indeed. I am expecting to take orders and soon, but I wish it to be secret till it comes about. Besides that it is the happiest and best way it practically is the only one. You know I once wanted to be a painter. But even if I could I wd. not I think, now, for the fact is that the higher and more attractive parts of the art put a strain upon the passions which I shd. think it unsafe to encounter. I want to write still and as a priest I very likely can do that too, not so freely as I shd. have liked, e.g. nothing or little in the verse way, but no doubt what wd. best serve the cause of my religion. But if I am a priest it will cause my mother, or she says it will, great grief and this preys on my mind very much and makes the near prospect quite black. The general result is that I am perfectly reckless about things that I shd. otherwise care about, uncertain as I am whether in a few months I may not be shut up in a cloister, and this state of mind, though it is painful coming to, when reached gives a great and real sense of freedom. Do you happen to know of any tutorship I cd. take for a few months after Easter? as I am anxious to leave this place then and also not to leave it without having secured something to live upon till, as seems likely, I take minor orders.°

Is it at Mrs Cunliffe's that you are staying? If so she has gone and renumbered herself again.—O that one shd. ever have been younger and more foolish! Do you know—my mother reminded me—that Mrs. Cunliffe once asked me to dinner and I refused, Puseyite that I was, because it was a Friday. I went to call there last summer but she was not in.

Wood is going or gone to America for a visit.

Now I think of it it is very unlikely that Garrett shd. have left England.

Is it true that Rogers° was mobbed out of his chair or on the contrary that he is incapable of reelection?

When this letter comes to hand you must be very corresponsive: you must, please, write news, criticism, confidences, and where I can get the above-mentioned employment.

There has come out a transl. of Horace in verse by one Mathews,° a Cambridge man, very good, the best I ever saw.

Have you read the *Pervigilium Veneris*?° It is about equal to the Atys and, I think, as beautiful as or more beautiful than anything of the same length in Latin.

Believe me always your affectionate friend,

Gerard M. Hopkins.

The Oratory. Feb. 12, 1868

To the Revd. Edward William Urquhart

[13 June 1868]

Dear Urquhart,—

. . . About the end of the month I am going to Switzerland for a month with Edward Bond and when I return shall be admitted at once to the Jesuit noviciate at Roehampton. It is enough to say that the sanctity has not departed fr. the order to have a reason for joining it. Since I made up my mind to this I have enjoyed the first complete peace of mind I have ever had. I am quite surprised—not that on reflection it is surprising—at the kind and contented way my parents have come to take the prospect.

With regard to the rejoinder you speak for I think argument is not only useless but tends to encourage the way of thinking of yr. position as if intellectual and not moral hindrance stood between you and the Catholic Church. If I tell you the truth it is that you are trying the forbearance of God and that the most terrible things our Lord uttered were spoken to some who had to all appearance more excuse than you. The way you write, peculiar so far as I know among your school to yourself, whether blindness or as I suppose irony, I can only call desperate. I know that living a moral life, with the ordinances of religion and yourself a minister of them, with work to do and the interest of a catholicwards movement to support you, it is most natural to say *all things continue as they were* and most hard to realise the silence and the severity of God, as Dr. Newman very eloquently and persuasively has said in a passage of the Anglican Difficulties; but this plea or way of thinking—all things continuing as they were—is the very character of infidelity. The difference between a state of grace and a state of reprobation, that difference to wh. all other differences of humanity are as the splitting of straws, makes no change in the outer world; faces, streets, and sunlight look just the same: it is therefore the more dangerous and terrible. And if God says that without faith it is impossible to please Him and will not excuse the best of heathens with the best of excuses for the want of it what is to be said of people who knowing it live in avowed doubt whether they are in His church or not? Will it comfort you at death not to have despaired of the English Church if by not despairing of it you are out of the Catholic Church?—a contingency which by the fact of doubt you contemplate. Will God thank you for yr. allegiance and will He excuse you for it? He asks obedience before everything else. Make half an hour's meditation on death and suppose you have received what you call the last sacrament: it will then occur—*perhaps* this is not a sacrament and if not it is a mockery to me and God; secondly, if it is, *perhaps* it is received in schism and I have wounded my soul with the 'instrument of salvation': this *perhaps* which gives little trouble on an ordinary Sunday will be very terrible then. Then if you add—but will not God allow for the possible mistake because I cd. not help being deceived? you will be able to answer—*certainly not*: I always knew there was a doubt. Dare to think of this fixedly even for three minutes if you will not make the longer meditation. And above all things say *Domine, quid vis ut faciam?* [Lord, what would you have me do?] Say it and force yourself to mean it. Until you prefer God to the world and yourself you have not made the first step. You see I do not apologise for this language: it is, I think, now my right and my duty to use it. In conclusion I earnestly beg you to say *Domine, quid vis ut faciam?* and, if you will, ask our Lady's help.

Believe me yr. affectionate friend—Gerard M. Hopkins.

Oak Hill, Hampstead, N.W. June 13, 1868.

To Kate Hopkins, sen.

[11 July 1868]

My dearest Mother,—

We° have had no time to write before. We are now at the Hôtel Brünig, Lungern, Oberwalden. We came by Dover, Ostende, Brussels the first day, to Cologne the next, up the Rhine to Mainz the next, by train to Basel the next. Basel we liked immensely and saw it by moonlight. Next day we reached Lucerne by train. Next day we went by steamboat to Küssnacht, walked across the neck of land to Immensee on the lake of Zug, went by steamboat to Arth and thence up the Rigi, where we saw an indifferent sunset and slept. Next morning we had a favourable sunrise and a grand view of the Alps on the south side. We went down to Wäggis and by steamer back to Lucerne. Next day we walked by the lake to Alpnach and there took a carriage on to Lungern. Next day, yesterday, we took a guide for the Wylerhorn, but cloud hanging on the top did not expect a view and dismissed him: we wandered up and nearly got to the top, which looked like clearing, but cloud coming on were frightened back—and then it became clear after all. Still we had grand views. Today we walked to Brienz and crossed here—to the Giessbach hotel—by rowboat. We have just seen the falls illuminated. Tomorrow we go by steamboat to Interlaken and on to Lauterbrunnen. If I am ever to get this letter off it must be by writing no more than this catalogue of things. The mountains fully satisfy me and today (Sunday) the costumes are most pretty. My cut finger is nearly well. In point of money we are getting on about as well as we expected. I have lost a pair of scissors and my toothbrush with its little cap, and the pills, which were in the soap-box, got soaked and looked like black currants, so I thew them out of window. We take to our exertions, we find, kindly. It is very hot. I must now cease.

With love to all believe me yr. loving son—

Gerard M. Hopkins.

Best address—*Poste restante*, Zermatt.

July 11, 1868.

The first page was blotted with the most dreadful pounce.

I got the letter at Lucerne, thank you.

To Robert Bridges

[7 August 1868]

Dear Bridges,—

I have been back since Saturday night. Yr. letter came before I started and yr. books were sent after I had gone. My mother directed of course that they shd. be paid for and I hope they were but we cannot ascertain till the carrier people send in their bill. I shd. be glad to hear also that they came safe.

I shall be here, I am expecting, till some time in September, when I shall enter the 30 days retreat which begins the noviciate. After the retreat I can always be seen by calling at Manresa House, Roehampton, S.W.—it is easily accessible—and can be written to but the letters will of course be read and I doubt whether I shall be able to write in answer. But I hope we shall now meet soon and for that reason I need not write much.

I cannot send my *Summa*° for it is burnt with my other verses: I saw they wd. interfere with my state and vocation. I kept however corrected copies of some things which you have and will send them that what you have got you may have in its last edition.

Write and say when and where you will be in town and believe me ever yr. affectionate friend Gerard M. Hopkins.

Oak Hill, Hampstead. Aug. 7, '68

P.S. I hope you will master the peculiar beat I have introduced into St. Dorothea.° The development is mine but the beat is in Shakspere—e.g.

Whý should thís desert be?°—

and

Thoú for whóm Jóve would swear°—where the rest of the lines are eight-syllabled or seven-syllabled.

To Kate Hopkins, sen.

[10 September 1868]

My dearest Mother,—

I was three quarters of an hour early for my train, as you will have heard, and in the meantime I went to Victoria Road, where I found Grandmamma unwell. Mrs Eden came in while I was there, which enabled Aunt Annie° to come with me to the station and see me off. Whether I was last in that night I cannot quite make out.

There are five novices besides myself now entered and another is expected. The odd thing is that one of them is called Hopkins, so that we must keep our Christian names to avoid confusion and on the other hand I must keep my surname because there is already a brother Jerrard with a J. At present we have two companions appointed us to get us into the rules etc, John Walford being one, but otherwise we do not as yet mix with the other novices. The retreat begins I believe on Monday but will be broken twice or more and this may perhaps give me the chance of writing. Just now I cannot write any more because of the post and disposition of our times and I thought you wd. rather have a short letter than none. All that occurs to me to say is that we have to keep our rooms tidy to an extraordinary degree. I may remark that just now I have a bedroom but in a short time shall move into one of the dormitories or, as they call them, Quarters.

I hope now that you will lose no time in getting yr. holiday: the weather may not last. Give my best love to all and believe me always yr. loving son— Gerard M. Hopkins.

P.S. Will you let me know fr. nurse exactly the number of pairs of socks I brought. I am sorry I changed coats with Cyril: the blue one wd. have done.

Manresa House, Roehampton, S.W.

I think if it is the same to you I wd. rather have my likeness enclosed in an envelope to E. Corry Esq., The Oratory, Edgbaston: there is no reason why it shd. go the roundabout course of coming here first. You can of course tell me how you liked them.

To Robert Bridges

[29 April 1869]

My dear Bridges,—

It is nearly a fortnight since my mother gave me the sad news of Mrs. Plow's death but I have not till today had an opportunity of writing to you, as I wished to do. I cannot help thinking that perhaps for her own sake she could not have much wished to live longer with such dreadful grief° upon her memory but it is different with you and with your mother: I have wondered with myself how Mrs. Molesworth would bear all these things. I know nothing but the fact of your sister's death, so that I can only speak generally. No doubt her health never really recovered the first shock. What suffering she had! Even during Mr Plow's life she had troubles, you told me, and it appeared in her face. But sufferings falling on such a person as your sister was are to be looked on as the marks of God's particular love and this is truer the more exceptional they are. I wonder what will become of her child: she had not more than one living, I think.

I am very sorry you had your journey here for nothing, as I afterwards found: at the time the community was unluckily in a three days' retreat. I wd. make this letter longer if I had more to say but as I know no particulars about yourself and I cd. not say anything else that wd. interest you I think it is better to send it off: as it is I have had it some time in my drawer. Let me assure you of my most earnest sympathy, which I can the more easily give as I had the happiness of a little knowing your sister, and believe me always

your affectionate friend Gerard M. Hopkins.

Manresa House, Roehampton, S.W. April 29, 1869.

To Robert Bridges

[2 April 1871]

My dear Bridges,—

I hear nothing whatever of you and the fault is certainly mine. I am going to address this to Rochdale, because you may have changed your lodgings° in town. I am now at Stonyhurst reading philosophy and mathematics: at present it is holidays. I shall be here some long time to come, I expect. Perhaps you have seen the place: it is bare and bleak but the rivers are beautiful. I shall not write more now, indeed I have nothing to say.° Please tell me all about yourself. I am sure I must have behaved unkindly when you came to Roehampton. Believe me always your affectionate friend

Gerard Hopkins.

Stonyhurst College, Whalley, Lancashire. April 2, 1871.

To Alexander William Mowbray Baillie

[10 April 1871]

My dear Baillie,—

Your letters are always welcome but often or always it is more pleasant to get them than easy to see how they are to be answered. So with today's dinner and tomorrow twelve month's butcher's bill. My time is short both for writing and reading, so that I can seldom write and when I do I have nothing to say. Don't you know, it is mainly about books and so on that I shd. be writing and I read so few. I am going through a hard course of scholastic logic (not just at present: it is holidays) which takes all the fair part of the day and leaves one fagged at the end for what remains. This makes the life painful to nature. I find now too late *how* to read—at least some books, e.g. the classics: now I see things, now what I read tells, but I am obliged to read by snatches.—I will not go a step further till I have explained that down to the bottom of the last page I was writing with the worst of steel pens and most of it with a dreadfully cold hand but now the grey goose and I are come to terms at the point of the knife—this to forestall your cuts and snarls at my material worsening.

I will tell you something about this place. Perpetual winter smiles. In the first place we have the highest rain-guage in England, I believe: this our observatory shews and a local rhyme expresses as much. Early in the year they told me there wd. be no spring such as we understood it in the south. When I asked about May they told me they had hail in May. Of June they told me it had one year been so cold that the procession could not be held on Corpus Christi. The country is also very bare and bleak—what its enemies say of Scotland, only that a young Campbell at Roehampton shewed me that Argyleshire was the warmest part of Great Britain, that greenhouse fuchsias grew in the open air, and that the pomegranate was for ever on the bough. But nevertheless it is fine scenery, great hills and 'fells' with noble outline often, subject to charming effects of light (though I am bound to say that total obscuration is the commonest effect of all), and three beautiful rivers. The clouds in particular are more interesting than in any other place I have seen. But they must be full of soot, for the fleeces of the sheep are quite black with it. We also see the northern lights to advantage at times. There is good fishing for those who do not see that after bad fishing the next worse thing is good fishing. At the College close by is a big library.

Let me see what books I can speak of.—I find nothing or nothing that I cd. at present say shortly and if I keep this longer I might perhaps never send it. I am glad to hear literary etc news as I am here removed from it and get much behind. I hope you find yourself happy in town: this life here though it is hard is God's will for me as I most intimately know, which is more than violets knee-deep. This sprig of rhetoric brings me to a close. Believe me always

your affectionate friend Gerard M. Hopkins.

Stonyhurst, Whalley, Lancashire. April 10, 1871.

To Robert Bridges

[2 August 1871]

My dear Bridges,—

Our holidays have begun, so I will write again. I feel inclined to begin by asking whether you are secretary to the International° as you seem to mean me to think nothing too bad for you but then I remember that you never relished 'the intelligent artisan'. I must tell you I am always thinking of the Communist future. The too intelligent artisan is master of the situation I believe. Perhaps it is what everyone believes, I do not see the papers or hear strangers often enough to know. It is what Carlyle has long° threatened and foretold. But his writings are, as he might himself say, 'most inefficacious-strenuous heaven-protestations, caterwaul, and Cassandra-wailings'. He preaches obedience but I do not think he has done much except to ridicule instead of strengthening the hands of the powers that be. Some years ago when he published his *Shooting Niagara* he did make some practical suggestions but so vague that they should rather be called '*too* dubious moonstone-grindings and on the whole impracticable-practical unveracities'. However I am afraid some great revolution is not far off. Horrible to say, in a manner I am a Communist. Their ideal bating some things is nobler than that professed by any° secular statesman I know of (I must own I live in bat-light and shoot at a venture). Besides it is just.—I do not mean the means of getting to it are. But it is a dreadful thing for the greatest and most necessary part of a very rich nation to live a hard life without dignity, knowledge, comforts, delight, or hopes in the midst of plenty—which plenty they make. They profess that they do not care what they wreck and burn, the old civilisation and order must be destroyed. This is a dreadful look out but what has the old civilisation done for them? As it at present stands in England it is itself in great measure founded on wrecking. But they got none of the spoils, they came in for nothing but harm from it then and thereafter. England has grown hugely wealthy but this wealth has not reached the working classes; I expect it has made their condition worse. Besides this iniquitous order the old civilisation embodies another order mostly° old and what is new in direct entail from the old, the old religion, learning, law, art, etc and all the history that is preserved in standing monuments. But as the working classes have not been educated they know next to nothing of all this and cannot be expected to care if they destroy it. The more I look the more black and deservedly black the future looks, so I will write no more.

I can hardly believe that this is August and your letter dated May. True there has been here and I believe elsewhere no summer between. There seems some chance now. In a fortnight we are going, also for a fortnight, to Inellan in Argyleshire on the Clyde. After that I expect to pay my people a short visit down near Southampton, where they have taken a cottage. None of them are turned Catholics: I do not expect it.—Believe me your affectionate friend

Gerard Hopkins, S.J.

Stonyhurst, Whalley, Lancashire. Aug. 2, 1871.

To Edward Bond

[4 August 1873]

Dear Edward,—

This letter is going to be quite short, as the paper shews. I am at Douglas in the Isle of Man again, same house as last year. Next year (from September) will be spent in teaching at Stonyhurst or elsewhere. Then I am to begin my theology and the course lasts four years. . . .

I have brought Mat Arnold's poems, the Empedocles volume, down here with me and read them with more interest than rapture, as you will easily understand, for they seem to have all the ingredients of poetry without quite being it—no ease or something or other, like the plum pudding at the English ambassador's, but still they do not leave off of being, as the French say, very beautiful. Besides he seems a very earnest man and distinctly seeing the difference between jest and earnest and a master in both, and this praise will also apply to you, I hope. But then very unhappily he jokes at the wrong things, as I see by a very profane passage quoted from his new book:° however that passage though profane is not blasphemous, for we are obliged to think of God by human thoughts and his account of them is substantially true. (I am obliged to go to broad guage paper.) This reminds me that I have been reading the *Grammar of Assent*:° have you? It is perhaps heavy reading. The justice and candour and gravity and rightness of mind is what is so beautiful in all he writes but what dissatisfies me (in point of style) is a narrow circle of instance and quotation—in a man too of great learning and of general reading—quite like the papers in the *Spectator* and a want, I think a real want, of brilliancy (which foolish people think every scribbler possesses, but it is no such thing). But he remains nevertheless our greatest living master of style—unless you think otherwise—and widest mind. Now I should be writing more carefully if it were not that people all about are reading extracts of the *Manx Sun* and *Mrs. Brown* and repeating a constructive pun I found my way into at supper and so on.

Besides all this have you read De Morgan's *Budget of Paradoxes*?° Now I have given you some matter to write about.

Tomorrow I am going up Snae Fell,° from which the Manx man can see the three kingdoms and reflect on the happiness of living under the House of Keys, which is what they call the national parliament.

Remember me very kindly to your people and believe me
yr. affectionate friend Gerard Hopkins S.J.

Derby Castle, Douglas, Aug. 4, '73.

Aug. 5—I had written the above when yr. letter containing your kind proposal came to hand, after slowly following me fr. Stonyhurst. I am sorry to have been thus unavoidably slow in answering. I am afraid that I must not avail myself of your kindness. On the score of time indeed there wd. be no difficulty on my side but leave for invitations to stay with friends who are not kindred without some more pressing reason than I could shew is so seldom given that I should not wish even to ask it. But it would have been a great pleasure to me if it had been possible.

To Robert Bridges

[22 January 1874]

My dear Bridges,—

My last letter to you was from Stonyhurst. It was not answered, so that perhaps it did not reach you. If it did I supposed then and do not know what else to suppose now that you were disgusted with the *red* opinions it expressed, being a conservative. I have little reason to be red: it was the red Commune that murdered five of our Fathers lately—whether before or after I wrote I do not remember. So far as I know I said nothing that might not fairly be said. If this was your reason for not answering it seems to shew a greater keenness about politics than is common.

I heard of you lately from an Eton and Oxford man I met—So and so, he told me, breeds fowls and Bridges writes—but nothing distinct. But in last week's *Academy* I came upon an appreciative review of a Mr. Bridges' poems, Robert Bridges the title shewed. And the characteristics the writer° found in the poems were true to you. Did I ever before see anything of yours? say in Coles' book? I cannot remember. But given that you write and have changed then I can fancy this yours—

> Next they that bear her, honoured on this night,
> And then the maidens in a double row.°

Short extracts from six poems were given. To have seen these gave me an occasion to write again. I think, my dear Bridges, to be so much offended about that red letter° was excessive.

One of my sisters,° who has become musical beyond the common, urged me to find her the music you wrote for 'O earlier shall the rose[bud]s blow'.° I hunted for it twice without finding it but I cannot have lost it. I never was quite reconciled to the freak of leaving off away from the keynote and have put imaginary endings to it several times. I myself am learning the piano now, self-taught alas! not for execution's sake but to be independent of others and learn something about music. I have very little time though. I am professor of rhetoric here since last September.

Always yr. affectionate friend Gerard M. Hopkins, S.J.

Manresa House, Roehampton, S.W. Jan. 22, 1874.

To Manley Hopkins

St. Beuno's, St. Asaph, North Wales. [29 August 1874]

My dearest Father,—

I came here yesterday, to begin my studies in theology. I had expected to have another year's teaching at Roehampton, but now my ordination and profession will be earlier. The house stands on a steep hillside, it commands the long-drawn valley of the Clwyd to the sea, a vast prospect, and opposite is Snowdon and its range, just now it being bright visible but coming and going with the weather. The air seems to me very fresh and wholesome. Holidays till the 2nd of October. After that hours of study very close—lectures in dogmatic theology, moral ditto, canon law, church history, scripture, Hebrew and what not. I have half a mind to get up a little Welsh: all the neighbours speak it. I have said nothing about the house. It is built of limestone, decent outside, skimpin within, Gothic, like Lancing College done worse. The staircases, galleries, and bopeeps are inexpressible: it takes a fortnight to learn them. Pipes of affliction convey lukewarm water of affliction to some of the rooms, others more fortunate have fires. The garden is all heights, terraces, Excelsiors, misty mountain tops, seats up trees called Crows' Nests, flights of steps seemingly up to heaven lined with burning aspiration upon aspiration of scarlet geraniums: it is very pretty and airy but it gives you the impression that if you took a step farther you would find yourself somewhere on Plenlimmon, Conway Castle, or Salisbury Craig. With best love to detachments stationed at Hampstead believe me your loving son

Gerard M. Hopkins S.J.

Aug. 29 1874.

To Kate Hopkins, sen.

St. Beuno's (not Bruno's), St. Asaph, North Wales | Sept. 20 1874.

My dearest Mother,—

I have been in an eight days' retreat ending on Friday night. On Friday, Saturday, and today ordinations have been going on here; sixteen priests were ordained this morning. I received the tonsure and the four minor orders yesterday. The tonsure consisted of five little snips but the bishop must have found even that a hard job, for I had cut my hair almost to the scalp, as it happened, just before. The four minor orders are those of Doorkeepers, Readers, Exorcists, and Acolytes: their use is almost obsolete. The holy orders are of Subdeacons, Deacons, and Priests.

I have got a yearning for the Welsh people and could find it in my heart to work for their conversion. However on consideration it seems best to turn my thoughts elsewhere. I say this because, though I am not my own master, yet if people among us shew a zeal and aptitude for a particular work, say foreign missions, they can commonly get employed on them. The Welsh round are very civil and respectful but do not much come to us and those who are converted are for the most part not very stanch. They are much swayed by ridicule. Wesleyanism is the popular religion. They are said to have a turn for religion, especially what excites outward fervour, and more refinement and pious feeling than the English peasantry but less steadfastness and sincerity. I have always looked on myself as half Welsh and so I warm to them. The Welsh landscape has a great charm and when I see Snowdon and the mountains in its neighbourhood, as I can now, with the clouds lifting, it gives me a rise of the heart. I ought to say that the Welsh have the reputation also of being covetous and immoral: I add this to forestall your saying it, for, as I say, I warm to them—and in different degrees to all the Celts.

The Provincial° was here a few days ago. It seems he wrote a letter giving me leave to spend a week with you at Lyme on my way or beside my way here, but I had already started. You will be vexed at this; at the same time it shews how thoughtful he is.

I fear my music has come to an end. I am very sorry, though practising (and I made singularly little way: I think I must be musically deficient somewhere) was a burden and here especially so, with a grunting harmonium that lived in the sacristy.

With best love to all believe me your loving son

Gerard M. Hopkins S.J.

Mind about BEUNO.

I see the *Academy* no more but among the last things I read in it was Tyndall's address.° I thought it interesting and eloquent, though it made me 'most mad'. It is not only that he looks back to an obscure origin, he looks forward with the same content to an obscure future—to be lost 'in the infinite azure of the past' (fine phrase by the by). I do not think, do you know, that Darwinism implies necessarily that man is descended from any ape or ascidian or maggot or what not but only from the common ancestor of maggots, and so on: these common ancestors, if lower animals, need not have been repulsive animals. What Darwin himself says about this I do not know. You should read St. George Mivart's *Genesis of Species*: he is an Evolutionist though he combats downright Darwinism and is very orthodox. To return to Tyndall—I notice that he has no sense of relative weights of authority: he quotes Draper, Whewell and other respectable writers for or against Aristotle, Bacon etc as if it were just the same thing and you were keeping at the same level—the Lord Chief Justice rules this way, his parlourmaid however says it should be the other, and so on. However Tyndall was kind to Edward and me at the foot of the Matterhorn.° I fear he must be called an atheist but he is not a shameless one: I wish he might come round.

This letter is quite long. Believe me your loving son

Gerard M. Hopkins S.J.

Monday now, Sept. 21. One of my late pupils has suddenly died.°

To Robert Bridges

St. Beuno's College, St. Asaph, North Wales. Feb. 20, 1875.

My dearest Bridges,—

The above address shews how impossible it is for me to execute your kind and welcome wish by calling at Maddox Street. There was never any moral difficulty, I could have got leave to spend more than an hour and a half with you, but a long crow-flight is between us—one over which the crowquill, to follow the lead of my own thoughts, does not carry. But if you had sent me such an invitation last year, when I really was at Roehampton, what a pleasure it would have been and what a break in the routine of rhetoric, which I taught so badly and so painfully!

You will wonder what I do under the sign of those Welsh saints. Study theology—for four years from last September. We live on a hillside of the beautiful valley of the Clwyd, but now the other side of the valley vanishes in mist and the ground is deep in snow.

Feb. 22—It was yesterday waistdeep in the drifts.

I have quite forgotten what I may have said in my last letter. What you write about yourself interests me of course but is beyond me: I have had no time to read even the English books about Hegel, much less the original, indeed I know almost no German. (However I think my contemporary Wallace° of Balliol has been translating him). I do not afflict myself much about my ignorance here, for I could remove it as far as I should much care to do, whenever it became advisable, hereafter, but it was with sorrow I put back Aristotle's Metaphysics in the library some time ago feeling that I could not read them now and so probably should never. After all I can, at all events a little, read Duns Scotus° and I care for him more even than Aristotle and more *pace tua* than a dozen Hegels. However this is me, not you. But it explains why I can do nothing more than say how much I like to hear about you and how glad I am you are as you say, nearer the top than the bottom of Hegel's or anybody else's bottomless pit.

I wd. have answered more promptly but I saw that you would not be in London for some little time. The close pressure of my theological studies leaves me time for hardly anything: the course is very hard, it must be said. Nevertheless I have tried to learn a little Welsh, in reality one of the hardest of languages.*

Believe me always your affectionate friend

Gerard M. Hopkins S.J.

To Kate Hopkins, sen.

St. Beuno's. Christmas Eve, 1875

My dearest Mother,—

Many thanks to you for your loving letter and presents and a very happy Christmas to you all. In particular thank Kate for her letter. I also return Grace's paper but I am persuaded that if she did write on the subject she would express herself far more simply and intelligibly than Mr. Nicholas Breakspear,° the effect of whose style on me is not, in his own words, 'the impartance of Emotional Pleasure': it is a great babble and he cannot say a plain thing in a plain way (I believe musical people never can). (I have just found that his name is Eustace, not Nicholas, by George.) When I next write to her I will add what little remains to be said. The nasty oilstain on the outside sheet was made in the post: this is the third paper here I have seen in that condition, but the others were worse.

I am obliged for the cuttings, nevertheless you made two oversights. You sent two duplicates, for one thing, and the other was that you omitted the most interesting piece of all, the account of the actual shipwreck:° fortunately I had read it but still I should have been glad to have had it by me to refer to again, for I am writing something on this wreck, which may perhaps appear but it depends on how I am speeded. It

* Hebrew is part of our curriculum.

made a deep impression on me, more than any other wreck or accident I ever read of.

My gas does flicker but I have ceased to care for it or notice it. My neighbour has got a new burner, lucky for him: it does not perceptibly lessen my light. On the other hand he has lost eight teeth.

Do you know if anything is said of a comet?° I have seen one three nights. It appears to be in Cancer. It is small and pale but quite visible. If it is not a comet it must be a nebula and then it is strange I should not have noticed it before but its appearance is in all respects that of a comet. At ten o'clock it is well visible in the northeast, not high; later it would be higher.

Have you guessed the charade in the Xmas *Illustrated?* I have.

Where is Aunt Anne spending her Christmas? and where Aunt Kate?°

With the best Christmas wishes to all I remain your loving son Gerard M. Hopkins S.J.

I want to write Everard a little note of congratulation. By the by he appeared unmistakeably in *Iced Tea.*

To Manley Hopkins

St. Beuno's, St. Asaph (not Asaph's), North Wales. | Aug. 6 1876.

My dearest Father,—

Many thanks for your kind letter and gift. I had no less than five birthday letters.

It is holidays with us. Half our community is at Barmouth: the rest of us are to go there in our turn. Tell my mother she has not the least reason to be alarmed about the drainage. There is nothing worse than this, that the town empties its sewage, like other well-watered shores, into Neptune's salt wash, and bathers have sometimes 'gone nigh to suspecting it'. . . .

Tell my mother that my poem° is not in the August *Month* and whether it will be in the September number or in any I cannot find out: altogether it has cost me a good deal of trouble. But if you care at once to see another poem by me, there is a little piece being published with Fr. Morris's° sermon on the Silver Jubilee, that is the 25th year of episcopate of Dr. James Brown first bishop of Shrewsbury. That event came off, I think, on my birthday but he did not visit us till the next day and on Sunday we presented him with an album containing a prose address and compositions, chiefly verse, in many languages, among which were Chinese and Manchoo, all by our people, those who had been or were to be ordained by his lordship. The Chinese and Manchoo (and perhaps there may have been some others) were by a little German very very learned, with a beaky nose like a bugle horn, and they were beautifully penned by himself. For the Welsh they had to come to me, for, sad to say, no one else in the house knows anything about it; I also wrote in Latin and English, and the English was the aforesaid Silver Jubilee.° Fr. Morris preached first, for the presentation took place in Church, and after mass the Bishop sat on a throne and received the address and album and a cheque for £100 with it. In the afternoon was a high dinner and music at dessert and the Silver Jubilee was set effectively by a very musical and very noisy member of the community and was sung as a glee by the choir. My little piece is only five short stanzas long and I might easily copy it out, so I will if you like, but it looks nicer in print.

I do not think my uncle can have known what he was doing when he went to Carlsbad. The waters are good for some complaints, but they are a kill-and-cure, they are very weakening; I know a strong man who goes there now every year but he finds himself pulled down for a month after the treatment, though after that he is set up, I suppose. It is true I have not heard that my uncle drank the waters, but why else should he go to Carlsbad?

The Silver Jubilee sermon is to be published next week (perhaps that meant this week) at Burns and Lambert's.

I am all right except some indigestion.

I have heard a great deal about *Joseph and his Brethren*° and want to see it but ca'nt.

Believe me your loving son Gerard M. Hopkins S.J.

Aug. 7.

I expect you will perish with cold at Whitby.

To Robert Bridges

St. Beuno's (and not Bruno's) College, St. Asaph (nor yet Asaph's), North Wales. Feb. 24, 1877.

Dearest Bridges,—

You have forgotten or else you never got a letter I wrote *from this place* a year or so ago: it was in answer to one of yours about Henry Heine and other things, and there too you, with the same kindness and futility as now, proposed to come and see me at Roehampton hundreds of miles away. Instead therefore of coming to see me° or, as your present letter proposes, my going to see you which would indeed be the greatest pleasure but cannot however be, write that long and interesting letter. And as for your letters being opened—you made an objection before, I remember—it is quite unreasonable and superstitious to let it make any difference. To be sure they are torn half open—and so for the most part as that one can see the letter has never been out of the envelope—but how can a superior have the time or the wish to read the flood of correspondence from people he knows nothing of which is brought in by the post? No doubt if you were offering me a wife, a legacy, or a bishopric on condition of leaving my present life, and someone were to get wind of the purpose of the correspondence, *then* our letters would be well read or indeed intercepted. So think no more of that.

And as your letter to which I am to answer has yet to be written and I am on Saturday to undergo a very serious examination° I will say no more now. The pamphlets,° you know, need not wait for the letter, only I shall not read them through this week: how I wonder what they are about!—

Always your affectionate friend Gerard M. Hopkins S.J.

Usen't you to call me by my christian name? I believe you did. Well if you did I like it better.

To Robert Bridges

St. Beuno's College, St. Asaph, North Wales, April 3, 1877

Dearest Bridges,—

You have no call to complain of my delay in writing, I could not help it: I am not a consulting physician° and have little time and now I am very very tired, yes 'a thousand times and yet a thousand times' and 'scarce can go or creep'.

As for this letter, it is to soothe you and stop your mouth; I will write more elsewhen.

The elegiacs are in my judgment most elegant and Latin, full of happiness. Nevertheless they are often obscure or crabbed. You cannot say you have reached the consummate smoothness of this sort of thing—

> Donec eris felix multos numerabis amicos
> Nubila si fuerint tempora solus eris.°

The subject has no interest° except in the quaintness of bringing all those folk in. The couplet that amuses me most, so far as I remember now, is the one—

> Quale animal nunquam etc.°

Foolish sneer at Rome near the beginning: making pilgrimages is *omnibus gentibus insitum*. The italic introductory verses are the smoothest, the last the hardest and worst. I don't know when I remember to have read so much good Latin verse together, still I look upon such a performance as a waste of time and money (a pretty penny it must have cost you printing).

. . . Hoc genus infidum etc°—Now how do you explain that? *This way of study is treacherous and the knowledge drops from the reader's mind before he goes to bed*—is that it? and in the next line *arte* means *practically*? It is . . . d obscure. . . . (I allow that 'ante cubantes' *sounds* very idiomatic but it cannot mean what you seem to want it to. Or do you mean *is slept off and so dies before the sleeper?*). More hereafter.

The sonnets are truly beautiful, breathing a grave and feeling genius, and make me proud of you (which by the by is not the same as for you to be proud of yourself: I say it because you always were and I see you still are given to conceit; witness your fussing about the 'Romana venustas' epigram and quoting 'Haec tua jam, dixit' etc.).* I have scarcely read them all yet but at present like the 5th best° (the thought however is the same as in *Winter's Tale*—'I wish you A wave of the sea that you might ever do Nothing but that' etc or words to that effect)—barring the weak third line:° you mean something more like—

Her fall of fold is daylight in my view—

and barring the barbarous rhyme of *prow* and *show*:° I can't abide bad rhymes and when they are spelt alike I hate them more—more by token, you hold also the hoary superstition of *love* and *prove*. In general I do not think you have reached finality in point of execution, words might be chosen with more point and propriety, images might be more brilliant etc. I will give some instances. In IV the personification is wrong:° in general it is a principle of grammar and language of old and of poetry now that what acts is masculine, what receives action feminine. The tongue cannot be feminine in a language where its gender is not fixed already as such. Rather the heart might as a queen send the tongue as an eloquent ambassador; but your image, I don't know what it means . . .

But the turns and recoils of your thought (which generally take place in the sestet) are admirable— . . .

About the rhythm. You certainly have the gift and vein of it, but have not quite reached your perfection. Most of your Miltonic rhythms (which by the by are not so very marked as your letter led me to suppose they would be, and I think many modern poets employ them, don't they?) are fine . . . But III° has scarcely enough justification (you will allow there must always be a reason and a call for the reversed rhythm); XIII° on the other hand might well be reinforced—

* At least, you know, it looks like it.

The happier gift to me cánnot belong—

(You mean *cánnot* of course, not *can nót*).

I have paid much attention to Milton's rhythm. By the by, calling Milton rough reminds me of what Garrett (do you remember him?) overheard at the King's Head—that inn at all events at the corner of Holywell Street. An undergraduate was entertaining some friends and had ordered port. 'Waiter, I think there is something dirty floating in this wine.' 'I see nothing but a piece of beeswing, sir.' Collapse. These are the lines, I suppose, which these folk think will not scan—

By the waters of life, where'er they sat—
Light from above, from the fountain of light—
But to vanquish by wisdom hellish wiles—
Home to his mother's house private returned—°

etc. The choruses of Samson Agonistes are still more remarkable: I think I have mastered them and may some day write on the subject. However J. A. Symonds has written a paper on Milton's verse° somewhere and it has, I see, received attention of late. His achievements are quite beyond any other English poet's, perhaps any modern poet's. It happened that the other day, before you had written to me on the matter, I composed two sonnets° with rhythmical experiments of the sort, which I think I will presently enclose. How our wits jump! Not but what I have long been on metrical experiments more advanced than these. You will see that my rhythms go further than yours do in the way of irregularity. The chiming of consonants I got in part from the Welsh, which is very rich in sound and imagery.

General remarks—In spite of the Miltonic rhythms and some other points your sonnets remind one more of Shakspere's. Milton's sonnets are not tender as Shakspere's are. Yours are not at all like Wordsworth's, and a good thing too, for beautiful as those are they have an odious goodiness and neckcloth about them which half throttles their beauty. The ones I like least are those that have a Tennysonian touch° about them, as VI and VII, not for want of admiring Tennyson to be sure but because it gives them a degree of neckcloth too. I have not yet *studied* them: at a first and second reading the drift and connection is very hard to find; you seem to mean it to be so. The Our Father sonnet is very beautiful, so is the one on your mother's picture, so is XXII,° so are they all and full of manly tenderness and a flowing and never-failing music. The more I read them the more I am delighted with them. Don't like what you say of Milton, I think he was a very bad man: those who contrary to our Lord's command both break themselves and, as St. Paul says, consent to those who break the sacred bond of marriage, like Luther and Milton, fall with eyes open into the terrible judgment of God. Crying up great names, as for instance the reviews do now Swinburne and Hugo, those plagues of mankind, is often wicked and in general is a great vanity and full of impious brag and a blackguard and unspiritual mind.

. . . The examination of which I spoke is called *ad audiendas confessiones*.

You say you don't like Jesuits. Did you ever see one?

Who was St. Beuno? Is he dead? Yes, he did that much 1200 years ago, if I mistake not. He was St. Winefred's uncle and raised her to life when she died in defence of her chastity and at the same time he called out her famous spring, which fills me with devotion every time I see it and wd. fill anyone that has eyes with admiration, the flow of ἀγλαὸν ὕδωρ [beautiful water] is so lavish and so beautiful: if you have not read her story (in Butler's *Lives* or elsewhere) you should, though you should treat it as fable, as no doubt you do the Gospels. As for St. Beuno he is a mythological centre to the Welsh and crystallises superstitions or till lately did, as for instance odd marks on cattle were called Beuno's Marks.

I hear this morning April 8 that poor Alexander Wood of Trinity is stark mad. He always had insanity in him.

Your affectionate friend Gerard M. Hopkins S.J.

And don't *you* say *my* lines don't scan. Observe that I treat *ng* as elisionable, like a Latin *m*.

To William Butterfield°

St. Beuno's St. Asaph | 26 April 1877

Dear Sir,

I am exceedingly obliged to you for your kind compliance with my wish, but now that your lists are in my hands I feel ashamed to have asked so much: I did not well realise how long the catalogue would have to be.

Keble College I am very likely to see and those of your buildings in London which I did not know of, the others I shall visit as chance puts me in the way. I hope you will long continue to work out yr beautiful and original style. I do not think this generation will ever much admire it. They do not understand how to look at a Pointed building as a whole having a single form governing it throughout, which they *would* perhaps see in a Greek temple: they like it to be a sort of farmyard and medley of ricks and roofs and dovecots. And very few people seem to care for pure beauty of line, at least till they are taught to.

Believe me, dear Sir, very gratefully yours

Gerard M. Hopkins S.J.

To Robert Bridges

St. Beuno's, St. Asaph. Aug. 21 1877.

Dearest Bridges,—

Your letter cannot amuse Father Provincial, for he is on the unfathering deeps outward bound to Jamaica: I shd. not think of telling you anything about his reverence's goings and comings if it were it not that I know this fact has been chronicled in the Catholic papers.

Enough that it amuses me, especially the story about Wooldridge and the Wagnerite, wh. is very good.

Your parody reassures me about your understanding the metre. Only remark, as you say that there is no conceivable licence I shd. not be able to justify, that with all my licences, or rather laws, I am stricter than you and I might say than anybody I know. With the exception of the *Bremen* stanza,° which was, I think, the first written after 10 years' interval of silence, and before I had fixed my principles, my rhymes are rigidly good—to the ear—and such rhymes as *love* and *prove* I scout utterly. And my quantity is not like 'Fĭfty̆twō Bĕdfŏrd Squāre',° where *fĭfty̆* might pass but *Bĕdfŏrd* I should never admit. Not only so but Swinburne's dactyls and anapaests are halting to my ear: I never allow e.g. *I* or *my* (that is diphthongs, for *I* = *a* + *i* and *my* = *ma* + *i*) in the short or weak syllables of those feet, excepting before vowels, semi-vowels, or *r*, and rarely then, or when the measure becomes (what is the word?) molossic [amphibrachic]—thus: ⏑–⏑|⏑–⏑|⏑–⏑, for then the first short is almost long. If you look again you will see. So that I may say my apparent licences are counterbalanced, and more, by my strictness. In fact all English verse, except Milton's, almost, offends me as 'licentious'. Remember this.

I do not of course claim to have invented *sprung rhythms* but only *sprung rhythm*; I mean that single lines and single instances of it are not uncommon in English and I have pointed them out in lecturing—e.g. 'why should this ⁚ desert be?'°—which the editors have variously amended; 'There to meet ⁚ with Macbeth' or 'There to meet with Mac ⁚ beth';° Campbell has some throughout the *Battle of the Baltic*—'and their fleet along the deep ⁚ proudly shone'—and *Ye Mariners*—'as ye sweep ⁚ through the deep' etc; Moore has some which I cannot recall; there is one in *Grongar Hill*;° and, not to speak of *Pom pom*, in Nursery Rhymes, Weather Saws, and Refrains they are very common—but what I do in the *Deutschland* etc is to enfranchise them as a regular and permanent principle of scansion.

There are no outriding feet in the *Deutschland*. An outriding foot is, by a sort of contradiction, a recognized extra-metrical effect; it is and it is not part of the metre; not part of it, not being counted, but part of it by producng a calculated effect which tells in the general success. But the long, e.g. seven-syllabled, feet of the *Deutschland*, are strictly metrical. Outriding feet belong to counterpointed verse,° which supposes a well-known and unmistakeable or unforgetable standard rhythm: the *Deutschland* is not counterpointed; counterpoint is excluded by sprung rhythm. But in some of my sonnets° I have mingled the two systems: this is the most delicate and difficult business of all.

The choruses in *Samson Agonistes* are intermediate between counterpointed and sprung rhythm. In reality they are sprung, but Milton keeps up a fiction of counterpointing the heard rhythm (which is the same as the mounted rhythm) upon a standard rhythm which is never heard but only counted and therefore really does not exist. The want of a metrical notation and the fear of being thought to write mere rhythmic or (who knows what the critics might not have said?) even unrhythmic prose drove him to this. Such rhythm as French and Welsh poetry has is sprung, counterpointed upon a counted rhythm, but it differs from Milton's in being little calculated, not more perhaps than prose consciously written rhymically, like orations for instance; it is in fact the *native rhythm* of the words used bodily imported into verse; whereas Milton's mounted rhythm is a real poetical rhythm, having its own laws and recurrence, but further embarrassed by having to count.

Why do I employ sprung rhythm at all? Because it is the nearest to the rhythm of prose, that is the native and natural rhythm of speech, the least forced, the most rhetorical and emphatic of all possible rhythms, combining, as it seems to me, opposite and, one wd. have thought, incompatible excellences, markedness of rhythm—that is rhythm's self—and naturalness of expression—for why, if it is forcible in prose to say 'lashed ⁚ rod',° am I obliged to weaken this in verse, which ought to be stronger, not weaker, into 'láshed birch-ród', or something?

My verse is less to be read than heard, as I have told you before; it is oratorical, that is the rhythm is so. I think if you will study what I have here said you will be much more pleased with it and may I say? converted to it.

You ask may you call it 'presumptious jugglery'. No, but only for this reason, that *presumptious* is not English.

I cannot think of altering anything. Why shd. I? I do not write for the public. You are my public and I hope to convert you.

You say you wd. not for any money read my poem again. Nevertheless I beg you will. Besides money, you know, there is love. If it is obscure do not bother yourself with the meaning but pay attention to the best and most intelligible stanzas, as the two last of each part and the narrative of the wreck. If you had done this you wd. have liked it better and sent me some serviceable criticisms, but now your criticism is of no use, being only a protest memorialising me against my whole policy and proceedings.

I may add for your greater interest and edification that what refers to myself in the poem is all strictly and literally true and did all occur; nothing is added for poetical padding.

Believe me your affectionate friend

Gerard M. Hopkins S.J.

To Kate Hopkins, sen.

St. Beuno's, St. Asaph. Oct. 9 1877.

My dearest Mother,—

I am glad that my dear grandfather's end° was peaceful and that all his children could be present to witness the last moments of an affectionate and generous father. But there is one circumstance about it which gives me the deepest consolation: I shall communicate it to you, think of it what you like. I had for years been accustomed every day to recommend him very earnestly to the Blessed Virgin's protection, so that I could say, if such a thing can ever be said without presumption, If I am disappointed who can hope? As his end drew near I had asked some people to pray for him and said to someone in a letter that I should take it as a happy token if he died on Sunday the Feast of the Holy Rosary. It is a day signalised by our Lady's overruling aid asked for and given at the victory of Lepanto.° This year the anniversary is better marked than usual, for Lepanto was fought on the 7th of October but the feast is kept on the first Sunday in the month whatever the day: this time they coincide. I receive it without questioning as a mark that my prayers have been heard and that the queen of heaven has saved a Christian soul from enemies more terrible than a fleet of infidels. Do not make light of this, for it is perhaps the seventh time that I think I have had some token from heaven in connection with the death of people in whom I am interested.

Since Saturday week I have been sick in bed, today I am up for the first time, in a few days' time I shall be completely recovered, and am then to go to Mount St. Mary's College, Chesterfield, Derbyshire (Chesterfield is the address). I cannot write more about it now. The work is nondescript—examining, teaching, probably with occasional mission work and preaching or giving retreats attached: I shall know more when I am there. The number of scholars is about 150, the community moderately small and family-like, the country round not very interesting but at a little distance is fine country, Sheffield is the nearest great town. The people call the place Spink Hill, Eckington is the station.

Believe me your loving son Gerard M. Hopkins S.J.

To Robert Bridges

Mount St. Mary's College, Chesterfield. [25 February 1878]

Dearest Bridges,—

The above has been my address since October and you may send the Deutschland to it or she will in course of time be lost.

I was pleased and flattered to hear of your calling at Oak Hill and Mrs. Molesworth with you, which was very kind, and that twice: nothing pleasanter could have happened. Remember me very kindly to her and say how glad I was.

Write me an interesting letter. I cannot do so. Life here is as dank as ditch-water and has some of the other qualities of ditch-water: at least I know that I am reduced to great weakness by diarrhoea, which lasts too, as if I were poisoned.

Today Feb. 25 [1878] is a holiday in honour of Pope Leo XIII, or else this note would have lain still longer no doubt.

Believe me your affectionate friend Gerard M. Hopkins.

To Robert Bridges

Mount St. Mary's College, Chesterfield. April 2 1878.

My dearest Bridges,—

Your last letter was very kind indeed, but I should have lost all shame if under any circumstances I had allowed such a thing to be as for you to come hundreds of miles to cure me.

I am overjoyed to hear of your and Mrs. Molesworth's intercourse with Oak Hill.

It was pleasing and flattering to hear that Mr. Pater remembers and takes an interest in me.

My muse turned utterly sullen in the Sheffield smoke-ridden air and I had not written a line till the foundering of the Eurydice the other day° and that worked on me and I am making a poem—in my own rhythm but in a measure something like Tennyson's *Violet*° (bound with *Maud*), e.g.—

They say who saw one sea-corpse cold
How hé was of lovely manly mould,
    Every inch a tar,
Of the bést we bóast séamen áre.

Look, from forelock down to foot he,
Strung by duty is strained to beauty
    And russet-of-morning-skinned
With the sún, sált, and whírling wínd.

Oh! his ními ble finger, his gnárled gríp!
Léagues, léagues of séamanshíp
    Slumber in his forsaken
Bones and will not, will not waken.

I have consistently carried out my rhyming system, using the first letter of the next line to complete the rhyme in the line before it.

Well, write those things that 'will tickle me'.

The Deutschland would be more generally interesting if there were more wreck and less discourse, I know, but still it is an ode° and not primarily a narrative. There is some narrative in Pindar but the principal business is lyrical. This poem on the Eurydice is hitherto almost all narrative however.

And what are you doing?

From notices in the *Athenaeum* it would appear that Gosse, Dobson, and Co. are still fumbling with triolets, villanelles, and what not.

Believe me your affectionate friend

Gerard M. Hopkins S.J.

April 3.

To Robert Bridges

Stonyhurst College, Blackburn (or Whalley). May 13 1878°

Dearest Bridges,—

Remark the above address. After July I expect to be stationed in town—111 Mount Street, Grosvenor Square. . . .

I enclose you my Eurydice, which the *Month* refused. It is my only copy. Write no bilgewater about it: I will presently tell you what that is and till then excuse the term. I must tell you I am sorry you never read the Deutschland again.

Granted that it needs study and is obscure, for indeed I was not over-desirous that the meaning of all should be quite clear, at least unmistakeable, you might, without the effort that to make it all out would seem to have required, have nevertheless read it so that lines and stanzas should be left in the memory and superficial impressions deepened, and have liked some without exhausting all. I am sure I have read and enjoyed pages of poetry that way. Why, sometimes one enjoys and admires the very lines one cannot understand, as for instance 'If it were done were 'tis done' sqq.,° which is all obscure and disputed, though how fine it is everybody sees and nobody disputes. And so of many more passages in Shakspere and others. Besides you would have got more weathered to the style and its features—not really odd. Now they say that vessels sailing from the port of London will take (perhaps it should be | used once to take) Thames water for the voyage: it was foul and stunk at first as the ship worked but by degrees casting its filth was in a few days very pure and sweet and wholesomer and better than any water in the world. However that maybe, it is true to my purpose. When a new thing, such as my ventures in the Deutschland are, is presented us our first criticisms are not our truest, best, most homefelt, or most lasting but what come easiest on the instant. They are barbarous and like what the ignorant and the ruck say. This was so with you. The Deutschland on her first run worked very much and unsettled you, thickening and clouding your mind with vulgar mudbottom and common sewage (I see that I am going it with the image) and just then unhappily you *drew off* your criticisms all stinking (a necessity now of the image) and bilgy, whereas if you had let your thoughts cast themselves they would have been clearer in themselves and more to my taste too. I did not heed them therefore, perceiving they were a first drawing-off. Same of the Eurydice—which being short and easy please read more than once.

Can you tell me who that critic in the *Athenaeum*° is that writes very long reviews on English and French poets, essayists, and so forth in a style like De Quincey's, very acute in his remarks, provoking, jaunty, and (I am sorry to say) would-be humorous? He always quotes Persian stories (unless he makes them up) and talks about Rabelaesian humour.

My brother's pictures, as you say, are careless and do not aim high, but I don't think it would be much different if he were a batchelor. But, strange to say—and I shd. never even have suspected it if he had not quite simply told me—he has somehow in painting his pictures, though nothing that the pictures express, a high and quite religious aim; however I cannot be more explanatory.

Your bodysnatch story is ghastly, but so are all bodysnatch stories. My grandfather° was a surgeon, a fellow-student of Keats', and once conveyed a body through Plymouth at the risk of his own.

Believe me your affectionate friend

Gerard M. Hopkins S.J.

May 21 1878

Please remember me very kindly to your mother.

To do the Eurydice any kind of justice you must not slovenly read it with the eyes but with your ears, as if the paper were declaiming it at you. For instance the line 'she had come from a cruise training seamen' read without stress and declaim is mere Lloyd's Shipping Intelligence; properly read it is quite a different thing. Stress is the life of it.

To Robert Bridges

Stonyhurst, Blackburn. May 30 1878

Dearest Bridges,—

It gave me of course great comfort to read your words of praise. But however, praise or blame, never mingle with your criticisms monstrous and indecent spiritual compliments like something you have said there.

I want to remark on one or two things.

How are hearts of oak furled?° Well, in sand and sea water. The image comes out true under the circumstances, otherwise it could not hold together. You are to suppose a stroke or blast in a forest of 'hearts of oak' (=, ad propositum, sound oak-timber) which at one blow both lays them low and buries them in broken earth. *Furling* (*ferrule* is a blunder for *furl*, I think) is *proper* when said of sticks and staves.

So too of *bole*, I don't see your objection here at all.° It is not only used by poets but seems technical and *proper* and in the mouth of timber merchants and so forth.

'This was that fell capsize' is read according to the above stresses—two cretics, so to say.°

I don't see the difficulty about the 'lurch forward'? Is it in the scanning? which is imitative as usual—an anapaest, followed by a trochee,° a dactyl, and a syllable, so that the rhythm is anacrustic or, as I should call it, 'encountering'.

'Cheer's death' = the death of cheer = the dying out of all comfort = despair.

'It is even seen'—You mistake the sense of this as I feared

it would be mistaken. I believed Hare to be a brave and conscientious man: what I say is that 'even' those who seem unconscientious will act the right part at a great push.

About 'mortholes' I do wince a little but can not now change it. What I dislike much more however is the rhyme 'foot he' to *duty* and *beauty*. In fact I cannot stand it and I want the stanza corrected thus—

> Look, foot to forelock, how all things suit! he
> Is strung by duty, is strained to beauty,
> And brown-as-dawning-skinned
> With brine and shine and whirling wind.

The difficulty about the Milky Way is perhaps because you do not know the allusion: it is that in Catholic times Walsingham Way was a name for the Milky Way, as being supposed a fingerpost to our Lady's shrine at Walsingham.

'O well wept' should be written asunder, not 'wellwept'. It means 'you do well to weep' and is framed like 'well caught' or 'well run' at a cricketmatch.

Obscurity I do and will try to avoid so far as is consistent with excellences higher than clearness at a first reading. This question of obscurity we will some time speak of but not now. As for affectation I do not believe I am guilty of it: you should point out instances, but as long as mere novelty and boldness strikes you as affectation your criticism strikes me as—as water of the Lower Isis.

I see I have omitted one or two things. If the first stanza is too sudden it can be changed back to what it was at first—

> The Eurydice—it concerned thee, O Lord:
> 4 5 1 2 3
> O alas! three hundred hearts on board—

But then it will be necessary to change the third stanza as follows, which you will hardly approve—

> Did she pride her, freighted fully, on
> Bounden bales or a hoard of bullion?—

About 'grimstones'° you are mistaken. It is not the remains of a rhyme to *brimstone*. I *could* run you some rhymes on it. You must know, we have a Father Grimstone in our province.

I shall never have leisure or desire to write much. There is one thing I should like to get done, an ode on the Vale of Clwyd begun therein.° It would be a curious work if done. It contains metrical attempts other than any you have seen, something like Greek choruses, a peculiar eleven-footed line for instance.

What you have got of mine you may do as you like with about shewing to friends.

Is your own ode on the Eurydice° done? Will you send it, as well as other things; which shall be returned.

Believe me your affectionate friend

Gerard M. Hopkins S.J.

You are kind enough to want me to dine with you on coming up to town. I should have to go to our house at once. I shall have, no doubt, little time when in London but still we shall manage to meet.

May 31.

To Richard Watson Dixon

Stonyhurst College, Blackburn. June 4 1878.

Very Rev. Sir,—

I take a liberty as a stranger in addressing you, nevertheless I did once have some slight acquaintance with you. You will not remember me but you will remember taking a mastership for some months at Highgate School,° the Cholmondeley School, where I then was. When you went away you gave, as I recollect, a copy of your book *Christ's Company*° to one of the masters, a Mr. Law° if I am not mistaken. By this means coming to know its name I was curious to read it, which when I went to Oxford I did. At first I was surprised at it, then pleased, at last I became so fond of it that I made it, so far as that could be, a part of my own mind. I got your other volume° and your little Prize Essay too.° I introduced your poems to my friends and, if they did not share my own enthusiasm, made them at all events admire. And to shew you how greatly I prized them, when I entered my present state of life, in which I knew I could have no books of my own and was unlikely to meet with your works in the libraries I should have access to, I copied out *St. Paul, St. John, Love's Consolation*, and others from both volumes and keep them by me.

What I am saying now I might, it is true, have written any time these many years back, but partly I hesitated, partly I was not sure you were yet living; lately however I saw in the *Athenaeum* a review of your historical work° newly published and since have made up my mind to write to you—which, to be sure, is an impertinence if you like to think it so, but I seemed to owe you something or a great deal, and then I knew what I should feel myself in your position—if I had written and published works the extreme beauty of which the author himself the most keenly feels and they had fallen out of sight at once and been (you will not mind my saying it, as it is, I suppose, plainly true) almost wholly unknown; then, I say, I should feel a certain comfort to be told they had been deeply appreciated by some one person, a stranger, at all events and had not been published quite in vain. Many beautiful works have been almost unknown and then have gained fame at last, as Mr. Wells' poem of *Joseph*,° which is said to be very fine, and his friend Keats' own, but many more must have been lost sight of altogether. I do not know of course whether your books are going to have a revival, it seems not likely, but not for want of deserving. It is not that I think a man is really the less happy because he has missed the renown which was his due, but still when this happens it is an evil in itself and a thing which ought not to be and that I deplore, for the good work's sake rather than the author's.

Your poems had a medieval colouring like Wm. Morris's and the Rossetti's and others but none seemed to me to have it so unaffectedly. I thought the tenderness of *Love's Consolation* no one living could surpass nor the richness of colouring in the 'wolfsbane' and other passages° (it is a mistake, I think, and you meant henbane) in that and *Mark and Rosalys*° nor the brightness of the appleorchard landscape in *Mother and*

Daughter.° And the Tale of Dauphiny and 'It is the time to tell of fatal love'° (I forget the title) in the other book are purer in style, as it seems to me, and quite as fine in colouring and drawing as Morris' stories in the *Paradise*, so far as I have read them, fine as those are. And if I were making up a book of English poetry I should put your ode to Summer next to Keats' on Autumn and the Nightingale and Grecian Urn. I do not think anywhere two stanzas so crowded with the pathos of nature and landscape could be found (except perhaps there are some in Wordsworth) as the little song of the Feathers of the Willow:° a tune to it came to me quite naturally. The extreme delight I felt when I read the line 'Her eyes like lilies shaken by the bees'° was more than any single line in poetry ever gave me and now that I am older I could not be so strongly moved by it if I were to read it for the first time. I have said all this, and could if there were any use say more, as a sort of duty of charity to make up, so far as one voice can do, for the disappointment you must, at least at times, I think, have felt over your rich and exquisite work almost thrown away. You will therefore feel no offence though you may surprise at my writing.

I am, Very Rev. Sir, your obedient servant

Gerard M. Hopkins S.J.

(I am, you see, in 'Christ's Company').

To Robert Bridges (Postcard)

[9 June 1878]

I forgot to answer about my metres° (rhythms rather, I suppose). Do by all means and you will honour them and me.

G. M. H.

June 9 1878

To Richard Watson Dixon

Stonyhurst, Blackburn. June 13 1878.

Very Reverend and Dear Sir, Pax Christi,—

I am very glad now to think I followed my impulse and wrote to you, since my writing could affect you so much and draw out so kind an answer.°

I suppose it is me that you remember at Highgate: I did get a prize for an English poem,° I do not well remember when; it may have been while you were there. In those days I knew poor Philip Worsley the poet;° he had been at school at Highgate himself; and spent some time at Elgin House (I suppose as Dr. Dyne's guest) when I was a boarder there; indeed he read over and made criticisms on my successful poem: I recollect that he knew you (perhaps you may have made the acquaintance then, but all these facts I recall detachedly, and cannot group them) and said you would praise Keats by the hour—which might well be: Keats' genius was so astonishing, unequalled at his age and scarcely surpassed at any, that one may surmise whether if he had lived he would not have rivalled Shakspere.

When I spoke of fame I was not thinking of the harm it does to men as artists: it may do them harm, as you say, but so, I think, may the want of it, if 'Fame is the spur that the clear spirit doth raise To shun delights and live laborious days'°—a spur very hard to find a substitute for or to do without. But I meant that it is a great danger in itself, as dangerous as wealth every bit, I should think, and as hard to enter the kingdom of heaven with. And even if it does not lead men to break the divine law, yet it gives them 'itching ears' and makes them live on public breath. (You have yourself said something of this—about 'seeking for praise in all the tides of air' in an ode, that 'on Departing Youth',° I think. Mr. Coventry Patmore, whose fame again is very deeply below his great merit, seems to have said something very finely about the loss of fame in his lately published odes (*The Hidden Eros*)—I speak from an extract in a review.

What I do regret is the loss of recognition belonging to the work itself. For as to every moral act, being right or wrong, there belongs, of the nature of things, reward or punishment, so to every form perceived by the mind belongs, of the nature of things, admiration or the reverse. And the world is full of things and events, phenomena of all sorts, that go without notice, go unwitnessed. I think you have felt this, for you say, I remember, in one of the odes: 'What though the white clouds soar Unmarked from the horizon-shore?'° or something like that. And if we regret this want of witness in brute nature much more in the things done with lost pains and disappointed hopes by man. But since there is always the risk of it, it is a great error of judgment to have lived for what may fail us. So that if Mr. Burne Jones works for a man who is to arise ages hence he works for what the burning of his pictures or the death of his admirer may for ever cut off.° However he in particular has surely many vehement admirers living and even men who have the ear of the public—detractors too no doubt, but who has not? that comes with admiration.

I am happy to think you have an admirer in Mr. Rossetti° (Gabriel Rossetti, I suppose): indeed if he read you it could not be otherwise. And I take the same for granted of Mr. Burne Jones.

Let me recommend you, if you have not seen them, my friend Dr. Bridges' poems—not his first little volume of roundels and so forth,° now so much the fashion, for I have not read it and he is ashamed of it and does not wish to be known by it, but a set of sonnets, a tiny anonymous work no bigger than a short pamphlet of two dozen pages, they are called *The Growth of Love* and are to be continued some day. They are strict in form and affect Miltonic rhythms (which are caviare to the general, so that his critics, I believe, think him rough) and seem to me, but I am prepossessed, very beautiful—dignified, both manly and tender, and with a vein of quaintness. In imagery he is not rich but excels in phrasing, in sequence of phrase and sequence of feeling on feeling. Milton is the great master of sequence of phrase. By sequence of feeling I mean a dramatic quality by which what goes before seems to necessitate and beget what comes after, at least after you have heard it it does—your own poems illustrate it, as 'Yes, one time in the church I think you mean' or 'It makes me mad' and 'It makes me very sad to think of all the bitterness he had'.° This little work is published by Pickering° and costs only a shilling, I think.

June 15—This letter has run to a greater length than the little time at my disposal makes justifiable.—It is sad to think what disappointment must many times over have filled your heart for the darling children of your mind. Nevertheless fame whether won or lost is a thing which lies in the award of a random, reckless, incompetent, and unjust judge, the public, the multitude. The only just judge, the only just literary critic, is Christ, who prizes, is proud of, and admires, more than any man, more than the receiver himself can, the gifts of his own making. And the only real good which fame and another's praise does is to convey to us, by a channel not at all above suspicion but from circumstances in this case much less to be suspected than the channel of our own minds, some token of the judgment which a perfectly just, heedful, and wise mind, namely Christ's, passes upon our doings. Now such a token may be conveyed as well by one as by many. Therefore, believing I was able to pass a fair judgment as people go, it seemed in the circumstances a charity to tell you what I thought. For disappointment and humiliations embitter the heart and make an aching in the very bones. As far as I am concerned I say with conviction and put it on record again that you have great reason to thank God who has given you so astonishingly clear an inward eye to see what is in visible nature and in the heart such a deep insight into what is earnest, tender, and pathetic in human life and feeling as your poems display.

Believe me, dear sir, very sincerely yours

Gerard Hopkins S.J.

My address will be after next month 111 Mount Street, Grosvenor Square, London W., where I am to be stationed. But a letter to Stonyhurst would find me.

To Robert Bridges

111 Mount Street, W. Tuesday afternoon. [16 July 1878.]

Dearest Bridges,—

You will learn that I have just called at Bedford Sq. I brought with me a basket of clean linen but did not deliver it. It comes now between these sheets. The Hurrahing Sonnet° was the outcome of half an hour of extreme enthusiasm as I walked home alone one day from fishing in the Elwy. I am going to send you a slightly amended copy of the Falcon sonnet.° The Curtal Sonnet° explains itself, for an experiment in metre (that is, in point of form it is an experiment). I have several things unfinished and one finished, if I could find it. I enclose a poem my father would like you to see. It appears to me that it echoes and expands the thought and in part the wording of 'The summer's rose is to the summer sweet' etc and Gray's 'Full many a flower' stanza; which is a great drawback.

I wanted to make some oral remarks on your Faded Flower song,° which is very charming, though not fully filed. Could you not end something like—

Sweet hues have marriage made
With as sweet scents—
or With sweeter scents—
and Thy death be that flower's death
And sky thy tomb—?

Also I wish the rhyme *exquisite* could be amended, especially as the next stanza contains a real rhyme to that word.

Believe me your affectionate friend

Gerard M. Hopkins S.J.

Send my father's poem back, please.

To Richard Watson Dixon

111 Mount Street, Grosvenor Square, W. Oct. 5 1878.

Very Reverend and Dear Sir,—

A visit to Great Yarmouth and pressure of work have kept me from answering before yr. very kind letter, and my reply will now not be written at once but as I shall find leisure.

I hope, to begin with, you have quite recovered from the effects of your accident. I escaped from such a one with very little hurt not long ago in Wales, but I witnessed a terrible and fatal coach-accident years ago in the Vale of Maentwrog.

I have forgotten not only what I said about 'Fr. Prout' but even that I ever read him. I always understood that he was a very amusing writer. I do remember that I was a very conceited boy.

I have quite lost sight of Mr. Lobb; I do not even know whether he is alive or dead. The truth is I had no love for my schooldays and wished to banish the remembrance of them, even, I am ashamed to say, to the degree of neglecting some people who had been very kind to me. Of Oxford on the other hand I was very fond. I became a Catholic there. But I have not visited it, except once for three quarters of an hour, since I took my degree. We have a church and house there now.

Oct. 6—The other day Dr. Bridges told me he had in vain tried to get yr. volumes of poems, for want of knowing the publisher. I promised I wd. enquire of you. Was it not Smith and Elder?

I quite agree with what you write about Milton. His verse as one reads it seems something necessary and eternal (so to me does Purcell's music). As for 'proper hue',° *now* it wd. be priggish, but I suppose Milton means *own hue* and they talk of *proper colours* in heraldry; not but what there is a Puritan touch about the line even so. However the word must once have had a different feeling. The Welsh have borrowed it for *pretty*; they talk of birds singing 'properly' and a little Welsh boy to whom I shewed the flowers in a green house exclaimed 'They *are* proper!'—Milton seems now coming to be studied better, and Masson° is writing or has written his life at prodigious length. There was an interesting review by Matthew Arnold in one of the Quarterlies of 'a French critic on Milton'—Scherer° I think. The same M. Arnold says Milton and Campbell are our two greatest masters of *style*. Milton's art is incomparable, not only in English literature but, I shd. think, almost in any; equal, if not more than equal, to the finest of Greek or Roman. And considering that this is shewn especially in his verse, his rhythm and metrical system, it is amazing that so great a writer as Newman should have fallen into the blunder of comparing the first chorus of the *Agonistes* with the opening of *Thalaba*° as instancing the gain in smoothness and correctness of versification made since Milton's time—Milton having been not only ahead of his own time as well as all aftertimes in verse-structure but these particular choruses being his own highwater mark. It is as if you were to compare the Panathenaic frieze and a teaboard and decide in the teaboard's favour.

I have paid a good deal of attention to Milton's versification and collected his latest rhythms: I did it when I had to lecture on rhetoric some years since. I found his most advanced effects in the *Paradise Regained* and, lyrically, in the *Agonistes*. I have often thought of writing on them, indeed on rhythm in general; I think the subject is little understood.°

You ask, do I write verse myself. What I had written I burnt before I became a Jesuit and resolved to write no more, as not belonging to my profession, unless it were by the wish of my superiors; so for seven years I wrote nothing but two or three little presentation pieces which occasion called for. But when in the winter of '75 the Deutschland was wrecked in the mouth of the Thames and five Franciscan nuns, exiles from Germany by the Falck Laws, aboard of her were drowned I was affected by the account and happening to say so to my rector he said that he wished someone would write a poem on the subject. On this hint I set to work and, though my hand was out at first, produced one. I had long had haunting my ear the echo of a new rhythm which now I realised on paper. To speak shortly, it consists in scanning by accents or stresses alone, without any account of the number of syllables, so that a foot may be but one strong syllable or it may be many light and one strong. I do not say the idea is altogether new; there are hints of it in music, in nursery rhymes and popular jingles, in the poets themselves, and, since then, I have seen it talked about as a thing possible in critics. Here are instances—'*Díng, dóng, béll;* Pússy's ín the wéll; *Whó pút* her ín? Líttle Jóhnny Thín. *Whó púlled* her óut? Líttle Jóhnny Stóut.' For if each line has three stresses or three feet it follows that some of the feet are of one syllable only. So too '*Óne, twó,* Búckle my shóe' *passim.* In Campbell you have 'Ánd their fléet alóng the *déep próudly* shóne'—'Ít was tén of Ápril *mórn bý* the chíme' etc; in Shakspere 'Whý shd. *thís* désert bé?' corrected wrongly by the editors; in Moore a little melody I cannot quote; etc. But no one has professedly used it and made it the principle throughout, that I know of. Nevertheless to me it appears, I own, to be a better and more natural principle than the ordinary system, much more flexible, and capable of much greater effects. However I had to mark the stresses in blue chalk, and this and my rhymes carried on from one line into another and certain chimes suggested by the Welsh poetry I had been reading (what they call *cynghanedd*) and a great many more oddnesses could not but dismay an editor's eye, so that when I offered it to our magazine the *Month,* though at first they accepted it, after a time they withdrew and dared not print it. After writing this I held myself free to compose, but cannot find it in my conscience to spend time upon it; so I have done little and shall do less. But I wrote a shorter piece on the Eurydice, also in 'sprung rhythm', as I call it, but simpler, shorter, and without marks, and offered the *Month* that too, but they did not like it either. Also I have written some sonnets and a few other little things; some in sprung rhythm, with various other experiments—as 'outriding feet', that is parts of which do not count in the scanning (such as you find in Shakspere's later plays, but as a licence, whereas mine are rather calculated effects); others in the ordinary scanning *counterpointed* (this is counterpoint: '*Hóme to* his móther's hóuse *príva*te retúrned' and '*Bút to vánquish* by wísdom héllish wíles'° etc); others, one or two, in common uncounterpointed rhythm. But even the impulse to write is wanting, for I have no thought of publishing.

I should add that Milton is the great standard in the use of counterpoint. In *Paradise Lost* and *Regained*, in the last more freely, it being an advance in his art, he employs counterpoint more or less everywhere, markedly now and then; but the choruses of *Samson Agonistes* are in my judgment counterpointed throughout; that is, each line (or nearly so) has two different coexisting scansions. But when you reach that point the secondary or 'mounted rhythm', which is necessarily a sprung rhythm, overpowers the original or conventional one and then this becomes superfluous and may be got rid of; by taking that last step you reach simple sprung rhythm. Milton must have known this but had reasons for not taking it.

I read Arnold's *Essays in Criticism* at Oxford and got Maurice de Guérin's Journal in consequence, admired it, but for some reason or other never got far in it. I should be glad to read it now if I had time. But I have no time for more pressing interests. I hear confessions, preach, and so forth; when these are done I have still a good deal of time to myself, but I find I can do very little with it. . . .

Believe me, dear Sir, very sincerly yours Gerard Hopkins.

Oct. 10.

To Robert Bridges

Catholic Church, St. Giles's, Oxford. Jan. 19 1879.

Dearest Bridges,—

In introducing yours and Mr. Dixon's Muses to each other I find myself crossed. I have just heard from him. He says his publishers are Smith, Elder, and Co. and as he says nothing about being out of print (indeed that would imply a run and a demand) no doubt you can still get his books, now you know where. He says *he* cannot get *yours*. Perhaps you told me the impression was sold—of the pamphlet, the G. of L. I mean. But if so you must have some copies. Could you not forward one 'with the author's compliments' to the Rev. R. W. Dixon, Hayton Vicarage, Carlisle? or else through me? I wish you would, and it is your own interest, for a poet is a public in himself.

Now Mr. Dixon having asked me whether I did not myself write, bearing in mind my prize poem at Highgate (where, I dare say I told you, I first knew him) I told him yes and what, and thereon he asks to see them, and so he shall when I have them to send. Which reminds me that I hope you forwarded the *Deutschland* as directed.

When we met in London we never but once, and then only for a few minutes before parting, spoke on any important subject, but always on literature. This I regret very much. If it had ended in nothing or consisted in nothing but your letting me know your thoughts, that is some of them, it would have been a great advantage to me. And if now by pen and ink you choose to communicate anything I shall be very glad. I should also like to say one thing. You understand of course that I desire to see you a Catholic or, if not that, a Christian or, if not that, at least a believer in the true God (for you told me something of your views about the deity, which were not as they should be). Now you no doubt take for granted that your already being or your ever coming to be° any of these things turns on the working of your own mind, influenced or uninfluenced by the minds and reasonings of others as the case may be, and on that only. You might on reflection expect me to suggest that it also might and ought to turn on something further, in fact on prayer, and that suggestion I believe I did once make. Still under the circumstances it is one which it is not altogether consistent to make or adopt. But I have another counsel open to no objection and yet I think it will be unexpected. I lay great stress on it. It is to give alms. It may be either in money or in other shapes, the objects for which, with your knowledge of several hospitals, can never be wanting. I daresay indeed you do give alms, still I should say give more: I should be bold to say / give, up to the point of sensible inconvenience. *Fieri non potest ut idem sentiant qui aquam et qui vinum bibant* [It is impossible for water-drinkers and wine-drinkers to feel the same]: the difference of mind and being between the man who finds comfort all round him unbroken unless by constraints which are none of his own seeking and the man who is pinched by his own charity is too great for forecasting, it must be felt: I do not say the difference between being pinched and being at one's ease, that one may easily conceive and most people know, willy-nilly, by experience, but the difference between paying heavily for a virtue and not paying at all. It changes the whole man, if anything can; not his mind only but the will and everything. For here something[2] applies[1] like the French bishop's question to his clergy whenever one of them came to tell him that he had intellectual difficulties and must withdraw from the exercise of his priestly functions—*What is her name?* in some such way a man may be far from belief in Christ or God or all he should believe, really and truly so; still the question to be asked would be (not *who is she?*, for that to him is neither here nor there) but *what good have you done?* I am now talking pure christianity, as you may remember, but also I am talking pure sense, as you must see. Now you may have done much good, but yet it may not be enough: I will say, it is not enough. I say this, you understand, on general grounds; I am not judging from particular knowledge, which I have no means to do and it would be very wrong and indiscreet.

Jan. 23—I feel it is very bold, as it is uncalled for, of me to have written the above. Still, if we care for fine verses how much more for a noble life!

I enclose some lines by my father, called forth by the proposal to fell the trees in Well Walk, (where Keats and other interesting people lived) and printed in some local paper. See what you think of them. And return them, please.

Believe me your affectionate friend

Gerard M. Hopkins S.J.

I forget if I ever told you that Addis had left the Oratory and become mission priest at Sydenham.

Our position here is quiet but we make a certain number of converts both from Town and Gown. Mrs. Paravicini, whose husband is Fellow of Balliol (he was my contemporary and is very kind) and her brother is Robert Williams, may be considered as belonging to both; she is a very sweet good creature. Small as Oxford compared to London is, it is far harder to set the Isis on fire than the Thames.

If you have any poetry to send I shall be very glad. If rough copy, I can mentally allow for the last touches. . . .

I have been holding back this letter as if it wd. mellow with keeping, but it is no good. Jan. 24.

To Robert Bridges

St. Giles's, Oxford. Jan. 29 1879.

Dearest Bridges,—

Morals and scansion not being in one keeping, we will treat them in separate letters and this one shall be given to the first named subject: the Preface° will wait.

You so misunderstand my words (it seems they ought never to have been written: if they meant what you take them to mean I should never have written them) that I am surprised, and not only surprised but put out. For amongst other things I am made to appear a downright fool.

Can you suppose I should send Pater a discipline wrapped up in a sonnet 'with my best love'? Would it not be mad? And it is much the same to burst upon you with an exhortation to mortification (under the name of 'sensible inconvenience')—which mortification too would be in your case aimless. So that I should have the two marks of the foolish counsellor—to advise what is bad to follow and what will not be followed.

But I said that my recommendation was not open to objection. I did not mean as the doctrine of the Real Presence, which is true and yet may be objected against; I meant what could not be and was not objected against. Unless you object to doing good and call it 'miserable' to be generous. All the world, so to speak, approves of charity and of the corporal works of mercy, though all the world does not practise what it approves of. Even Walt Whitman nurses the sick.

I spoke, then, of alms—alms whether in money or in medical or other aid, such as you from the cases you come across at the hospital might know to be called for. And I said 'sensible inconvenience'; that is, for instance, you might know of someone needing and deserving an alms to give which would require you in prudence to buy no books till next quarter day or to make some equivalent sacrifice of time. These are sensible inconveniences. And to submit to them you cannot, nevertheless, call the reverse of sensible. But to 'derweesh' yourself (please see the Cairo letter in the last *Athenaeum*—or possibly *Academy*),° that would *not* be sensible and that is what you took me to mean and that is what it would have been supremely senseless of me to mean.

I added something about it needing the experience to know what it feels like to have put oneself out for charity's sake (or one might say for truth's sake, for honour's sake, for chastity's sake, for any virtue's sake). I meant: everybody knows, or if not can guess, how it feels to be short of money, but everybody may not know, and if not cannot well guess, how it feels to be short of money for charity's sake, etc as above.

All the above appears to me to be put plainly. It reads to me in the blustering bread-and-cheese style. You will ask why I was not as plain at first. Because the blustering bread-and-cheese style is not suited for giving advice, though it may be for defending it. Besides I did not foresee the misunderstanding. What I did fear, and it made me keep the letter back, was that you would be offended at my freedom, indeed that you would not answer at all. Whereas, for which I heartily thank you, you have answered three times.

It is true I also asked you to give me, if you liked, an account of your mind—which wd. call for, you say, self examination, and at all events one cannot say what one thinks without thinking. But this and the almsgiving are two independent things mentioned in one letter. No doubt I see a connection, but I do not need you to.

However if I must not only explain what I said but discover what I thought, my thoughts were these—Bridges is all wrong, and it will do no good to reason with him nor even to ask him to pray. Yet there is one thing remains—if he can be got to give alms, of which the Scripture says (I was talking to myself, not you) that they resist sins and that they redeem sins and that they will not let the soul go out into darkness, to give which Daniel advised Nabuchodonosor° and Christ the Pharisees,° the one a heathen, the other antichristians, and the whole scripture in short so much recommends; of which moreover I have heard so-and-so, whose judgment I would take against any man's on such a point, say that the promise is absolute and that there is for every one a fixed sum at which he will ensure his salvation, though for those who have sinned greatly it may be a very high sum and very distressing to them to give—or keep giving: and not to have the faith is worse than to have sinned deeply, for it is like not being even in the running. Yet I will advise something and it must improve matters and will lead to good. So with hesitation and fear I wrote. And now I hope you see clearly, and when you reply will make your objections, if any, to the practice of almsgiving, not to the use of hairshirts. And I take leave to repeat and you cannot but see, that it is a noble thing and not a miserable something or other to give alms and help the needy and stint ourselves for the sake of the unhappy and deserving. Which I hope will take the bad taste away. And at any rate it is good of you only to misunderstand and be vexed and not to bridle and drop correspondence. Still I do enclose some lines I wrote some years ago in honour of the Bp. of Shrewsbury's 26th year of episcopate,° which I say (but wrongly) to have been the 25th of the reestablishment of the hierarchy: it was the 26th. And though the subject may not interest you the lines may and may take tastes out. I have nothing newer. Yes, I will send also a May piece° meant for the 'Month of Mary' at Stonyhurst, in which I see little good but the freedom of the rhythm.

And now no more at present: I assure you I have little time for writing.

Believe me your affectionate friend

Gerard M. Hopkins S.J.

Jan. 30 Remember me very kindly to your mother.

To Kate Hopkins, sen.

St. Aloysius', St. Giles's, Oxford. | Feb. 12 1879.

My dearest Mother,—

The long frost, severer, it is said, at Oxford than elsewhere, has given place to great rains and those to fine weather. The floods are high: they were high before the frost too, so that the great expanse of Port Meadow was covered over and the room for skaters above and below Oxford was perhaps as much as you could get anywhere.

I went yesterday to dine with the Paters.° This morning I

took a visitor to see Keble College,° which hitherto I had not seen myself from within.

On Monday evening we had a small parochial concert—the third. Neither voices nor choice of music was very good, still the effect is humanising, as they say. There was some recitation also. It was given by our Young Men's Association: they are shopkeepers and so on, a fine wellmannered set of young men, but their peculiarity and all our congregation's (excepting the University men and some of the gentry) is that they have a stiff respectful stand-off air which we can scarcely make our way through nor explain, but we believe it to be a growth of a University, where Gown holds itself above and aloof from Town and Town is partly cowed by, partly stands on its dignity against Gown. These young men rally to us, frequent and take parts in our ceremonies, meet a good deal in the parishroom, and so on, but seem as if a joke from us would put them to deep and lasting pain.

Bridges' new book° is just coming out and I am every day expecting a copy.

I went to call on Mr. Green,° fellow of Baliol, professor of Moral Philosophy. His wife, a very kind creature, is sister to John Addington Symonds the critic.

We had a meeting on Charity Organisation at the town-hall yesterday, Lord Jersey presiding. Mr. Alsager Hill° came up and spoke much but I could not well follow his drift. Thorold Rogers° after some hesitation replied in a vigorous and trenchant style. No resolutions were made nor anything done, partly I think because there is not much distress at Oxford and plenty of people to relieve it: the relievers therefore do not need nor probably at all wish to be organised. Mr. Hill also appeared to me to be combating the kind of objections which nobody in the room wanted to make. One gentleman was terribly severe on him for saying that employers ought to support their aged workmen. He had expected sentimental objections and met the opposite sort. By the by it was not on Mr. Hill the employer of labour was so severe but on my friend 'Silver Spooner'° (I do not know if you ever saw and heard him, but if you have you will find an extreme felicity in this name).

Sir Gore Ouseley° came up the other day to give the last of

a course of lectures on organ-music (illustrated) at the Sheldonian Theatre. The organ is new; the organist said to be a genius: he cries (like Du Maurier's man) over his own playing. The audience, which was large and brilliant, included Miss Lloyd in a black bonnet and yellow ribbons. Sir Gore (ghastly as this is, what else can you say?—his name in a book of Mallock's° would become Sir Bloodclot Reekswell) wanted us to agree with him that such and such an example was in a better style than such and such another, livelier, one, but we were naughty and would not; the more griggish the piece the more we clapped it.

I hope the Well Walk trees are saved.° I do not know if my father wants the printed copy of his choicely phrased lines back again.

Believe me your loving son Gerard Hopkins.

To Robert Bridges

[Incomplete letter]

St. Giles's, Oxford. Feb. 15 '79.

Dearest Bridges,—

I should have added in my last that the *Silver Jubilee* had been published. It was printed at the end of a sermon, bearing the same title and due to the same occasion, of Fr. John Morris's of our Society. I have found it since I wrote and the copy I sent you from memory is not quite right. The third stanza should stand fourth and run—

Not today we need lament
Your lot of life is some way spent:
    Toil has shed round your head
Silver, but for Jubilee.°

The thought is more pointed. Please correct it if you put it into your album.

No, do not ask Gosse anything of the sort.° (1) If I were going to publish, and that soon, such a mention would be 'the puff preliminary', which it wd. be dishonourable of me to allow of. (2) If I did, a mention in one article of one review would do very little indeed, especially as publishing now is out of the question. (3) When I say that I do not mean to publish I speak the truth. I have taken and mean to take no steps to do so beyond the attempt I made to print my two wrecks in the *Month*. If some one in authority knew of my having some poems printable and suggested my doing it I shd. not refuse, I should be partly, though not altogether, glad. But that is very unlikely. All therefore that I think of doing is to keep my verses together in one place—at present I have not even correct copies—, that, if anyone shd. like, they might be published after my death. And that again is unlikely, as well as remote. I could add other considerations, as that if I meant to publish at all it ought to be more or ought at least to be followed up, and how can that be? I cannot in conscience spent time on poetry, neither have I the inducements and inspirations that make others compose. Feeling, love in particular, is the great moving power and spring of verse and the only person that I am in love with seldom, especially now, stirs my heart sensibly and when he does I cannot always 'make capital' of it, it would be a sacrilege to do so. Then again I have of myself made verse so laborious.

No doubt my poetry errs on the side of oddness. I hope in time to have a more balanced and Miltonic style. But as air, melody, is what strikes me most of all in music and design in painting, so design, pattern or what I am in the habit of calling 'inscape' is what I above all aim at in poetry. Now it is the virtue of design, pattern, or inscape to be distinctive and it is the vice of distinctiveness to become queer. This vice I cannot have escaped. However 'winding the eyes'° is queer only if looked at from the wrong point of view: looked at as a motion in and of the eyeballs it is what you say, but I mean that the eye winds / only in the sense that its focus or point of sight winds and that coincides with a point of the object and winds with that. For the object, a lantern passing further and further away and bearing now east, now west of one right line, is truly and properly described as winding. That is how it should be taken then.

To Richard Watson Dixon

St. Aloysius' Presbytery, St. Giles's, Oxford. Feb. 27 1879.

Very Reverend and dear Sir,—

You will see that I have again changed my abode and am returned to my Alma Mater. . . . We have passed here a bitter winter, which indeed still holds out, and Oxford is but its own skeleton in wintertime. March. 4. I have parish work to do, am called one way and another, and can find little time to write.

I am glad to hear that Dr. Bridges has sent you his *Growth of Love* (his last copy) and the new book and that you were pleased with them.

In the new book three poems, the 'Passer By', the 'Downs', and a sonnet beginning 'So hot the noon was' are written in a mitigated sprung rhythm. But to understand a new thing, such as this rhythm is, it is best to see it in an extreme example: you will then rather appreciate their peculiarities from it than that from them. March 7. I cannot just now get at Coleridge's preface to *Christabel*. So far as I can gather from what you say and I seem to have seen elsewhere, he was drawing a distinction between two systems of scanning the one of which is quite opposed to sprung rhythm, the other *is not, but might be developed into*, that. For though it is only a step from many popular and many literary cadences now in being to sprung rhythm and nature even without that help seems to prompt it of itself, yet the step has never, that I know of, been taken. The distinction Coleridge, as I suppose, was drawing (though it is a great abuse of terms and usage to make it by the words Accent and Quantity) is between strictly *counted rhythm*, in which, if iambic, e.g., each foot has two syllables only and is an iamb; if anapaestic, each foot has three syllables and is an anapaest—this on the one hand, and, on the other, mixed rhythm, in which feet of the same kind maybe used interchangeably, as iambs with anapaests, because both belong to *rising rhythm*, or trochees with dactyls, because both belong to *falling rhythm*. And this mixture maybe of two sorts—*equal-timed*, as in the hexameter, where the spondee is used as the alternative of the dactyl, because it is of equal length; or *logaoedic*, as when in classical and therefore strictly timed metres dactyls are mixed with trochees, which feet are of unequal length. (I leave out here all consideration of the still freer mixed lyric rhythms of antiquity.) However this last division is of little importance or meaning in English verse. It is enough that we can interchange two-syllabled with three-syllabled feet. This is freely done in ballad-measures and Coleridge does it in *Christabel*. In the more stately metres the poets of the last century as well as others before and since employ only the stricter counted rhythm,* but even in the fivefoot iambic Tennyson and other modern poets often make two light syllables count for one.

This practice is founded upon an easily felt principle of *equal strengths*, as in the classic hexameter the substitution of spondees for dactyls is founded on the principle of equal lengths (or times). To go a little deeper, it supposes not only that, speaking in the abstract, any accent is equal to any other (by accent I mean *the* accent of a word) but further that each accent may be considered to be accompanied by an equal quantity of slack or unaccented utterance, one, two, or more such unaccented syllables; so that wherever there is an accent or stress, there there is also so much unaccentuation, so to speak, or slack, and this will give a foot or rhythmic unit, viz. a stress with its belonging slack. But now if this is so, since there are plenty of accented monosyllables, and those too immediately preceded and followed by the accents of other words, it will come about that a foot may consist of one syllable only and that one syllable has not only the stress of its accent but also the slack which another word wd. throw on one or more additional syllables, though here that may perhaps be latent, as though the slack syllables had been absorbed. What I mean is clearest in an antithesis or parallelism, for there the contrast gives the counterparts equal stress; e.g. 'sanguinary consequences, terrible butchery, frightful slaughter, fell swoop': if these are taken as alternative expressions, then the total strength of *sanguinary* is no more

* Even to the absurdities of 'fond mem'ry's voice' and 'th' umbrageous grove'.

than that of *terrible* or of *frightful* or of *fell* and so on of the substantives too.

Now granting this, if the common ballad measure allows of our having (say) in a fourfoot line 'Terrible butchery, frightful slaughter' why, on principle, shd. we not say 'Terrible butchery, fell swoop' and that be four feet? or further why not 'Sanguinary consequences, terrible butchery'?—except indeed, what of course in practice and actual versewriting is important, that *consequences* is a clumsy halting word which makes the line lag. This then is the essence of sprung rhythm: *one stress makes one foot*, no matter how many or few the syllables. But all that I have said is of course shewing you the skeleton or flayed anatomy, you will understand more simply and pleasantly by verses in the flesh.

March 10—You are kind enough to ask to see my poems. You shall do so when I have got the two shipwreck-pieces back, which are not at hand, and have copied the sonnets out fair. But though the number is small I find this no easy matter.

Reading over what I have written above I find it very hurried and confused: I hope you may gather some meaning out of it. I shd. add that the word Sprung which I use for this rhythm means something like *abrupt* and applies by rights only where one stress follows another running, without syllable between. Besides the bare principle which I have been explaining I employ various artifices which you will see in reading.

To turn to your letter—I am not surprised at what Arnold says of Campbell. Cold and dull as the *Pleasures of Hope* is and much more that he wrote, there is always the 'freehand' of a master in his work beyond almost all our poets, and when one turns from his frigidities to what are held his masterpieces and will always keep his name green, the *Battle of the Baltic* and so forth, one finds a kind of inspired felicity seen no where else that he himself could not have analysed or justified. An inversion and a phrase like 'On the deck of fame that died' or the lines 'But the might of England flushed To anticipate the scene' seem to me as if the words had fallen into their places at a magic signal and not by any strain and continuance of thought.

Marvel, of whom I have only read extracts, is a most rich and nervous poet. Thomas Vaughan's poems were reprinted not so long ago.° He was a follower of Herbert both in life and style: he was in fact converted from worldly courses by reading Herbert's poems on a sickbed and even his muse underwent a conversion (for he had written before). He has more glow and freedom than Herbert but less fragrant sweetness. Somewhere he speaks of some spot 'primrosed and hung with shade'° and one piece end

> And here in dust and dirt, O here
> The lilies of his love appear.°

(I am assuming that you have not got the book.) Still I do not think him Herbert's equal.

You call Tennyson 'a great outsider'; you mean, I think, to the soul of poetry. I feel what you mean, though it grieves me to hear him depreciated, as of late years has often been done. Come what may he will be one of our greatest poets. To me his poetry appears 'chryselephantine'; always of precious mental material and each verse a work of art, no botchy places, not only so but no half wrought or low-toned ones, no drab, no brown-holland; but the form, though fine, not the perfect artist's form, not equal to the material. When the inspiration is genuine, arising from personal feeling, as in *In Memoriam*, a divine work, he is at his best, or when he is rhyming pure and simple imagination, without afterthought, as in the *Lady of Shalott*, *Sir Galahad*, the *Dream of Fair Women*, or *Palace of Art*. But the want of perfect form in the imagination comes damagingly out when he undertakes longer works of fancy, as his Idylls: they are unreal in motive and incorrect, uncanonical so to say, in detail and keepings. He shd. have called them *Charades from the Middle Ages* (dedicated by permission to H. R. H. etc). The Galahad of one of the later ones is quite a fantastic charade-playing trumpery Galahad, merely playing the fool over Christian heroism. Each scene is a triumph of language and of bright picturesque, but just like a charade—where real lace and good silks and real jewelry are used, because the actors are private persons and wealthy, but it is acting all the same and not only so but the make-up has less pretence of correct keeping than at Drury Lane. His opinions too are not original, often not independent even, and they sink into vulgarity: not only *Locksley Hall* but *Maud* is an ungentlemanly row and *Aylmer's Field* is an ungentlemanly row and the *Princess* is an ungentlemanly row. To be sure this gives him vogue, popularity, but not that sort of ascendancy Goethe had or even Burns, scoundrel as the first was, not to say the second; but then they spoke out the real human rakishness of their hearts and everybody recognised the really beating, though rascal, vein. And in his rhetorical pieces he is at his worst, as the *Lord of Burleigh* and *Lady Clare Vere de Vere* (downright haberdasher). But for all this he is a glorious poet and all he does is chryselephantine. Though by the by I owe him a grudge for *Queen Mary*, written to please the mob, and for that other drama where a portent of a man in flaxen locks and ring-mail mouths rationalism 'to torment us before the time'.

I remember what I said about Latin elegiacs but I think I was wrong. Ovid carried the elagiac couplet to a perfection beyond which it could not go and his work remains the standard of excellence. He fixed the system of counterpoint for the elegiac couplet, as Horace for the Sapphic and Alcaic stanzas. This is a long intricate matter, to which I have paid some attention but I can write little about it now. It shd. however be said that in the *Fasti* Ovid does now and then employ the three-syllable ending. To shew the advance made in the counterpointing of the elegiac couplet take the following small point. Words with *-que, -ne, -ve* attached were always accented on the syllable before, whereas when the *-que* etc was part of the word itself (as in *utique, itaque* it may be) it followed the usual accentuation. In such a dactyl then as *armaque* the accent of the word would not in elegiac verse agree with the accent of the verse, the stress; which shd. fall on the first syllable. Here at once is counterpoint. Now in the sensitive places of the couplet, the fifth foot of the hexameter and the second half of the pentameter, Propertius never ventures on this counterpointing except once in all his works. Ovid employs and parades it: the first pentameter of the *Fasti* is

Lapsáque sub térras ortáque sígna cánam—

in which the word-accent only once (in *signa*) agrees with the stress of the rhythm. The accentuation is the same as in English would be

The rísings and séttings of stárs I méan to síng of—

which is nothing like a pentameter.

I have just got back my two wreck-pieces, which with the sonnets I hope to send you in a few days. This letter is longer than I had any business to write.

Believe me your sincere friend Gerard M. Hopkins S.J.

March 12 1879.

March 13—I have been up to Godstow this afternoon. I am sorry to say that the aspens that lined the river are everyone felled.°

To Richard Watson Dixon

The Catholic Church, St. Giles's, Oxford. March 29 1879.

Very Reverend and dear Sir,—

I now send my pieces: please return them when done with, as I have no other copies. It is best to read the *Eurydice* first, which is in plain sprung rhythm and will possess you with the run of it. The *Deutschland*, earlier written, has more variety but less mastery of the rhythm and some of the sonnets are much bolder and more licentious. The two pieces written here at Oxford have not their last finish.°

I hope you will like them.

Believe me your sincere friend Gerard M. Hopkins S.J.

To Robert Bridges

Catholic Church, St. Giles's, Oxford. April 22 1879.

Dearest Bridges,—

I fully answered your question about the 'one' in the Eurydice. You seem to have meant to ask two questions about it, but you did ask only one (You asked also about one of the sonnets.) What you now say shews me that you must have fallen into some unaccountable misunderstanding about the 'hero' stanza.° The words are put into the mouth of a mother, wife, or sweetheart who has lost a son, husband, or lover respectively by the disaster and who prays Christ, whom she addresses 'Hero savest', that is, 'Hero that savest', that is, Hero of a Saviour, to save (that is, have saved) her hero, that is, her son, husband, or lover: 'Hero of a Saviour' (the line means) 'be the saviour of my hero'. There is no connection with the 'one' before the aposiopesis; I cannot think how you came to suppose any . . .

I think I have seen nothing of Lang's° but in some magazine; also a sonnet prefixed to his translation of the Odyssey. I liked what I read, but not so that it left a deep impression. It is in the Swinburnian kind, is it not? (I do not think that kind goes far: it expresses passion but not feeling, much less character. This I say in general or of Swinburne in particular. Swinburne's genius is astonishing, but it will, I think only do one thing.) Everybody cannot be expected to like my pieces. Moreover the oddness may make them repulsive at first and yet Lang might have liked them on a second reading. Indeed when, on somebody returning me the *Eurydice*, I opened and read some lines, reading, as one commonly reads whether prose or verse, with the eyes, so to say, only, it struck me aghast with a kind of raw nakedness and unmitigated violence I was unprepared for: but take breath and read it with the ears, as I always wish to be read, and my verse becomes all right. I do warm to that good Mr. Gosse for liking and, you say, 'taking' my pieces: I may then have contributed fuel to his Habitual Joy.

No, I was thinking of myself when I warned you of your

danger and there was no need. Your only obligations to me you expressed in the discarded preface.° 'Hail is hurling'° did remind me of myself but I do not well know why: I have something about hail and elsewhere several things about hurling, but that does not amount to hail hurling. 'Father fond'° wd. never have occurred to me, at all events it never had. Beyond this I do not think it desirable that I shd. be wholly uninfluenced by you or you by me; one ought to be independent but not unimpressionable: that wd. be to refuse education.

I now enclose two sonnets and 'Binsey Poplars' (in which, more by token, you might say that 'wind-wandering' came from your 'wind-wavering'—which latter is found in Burns and, I suppose elsewhere). What do you think of the effect of the Alexandrines?° That metre unless much broken, as I do by outrides, is very tedious.

I do not much expect to be long at Oxford. I shd. like however to see the Spring out: hitherto there is none . . .

Your affectionate friend Gerard M. Hopkins S.J.

To Richard Watson Dixon

St. Aloysius' Clergy House, St. Giles's, Oxford. May 12 1879.

Reverend and dear Sir,—

Let me first apologise for mis-styling you: it is a blunder I ought not to have made, but our Canons are styled Very Reverend, I daresay by a modern usage, and without enquiring to set myself right I followed that example.

I should have written before but that my superior had a carriage-accident (like you not long since), broke his collarbone, and was at the hardest time of our year laid up in the country, all the work falling on me, and so in great measure it does still after he has returned, for he is laid up with another complaint. The work I find very tiring and it leaves me no time for reading and makes letterwriting hard. This is my excuse for not acknowledging your very kind words sooner.

It was of course a very great pleasure to have so high an opinion expressed of my poems and by you.

But for what concerns the notice you kindly offer to make of me in your forthcoming volume,° it would not at all suit me. For this there are several reasons, any one sufficient; but it is enough to say now that (1) I have no thought of publishing until all circumstances favour, which I do not know that they ever will, and it seems that one of them shd. be that the suggestion to publish shd. come from one of our own people; (2) to allow such a notice would be on my part a sort of insubordination to or doubledealing with my superiors. But nevertheless I sincerely thank you for your kind willingness to do me a service.

The life I lead is liable to many mortifications but the want of fame as a poet is the least of them. I could wish, I allow, that my pieces could at some time become known but in some spontaneous way, so to speak, and without my forcing.

Believe me, with many thanks for the kindness which your letters always breathe, your sincere friend

Gerard M. Hopkins S.J.

To Robert Bridges

St. Giles's, Oxford. Aug. 14 1879.

My dearest Bridges,—

I must try and tersely scribble you something.

That German word is *sache*, not *sach*,° except in compounds: you should have set me right.

Your Picnic verses are very good, the rhymes capital, beyond the ingenuity I credited you with. Some lines however are faulty, as 'Anything more delicious'.°

Muirhead,° who called here on Sunday, was on that party. I mean Muirhead, who was on that party, called etc.

I wish you would send me all the music you have,° to try. I wd. return it. I do not yet the present piece nor comment on it, as I have not had an opportunity of hearing it. I feel sure you have a genius in music—on the strength of the only piece

I know 'O earlier:'° it is an inspiration of melody, but somewhat 'sicklied o'er', as indeed the words are.

To rejoin on some points of your criticisms. Though the analogy in the Candle sonnet° may seem forced, yet it is an 'autobiographical' fact that I was influenced and acted on the way there said.

I send a recast° of the Handsome Heart. Nevertheless the offence of the rhymes° is repeated. I felt myself the objection you make and should only employ the device very sparingly, but you are to know that it has a particular effect, an effect of climax, and shd. so be read, with a rising inflection, after which the next line, beginning with the enclitic, gracefully falls away. And in like manner with proclitics and so on: if a strong word and its epithet or other appendage are divided so that the appendage shall end one line and the supporting word begin the next, the last becomes emphasised by position and heads a fall-away or diminuendo. These little graces help the 'over-reaving' of the verse at which I so much aim, make it flow in one long strain to the end of the stanza and so forth.

I am somewhat surprised at your liking this sonnet so much. I thought it not very good. The story was that last Lent, when Fr. Parkinson was laid up in the country,° two boys of our congregation gave me much help in the sacristy in Holy Week. I offered them money for their services, which the elder refused, but being pressed consented to take it laid out in a book. The younger followed suit; then when some days after I asked him what I shd. buy answered as in the sonnet. His father is Italian and therefore sells ices. I find within my professional experience now a good deal of matter to write on. I hope to enclose a little scene that touched me at Mount St. Mary's.° It is something in Wordsworth's manner; which is, I know, inimitable and unapproachable, still I shall be glad to know if you think it a success, for pathos has a point as precise as jest has and its happiness 'lies ever in the ear of him that hears, not in the mouth of him that makes'. I hope also soon to shew you a finer thing, in a metre something like the Eurydice,° not quite finished yet; also a little song° not unlike 'I have loved flowers that fade'. I have added some strokes to the Vale of Clwyd° and have hopes of some day finishing it: it is more like your Hymn to Nature than anything else I can think of, the rhythm however widely unlike. Lastly I enclose a sonnet° on which I invite minute criticism. I endeavoured in it at a more Miltonic plainness and severity than I have anywhere else. I cannot say it has turned out severe, still less plain, but it seems almost free from quaintness and in aiming at one excellence I may have hit another.

I had quite forgotten the sonnet you have found, but can now recall almost all of it; not so the other piece, birthday lines° to me sister, I fancy.

Baliol is the old spelling and the one I prefer, but they have adopted Balliol and one must conform.

I was almost a great admirer of Barnes' Dorset (not Devon) poems.° I agree with Gosse, not with you. A proof of their excellence is that you may translate them and they are nearly as good—I say nearly, because if the dialect plays any lawful part in the effect they ought to lose something in losing that. Now Burns loses prodigiously by translation. I have never however read them since my undergraduate days except the one quoted in Gosse's paper,° the beauty of which you must allow. I think the use of dialect a sort of unfair play, giving, as you say, 'a peculiar but shortlived charm', setting off for instance a Scotch or Lancashire joke which in standard English comes to nothing. But its lawful charm and use I take to be this, that it sort of guarantees the spontaneousness of the thought and puts you in the position to appraise it on its merits as coming from nature and not books and education. It heightens one's admiration for a phrase just as in architecture it heightens one's admiration of a design to know that it is old work, not new: in itself the design is the same but as taken together with the designer and his merit this circumstance makes a world of difference. Now the use of dialect to a man like Barnes is to tie him down to the things that he or another Dorset man has said or might say, which though it narrows his field heightens his effects. His poems used to charm me also by their Westcountry 'instress', a most peculiar product of England, which I associate with airs like Weeping Winefred, Polly Oliver, or Poor Mary Ann, with Herrick and Herbert, with the Worcestershire, Herefordshire, and Welsh landscape, and above all with the smell of oxeyes and applelofts: this instress is helped by particular rhythms and these Barnes employs; as, I remember, in 'Linden Ore'° and a thing with a refrain like 'Alive in the Spring'.°

By the by I have seen a Westcountryman—V.
S.
S.
Coles—°
for the first time since I went down. I am truly fond of him and wish . . . except these bonds.

I should be very glad to see your prose of Michelangelo's sonnets and also your verse,° for though I do not like verse-renderings of verse (according to the saying *Traduttore traditore* [the translator is a traitor]), yet I think you could do them if anyone can. I have seen something of them, in particular a most striking one beginning—

Non ha l'ottimo artisa alcun concetto.°

By the by, inversions—As you say, I do avoid them, because they weaken and because they destroy the earnestness or in-earnestness of the utterance. Nevertheless in prose I use them more than other people, because there they have great advantages of another sort. Now these advantages they should have in verse too, but they must not seem to be due to the verse: that is what is so enfeebling (for instance the finest of your sonnets to my mind has a line enfeebled by inversion plainly due to the verse, as I said once before ''Tis joy the falling of her fold to view'°—but how it should be mended I do not see). As it is, I feel my way to their use. However in a nearly finished piece I have a very bold one indeed. So also I cut myself off from the use of *ere, o'er, wellnigh, what time, say not* (for *do not say*), because, though dignified, they neither belong to nor ever cd. arise from, or be the elevation of, ordinary modern speech. For it seems to me that the poetical language of an age shd. be the current language heightened, to any degree heightened and unlike itself, but not (I mean normally: passing freaks and graces are another thing) an obsolete one. This is Shakespeare's and Milton's practice and the want of it will be fatal to Tennyson's Idylls and plays, to Swinburne, and perhaps to Morris.

21 Trenchard Street, Bristol. Aug. 21. I am spending a few days here. I have roughly finished the little song and enclose it.

Remember me very kindly to Mrs Molesworth and believe me your loving friend

Gerard M. Hopkins S.J.

To Robert Bridges

St. Joseph's, Bedford Leigh, near Manchester. | Oct. 22 1879.

(you will be surprised at this hand: I employ it sometimes with steel pens).

Dearest Bridges,—

One thing you say in your last is enough to make me quite sad and I see that I shall have to write at some length in order to deal with it. You ask whether I really think there is any good in your going on writing poetry. The reason of this question I suppose to be that I seemed little satisfied with what you then sent and suggested many amendments in the sonnet on Hector.° I do still think 'nor he the charms' and its context obscure and cumbersome. The other° I thought very beautiful (I said so), full of feeling and felicities, as 'The breathing Summer's sloth, the scented Fall' and 'sweet jeopardy'; only I called one part obscure. I find it so after your explanation: it is the 8th line that is most in fault, for the rest would bear your meaning if that did. To my mind you cannot be understood unless you write something like 'Last' did something-or-other 'and last had hope in thrall'. The present line is so vague, it might conceivably mean so many things, it stamps the mind with nothing determinate. But you are to know, indeed very likely you experience the same thing, I see your work to its very least advantage when it comes to me on purpose to be criticised. It is at once an unfinished thing, in my eyes, and any shortcoming or blemish that in print I should either not notice or else easily digest with the excellence of the context becomes a rawness and a blot, to be removed before my mind can even sit down to receive an impression of the whole or form a final judgment about it. It is just as if I had written it myself and were dissatisfied, as you know that in the process of composition one almost always is, before things reach their final form. And things you shewed me at Bedford Square in MS and I did not so much care for then, when I came to see them in print I read in a new light and felt very differently about them. Before that they are too near the eye; then they fall into focus. Oct. 23—Therefore in your book almost everything seems perfect and final and exercises its due effect and the exceptions prove the rule, such as the pieces in sprung rhythm, or some of them, and that is just because they *are* experimental and seem submitted to revision, and also the song, truly beautiful as it is, 'I have loved flowers';° but I was not satisfied with the music and mentally altered it: now it comes to me like a thing put by for repairs. And while on repairs and before going further I will say that I think it wd. be better to write 'one irrevocable day'.° 'That . . . day' is ambiguous: you mean *ille dies*, the particular day which in fact did etc; I took it for *is dies*, a day such that, whenever it shall come, it is doomed to etc. You see, perfects in dependent sentences, like *held* there, need not be historical pasts; they may also be subjunctives of present or any date, and so I took it.

But now in general. And first to visit the workhouse. Oct. 25—You seem to want to be told over again that you have genius and are a poet and your verses beautiful. You have been told so, not only by me but very spontaneously by Gosse, Marzials,° and others; I was going to say Canon Dixon, only, as he was acknowledging your book, it was not so spontaneous as Gosse's case. You want perhaps to be told more in particular. I am not the best to tell you, being biassed by love, and yet I am too. I think then no one can admire beauty of the body more than I do, and it is of course a comfort to find beauty in a friend or a friend in beauty.° But this kind of beauty is dangerous. Then comes the beauty of the mind, such as genius, and this is greater than the beauty of the body and not to call dangerous. And more beautiful than the beauty of the mind is beauty of character, the 'handsome heart'. Now every beauty is not a wit or genius nor has every wit or genius character. For though even bodily beauty, even the beauty of blooming health, is from the soul, in the sense, as we Aristotelian Catholics say, that the soul is in the form of the body, yet the soul may have no other beauty, so to speak, than that which it expresses in the symmetry of the body—barring those blurs in the cast which wd. not be found in the die or the mould. This needs no illustration, as all know it. But what is more to be remarked is that in like manner the soul may have no further beauty than that which is seen in the mind, that there may be genius uninformed by character. I sometimes wonder at this in a man like Tennyson: his gift of utterance is truly golden, but go further home and you come to thoughts commonplace and wanting in nobility (it seems hard to say it but I think you know what I mean). In Burns there is generally recognized on the other hand a richness and beauty of manly character which lends worth to some of his smallest fragments, but there is a great want in his utterance; it is never really beautiful, he had no eye for pure beauty, he gets no nearer than the fresh picturesque expressed in fervent and flowing language (the most strictly beautiful lines of his that I remember are those in Tam o' Shanter: 'But pleasures are like poppies spread' sqq. and those are not). Between a fineness of nature which wd. put him in the first rank of writers and a poverty of language which puts him in the lowest rank of poets, he takes to my mind, when all is balanced and cast up, about a middle place. Now after all this introduction I come to what I want to say. If I were not your friend I shd. wish to be the friend of the man who wrote your poems. They shew the eye for pure beauty and they shew, my dearest, besides, the character which is much more rare and precious. Did time allow I shd. find a pleasure in dwelling on the instances, but I cannot now. Since I must not flatter or exaggerate I do not claim that you have such a volume of imagery as Tennyson, Swinburne, or Morris, though the feeling for beauty you have seems to me pure and exquisite; but in point of character, of sincerity or earnestness, of manliness, of tenderness, of humour, melancholy, human feeling, you have what they have not and seem scarcely to think worth having (about Morris I am not sure: his early poems had a deep feeling). I may then well say, like St. Paul, *aemulor te Dei aemulatione*.° To have a turn for sincerity has not made you sincere nor a turn for earnest / in earnest; Sterne had a turn for compassion, but he was not compassionate; a man may have natural courage, a turn for courage, and yet play the coward.

I must now answer the rest of your letter. The Ship° is very striking and beautiful in your manner. Only who is to take the advice? parents? I shd. like something more like 'And let him deep in memory's hold have stored'. However I am not to make amendments of this sort. The other° is beautiful too, but not quite satisfactory in point of finish. The image of the saplings is perhaps not so pointed as some other might have been. (By the by I see nothing to object to in the *rhythm* of 'The careless ecstasy of leafy May';° so far as run goes it runs well enough. I should not alter the line 'Ride o'er the seas'° etc.).

I hardly know what you allude to at Oxford, it is better that I should not. I used indeed to fear when I went up about this time last year that people wd. repeat against me what they remembered to my disadvantage. But if they did I never heard of it. I saw little of University men: when you were up it was an exceptional occasion, which brought me into contact with them. My work lay in St. Clement's, at the Barracks, and so on. However it is perhaps well I am gone; I did not quite hit it off with Fr. Parkinson and was not happy. I was fond of my people, but they had not as a body the charming and cheering heartiness of these Lancashire Catholics, which is so deeply comforting; they were far from having it. And I believe they criticised what went on in our church a great deal too freely, which is d—d impertinence of the sheep towards the shepherd, and if it had come markedly before me I shd. have given them my mind.

I doubt whether I shall ever get to Liverpool, but if I settle there I will avail myself of your kind offer.° Tomorrow I am going to Wigan (St. John's) for eight days. Today is Nov. 18.

I cannot stop to defend the rhymes in the Bugler.° The words 'came down to us after a boon he on My late being there begged of me' mean 'came into Oxford to our Church in quest of (or to get) a blessing which, on a late occasion of my being up at Cowley Barracks, he had requested of me': there is no difficulty here, I think. But the line 'Silk-ashed' etc in the Sacrifice° is too hard and must be changed to 'In silk-ash kept from cooling'.° I meant to compare grey hairs to the flakes of silky ash which may be seen round wood embers burnt in a clear fire and covering a 'core of heat', as Tennyson calls it. But *core* there is very ambiguous, as your remark shews. 'Your offer, with despatch, of' is said like 'Your ticket', 'Your reasons', 'Your money or your life', 'Your name and college': it is 'Come, your offer of all this (the matured mind), and without delay either!' (This should now explode.) Read the last tercet 'What Death dare lift the latch of, What Hell hopes soon the snatch of, Your offer, with despatch, of!'

It was embarrassment made Grace odd that night, I have no doubt: you think she only cares for learned music and she thinks so of you. No question she admires Handel. She stands in dread of your judgment probably.

I sent her your hymn. I mentioned it and she begged to see it. She said it was not original-sounding but it was very sweet: she wd. not be pleased if she knew I repeated her criticism. If I could have found her the music to 'O earlier shall the rose buds blow' she would have thought it original-sounding as well as sweet. Yet it was youthful too. I return the hymn.

Do you like Weber? For personal preference and fellow feeling I like him of all musicians best after Purcell. I feel as if I cd. have composed his music in another sphere.° I do not feel that of Handel or Mozart or Beethoven. Moreover I do not think his great genius is appreciated. I shd. like to read his life. He was a good man, I believe, with no hateful affectation of playing the fool and behaving like a blackguard.

I cannot undertake to find a motto for the ring.

Remember me very kindly to Mrs. Molesworth. And when is your brother's book coming?

Believe me your loving friend Gerard Hopkins S.J.

Nov 18 1879.

To Richard Watson Dixon

St. Joseph's, Bedford Leigh, near Manchester. Oct. 24 1879.

Reverend and dear Sir,—

I have left Oxford and am appointed to Liverpool (St. Francis Xavier's, Salisbury Street). I am uncertain how long I shall be at Leigh. The place is very gloomy but our people hearty and devoted.

I cannot be quite sure from your words whether you have sent the verses to the paper or only were thinking of sending; I suppose however that they are sent.° If it is too late to recall them the matter can not be helped. I am troubled about it because it may come to the knowledge of some of ours and an unpleasant construction be put upon it. It would be easy to explain it to the Provincial, but not so easy to guard myself against what others might say. However we have no house at or near Carlisle, so that I daresay it may pass without notice taken. You, I know, acted out of pure kindness, but publication of my lines except by the ordinary channels cannot serve me. You would not, I hope, think I secretly wished to steal a march upon my superiors: that would be in me a great baseness. I believe after all that no great harm will have been done, since Carlisle papers are not likely to have more than a local circulation; but do not send them any more pieces.

The learned Fr. Joseph Stevenson,° who joined our body two years ago very late in life, and his friend the Rev. Mr. Sole, late of Oscot, also an antiquary, by my persuasion made themselves acquainted with the first volume of your history (I have not looked at it myself, I have no time for study, at least at Oxford I had none) and reported to me highly of its learning and spirit. I hope it is going on well.

Believe me affectionately your friend

Gerard M. Hopkins, S. J.

To Richard Watson Dixon

St. Joseph's, Bedford Leigh, Oct. 31 1879

My dear Canon,—

Pray do not send the piece to the paper: I cannot consent to, I forbid its publication. You must see that to publish my manuscript against my expressed wish is a breach of trust. Ask any friend and he will tell you the same.

Moreover this kind of publication is very unlikely to do the good that you hope and very likely to do the harm that I fear. For who ever heard of fame won by publication in a local paper, and of one piece? If everything of its intrinsic goodness gravitated to fame your poems wd. long since have been famous. Were Tennyson, putting aside marks of style by which he might be recognised, to send something to the *Nineteenth Century* or best circulated London magazine *without his name* it wd. be forgotten in a month: now no name and an unknown name is all one. But what is not near enough for public fame may be more than enough for private notoriety, which is what I dread.

You say truly that our Society fosters literary excellence. Why then it may be left to look to its own interests. It could not approve of unauthorised publication, for all that we publish must be seen by censors first.

Then again if you were to print my piece you would surely not mutilate it. And yet you must; for with what grace could you, a clergyman of the Church of England, stand godfather to some of the stanzas in that poem? And besides I want to alter the last stanza.

Nov. 1—This letter, which the pressure of parish work has delayed, will now, I daresay, be too late and the Eurydice may have appeared. You will see that your warmhearted but much mistaken kindness will be unavailing: if the paper takes the piece (which it is sure to misprint) few will read it and of those few fewer will scan it, much less understand or like it. (To be sure the scanning is plain enough, but people cannot, or they will not, take in anything however plain that departs from what they have been taught and brought up to expect: I know from experience.) Indeed I am in hopes that the matter may even escape the notice of our own people.

Believe me affectionately your friend

Gerard M. Hopkins S. J.

To Richard Watson Dixon

St. Joseph's, Bedford Leigh, near Manchester, Nov. 5 1879.

My dear Canon,—

I am very glad that all has blown over and no harm done. You are very welcome to shew my poems to anyone you like so long as nothing gets into print.

I will, when I can feel that I can spare the time, send you a few more pieces composed since what you have, and you can keep the copies. I am thinking of a tragedy on St Winefred's Martyrdom° and have done a little and of another on Margaret Clitheroe,° who suffered by pressing to death at York on Ouse Bridge, Lady Day 1586 (I think): her history is terrible and heartrending.

Have you any thoughts of publishing another volume of poems?

Believe me your affectionate friend

Gerard M. Hopkins S. J.

To Alexander William Mowbray Baillie

8 Salisbury Street, Liverpool. May 22 1880

Dearest Baillie,—

I do not know how it is, when your letters give me so much pleasure to get, I am so slow in answering them. At least I can say my Liverpool work is very harassing and makes it hard to write. Tonight I am sitting in my confessional, but the faithful are fewer than usual and I am unexpectedly delivered from a sermon which otherwise I should have had to be delivered of. Here comes someone.

You say it is something of an affectation for me to run up the Lancashire people and run down 'Oxonians'—unpleasant word, let us say the Oxford ones. I do not remember quite what I said; are you sure it was, as you assume, of Gown, not Town I was speaking? Now I do like both. Not to love my University would be to undo the very buttons of my being and as for the Oxford townspeople I found them in my 10 months' stay among them very deserving of affection—though somewhat stiff, stand-off, and depressed. And in that stay I saw very little of the University. But I could not but feel how alien it was, how chilling, and deeply to be distrusted. I could have wished, and yet I could not, that there had been no one that had known me there. As a fact there were many and those friendly, some cordially so, but with others I cd. not feel at home. With the Lancastrians it is the reverse; I felt as if [I] had been born to deal with them. Religion, you know, enters very deep; in reality it is the deepest impression I have in speaking to people, that they are or that they are not of my religion. And then it is sweet to be a little flattered and I can truly say that except in the most transparently cringing way I seldom am. Now these Lancashire people of low degree or not of high degree are those who most have seemed to me to welcome me and make much of me. This is, I suppose, what was on my mind.

If you have set to work in earnest on the fascinating study of hieroglyphics, or rather, of Egyptian, perhaps you will come to translate texts, and then you will do it better than they do in the Biblical Archaeological Society and that slipshod publication, the 'Ancient Texts' I think it is called. I have been reading the first Egyptian volume of the issue (the right name is 'Records of the Past', I find) and the translations are a very bad business. Allowance must be made for a little known language but, making it, still they are bad. The most curious thing in this volume is called the Travels of an Egyptian: it is in reality, as it would appear, a sarcastic criticism, and meant to be published too, on a journal or account of his Syrian travels by a man calling himself and laying a great stress on being, a Mohar, whatever a Mohar is.

The critic, just like a modern Reviler or Athenaeum, asks why he makes no mention of such and such places, quoting a learned string of names. He also ridicules his pomposity and wd. seem to parody his style. Altogether it is condemned modern in spirit and levels all up or all down surprisingly. I daresay you have read it in the original.

June 9—I had written a great deal more, about this place (to which I came on Dec. 30), but have suppressed it all after keeping it by me and reading it with my head first on one side, then on the other, at various distances and in various lights, many times over. I do not think I can be long here; I have been long nowhere yet. I am brought face to face with the deepest poverty and misery in my district. On this theme I could write much, but it would do no good.

What you write of Apuleius is interesting. But when you have a parish you can no longer read nor have intellectual interests.

Garrett went to Tasmania and was at his mother's death-bed. He asked me to write to him at Hobart Town, but I unluckily let the time pass and do not now know where he is. Perhaps the Chowringhe address might find him.

By the by when I was at Oxford Pater was one of the men I saw most of.

June 18—This is a dull letter, but you can answer it by a livelier one.

What do you think of Wagner? I heard a concert of his music in the winter. He loses greatly, I fancy, off the stage. The Germans call him the Master of Masters and Hartmann the greatest of philosophers and the last new thing everywhere the greatest that ever was. This is a barbarous business of greatest this and supreme that that Swinburne and others practise. What is the thing that has been? The same that shall be. Everything is vanity and vexation of spirit.

Believe me your affectionate friend

Gerard M. Hopkins S. J.

P.S. What is the origin of *wean*? Some people say *wee 'un*, but I do not think it can be so. The common people in this town talk of 'a little weany bit'.

I see with sorrow that it is *half a year* since you wrote. Return good for evil.

To Richard Watson Dixon

8 Salisbury Street, Liverpool. Dec. 22 1880.

My dear Friend,

A letter was already owing from me to you and I had long been meaning to write and had your name on a list before me, when your last, now five weeks old, overtook me in the midst of my lingerings and my hinderings. I began to answer it, but that answer was never finished: perhaps this happened more than once. My parish work has been very wearisome; of late especially; it appeared to me at last that I never should be able to get my letters written. Now I am flattering myself that this big paper helps me on.

I thank you very much for your comforting praises. I cannot see what should make me overrate your poems:° I had plenty of poetry old and new to compare with them and to guide my taste, I read them of my own choice years before I ever thought of communicating with you. I did not, it is true, care very much for some of them, such as the Romance beginning 'Rightly be swift',° and there are passages in most of them, even in those I value most, which I could not and can not understand, obscurities of expression which are, I think, of themselves and not through the reader's want of apprehension faulty; but against these I set their extreme beauties—imagery inheriting Keats's mantle, the other-world of imagination (constructive imagination is rare even among poets), the 'instress' of feeling, and a pathos the deepest, I think, that I have anywhere found. (By the by there is one thing that Keats's authority can never excuse, and that is rhyming open vowels to silent *rs*, as *higher* to *Thalia*: as long as the *r* is pronounced by anybody, and it is by a good many yet, the feeling that it is there makes this rhyme most offensive, not indeed to the ear, but to the mind.) Your second volume I never knew so well as the first nor did the historic odes themselves interest me so much as the pieces of Christ's Company, not that they do not mark an advance in power, but for just the reason that their subjects or motives had less interest and also perhaps because they were transitional and you had not altogether made your own some new ground you seemed moving on to. But pieces like the Ode to Summer° in that volume are in point of art and execution more perfect than any in the older one.

Bridges of course told me about his visit° to you when I saw him in town in the summer. He spoke of your epic on some legend of the northern mythology,° and praised its beauties, but said he had pointed out to you that it too much resembled *Hyperion*. I had thought of asking you to let me see it but held back for want of time. Now however I shall be only too happy to see the pieces you offer to send and will, if you wish, make what remarks may occur to me as opportunity shall serve. I read some beautiful pieces of yours in his book—the Murder in the Dark, some sonnets on Man, a reflective Ode on the pleasures of learning and the sorrows of sympathy° (I forget its name), perhaps some other things I cannot now recall. This Ode expresses something of what your letter speaks of in the case of Tennyson, the loss of taste, of relish for what once charmed us. I understand that state of mind well enough; it used at one time to dismay and dishearten me deeply, it made the best of things seem empty. I think that many things contribute to it and play a part. One is a real disenchantment, the correction of the earlier untrained judgment or taste by the maturer one—as, suppose a child thought Macaulay's Lays the finest poetry that ever was penned: I daresay many do. Another is the shortcoming of faculty in us, because the enchanting power in the work is finite or because the mind after a certain number of shocks or stimuli, as the physiologists would say, is spent and flags; and this is plainly the case with jokes, however witty and whimsical: you know that they *are* good, you laughed and were right to laugh heartily when you first heard them, but now they are stale to you and you could laugh no more. Another is that insight is more sensitive, in fact is more perfect, earlier in life than later and especially towards elementary impressions: I remember that crimson and pure blues seemed to me spiritual and heavenly sights fit to draw tears once; now I can just see what I once saw, but can hardly dwell on it and should not care to do so. Another is—or it comes to one of the above—the greater demand for perfection in the work, the greater impatience with technical faults. In the particular case of Tennyson's Ode to Memory I find in my own case all these: it has a mysterious stress of feeling, especially in the refrain—I am to my loss less sensitive to that; it had no great meaning of any importance nor power of thought—I am to my advantage more alive to that; from great familiarity with the style I am deadened to its individuality and beauty, which is again my loss; and I perceive the shortcomings of the execution, which is my own advance in critical power. Absolutely speaking, I believe that if I were now reading Tennyson for the first time I should form the same judgment of him that I form as things are, but I should not feel, I should lose, I should never have gone through, that boyish stress of enchantment that this Ode and the *Lady of Shalott* and many other of his pieces once laid me under. Rose Hall, Lydiate (a country house where I sometimes spend a night as occasion requires and take the opportunity to write my letters). Jan. 11 1880. And here I stop for tonight.

Jan. 14 8 Salisbury Street, Liverpool—The new prosody, Sprung Rhythm, is really quite a simple matter and as strict as the other rhythm. Bridges treats it in theory and practice as something informal and variable without any limit but ear and taste, but this is not how I look at it. We must however distinguish its *εἶναι* [being] and its *εὖ εἶναι* [well-being], the writing it somehow and the writing it as it should be written; for written anyhow it is a shambling business and a corruption, not an improvement. In strictness then and simple *εἶναι* it is a matter of accent only, like common rhythm, and not of quantity at all. Its principle is that all rhythm and all verse consists of feet and each foot must contain one stress or verse-accent: so far is common to it and Common Rhythm; to this it adds that the stress alone is essential to a foot and that therefore even one stressed syllable may make a foot and consequently two or more stresses may come running, which in common rhythm can, regularly speaking, never happen. But there may and mostly there does belong to a foot an unaccented portion or 'slack': now in common rhythm, in which less is made of stress, in which less stress is laid, the slack must be always one or else two syllables, never less than one and never more than two, and in most measures fixedly one or fixedly two, but in sprung rhythm, the stress being more *of* a stress, being more important, allows of greater variation in the slack and this latter may range from three syllables to none at all—*regularly*, so that paeons (three short syllables and one long or three slack and one stressy) are regular in sprung rhythm, but in common rhythm can occur only by licence; moreover may in the same measure have this range. Regularly then the feet in sprung rhythm consist of one, two, three, or four syllables and no more, and if for simplicity's sake we call feet by Greek names, taking accent for quantity, and also scan always as for rising rhythm (I call *rising rhythm* that in which the slack comes first, as in iambs and anapaests, *falling* that in which the stress comes first, as in trochees and dactyls), scanning thus, the feet in sprung rhythm will be monosyllables, iambs, anapaests, and fourth paeons, and no others. But for particular rhythmic effects it is allowed, and more freely than in common rhythm, to use any number of slack syllables, limited only by ear. And though it is the virtue of sprung rhythm that it allows of 'dochmiac' or 'antispastic' effects or cadences, when the verse suddenly changes from a rising to a falling movement, and this too is strongly felt by the ear, yet no account of it is taken in scanning and no irregularity caused, but the scansion always treated, conventionally and for simplicity, as rising. Thus the line 'She had cóme from a crúise, tráining, séaman'°has a plain reversed rhythm, but the scanning is simply 'She had cóme | from a crúise | tráin | ing séa | men'—that is / rising throughout, having one monosyllabic foot and an overlapping syllable which is counted to the first foot of the next line. Bridges in the preface to his last issue says something to the effect that all sorts of feet may follow one another, an anapaest a dactyl for instance (which would make four slack syllables running): so they may, if we look at the real nature of the verse; but for simplicity it is much better to recognize, in scanning this new rhythm, only one movement, either the rising (which I choose as being commonest in English verse) or the falling (which is perhaps better in itself), and always keep to that.

In lyric verse I like sprung rhythm also to be *over-rove*, that is the scanning to run on from line to line to the end of the stanza. But for dramatic verse, which is looser in form, I should have the lines 'free-ended' and each scanned by itself.

Sprung rhythm does not properly require or allow of counterpoint. It does not require it, because its great variety amounts to a counterpointing, and it scarcely allows of it, because you have scarcely got in it that conventionally fixed form which you can mentally supply at the time when you are actually reading another one—I mean as when in reading 'Bý the wáters of life where'er they sat' you mentally supply 'By thé watérs', which is the normal rhythm. Nevertheless in dramatic verse I should sparingly allow it at the beginning of a line and after a strong caesura, and I see that Bridges does this freely in *London Snow* for instance. However by means of the 'outrides' or looped half-feet you will find in some of my sonnets and elsewhere I secure a strong effect of double rhythm, of a second movement in the verse besides the primary and essential one, and this comes to the same thing or serves the same purpose as counterpointing by reversed accents as in Milton.

But for the εὖ εἶναι of the new rhythm great attention to quantity is necessary. And since English quantity is very different from Greek or Latin a sort of prosody ought to be drawn up for it, which would be indeed of wider service than for sprung rhythm only. We must distinguish strength (or gravity) and length. About length there is little difficulty: plainly *bidst* is longer than *bids* and *bids* than *bid*. But it is not recognized by everybody that *bid*, with a flat dental, is graver or stronger than *bit*, with a sharp. The strongest and, other things being alike, the longest syllables are those with the circumflex, like *fire*. Any syllable ending in *ng*, though *ng* is only a single sound, may be made as long as you like by prolonging the nasal. So too *n* may be prolonged after a long vowel or before a consonant, as in *soon* or *and*. In this way a great number of observations might be made: I have put these down at random as samples. You will find that Milton pays much attention to consonant-quality or gravity of sound in his line endings. Indeed every good ear does it naturally more or less / in composing. The French too say that their feminine ending is graver than the masculine and that pathetic or majestic lines are made in preference to end with it. One may even by a consideration of what the music of the verse requires restore sometimes the pronunciation of Shakspere's time where it has changed and shew for instance that *cherry* must have been *cher-ry* (like *her, stir, spur*) or that *heavy* was *heave-y* in the lines 'Now the heavy ploughman snores All with weary task foredone'. You speak of the word *over*. The *o* is long no doubt, but long *o* is the shortest of the long vowels and may easily be used in a weak place; I do not however find that Tennyson uses it so in the Ode to Memory: in the line 'Over the dewy dark [or "dark dewy"] earth forlorn' it seems to be in a strong place.

I will inclose a little piece° I composed last September in walking from Lydiate. It is to have some plainsong music to it. I found myself quite unable to redeem my promise of copying you out the pieces you had not seen: time would not allow it. However I think you have seen them since in Bridges' book. Liverpool is of all places the most museless. It is indeed a most unhappy and miserable spot. There is moreover no time for writing anything serious—I should say for composing it, for if it were made it might be written.

I do not despair of our coming to meet, for business might perhaps bring you here. Meanwhile believe me

your affectionate friend Gerard M. Hopkins S. J.

Jan. 14 1881.

You will then send the poems, I hope, as soon as possible.

Jan. 16—I have added another piece, the *Brothers*.°

To Robert Bridges

8 Salisbury Street, Liverpool. [26 January 1881]

Dearest Bridges,

. . . You should never say 'standpoint': 'Point of view'.

I agree that the *Eurydice* shews more mastery in art, still I think the best lines in the *Deutschland* are better than the best in the other. One may be biassed in favour of one's firstborn though. There are some immaturities in it I should never be guilty of now.

I think I remember that Patmore pushes the likeness of musical and metrical time too far—or, what comes to the same thing, not far enough: if he had gone quite to the bottom of the matter his views would have been juster. He might remember that for more than half the years music has been in the world it had perhaps *less* time than verse has, as we see in plainchant now. Sir Oozy Gore° (so to say) says, and I believe him, that strict musical time, modern time, arose from dance music. Now probably verse-time arose from the dance too. The principle, whether necessary or not, which is at the bottom of both musical and metrical time is that everything shd. go by twos and, where you want to be very strict and effective, even by fours. But whereas this is insisted[2] on and recognised[1] in modern music it is neither in verse. It exists though and the instance Pat gives° is good and bears him out. For it is very noticeable and cannot be denied that to three foot lines you can add one syllable or two syllables, which makes four feet, with pleasure, and then no more; but that to four foot lines you can comfortably add nothing. Why, but because we carry mentally a frame of fours, which being filled allows of no more? Thus—

'Twas when the seas did roar
With hollow blasts of wind:
A damsel did deplore
All on a rock reclined—

This is in threes. Add a syllable—

'Twas when the seas were roaring
With hollow blasts of wind:
A damsel lay deploring
All on a rock reclined—

This is three and a half and still runs smooth. Add one more—

'Twas when the seas were roaring, sir—

and so on with 'deploring, sir'. It flows smoothly still and is now four feet. But add one more—

> 'Twas when the seas were roaring, madam,
> With hollow blasts of wind—

And so on. *Now* it overlaps, limps, and is spoilt. And so in practice I find; for whereas in my lyrics in sprung rhythm I am strict in overreaving the lines when the measure has four feet, so that if one line has a heavy ending the next must have a sprung head (*or begin with a falling cadence*) as—

> Márgarét, áre you *gríeving*
> *Óver* Góldengróve

[*and not e.g.* Concérning Góldengróve] unléaving?°—
when it has only three I take no notice of it, for the heavy ending or falling cadence of one line does not interfere with the rising cadence of the next, as you may see in the *Brothers*. Now this principle of symmetry and quadrature has, as I think, been carried in music to stifling lengths and in verse not far enough and both need reforming; at least there is room, I mean, for a freer musical time and a stricter verse-prosody.

But about Patmore you are in the gall of bitterness.

Italics do look very bad in verse. But people will *not* understand where the right emphasis is. However they shall not be.

About Wyatt you are very unsatisfactory. On the fragment 'it sitteth me near' you may be right, and as likely as not it is 'sitth', for both will scan, and in Chaucer certainly *all* inflexions are open or contracted at choice. But for the whole you suggested a scanning which I believed, and believe, (no doubt without your materials for judging) to be untenable, and I think I gave reasons why. I suggested another,° of which you say nothing; but now, does it not meet the case? *does it not do?* Well to be sure if this one piece were all it does; but look at Wyatt, which you have before you, and see whether the principle I employed does not explain others too.

By Surrey's 'couplets of long twelves and thirteens'—a

mistake for 'fourteens'—I meant the same as your '6 + 6 and 8 + 6'. It is difficult to say what makes a stanza, but I think the writer's own intention shd. decide it, which is signified by his writing or not writing in stanza-form. One certainly has a different feeling towards two lines and the same words treated as one line.

And so much for your letter of alas! Sept. 15, a very flattering and endearing one indeed. Jan. 29 1881 . . .

. . . About the echos I believe I have already replied. Some of them I ought not to have thought echos at all perhaps and one, which you grant to be, I said and say does not matter. I say the same of 'the white-mossed wonder' line, that it does not matter; I cannot help fancying nevertheless that you did have in your memory the line 'For though he is under the world's spendour and wonder', the ryhmes being identical and the rhythm almost so. But it is a trifle.

The Dead Child° is a fine poem, I am aware, but I am not bound to like it best; I do not in fact like it best nor think it the best you have written, as you say it is. I do not think either the rhythm or the thought flowing enough. The diction is not exquisite, as yours can be when you are at ease. No, but you say it is severe: perhaps it is bald. But indeed 'wise, sad head' and 'firm, pale hands' do not strike me as severe at all, nor yet exquisite. Rather they belong to a familiar commonplace about 'Reader, have you never hung over the pillow of. . . . pallid cheek, clammy brow. . . . long, long night-watches. . . . surely, Sir Josiah Bickerstaff, there is *some* hope! O say not all is over. It cannot be'—You know.

I have a few suggestions to make about the rhythm of *London Snow*, which would make it perfect.° In 2. for 'the city' read 'London'. Then for 'Hushing' 'It hushed'. Then 'Difference hiding, making uneven even', since 'unevenness', in which the *n* is really doubled, is an awkward word. Then 'To crevices and angles' or 'To crevice and angle'. I suppose you scan 'The éye márvelled—márvelled at the dázzling whíteness; The éar hearkened to the stíllness of the sólemn áir': this is well enough when seen, but the following is easier to catch and somewhat better in itself—'Eye márvelled—márvelled át the dázzling whíteness; Ear heárkened to the stíllness ín the sólemn áir'. Then for 'nor of foot' read 'or foot'. For 'awhile no thoughts' better 'no thoughts awhile'. 'Is unspoken': 'is' perhaps is better omitted. In the last line omit 'for'. I know that some of the words thus omitted might on my principles as well be in, with underloopings; but there it is: I put the loops, you do not. Now it makes all the difference with a wheelbarrow whether you do or do not cry 'By leave, Sir!' . . .

To Richard Watson Dixon

April 6 1881. 8 Salisbury Street, Liverpool.

My dear friend,

I sent Mr Hall Caine° a choice of three sonnets, which he acknowledged and is to write 'at some length' shortly.

I take the opportunity to say something about the batch of poems you sent me. Time has been very short, especially since Lent came in, but I hope before very long to have studied them well.

The present remarks will be disjointed . . .

The poem 'Rise in their place the woods'° is beautiful in the same mournful vein as the Ode to Summer and there are others in the same. It contains one of the inimitable pathetic turns which attract me so much: 'They not regard thee, neither do they send' etc.

However the longest criticism I have to make at present is upon *Love's Casuistry*.°

You say that the plot of this piece is your own. It seems to me in general a hazardous thing, a pity, to make one's own plots: one cannot well have the independence, the spontaneousness of production which one gets from a true story or from a fiction that comes to one as a fresh whole not of one's own feigning. This piece it is plain has a *motive* and is planned to exhibit a certain situation, the situation which is darkly described in the opening. The consequence has been, as it seems to me, that you have invented *only just enough plot* to bring out the required situation. And this takes away from the interest. Besides motive a plot should have these two things, scenes and intrigue. By scenes I mean localisation, with local colour and particular details and keepings. These are things in which you naturally excel, as in the other tales of the set. But here there are scarcely any. If you had been treating some one else's plot you would have said something of what Basilis' house was like and where, but now you do not even tell us how she managed to get out of Venice into the wood without, as it would seem, crossing the water. There is also no intrigue. One wants to know how Madaline happened to come up just when the two men had been fighting, and the hermit too, how he was there. The hermit is almost as bad as 'in the Queen's name I command you all to drop your swords and daggers'. I am afraid I shall have vexed you; nevertheless I believe you will see that I have hit a defect.

Easter Eve, which the Irish miscall Easter Saturday—In 'Margaret, are you grieving'° will the following alteration do?—

Nor mouth had, no, nor mind, expressed
What héart heard of, ghóst gúessed.

The *Brothers* I have rewritten in deference to both yours and Bridges' criticisms and now he is not satisfied and wishes it back again. But I do not think I shall be able to send a corrected copy now. According to your wish I make it begin

How lovely the elder brother's
Life all laced in the other's!
Love-laced; as once I well
Witnessed, so fortune fell—

or something like that.

Mr. Hall Caine has not again been heard of.

Wishing you Paschal joy and a speedy conversion I remain
affectionately yours Gerard M. Hopkins S.J.

To the Bishop of Liverpool°

St. Joseph's, 40 North Woodside Road, Glasgow. | Aug. 12 1881.

My Lord,

Thomas Murphy of 45 B Bidder Street, Liverpool, and Mary Hennessy of the same, both Catholics, humbly petition your Lordship for leave to be secretly married.

Thomas Murphy was in the year 1871 acquainted with one Ellen Smith, who was or was said to be with child by him. To cover her shame, a marriage, and at a Protestant church, was forced on by her uncle, since dead, being a Catholic, and this took place at St. Peter's; but the day and month are not remembered. Thomas Murphy however neither then nor after looked upon her as his wife. The circumstances of the ceremony favoured this dissimulation. Many, perhaps fifty, persons were that morning married; all the rites, including the words of contract, were gone through for and by all the couples together; and these words Murphy neither heeded nor pronounced. Nor would he put the ring fully and properly on the woman's finger, so acting throughout as to hold himself free and withold consent. And this, so far as I can sift him, appears to have been his real mind, though he is too little of a scholar to express himself clearly: only this he says plainly, that he does not and never did think Ellen Smith his wife. The marriage therefore appears null from want both of form and intention.

The union thus iniquitously entered into was unhappy. The woman bore at least one child which Murphy takes to be none of his and forsook him thrice, for spaces of 9, 12, and 15 months respectively, more or less; after each of which he took her back for the children's sake. She then left him for a fourth and last time and became and now is a prostitute.

About Whitsuntide 1879 Murphy took up with Mary Hennessy, who is believed to be married to him; for it was well known to his acquaintance that he held the women Ellen Smith not to be his lawful wife. She has borne him one child, since dead, and is now big with another.

The grounds for asking this grace are the saving of the petitioners' reputation, the prevention of incontinence, and the prevention of public scandal. Awaiting your Lordship's judgment the petitioners promise to live as brother and sister. They behave themselves humbly and sincerely so far as I have dealt with them. If your Lordship should wish further to sound Murphy's mind upon the invalidity of his marriage he can be summoned: he is unlearned but not stupid.

I am your Lordship's humble servant in Christ

Gerard M. Hopkins S. J.

The petitioners live in my district. The above facts are none of them known to me from confession. The first information came to me from an unknown source.

I should add that I had already, with my Rector's approval, waited on your Lordship at Rodney Street, but your Lordship being from home have had to draw up the case on paper.

To Robert Bridges

St. Joseph's, North Woodside Road, Glasgow. | Sept. 16 1881.

Dearest Bridges,—

How is it you do not know I am here? On Oct. 10 I am to be at Roehampton (Manresa House, as of old) to begin, my 'tertianship', the third year (really ten months) of noviceship which we undergo before taking our last vows. Till then I expect to be here mostly, but must go to Liverpool to pack; for I came for a fortnight or so only and left my things: indeed I am going to pieces as I stand.

I began a letter to you a short while ago, but tore it up. Meant to write I have every day for long.

I am very glad you do improve.° Still your recovery is very slow and I cannot understand it. You did run well, like the Galatians:° how has your good constitution been so unhappily bewitched? I hope nevertheless that all your strength will return.

And the good Canon too lies like a load on my heart. To

him I am every day meaning to write and last night it was I began, but it would not do; however today I shall. Besides I have his poems—some here, some left behind at Liverpool. I have some hopes of managing an interview on my way south.

Things are pleasanter here than at Liverpool. Wretched place too Glasgow is, like all our great towns; still I get on better here, though bad is the best of my getting on. But now I feel that I need the noviceship very much and shall be every way better off when I have been made more spiritual minded.

There, I mean at Roehampton, I am pretty well resolved, I will altogether give over composition for the ten months, that I may *vacare Deo* [to be available for God] as in my noviceship proper. I therefore want to get some things done first, but fear I never shall. One is a great ode on Edmund Campion S. J.° For the 1st of December next is the 300th anniversary of his, Sherwin's and Bryant's martyrdom, from which I expect of heaven some, I cannot guess what, great conversion or other blessing to the Church in England. Thinking over this matter my vein began to flow and I have by me a few scattered stanzas, something between the *Deutschland* and *Alexander's Feast*, in sprung rhythm of irregular metre. But the vein urged by any country sight or feeling of freedom or leisure (you cannot tell what a slavery of mind or heart it is to live my life in a great town) soon dried and I do not know if I can coax it to run again. One night, as I lay awake in a fevered state, I had some glowing thoughts and lines, but I did not put them down and I fear they may fade to little or nothing. I am sometimes surprised at myself how slow and laborious a thing verse is to me when musical composition comes so easily, for I can make tunes almost at all times and places and could harmonise them as easily if only I could play or could read music at sight. Indeed if I could play the piano with ease I believe I could improvise on it. I have of late been finishing the air, but only the air, of *I have loved flowers that fade*. I find now I can put a second part satisfactorily to myself, but about fuller chords I am timid and incapable as yet. It is besides very difficult to get at a piano. I have now also a certain power of counterpointing (I will not say harmonising) without an instrument: I do not, in my mind's ear, as a musician would do, hear the chords, but I have an instinct of what will do and verify by rule and reckoning the air which I do hear: this suggests itself and springs from the leading air which is to be accompanied.—I got a young lady this evening to play me over some of my pieces, but was not well pleased with them. What had sounded rich seemed thin. I had been trying several of them as canons, but this I found was unsatisfactory and unmeaning and the counterpoint drowns the air. If I could only get good harmonies to *I have loved flowers* it would be very sweet, I think; I shd. then send it you and should like Woolrych [Wooldridge] to see it too.

I am now writing to Canon Dixon.

I am promised before I leave Scotland two days to see something of the Highlands.

I can well understand that 'what there is unusual in expression in my verse is less pleasant when you are in that sort of weak state', for I find myself that when I am tired things of mine sound strange, forced, and without idiom which had pleased me well enough in the fresh heat of composition. But then the weaker state is the less competent and really critical. I always think however that your mind towards my verse is like mine towards Browning's: I greatly admire the touches and the details, but the general effect, the whole, offends me, I think it repulsive.

Your letters addressed to Liverpool were forwarded very leisurely.

Believe me your affectionate friend

Gerard M. Hopkins S.J.

Sept. 17 1881.

To Richard Watson Dixon

Manresa House, Roehampton, London S.W. | (By the by have you read Lothair?° because this house is the divine Theodora's: some of the scenes are laid here.) Oct. 12 1881.

My dear friend,—

Some of the sonnets are very, I must say unpardonably, licentious in form. I recognise stricter and looser forms and the Shakespearian sonnet, though it is sonnet only *in genere* and not one if by sonnet you mean the Italian sonnet, which is the sonnet proper—but this is a question of names only—the Shakespearian sonnet is a very beautiful and effective species of composition in the kind. But then, though simpler, it is as strict, regular, and specific as the sonnet proper. Moreover it has the division into the two parts 8 + 6, at all events 4 + 4 + 4 + 2. Now it seems to me that this division is the real characteristic of the sonnet and that what is not so marked off and moreover has not the octet again divided into quatrains is not to be called a sonnet at all. For in the cipher 14 is no mystery and if one does not know nor avail oneself of the opportunities which it affords it is a pedantic encumbrance and not an advantage. The equation of the best sonnet is

$$(4 + 4) + (3 + 3) = 2.4 + 2.3 = 2(4 + 3) = 2.7 = 14.$$

This means several things—(A) that the sonnet is one of the works of art of which the equation or construction is unsymmetrical in the shape $x + y = a$, where x and y are unequal in some simple ratio, as 2 : 1, 3 : 2, 4 : 3: perhaps it would be better to say $mx + nx = a$. Samples of this are the Hexameter and Ionic Trimeter, divided by their caesura, as St. Austin *De Musica* suggests, so as to give the equation $3^2 + 4^2 = 5^2$ (it is not very clear how he makes it out, but all events they give the equation 2½ + 3½ = 6 or 5 + 7 = 12). The major and minor scales again consist of a pentachord + a tetrachord and in Plainsong music all the 'Authentic' Modes have this order and all the 'Plagal' the reverse, the tetrachord first. And I could shew, if there were time, that it would be impracticable to have a ratio of the sort required with numbers higher than 4 and 3. Neither would 4 : 2 do, for it wd. return to 2 : 1, which is too simple. (B) It is divided symmetrically too in multiples of two, as all effects taking place in time tend to be, and all very regular musical composition is: this raises the 7 to 14. (C) It pairs off even or symmetrical members with symmetrical (the quatrains) and uneven or unsymmetrical with uneven (the tercets). And even the rhymes, did time allow, I could shew are founded on a principle of nature and cannot be altered without loss of effect. But when one goes so far as to run the rhymes of the octet into the sestet a downright prolapsus or hernia takes place and the sonnet is crippled for life.

I have been longer and perhaps more dogmatic than I shd. have been over this point. Of the sonnets themselves° those on the World, except for happy touches, do not interest me very much and that to Corneille has a certain stiffness, as the majority of Wordsworth's have, great sonneteer as he was, but he wrote in 'Parnassian', that is the language and style of poetry mastered and at command but employed without any fresh inspiration: and this I feel of your sonnet here. The rest, that to George Sand and those on Shakespeare and Milton, are rich in thought, feeling, and diction. . . .

Ode on the Death of Dickens° is fine and stirring; the Aryan image of the cloud cows and the dog particularly striking; but the anapaests are heavily loaded. For myself I have been accustomed to think, as many critics do, that Dickens had no true command of pathos, that in his there is something mawkish; but perhaps I have not read the best passages. Just such a gale as this poem paints is blowing today (Oct. 14) and two of my fellow Tertians have been injured by the fall of almost half a tall cedar near my room, which wrecked the woodshed where they happened to be and battered and bruised them with a rain of tiles.

The Fall of the Leaf—I have spoken of this beautiful poem before.

I cannot remember if I spoke of *Nature and Man*,° the one beginning 'Blue in the mists all day'. At all events it is one of the most perfect of all, both in thought and expression. The thing had to be said. I suppose 'pod' means some pod-like bud, for I think, scientifically speaking, the pod is only a seed vessel.

There only remain the two tales; of which I will write another day, though it must be less fully than they deserve. I will finish with remarks called out by your most welcome letter of yesterday.

In speaking of 'frigid fancy'° I referred to the particular passage only. But Browning has, I think, many frigidities. Any untruth to nature, to human nature, is frigid. Now he has got a great deal of what came in with Kingsley and the

Broad Church school, a way of talking (and making his people talk) with the air and spirit of a man bouncing up from table with his mouth full of bread and cheese and saying that he meant to stand no blasted nonsense. There is a whole volume of Kingsley's essays which is all a kind of munch and a not standing of any blasted nonsense from cover to cover. Do you know what I mean? The *Flight of the Duchess*, with the repetition of 'My friend', is in this vein. Now this is *one* mood or vein of human nature, but they would have it all and look at all human nature through it. And Tennyson in his later works has been 'carried away with their dissimulation.'° The effect of this style is a frigid bluster. A true humanity of spirit, neither mawkish on the one hand nor blustering on the other, is the most precious of all qualities in style, and this I prize in your poems, as I do in Bridges'. After all it is the breadth of his human nature that we admire in Shakespeare.

I read some, not much, of the *Ring and the Book*, but as the tale was not edifying and one of our people, who had been reviewing it, said that further on it was coarser, I did not see, without a particular object, sufficient reason for going on with it. So far as I read I was greatly struck with the skill in which he displayed the facts from different points of view: this is masterly, and to do it through three volumes more shews a great body of genius. I remember a good case of 'the impotent collection of particulars' of which you speak in the description of the market place at Florence where he found the book of the trial: it is a pointless photograph of still life, such as I remember in Balzac, minute upholstery description; only that in Balzac, who besides is writing prose, all tells and is given with a reserve and simplicity of style which Browning has not got. Indeed I hold with the oldfashioned criticism that Browning is not really a poet, that he has all the gifts but the one needful and the pearls without the string; rather one should say raw nuggets and rough diamonds. I suppose him to resemble Ben Jonson, only that Ben Jonson has more real poetry.

As for Carlyle; I have a letter by me never sent, in answer to a pupil of mine, who had written about him, and I find I there say just what you do about his incapacity of general truths. And I always thought him morally an impostor, worst of all impostors a false prophet. And his style has imposture or pretence in it. But I find it difficult to think there is imposture in his genius itself. However I must write no more criticism.

I see you do not understand my position in the Society. This Tertianship or Third Year of Probation or second Noviceship, for it is variously called in the Institute, is not really a noviceship at all in the sense of a time during which a candidate or probationer makes trial of our life and is free to withdraw. At the end of the noviceship proper we take vows which are perpetually binding and renew them every six months (not *for* every six months but for life) till we are professed or take the final degree we are to hold, of which in the Society there are several. It is in preparation for these last vows that we make the tertianship; which is called a *schola affectus* [school of the love of God] and is meant to enable us to recover that fervour which may have cooled through application to study and contact with the world. Its exercises are however nearly the same as those of the first noviceship. As for myself, I have not only made my vows publicly some two and twenty times but I make them to myself every day, so that I should be black with perjury if I drew back now. And beyond that I can say with St. Peter: To whom shall I go? *Tu verba vitae aeternae habes*.° Besides all which, my mind is here more at peace than it has ever been and I would gladly live all my life, if it were so to be, in as great or a greater seclusion from the world and be busied only with God. But in the midst of outward occupations not only the mind is drawn away from God,° which may be at the call of duty and be God's will, but unhappily the will too is entangled, worldly interests freshen, and worldly ambitions revive. The man who in the world is as dead to the world as if he were buried in the cloister is already a saint. But this is our ideal.

Our Rector Fr. Morris° shd. be known to you as a historian in your own field and epoch of history.

Believe me your affectionate friend

Gerard M. Hopkins S.J.

Oct. 17 1881.

To Richard Watson Dixon

Manresa House, Roehampton, S.W. Oct. 29 1881.

My dear friend,—

. . . On the Sonnet and its history a learned book or two learned books have been published of late and all is known about it—but not by me. The reason why the sonnet has never been so effective or successful in England as in Italy I believe to be this: it is not so long as the Italian sonnet; it is not long enough, I will presently say how. Now in the form of any work of art the intrinsic measurements, the proportions, that is, of the parts to one another and to the whole, are no doubt the principal point, but still the extrinsic measurements, the absolute quantity or size goes for something. Thus supposing in the Doric Order the Parthenon to be the standard of perfection, then if the columns of the Parthenon have so many semidiameters or modules to their height, the architrave so many, and so on these will be the typical proportions. But if a building is raised on a notably greater scale it will be found that these proportions for the columns and the rest are no longer satisfactory, so that one of two things—either the proportions must be changed or the Order abandoned. Now if the Italian sonnet is one of the most successful forms of composition known, as it is reckoned to be, its proportions, inward and outward, must be pretty near perfection. The English sonnet has the same inward proportions, 14 lines, 5 feet to the line, and the rhymes and so on may be made as in the strictest Italian type. Nevertheless it is notably shorter and would therefore appear likely to be unsuccessful, from want not of comparative but of absolute length. For take any lines from an Italian sonnet, as

Non ha l'ottimo‿artista‿alcun concetto
Che‿un marmor solo‿in se non circonscriva.°

Each line has two elisions and a heavy ending or 13 syllables, though only 10 or, if you like, 11 count in the scanning. An Italian heroic line then and consequently a sonnet will be longer than an English in the proportion 13 : 10, which is considerable. But this is not all: the syllables themselves are longer. We have seldom such a delay in the voice as is given to the syllable by doubled letters (as *ottimo* and *concetto*) or even by two or more consonants (as *artista* and *circonscriva*) of any sort, read as Italians read. Perhaps then the proportions are nearer 4 : 3 or 3 : 2. The English sonnet is then in comparison with the Italian short, light, tripping, and trifling.

This has been instinctively felt and the best sonnets shew various devices successfully employed to make up for the shortcoming. It may be done by the mere gravity of the thought, which compels a longer dwelling on the words, as in Wordsworth (who otherwise is somewhat light in his versification), e.g.

> Earth has not anything to shew more fair°—etc;

or by inversion and a periodic construction, which has something the same effect: there is a good deal of this in Bridges' sonnets; or by breaks and pauses, as

> Captain or colonel or knight-at-arms;°

or by many monosyllables, as

> Both them I serve and of their train am I:°

this is common with τοὺς περὶ [followers of] Swinburne; or by the weight of the syllables themselves, strong or circumflexed and so on, as may be remarked in Gray's sonnet, an exquisite piece of art, whatever Wordsworth may say,

> In vain to me the smiling mornings shine—°

(this sonnet is remarkable for its falling or trochaic rhythm—

> In | vain to | me the | smiling | mornings | shine—

and not

In vain | to me | the smil | ing morn | ings shine),

and it seems to me that for a mechanical difficulty the most mechanical remedy is the best: none, I think, meet it so well as these 'outriding' feet I sometimes myself employ, for they more than equal the Italian elisions and make the whole sonnet rather longer, if anything, than the Italian is. Alexandrine lines (used throughout) have the same effect: this of course is a departure from the Italian, but French sonnets are usually in Alexandrines.

The above reasoning wd. shew that any metre (in the same rhythm) will be longer in Italian than in English and this is in fact, I believe, the case and is the reason perhaps why the *ottava rima* has never had the success in England it has had in Italy and why Spencer° found it necessary to lengthen it in the ratio from 20 to 23 (= 80 to 92).

Surrey's sonnets are fine, but so far as I remember them they are strict in form. I look upon Surrey as a great writer and of the purest style. But he was an experimentalist, as you say, and all his experiments are not successful. I feel ashamed however to talk of English or any literature, of which I was always very ignorant and which I have ceased to read.

The alteration 'seek a part' will meet the difficulty of the mixed metaphor. 'Love's mast' will then be the post. But I had imagined that you were speaking of that mast itself as a place of danger, subject to the storms of speculation, panics, failures, inflations, depressions, 'bears', 'bulls', and swindles.

This must be my last letter on literary matters while I stay here, for they are quite out of keeping with my present duties. I am very glad my criticisms should be of any service to you: they have involved a labour of love.

Nov. 2—My sister is unwilling to send you the music, with which she is not satisfied, till I have seen it. It must therefore wait awhile.

I am ashamed at the expression of high regard which your last letter and others have contained, kind and touching as they are, and do not know whether I ought to reply to them or not. This I say: my vocation puts before me a standard so high that a higher can be found nowhere else. The question then for me is not whether I am willing (if I may guess what is in your mind) to make a sacrifice of hopes of fame (let us suppose), but whether I am not to undergo a severe judgment from God for the lothness I have shewn in making it, for the reserves I may have in my heart made, for the backward glances I have° given with my hand upon the plough, for the waste of time the very compositions you admire may have caused and their preoccupation of the mind which belonged to more sacred or more binding duties, for the disquiet and the thoughts of vainglory they have given rise to. A purpose may look smooth and perfect from without but be frayed and faltering from within. I have never wavered in my vocation, but I have not lived up to it. I destroyed the verse I had written when I entered the Society and meant to write no more;° the *Deutschland* I began after a long interval at the chance suggestion of my superior, but that being done it is a question whether I did well to write anything else. However I shall, in my present mind, continue to compose, as occasion shall fairly allow, which I am afraid will be seldom and indeed for some years past has been scarcely ever, and let what I produce wait and take its chance; for a very spiritual man once told me that with things like composition the best sacrifice was not to destroy one's work but to leave it entirely to be disposed of by obedience. But I can scarcely fancy myself asking a superior to publish a volume of my verses and I own that humanly there is very little likelihood of that ever coming to pass. And to be sure if I chose to look at things on one side and not the other I could of course regret this bitterly. But there is more peace and it is the holier lot to be unknown than to be known.—In no case am I willing to write anything while in my present condition: the time is precious and will not return again and I know I shall not regret my forbearance. If I do get hereafter any opportunity of writing poetry I could find it in my heart to finish a tragedy of which I have a few dozen lines written and the leading thoughts for the rest in my head on the subject of St. Winefred's martyrdom: as it happens, tomorrow is her feastday.

I hope you may have all happiness in your marriage.° You have, I think, no children of your own, but Bridges told me he met your two step daughters at Hayton.

I am afraid our retreat will not begin tonight after all.

Believe me always your affectionate friend

Gerard M. Hopkins S.J.

I should tell you that my letters now are opened.

To Richard Watson Dixon

Manresa House, Roehampton, S.W. Dec. 1 1881 | (the very day 300 years ago of Father Campion's martyrdom).

My dear friend,—

I am heartily glad you did not make away with, as you say you thought of doing, so warm and precious a letter as your last. It reached me on the first break or day of repose in our month's retreat; I began answering it on the second, but could not finish; and this is the third and last of them.

When a man has given himself to God's service, when he has denied himself and followed Christ, he has fitted himself to receive and does receive from God a special guidance, a more particular providence. This guidance is conveyed partly by the action of other men, as his appointed superiors, and partly by direct lights and inspirations. If I wait for such guidance, through whatever channel conveyed, about anything, about my poetry for instance, I do more wisely in every way than if I try to serve my own seeming interests in the matter. Now if you value what I write, if I do myself, much more does our Lord. And if he chooses to avail himself of what I leave at his disposal he can do so with a felicity and with a success which I could never command. And if he does not, then two things follow; one that the reward I shall nevertheless receive from him will be all the greater; the other that then I shall know how much a thing contrary to his will and even to my own best interests I should have done if I had taken things into my own hands and forced on publication. This is my principle and this in the main has been my practice: leading the sort of life I do here it seems easy, but when one mixes with the world and meets on every side its secret solicitations, to live by faith is harder, is very hard; nevertheless by God's help I shall always do so.

Our Society values, as you say, and has contributed to literature, to culture; but only as a means to an end. Its history and its experience shew that literature proper, as poetry, has seldom been found to be to that end a very serviceable means. We have had for three centuries often the flower of the youth of a country in numbers enter our body: among these how many poets, how many artists of all sorts, there must have been! But there have been very few Jesuit poets and, where they have been, I believe it would be found on examination that there was something exceptional in their circumstances or, so to say, counterbalancing in their career. For genius attracts fame and individual fame St. Ignatius looked on as the most dangerous and dazzling of all attractions. There was a certain Fr. Beschi° who in Southern Hindustan composed an epic which has become one of the Tamul classics and is spoken of with unbounded admiration by those who can read it. But this was in India, far from home, and one can well understand that fame among Hindu pundits need not turn the head of an Italian. In England we had Fr. Southwell° a poet, a minor poet but still a poet; but he wrote amidst a terrible persecution and died a martyr, with circumstances of horrible barbarity: this is the counterpoise in his career. Then what a genius was Campion° himself! was not he a poet? perhaps a great one, if he had chosen. His History of Ireland, written in hiding and hurrying from place to place, Mr. Simpson in his Life° says, and the samples prove it, shews an eloquence like Shakspere's; and in fact Shakspere made use of the book. He had all and more than all the rhetoric of that golden age and was probably the most vigorous mind and eloquent tongue engaged in theological strife then in England, perhaps in Europe. It seems in time he might have done anything. But his eloquence died on the air, his genius was quenched in his blood after one year's employment in his country. Music is more professional than poetry perhaps and Jesuits have composed and well, but none has any fame to speak of. We had one painter who reached excellence, I forget his name, he was a laybrother; but then he only painted flower pieces.° You see then what is against me, but since, as Soloman says, there is a time for everything, there is nothing that does not some day come to be, it may be that the time will come for my verses. I remember, by the by, once taking up a little book of the life of St. Stanislaus° told or commented on under emblems; it was much in the style of Herbert and his school and about that date; it was by some Polish Jesuit. I was astonished at their beauty and brilliancy, but the author is quite obscure. Brilliancy does not suit us. Bourdaloue° is reckoned our greatest orator: he is severe in style. Suarez° is our most famous theologian: he is a man of vast volume of mind, but without originality or brilliancy; he treats everything satisfactorily, but you never remember a phrase of his, the manner is nothing. Molina° is the man who *made* our theology: he was a genius and even in his driest dialectic I have remarked a certain fervour like a poet's. But in the great controversy on the Aids of Grace, the most dangerous crisis, as I suppose, which our Society ever went through till its suppression, though it was from his book that it had arisen, he took, I think, little part. The same sort of thing may be noticed in our saints. St. Ignatius° himself was certainly, every one who reads his life will allow, one of the most extraordinary men that ever lived; but after the establishment of the Order he lived in Rome so ordinary, so hidden a life, that when after his death they began to move in the process of his canonisation one of the Cardinals, who had known him in his later life and in that way only, said that he had never remarked anything in him more than in any edifying priest. St. Stanislaus Kostka's life and vocation is a bright romance—till he entered the noviceship, where after 10 months he died, and at the same time its interest ceases. . . . I quote these cases to prove that show and brilliancy do not suit us, that we cultivate the commonplace outwardly and wish the beauty of the king's daughter the soul to be from within.

I could say much more on all this, but it is enough and I must go on to other things. Our retreat ended on the 8th. The 'hoity toity' passage I have not seen; indeed I have never even had your book° in my hands except one day when waiting to see Bridges in his sickness I found it on the table and was just going to open it—but to the best of my remembrance I did not then open it either. I have for some years past had to put aside serious study. It is true if I had been where your book was easy of access I should have looked at it, perhaps read it all, but in Liverpool I never once entered the public library. However if, as I hope, the time for reading history should ever come I shall try to read this one. You said once you did not pretend not to have a side and that you must write as an Anglican: this is of course and you could not honestly be an Anglican and not write as one. Do you know Cobbett's *Reformation*?° Cobbett was a most honest man but not an honest Anglican; I shd. rather say that he was an honest thinker and an honest speaker but not an honest actor-out of his convictions but is a conspicuous 'bell in a bellcot' and 'signpost on a road'. The book is written with the greatest violence of language; I must own that to me the strength seems not at all too strong; but from the point of view of expediency it is far too much so, it has overshot its mark, and those for whom it is meant will not read it. I much wish some learned Catholic would reëdit it and bring it up to date.° The most valuable and striking part of it to me is the doctrine about the origin of pauperism:° I shd. much myself like to follow this out. My Liverpool and Glasgow experience laid upon my mind a conviction, a truly crushing conviction, of the misery of town life to the poor and more than to the poor, of the misery of the poor in general, of the degradation even of our race, of the hollowness of this century's civilisation: it made even life a burden to me to have daily thrust upon me the things I saw.

I have found to my dismay what I suspected before, that my sister only sent you the music to two stanzas of your Song,° whereas I made it for six. How she came to make so dreadful an oversight I cannot tell: the music changes and she had remarked on the change. But I must get her to send the rest and then you will be able to judge of the whole. I do not believe that my airs—if I can compare them with the work of an accomplished musician—would really be found to be like Mr. Metcalf's°—to judge by the two pieces of his that you sent me.

About sonnet-writing I never meant to override your own judgment. I have put the objections to licentious forms and I believe they hold. But though many sonnets in English may in point of form be great departures from and degenerations of the type, put aside the reference to the type, and they may in themselves be fine poems of 14 lines. Still that fact, that the poet has tied himself within 14 lines and calls the piece a sonnet, lays him open to objection.

I must hold that you and Morris° belong to one school, and that though you should neither of you have read a line of the other's. I suppose the same models[2], the same masters[1], the same tastes, the same keepings, above all, make the school. It will always be possible to find differences, marked differences, between original minds; it will be necessarily so. So the species in nature are essentially distinct, nevertheless they are grouped into genera: they have one form in common, mounted on that they have a form that differences them. I used to call it the school of Rossetti: it is in literature the school of the Praeraphaelites. Of course that phase is in part past, neither do these things admit of hard and fast lines; still consider yourself, that you know Rossetti and Burne Jones, Rossetti through his sympathy for you and Burne Jones—was it the same or your sympathy for him? This modern medieval school is descended from the Romantic school (Romantic is a bad word) of Keats, Leigh Hunt, Hood, indeed of Scott early in the century. That was one school; another was that of the Lake poets and also of Shelley and Landor; the third was the sentimental school, of Byron, Moore, Mrs. Hemans, and Haynes Bailey [Bayly]. Schools are very difficult to class: the best guide, I think, are keepings. Keats' school chooses medieval keepings, not pure nor drawn from the middle ages direct but as brought down through that Elizabethan tradition of Shakspere and his contemporaries which died out in such men as Herbert and Herrick. They were also great realists and observers of nature. The Lake poets and all that school represent, as it seems to me, the mean or standard of English style and diction, which culminated in Milton but was never very continuous or vigorously transmitted, and in fact none of these men unless perhaps Landor were great masters of style, though their diction is generally pure, lucid, and unarchaic. They were faithful but not rich observers of nature. Their keepings are their weak point, a sort of colourless classical keepings: when Wordsworth wants to describe a city or a cloudscape which reminds him of a city it is some ordinary rhetorical stage-effect of domes, palaces, and temples. Byron's school had a deep feeling but the most untrustworthy and barbarous eye, for nature; a diction markedly modern; and their keepings any gaud or a lot of Oriental rubbish. I suppose Crabbe to have been in form a descendant of the school of Pope with a strong and modern realistic eye; Rogers something between Pope's school and that of Wordsworth and Landor; and Campbell between this last and Byron's, with a good deal of Popery too, and a perfect master of style. Now since this time Tennyson and his school seem to me to have struck a mean or compromise between Keats and the medievalists on the one hand and Wordsworth and the Lake School on the other (Tennyson has some jarring notes of Byron in *Lady Clare Vere de Vere*, *Locksley Hall* and elsewhere). The Lake School expires in Keble and Faber and Cardinal Newman. The Brownings may be reckoned to the Romantics. Swinburne is a strange phenomenon: his poetry seems a powerful effort at establishing a new standard of poetical diction, of the rhetoric of poetry; but to waive every other objection it is essentially archaic, biblical a good deal, and so on: now that is a thing that can never last; a perfect style must be of its age. In virtue of this archaism and on other grounds he must rank with the medievalists.

This is a long ramble on literary matters, on which I did not want to enter.

At Torquay Bridges made at last a sudden and wonderful recovery: so I am told, for he has not written. He then went abroad with a common friend of ours, Muirhead,° and is, I suppose, likely to be abroad for the winter. And I am afraid when he returns I shall not see him; for I may now be called away at any time.

Earnestly thanking you for your kindness and wishing you all that is best I remain your affectionate friend

Gerard M. Hopkins S.J.

Dec. 16 1881.

To Robert Bridges

Manresa House, Roehampton, S.W. June 10 1882.

Dearest Bridges,—

It was a needless and tedious frenzy (no, the phrase is *not* like Flatman's 'serene and rapturous joys' to which poor Purcell had to drudge the music):° another train came up on that train's tail, and indeed it was a dull duncery that overhung us both not to see that its being Ascot day ensured countless more trains and not fewer. There was a lovely and passionate scene (for about the space of the last trump) between me and a tallish gentleman (I daresay he was a cardsharper) in your carriage who was by way of being you; I smiled, I murmured with my lips at him, I waved farewells, but he would not give in, till with burning shame (though the whole thing was, as I say, like the duels of archangels) I saw suddenly what I was doing.

I wish our procession, since you were to see it, had been better: I find it is agreed it was heavy and dead. Now a Corpus Christi procession shd. be stately indeed, but it shd. be brisk and joyous. But I grieve more, I am vexed, that you had not a book to follow the words sung: the office is by St. Thomas and contains all his hymns, I think. These hymns, though they have the imperfect rhetoric and weakness in idiom of all medieval Latin verse (except, say, the Dies Irae: I do not mean weakness in classical idiom—that does not matter—but want of feeling for or command of *any* idiom), are nevertheless remarkable works of genius and would have given meaning to the whole, even to the music, much more to the rite.

It is long since such things had any significance for you. But what is strange and unpleasant° is that you sometimes speak as if they had in reality none for me and you were only waiting with a certain disgust till I too should be disgusted with myself enough to throw off the mask. You said something of the sort walking on the Cowley Road when we were last at Oxford together—in '79 it must have been. Yet I can hardly think you do not think I am in earnest. And let me say, to take no higher ground, that without earnestness there is nothing sound or beautiful in character and that a cynical vein much indulged coarsens everything in us. Not that you do overindulge this vein in other matters: why then does it bulk out in that diseased and varicose way in this?

Believe me your affectionate friend

Gerard Hopkins S.J.

June 11—Since writing the above I have luckily come across the enclosed, which contains some of the hymns.

Remember me very kindly to Mrs Molesworth, who is, I hope, better. Also to Mr Woolrych [Wooldridge]. Must meet him next time I am at—but I shall never be there by the by now.

I am just starting for Brentford.

To Robert Bridges

Stonyhurst College, Blackburn. Oct. 18 1882.

Dearest Bridges,—

I have read of Whitman's (1) 'Pete' in the library at Bedford Square (and perhaps something else; if so I forget), which you pointed out; (2) two pieces in the *Athenaeum* or *Academy*, one on the Man-of-War Bird, the other beginning 'Spirit that formed this scene'; (3) short extracts in a review by Saintsbury in the *Academy*:° this is all I remember. I cannot have read more than half a dozen pieces at most.

This, though very little, is quite enough to give a strong impression of his marked and original manner and way of thought and in particular of his rhythm. It might be even enough, I shall not deny, to originate or, much more, influence another's style: they say the French trace their whole modern school of landscape to a single piece of Constable's exhibited at the Salon° early this century.

The question then is only about the fact. But first I may as well say what I should not otherwise have said, that I always knew in my heart Walt Whitman's mind to be more like my own than any other man's living. As he is a very great scoundrel this is not a pleasant confession. And this also makes me the more desirous to read him and the more determined that I will not.

Nevertheless I believe that you are quite mistaken about this piece° and that on second thoughts you will find the fancied resemblance diminish and the imitation disappear.

And first of the rhythm. Of course I saw that there was to the eye something in my long lines like his, that the one would remind people of the other. And both are in irregular rhythms. There the likeness ends. The pieces of his I read were mostly in an irregular rhythmic prose: that is what they are thought to be meant for and what they seemed to me to be. Here is a fragment of a line I remember: 'or a handkerchief designedly dropped'.° This is in a dactylic rhythm—or let us say anapaestic; for it is a great convenience in English to assume that the stress is always at the end of the foot; the consequence of which assumption is that in ordinary verse there are only two English feet possible, the iamb and the anapaest, and even in my regular sprung rhythm only one additional, the fourth paeon: for convenience' sake assuming this, then the above fragment is anapaestic—'or a hánd | kerchief . . . | . desígn | edly drópped'—and there is a break down, a designed break of rhythm, after 'handkerchief', done no doubt that the line may not become° downright verse, as it would be if he had said 'or a handkerchief purposely dropped'. Now you can of course say that he meant pure verse and that the foot is a paeon—'or a hánd | kerchief desígn | edly drópped'; or that he means, without fuss, what I should achieve by looping the syllable *de* and calling that foot an outriding foot—for the result might be attained either way. Here then I must make the answer which will apply here and to all like cases and to the examples which may be found up and down the poets of the use of sprung rhythm—*if they could have done it they would*: sprung rhythm, once you hear it, is so eminently natural a thing and so effective a thing that if they had known of it they would have used it. Many people, as we say, have been 'burning', but they all missed it; they took it up and mislaid it again. So far as I know—I am enquiring and presently I shall be able to speak more decidedly—it existed in full force in Anglo saxon verse and in great beauty; in a degraded and doggrel shape in *Piers Ploughman* (I am reading that famous poem and am coming to the conclusion that it is not worth reading); Greene° was the last who employed it at all consciously and he never continuously; then it disappeared—for one cadence in it here and there is not sprung rhythm and one swallow does not make a spring. (I put aside Milton's case, for it is altogether singular.) In a matter like this a thing does not exist, is not *done* unless it is wittingly and willingly done; to recognise the form you are employing and to mean it is everything. To apply this: there is (I suppose, but you will know) no sign that Whitman means to use paeons or outriding feet where these breaks in rhythm occur; it seems to me a mere extravagance to think he means people to understand of themselves what they are slow to understand even when marked or pointed out. If he does not mean it then he does not do it; or in short what he means to write—and writes—is rhythmic prose and that only. And after all, you probably grant this.

Good. Now prose rhythm in English is always one of two things (allowing my convention about scanning upwards or from slack to stress and not from stress to slack)—either iambic or anapaestic. You may make a third measure (let us call it) by intermixing them. One of these three simple measures then, all iambic or all anapaestic or mingled iambic and anapaestic, is what he in every case means to write. He dreams of no other and he *means* a rugged or, as he calls it in that very piece 'Spirit that formed this scene' (which is very instructive and should be read on this very subject), a 'savage' art and rhythm.

Extremes meet, and (I must for truth's sake say what sounds pride) this savagery of his art, this rhythm in its last ruggedness and decomposition into common prose, comes near the last elaboration of mine. For that piece of mine is very highly wrought. The long lines are not rhythm run to seed: everything is weighed and timed in them. Wait till they have taken hold of your ear and you will find it so. No, but what it *is* like is the rhythm of Greek tragic choruses or of Pindar: which is pure sprung rhythm. And that has the same changes of cadence from point to point as this piece. If you want to try it, read one till you have settled the true places of the stress, mark these, then read it aloud, and you will see. Without this these choruses are prose bewitched; with it they are sprung rhythm like that piece of mine.

Besides, why did you not say *Binsey Poplars* was like Whitman? The present piece is in the same kind and vein, but developed, an advance. The lines and the stanzas (of which there are two in each poem and having much the same relation to one another) are both longer, but the two pieces are greatly alike: just look. If so how is this a being untrue to myself? I am sure it is no such thing.

The above remarks are not meant to run down Whitman. His 'savage' style has advantages, and he has chosen it; he says so. But you cannot eat your cake and keep it: he eats his offhand, I keep mine. It makes a very great difference. Neither do I deny all resemblance. In particular I noticed in 'Spirit that formed this scene' a preference for the alexandrine. I have the same preference: I came to it by degrees, I did not take it from him.

About diction the matter does not allow me so clearly to point out my independence as about rhythm. I cannot think that the present piece owes anything to him. I hope not, here especially, for it is not even spoken in my own person but in that of St. Winefred's maidens. It ought to sound like the thoughts of a good but lively girl and not at all like—not at all like Walt Whitman. But perhaps your mind may have changed by this.

I wish I had not spent so much time in defending the piece.

Believe me your affectionate friend Gerard.

Oct. 19 1882. I am not sure I shall not ask C[anon]. D[ixon]. to let me see at least one packet of Mano. He should, every one should now, use one of these reproductive processes: it is next to printing and at least it secures one against irretrievable loss by the post. All our masters here use the gelatine process for flying sheets etc.

To Robert Bridges

4 Nov. 1882.

. . . Although on the one hand the action is so good and its unity so well kept and on the other hand the style so beautiful I have doubts about the play's acting.° Experience only can decide; but I do not think it has in a high degree a nameless quality which is of the first importance both in oratory and drama: I sometimes call it *bidding*. I mean the art or virtue of saying everything right *to* or *at* the hearer, interesting him, holding him in the attitude of correspondent or addressed or at least concerned, making it everywhere an act of intercourse—and of discarding everything that does not bid, does not tell. I think one may gain much of this by practice. I do not know if I make myself plain. It is most difficult to combine this bidding, such a fugitive thing, with a monumental style. Your style is monumental. But it can be done: witness Greek plays—and Shakspere's, but those are more monumental and less in bidding, his more bidding and less monumental. I fancy the French drama eminently succeeds in this combination, but the success is not what we should be content with, the rank of the result not being very high. This will be of more importance in your Nero. . . .

Believe me your affectionate friend

Gerard M. Hopkins S.J.

To Robert Bridges

Stonyhurst, Blackburn. Dec. 1 1882.

Dearest Bridges,—

. . . I agree with you that English compounds° do not seem real single words or properly unified till by some change in form or spelling or slur in pronunciation their construction is disguised. This seems in English a point craved for and insisted on, that words shall be single and specific marks for things, whether self-significant or not; and it is noticeable how unmeaning our topographical names are or soon become, while those in Celtic languages are so transparent—not that their unmeaningness is any virtue, rather a vice; still it shews the tendency. But your instances are not fair: if icebergs had been common in British seas a name would have been found for them either not compounded at all° or if compound as good as *iceberg* is or better and certainly a great deal better than *icelump*, which is caricature. *Thimble* is singler than *thumbstall* (I do not believe it comes from that but from *thumble*), but it is a meaner word. The absurdity of 'finger hut' is not in its being a compound but in its impropriety, in the particular trope employed. *Fingerhood* or indeed *fingerstall* seem to me to be well enough. *Potato* is certainly one of the ugliest and most laughable words in the language and cannot well be used in verse, whereas *earthapple* is stately: *potato* has one virtue only, the being specific . . .

To Robert Bridges

Stonyhurst College, Blackburn. Jan. 4 1883.

Dearest Bridges,—

Since our holidays began I have been in a wretched state of weakness and weariness, I can't tell why, always drowsy and incapable of reading or thinking to any effect. And this must be why I was, before that, able to do so little on your *Prometheus*.°

I think the sonnet° a fine work, but should like the phrasing to be more exquisite in lines 2, 4, and perhaps elsewhere. Still it has to me an unspontaneous artificial air. I cannot consider the goblet and 'golden foil' a success. It is out of keeping with sons of toil and the unadornment of their brides. It is obscure too: it means, I suppose, that the goblet is of gold and that this gold sets off and is set off by the colour of the wine. This much resemblance there is, that as the goblet draws or swallows up and sort-of-drinks the liquid and the liquid at the same time swallows up and sort-of-drinks the material of the goblet so the body absorbs sleep and sleep the body. But the images of gold and crimson are out of keeping: brilliancy is only in the way. You were, you say, driven to it: I protest, and with indignation, at your saying I was driven to the same image. With more truth might it be said that my sonnet might have been written expressly for the image's sake.° But the image is not the same as yours and I do not mean by foil set-off at all; I mean foil in its sense of leaf or tinsel, and no other word whatever will give the effect I want. Shaken goldfoil gives off broad glares like sheet lightning and also, and this is true of nothing else, owing to its zigzag dints and creasings and network of small many cornered facets, a sort of fork lightning too. Moreover as it is the first rhyme, presumably it engendered the others and not they it. This reminds me that I hold you to be wrong about 'vulgar', that is obvious or necessary, rhymes. It follows from your principle that if a word has only one rhyme in the language it cannot be used in selfrespecting poetry at all. The truth seems to me that a problem is set to all, how to use that same pair (or triplet or any set) of rhymes, which are invariable, to the finest and most natural effect. It is nothing that the reader can say / He had to say it, there *was* no other rhyme: you answer / shew me what better I could have said if there had been a million. Hereby, I may tell you, hangs a very profound question treated by Duns Scotus, who shews that freedom is compatible with necessity. And besides, common sense tells you that though if you say A_1 you cannot help saying A_2 yet you can help saying $A_1 + A_2$ at all; you could have said $B_1 + B_2$ or $C_1 + C_2$ etc. And is not music a sort of rhyming on seven rhymes and does that make it vulgar? The variety is more, but the principle the same. Come, you are as much cast in this matter as Lawes was in the Belt case—though I am grievously afraid there was a miscarriage of justice in that trial; not that I like to side against a judge's sentence.°

Jan. 5—Hall Caine's 'Disquisition' on Rossetti's picture of Dante's Dream bought by the city of Liverpool reached me this morning, I suppose from the author. Noel Paton° is quoted as saying, with goodnatured gush, that it may be ranked with the Madonna di San Sisto. Now,you know, it may *not*, and I am considering whether I shall tell Hall Caine so.

To return to your sonnet, could you not find another rhyme? there is *spoil, despoil, turmoil* not to speak of *coil, boil, parboil*, and Hoyle on whist—the very sight of which dreary jugglery brings on yawns with me.

You speak of writing the sonnet in prose first. I read the other day that Virgil wrote the Aeneid in prose. Do you often do so? Is it a good plan? If it is I will try it; it may help on my flagging and almost spent powers. Years ago one of ours, a pupil of mine, was to write some English verses for me, to be recited: he had a real vein. He said he had no thoughts, but that if I would furnish some he would versify them. I did so and the effect was very surprising to me to find my own thoughts, with no variation to speak of, expressed in good verses quite unlike mine.

The sonnet on Purcell means this: 1–4. I hope Purcell is not damned for being a Protestant, because I love his genius. 5–8. And that not so much for gifts he shares, even though it shd. be in higher measure, with other musicians as for his own individuality. 9–14. So that while he is aiming only at impressing me his hearer with the meaning in hand I am looking out meanwhile for his specific, his individual markings and mottlings, 'the sakes of him'. It is as when a bird thinking only of soaring spreads its wings: a beholder may happen then to have his attention drawn by the act to the plumage displayed.—In particular, the first lines mean: May Purcell, O may he have died a good death and that soul which I love so much and which breathes or stirs so unmistakeably in his works have parted from the body and passed away, centuries since though I frame the wish, in peace with God! so that the heavy condemnation under which he outwardly or nominally lay for being out of the true Church may in consequence of his good intentions have been reversed. 'Low lays him' is merely 'lays him low', that is / strikes him heavily, weighs upon him. (I daresay this will strike you as more professional than you had anticipated.) It is somewhat dismaying to find I am so unintelligible though, especially in one of my very best pieces. 'Listed', by the by, is 'enlisted'. 'Sakes' is hazardous: about that point I was more bent on saying my say than on being understood in it. The 'moonmarks' belong to the image only of course, not to the application; I mean not detailedly: I was thinking of a bird's quill feathers. One thing disquiets me: *I meant* 'fair fall' to mean *fair (fortune be) fall*; it has since struck me that perhaps 'fair' is an adjective proper and in the predicate and can only be used in cases like 'fair fall the day', that is, *may the day fall, turn out, fair*. My line will yield a sense that way indeed, but I never meant it so. Do you know any passage decisive on this?

Would that I had Purcell's music here.

Did you see Vernon Lee's paper in the December *Contemp*.?° I don't like it. She professes herself a disciple of a Mr. Edmund Gurney, who by way of reaction against the gush of programmes ('sturdy old tone-poet'—'inimitable drollery of the semi demiquavers in the dominant minor' and so on) says that we enjoy music because our apish ancestors serenaded their Juliet-apes of the period in rudimentary recitatives and our emotions are the survival—that sexual business will in short be found by roking° the pot. This is to swing from pap to poison. Would that I had my materials ready to talk sense.

Yours affectionately Gerard Hopkins S.J.

Jan. 5 1883.

To Alexander William Mowbray Baillie

Stonyhurst College, Blackburn. Jan. 14 1883.

Dearest Baillie,—

I believe I am writing chiefly to withdraw something I said at our last meeting, though if there had been nothing to withdraw still I ought to write; but blackguardry stamps my whole behaviour to you from first to last.

Strong words are seldom much good and the more of heat the less of reason. The strong word I repent of using was that if ever there was a humbug it was Swedenborg. What I might reasonably have said (and what I really meant) was that Swedenborgianism (what a word!) is humbug. But I ought not to have seemed to imply that Swedenborg° himself was an impostor or anything of the nature of Cagliostro, for so far as I know there is no ground for saying this. He had some very strange experiences: how he came by them no matter, but he may have related them faithfully. It is however a great folly of his followers to build on them. His first dealing with the other world took place at an eating-house in London, where after a very heavy dinner (so he is quoted as saying in his journal) he saw the cieling [sic] (or the floor) covered with hideous reptiles. Then he was aware of a light in a corner of the room and of a luminous figure which sternly said to him 'Do not eat so much'. After that he began to receive communications. The circumstances suggest delirium tremens, as everyone must feel. Whatever the explanation, no sensible man would feel happy in a religion which began to be revealed in that way.

I am here to coach classics for the London University Intermediate (say Moderations) and B.A. (say Greats) examinations. I like my pupils and do not wholly dislike the work, but I fall into or continue in a heavy weary state of body and mind in which my go is gone (the elegance of that phrase! as Thackeray says, it makes one think what vast sums must have been spent on my education!), I make no way with what I read, and seem but half a man. It is a sad thing to say. I try, and am even meant to try, in my spare time (and if I were fresher or if it were anyone but myself there would be a good deal of spare time taking short and long together) to write some books; but I find myself so tired or so harassed I fear they will never be written. The one that would interest you most is on the Greek Lyric Art or on, more narrowly, the art of the choric and lyric parts of the Gk. plays. I want it to be in two parts, one the metre, the other the style. It is, I am afraid, too ambitious of me, so little of a scholar as I am; only I think what I should say would throw a new light and that if I did not perhaps no one else would. But it is a laborious business and why shd. I undertake it? There are, I believe, learned books lately written in Germany on the choric metres and music, which if I could see and read them would either serve me or quench me; but on the other head I do not anticipate being anticipated—so to say. My thought is that in any lyric passage of the tragic poets (perhaps not so much in Euripides as the others) there are—usually; I will not say always, it is not likely—two strains of thought running together and like counterpointed; the overthought that which everybody, editors, see (when one does see anything—which in the great corruption of the text and original obscurity of the diction is not everywhere) and which might for instance be abridged or paraphrased in square marginal blocks as in some books carefully written; the other, the underthought, conveyed chiefly in the choice of metaphors etc used and often only half realised by the poet himself, not necessarily having any connection with the subject in hand but usually having a connection and suggested by some circumstance of the scene or of the story. I cannot prove that this is really so except by a large induction of examples and perhaps not irrefragably even then nor without examples can I even make my meaning plain. I will give only one, the chorus with which Aeschylus' *Suppliants* begins. The underthought which plays through this is that the Danaids flying from their cousins are like their own ancestress Io teazed by the gadfly and caressed by Zeus and the rest of that foolery. E.g. *δίαν δὲ λιποῦσαι | χθόνα σύγχορτον Συρίᾳ φεύγομεν* [for we have fled the land of Zeus whose pastures border upon Syria, and are fugitives]. the suggestion is of a herd of cows feeding next a herd of bulls. Shortly follows a mention of Io and her story. Then comes *δέξαισθ' ἱκέτην | τὸν θηλυγενῆ στόλον αἰδοίῳ | πνεύματι χώρας* [receive as suppliants this company of womankind with the reverent spirit of the land]: this alludes to the *ἐπίπνοια* [engendering breath] by which Epaphus was conceived—*ἀρσενοπληθῆ δ' | ἑσμὸν ὑβριστὴν Αἰγυπτογενῆ* [but the thronging swarm of wanton men born of Aegyptus] etc: this suggests the gadfly. Perhaps what I ought to say is that the underthought is commonly an echo or shadow of the overthought, something like canons and repetitions in music, treated in a different manner, but that sometimes it may be independent of it. I find this same principle of composition in St. James' and St. Peter's and St. Jude's Epistles, an undercurrent of thought governing the choice of images used. Perhaps I spoke of this to you before.

I could write more, but have written enough now. Tell me about the Rossetti exhibition; but you need not enlarge on

Dante's Dream or on Mr Rae's pictures,° for these I have seen. In an old letter of yours, many years old (I have been reading them again), you speak of Pindar, taking exception to some things and giving examples. I do not on the whole agree with your objections and should defend the *examples. This sort of thing I should explain in that book if it were written. I shd. also give some fancy music to some choruses and odes, plainchant, not an attempted reproduction of Gk. music but as a means of bringing out the rhythm.

Be very interesting and entertaining: what else could a letter of yours be? Meanwhile and ever after believe me your affectionate and grateful friend Gerard Hopkins S.J.

To Robert Bridges

Stonyhurst College, Blackburn. Feb. 3 1883.

Dearest Bridges,—

I cd. not venture to ask that our library should subscribe half a sovereign for an *édition de luxe* of a new book° by an almost unknown author; still less could I expect, nor shd. I like, you to present me, that is our library, with a copy. Here then is a downright deadlock and there is nothing for it but for me to wait for the second edition and then, like Brewer in the *Mutual Friend*, 'see how things look'.

Many thanks for the anthems. I remember now that I heard the first at Magdalen. Did you remark that the first 9 notes of the Hallelujah are, with a slight change, the beginning of *Cease your funning*?

This is a terrible business about my sonnet° 'Have fair fallen', for I find that I still 'make myself misunderstood'. *Have* is not a plural at all, far from it. It is the singular imperative (or optative if you like) of the past, a thing possible and actual both in logic and grammar, but naturally a rare one. As in the second person we say 'Have done' or in making appointments 'Have had your dinner beforehand', so one can say in the third person not only 'Fair fall' of what is present

* It turns on their explanation. If the explanation suits them it defends them.

or future but also 'Have fair fallen' of what is past. The same thought (which plays a great part in my own mind and action) is more clearly expressed in the last stanza but one of the *Eurydice*, where you remarked it.

I quite understand what you mean about gentlemen and 'damfools'; it is a very striking thing and I could say much on the subject. I shall not say that much, but I say this: if a gentleman feels that to be what we call a gentleman is a thing essentially higher than without being a gentleman to be ever so great an artist or thinker or if, to put it another way, an artist or thinker feels that were he to become in those ways ever so great he wd. still essentially be lower than a gentleman that was no artist and no thinker—and yet to be a gentleman is but on the brim of morals and rather a thing of manners than of morals properly—then how much more must art and philosophy and manners and breeding and everything else in the world be below the least degree of true virtue. This is that chastity of mind which seems to lie at the very heart and be the parent of all other good, the seeing at once what is best, the holding to that, and the not allowing anything else whatever to be even heard pleading to the contrary. Christ's life and character are such as appeal to all the world's admiration, but there is one insight St. Paul gives us° of it which is very secret and seems to me more touching and constraining than everything else is: This mind he says, was in Christ Jesus—he means as man: being in the form of God—that is, finding, as in the first instant of his incarnation he did, his human nature informed by the godhead—he thought it nevertheless no snatching-matter for him to be equal with God, but annihilated himself, taking the form of servant; that is, he could not but see what he was, God, but he would see it as if he did not see it, and be it as if he were not and instead of snatching at once at what all the time was his, or was himself, he emptied or exhausted himself so far as that was possible, of godhead and behaved only as God's slave, as his creature, as man, which also he was, and then being in the guise of man humbled himself to death, the death of the cross. It is this holding of himself back, and not snatching at the truest and highest good, the good that was his right, nay his possession from a past eternity in his other nature, his own being and self, which seems to me the root of all his holiness and the imitation of this the root of all moral good in other men. I agree then, and vehemently,° that a gentleman, if there is such a thing on earth, is in the position to despise the poet, were he Dante or Shakspere, and the painter, were he Angelo or Apelles, for anything in him that shewed him *not* to be a gentleman. He is in the position to do it, I say, but if he is a gentleman perhaps this is what he will not do. Which leads me to another remark.

The quality of a gentleman is so very fine a thing that it seems to me one should not be at all hasty in concluding that one possesses it. People assume that they have it, take it quite for granted, and claim the acknowledgment from others: now I should say that this also is 'no snatching-matter'. And the more a man feels what it means and is—and to feel this is certainly some part of it—the more backward he will be to think he can have realised in himself anything so perfect. It is true, there is nothing like the truth and 'the good that does itself not know scarce is';° so the perfect gentleman will know that he is the perfect gentleman. But few can be in the position to know this and, being imperfect gentlemen, it will perhaps be a point of their gentlemanliness, for a gentleman is modest, to feel that they are not perfect gentlemen.

By the by if the English race had done nothing else, yet if they left the world the notion of a gentleman, they would have done a great service to mankind.

As a fact poets and men of art are, I am sorry to say, by no means necessarily or commonly gentlemen. For gentlemen do not pander to lust or other basenesses nor, as you say, give themselves airs and affectations nor do other things to be found in modern works. And this adds a charm to everything Canon Dixon writes, that you feel he is a gentleman and thinks like one. But now I have prosed my prose and long enough.

Believe me your affectionate friend

Gerard M. Hopkins S.J.

Feb. 10 1883.

I am rueful and remorseful about P. F. But what else could

come of handmade Dutch paper? I regret that Daniel made his offer. And I hope the 2nd edition will be this one's Jacob.°

To Robert Bridges

Stonyhurst College, Blackburn. May 11 1883.

Dearest Bridges,—

Here then is this blessed thing, which has cost more trouble than it is worth.° Try it yourself. Sometimes when I play it at my own pace and with my own expression I think it very good in parts and at other times and when somebody else plays it it seems to me a meaningless maundering and a wandering in a wilderness.

I think from what you say it had better not go to Stainer,° though as he was my contemporary and I knew him by sight I feel drawn to him.

We hang up polyglot poems in honour of the Blessed Virgin this month. I am on one in English in three-foot couplets.° I do not suppose I shall find it either convenient or desirable to send you a copy. It is partly a compromise with popular taste, and it is too true that the highest subjects are not those on which it is easy to reach one's highest.

The cold half kills me.

Your affectionate friend Gerard Hopkins S.J.

Though the favour will be, directly speaking, to you I shall be very grateful to your friend.° What I want is that he should mark any mistakes he may find and make any remarks he may think proper, on the margin or elsewhere. Whitsunday. I have sealed it up, but you may put onto it that the bass sounds better an octave lower or doubled.

Your letter has come, on which I have to remark—

Some of my rhymes I regret, but they are past changing, grubs in amber: there are only a few of these;

Others are unassailable;

Some others again there are which *malignity may munch at* but the Muses love. To this class belongs what you quote. You will grant that there are things in verse which may be read right or wrong, which depend for their effect upon pronunciation. For instance here if I had rhymed *drew her* to *to her* I should have meant it to be read *tó her* and not *to hér*, though in itself the latter is just as possible. You will also grant that in *drew her*, rightly read, the *h* is evanescent. Good. Now then *endured*° may be read with little or with well marked circumflex—*endũred* like *en-dew-ered*. And°

To Robert Bridges

Stonyhurst College, Blackburn. May 18 1883.

(fine day, with a solar halo; holiday; our boys to have a match)

Dearest Bridges,—

Fine bass! I should think so. But did you never hear *Pray Goody* before? I am glad I have introduced it to you. (I think it far better to take fine things like that to practise on than the maundering exercises in books.) And it is but one out of a host of such masculine and (what some one called) earnest melodies, little known here and abroad I suppose totally unknown. It is simple truth that no German since Mozart has been capable of anything of the sort. The Germans are great and I believe unsurpassable in expressing mood and feeling, but for the bone, frame, and *charpente* [frame (work)] of music they cannot come up to this kind of thing.

On the contrary anything that Simcox° says is important. But for rhymes like those search the scriptures, thumb the poets, and you will find they readily allow monosyllables and dissyllables like *higher* and *fire* to rhyme.* It is true it is not very consistent of me to appeal to them when I profess to follow a more excellent way; still when I am told so and so is indefensible I must shew that it is defensible. Authority justifies it and the pronunciation can be so adjusted as to

* You will say a monosyllable cannot rhyme to a monosyllable and a disyllable both at once, in the same stanza, that is. But if it can ever, then one of the two is accommodated to the other; and if one can be so can two or if one to one then one or two. Do you see the reasoning?

satisfy the ear. What is serious, you seem to think I took the objection overseriously. And now I think I am going out by woods and waters alone.

Yours Gerard.

To Richad Watson Dixon

Stonyhurst, Blackburn. June 25 1883.

My dear Friend,—

I am ashamed to think how long I have let you go unanswered: it was bitter winter weather, I remember you said, when you wrote; but the winter was very late this year. It came March 20.

I have little to say. I enclose one sonnet,° meant as a companion to one beginning 'I remember a house',° which perhaps you have. You will see that the first words begin a lyric of yours—or perhaps those are 'Earth, *sad* Earth'.° During May I was asked to write something in honour of the Blessed Virgin, it being the custom to hang up verse-compositions 'in the tongues' (which sometimes are far fetched, for people gravitate to us from odd quarters): I did a piece° in the same metre as 'Blue in the mists all day',° but I have not leisure to copy it.

Both your new poem and Bridges' linger.°

We have duly got your History, but till holiday time I shall not look at it. Reading history is very laborious to me: I can only digest or remember a little at a time.

My time, as I have said before this, is not so closely employed but that someone else in my place might not do a good deal, but I cannot, and I see no grounded prospect of my ever doing much not only in poetry but in anything at all. At times I do feel this sadly and bitterly, but it is God's will and though no change that I can foresee will happen yet perhaps some may that I do not foresee.—I fumble a little at music, at counterpoint, of which in course of time I shall come to know something; for this, like every other study, after some drudgery yields up its secrets, which seem inpenetrable at first. If I could get to accompany my own airs I should, so to say, enter into a new kingdom at once, for I have plenty of tunes ready.

Your health is, I hope, good, for when you wrote you were suffering greatly from the cold. We have had drought in Lancashire, a rare thing: now the fine weather is broken up and there is much rain.

In the sonnet enclosed 'louchéd'° is a coinage of mine and is to mean much the same as *slouched, slouching*. And I mean 'throng' for an adjective as we use it here in Lancashire.

This is but a scrub of a letter, but I could not make it longer or better now.

Believe me your affectionate friend

Gerard M. Hopkins S.J.

June 28 1883.

To Richard Watson Dixon

The Holy Name, Oxford Road, Manchester. Aug. 15 1883

My dear friend,—

Your letter was brought me from Stonyhurst by hand yesterday and your book° came by parcel post today: for both I heartily thank you. I have nearly finished the first Book, but at a first reading it would be too soon to speak. The style is more consistently archaic than I had expected: this style easily lends itself to pathetic effects but not so easily to powerful ones. A pageant of beauties passes before my mind as I read, but, much as Mr. Patmore said, I need time and rereading to take the effect fairly in. So I will wait a while before writing further.

By 'unity of action'° I understand (but I am not advised of the subject) not simplicity of plot (in the ordinary sense of simple, that is the opposite of complex) but connectedness of plot. There is unity of action, as I understand, if the plot turns on one event, incident, or, to speak more technically, motive and all its parts and details bear on that and are relevant to that: if they are irrelevant or disconnected or involve by-issues then the unity of action is impaired. So I have been accustomed to understand the phrase. The plot in some Greek plays is simple, slight, in the extreme: the *Agamemnon* for instance is what we should call rather a scene than a plot, a scene leading up to and then leading off from one incident, the hero's murder; but the unity of action is also extreme, for almost every word said and thing done leads up to, turns on, influences, or is influenced by this. But in this play there is also the 'unity of place' and, by a conventional abridgment, the semblance of 'unity of time'. Where, as in the *Eumenides*, these two unities are not observed the plot becomes more complicated. The plot, quite in our modern sense of plot, is well enough marked in the *Oedipus King* though the unities of time and place are there observed. In general I take it that other things being alike unity of action is higher the more complex the plot; it is the more difficult to effect and therefore the more valuable when effected. We judge so of everything. In practice something must be sacrificed, and on what shall be sacrificed temperaments differ and discover their differences. The incidents for instance of Goethe's *Faust* are fascinating, but the unity of action, the bearing of all these on one common lesson the play is to teach or effect it is to produce, is not telling at first sight and is perhaps—I have no opinion—really defective. The Gk. dramas are on the other hand well concentrated, but the play of incident and character is often slight: one does not quote from them either stage-effects or types of character. But my thoughts are unverified and undigested.

A friend recommended me if I met with them to read L. Stevenson's stories, the *New Arabian Nights*° and others since. I read a story by him in *Longman's*, I think, and a paper by him on Romance.° His doctrine, if I apprehend him, is something like this. The essence of Romance is incident and that only, the type of pure Romance the *Arabian Nights*: those stories have no moral, no character-drawing, they turn altogether on interesting incident. The incidents must [of] course have a connection, but it need be nothing more than that they happen to the same person, are aggravations and so on. As history consists essentially of events likely or unlikely, consequences of causes chronicled before or what may be called chance, just retributions or nothing of the sort, so Romance, which is fictitious history, consists of event, of incident. His own stories are written on this principle: they are very good and he has all the gifts a writer of fiction should have, including those he holds unessential, as characterisation, and at first you notice no more than an ordinary well told story, but on looking back in the light of this doctrine you see that the persons illustrate the incident or strain of incidents, the plot, *the story*, not the story and incidents the persons. There was a tale of his called the *Treasure of Fourvières*° or something like that; it is the story of an old treasure found, lost, and found again. The finding of the treasure acts of course and rather for the worse upon the finder, a retired French doctor, and his wife; the loss cures them; you wait to see the effect of the refinding: but not at all, the story abruptly ends—because its hero was, so to say, this triplet of incidents. His own remarks on the strength and weakness of the Waverleys are excellent. But I have been giving my own version of the doctrine (which is, I think, clearly true) rather than his for I do not remember well enough what he says.

Now I think Shakspere's drama is more in this sense romantic than the Greek and that if the unity of action is not so marked (as it is not) the *interest of romance*, arising from a well calculated strain of incidents, is greater. You remember the scene or episode of the little Indian boy in the *Midsummer Night*: it is, I think, an allegory, to which, in writing once on the play, I believed I had found the clue, but whether I was right or wrong the meaning must have in any case been, and Shakspere must have known it wd. be, dark or invisible to most beholders or readers; yet he let it stand, just, as I suppose, because it is interesting as an incident in the story, not that it throws any light on the main plot or helps the unity of action, but rather, at all events superficially, hinders it. I could write much more but must stop. I am shortly starting for London, where my address is Oak Hill, Hampstead, N.W. I am going to let Mr. Patmore know *Mano* is out: I heard from him this morning.

Believe me gratefully and affectionately your friend

Gerard Hopkins S.J.

Aug. 16.

To Coventry Patmore

Stonyhurst. Sept. 24 1883

My dear Mr. Patmore,—

I have found since writing yesterday that the line 'Her virtue all virtue so endears'° may with forethought be so read as to run smoothly, even with a stress on 'all'. I think however that how to do this will not strike everybody and that the line will mostly be a stumbling-block in reading aloud.

. . . Also I am dissatisfied with 'Beauty'° p. 159 sq. The text and principle stated is noble and deeply true, the development seems to me a decline and a surrender. It comes to this: beautiful evil is found, but it is nature's monstrosity. Then *is qui supplet locum idiotae* [he who supplies the place of the ignorant man], the worldling, Philistine (or whatever he is to be called) answers: and all I have to add is that the monstrosity is very common, and so we are agreed. And so it wd. come to the same thing to say Beauty deludes or Ugliness does.° This was not to be granted. It is certain that in nature outward beauty is the proof of inward beauty, outward good of inward good. Fineness, proportion, of feature comes from a moulding force which succeeds in asserting itself over the resistance of cumbersome or restraining matter; the bloom of health comes from the abundance of life, the great vitality within. The moulding force, the life, is the form in the philosophic sense, and in man this is the soul. But because its available activity is limited the matter it has to struggle with may be too much for it and the wax is either too cold and doughy (so to speak) and will not take or is too hot and boiling blots out the stamp of the seal—I speak under an old but a very apposite image not easily improved. This explains why 'ugly good' is found. But why do we find beautiful evil? Not by any freak of nature, nature is incapable of producing beautiful evil. The explanation is to be sought outside nature; it is old, simple, and the undeniable fact. It comes from wicked will, freedom of choice, abusing the beauty, the good of its nature. 'Thou wert' the Scripture says and great writers apply it to the Devil 'the seal of resemblance'. The instance is palmary and shews how far evil can be beautiful or beauty evil and what the phenomenon means when it occurs.—This at least is how the subject strikes me and I find it more interesting and pathetic so; it maybe however that you think no otherwise, only that I have missed the turn of your thought.

Whether you agree with me or not about the above points they are all trifles and altered or let stand little affect the poem. The following is the matter where I have to make a serious objection.

P. 202 'Women *should* be vain',° p. 217 'The Koh-i-noor'° no. 1, p. 251 'Because, although in act and word, . . . unattain'd desert'°—In the midst of a poem undertaken under a kind of inspiration from God & to express what, being most excellent, most precious, most central and important and even obvious in human life, nevertheless no one has ever yet, unless passingly thought of expressing you introduce a vice, the germ of widespread evils, and make the highest relish of pure love come from the base 'smell of mortality'. Everyone has some one fault he is tender to and vice he tolerates. We do this ourselves, but when another does it towards another vice not our own favourite (of tolerance, I do not say of commission) we are disgusted. The *Saturday Review* contrasting the Catholic and Protestant ideal of a schoolboy° came out with the frank truth, that it looked on chastity as a feminine virtue (= lewdness a masculine one: it was not quite so raw as I put it, but this was the meaning). Mommsen a brilliant historian I find thinks great nations should break treaties. Dr Ward (in his younger days) said candour was anything but a saintly virtue (perhaps he did not but is misquoted: let it at least serve as an illustration). Then violence is admired and, above all, insolence and pride. But it is our baseness to admire anything evil. It seems to me we shd. in everything side with virtue, even if we do not feel its charm, because good is good.

In particular how can anyone admire or (except in charity, as the greatest of sins, but in judgment and approval) tolerate vanity in women? Is it not the beginning of their saddest and most characteristic fall? What but vanity makes them first publish, then prostitute their charms? In Leonardo's [Titian's] famous picture 'Modesty and *Vanity*' is it not almost taken for granted that the one figure is that of a virgin, the other that of a courtezan? If modesty in women means two things at once, purity and humility, must not the pair of opposites be no great way apart, vanity from impurity? Who can think of the Blessed Virgin and of vanity? Then in one's experience, in my own, it seems to me that nothing in good women is more beautiful than just the absence of vanity and an earnestness of look and character which is better than beauty. It teaches me (if I may give such an instance—I cannot easily give others) in my own sisters that when they let me see their compositions in music or painting, which I, with a brother's biassed judgment but still sincerely, admire, they seem to be altogether without vanity—yet they might be with reason vainer of these than of their looks, and towards a brother not be ashamed to shew it (and I towards them can hardly conceal mine): they are glad when I admire nevertheless. It is the same in literature as in life: the vain women in Shakspere are the impure minded too, like Beatrice (I do not know that I may not call her a hideous character); those whose chastity one could have trusted, like Desdemona, are free from vanity too.

It is a lover who speaks in the 'Koh-i-noor', but that proves very little. He happens to be a good one, and therefore tolerates nothing worse than carelessness, talkativeness, and vanity;° but take a bad one: he will want the smell of mortality stronger. What does the adulterer love in his neighbour's wife but her obligingness in committing adultery? Tennyson makes Guenevere say 'The low sun makes the colour'°: it is a happy touch and the whole passage is instructive. Those also who write of moral monsters born without a fault and 'Let other bards of angels sing [in the House or elsewhere] Bright suns without a spot; But thou art no such perfect thing: Rejoice that thou art not', these people never saw and had lost the idea of holiness / and are no authority.

You will say that everything else, her own words and what others say of her, shew that in Honoria there was in reality no vanity and that your lines are not be taken in such grim earnest. But the truth seems to me to be that in writing you were really in two inconsistent moods, a lower and a higher, and that the record of both is in your pages.

Naturally a lurking error appears in more places than one and a false principle gives rise to false consequences. An ideal becomes an idiol and false worship sets in. So I call it at p. 251, where it is said that a wife calls her husband lord by courtesy,° meaning, as I understand, only by courtesy and 'not with her least consent of will' to his being so. But he *is* her lord. If it is courtesy only and no consent then a wife's lowliness is hypocrisy and Christian marriage a comedy, a piece of pretence. How much more truly and touchingly did you make Mrs. Graham° speak! But if she was right then the contrary is wrong. Perhaps I misunderstand the passage: I hope I do, but then I hope you will prevent other people misunderstanding it. And now pernicious doctrines and practice are abroad and the other day the papers said a wretched being refused in church to say the words 'and obey': if it had been a Catholic wedding and I the priest I would have let the sacrilege go no further.

Honoria's letter in the 'Love-letters' pp. 202, 203 by itself would be well enough, it contains its own correction ('I hope in jest'), though the incident always struck me as very trivial if also very natural, and I on no account want to lose the lovely turn 'But I was very dull, dear friend' and what follows; but the other two convey, it seems to me, though in small quantities, a poison. And they may be quoted in support of evil and do mischief commended by the lustre of your name (I hope it will be illustrious then) years after you are dead.

If I have written strongly I am sure it is in a zeal for the poem.

Believe me yours very sincerely

Gerard Manley Hopkins S.J.

To Robert Bridges

Stonyhurst, Blackburn. Oct. 24 1883.

Dearest Bridges,—

Thank you first for very kindly copying out the poem on the Blessed Virgin° and then for your letter.

You always do misunderstand me on matters like that prayer for Mrs. Waterhouse. I was not thinking of you and her, not, I mean, as using the prayers in that book or of your opinions as mirrored in them, but of the buyers of the book and the public it was meant for; which public I suppose you and Mrs. W. to know the mind and need of better than I do and therefore to be right in admitting one thing and excluding another: now in that public I regret, and surely I may, that it can no longer be trusted to bear, to stomach, the clear expression of or the taking for granted even very elementary Christian doctrines. I did not realise this well enough, did not realise that distinct Christianity damages the sale and so the usefulness of a well meant book; but now that I do what ought I to be but sorry?

But by the way you say something I want to remark on: 'Even such a doctrine as the Incarnation may be believed by people like yourself', as a mystery, till it is formulated, but as soon as it is it seems dragged down to the world of pros and cons, and '*as its mystery goes*, so does its hold on their minds'. Italics the present writer's. You do not mean by mystery what a Catholic does. You mean an interesting uncertainty: the uncertainty ceasing interest ceases also. This happens in some things; to you in religion. But a Catholic by mystery means an incomprehensible certainty: without certainy, without formulation there is no interest (of course a doctrine is valuable for other things than its interest, its interestingness, but I am speaking now of that); the clearer the formulation the greater the interest. At bottom the source of interest is the same in both cases, in your mind and in ours; it is the unknown, the reserve of truth beyond what the mind reaches and still feels to be behind. But the interest a Catholic feels is, if I may say so, of a far finer kind than yours. Yours turns out to be a curiosity only; curiosity satisfied, the trick found out (to be a little profane), the answer heard, it vanishes at once. But you know there are some solutions to, say, chess problems so·beautifully ingenious, some resolutions of suspensions so lovely in music that even the feeling of interest is keenest when they are known and over, and for some time survives the discovery. How must it then be when the very answer is the most tantalising statement of the problem and the truth you are to rest in the most pointed putting of the difficulty! For if the Trinity, as Francis Newman° somewhere says, is to be explained by grammar and by tropes, why then he could furnish explanations for himself; but then where wd. be the mystery? the true mystery, the incomprehensible one. At that pass one should point blank believe or disbelieve: he disbelieved; his brother, at the same pass, believed. There are three persons, each God and each the same, the one, the only God: to some people this is a 'dogma', a word they almost chew, that is an equation in theology, the dull algebra of schoolmen; to others it is news of their dearest friend or friends, leaving them all their lives balancing whether they have three heavenly friends or one—not that they have any doubt on the subject, but that their knowledge leaves their minds swinging; poised, but on the quiver. And this might be the ecstasy of interest, one would think. So too of the Incarnation, a mystery less incomprehensible, it is true: to you it comes to: Christ is in some sense God, in some sense he is not God—and your interest is in the uncertainty; to the Catholic it is: Christ is in every sense God and in every sense man, and the interest is in the locked and inseparable combination, or rather it is in the person in whom the combination has its place. Therefore we speak of the events of Christ's life as the mystery of the Nativity, the mystery of the Crucifixion and so on of a host; the mystery being always the same, that the child in the manger is God, the culprit on the gallows God, and so on. Otherwise birth and death are not mysteries, nor is it any great mystery that a just man should be crucified, but that God should fascinates—with the interest of awe, of pity, of shame, of every harrowing feeling. But I have said enough. . . .

Oct. 25—. . . .

[A leaf cut from MS at this point]

The expectations I raised in Mr. Patmore about Mano were my own and got from you: I had not then seen it. Afterwards however, when I had, I wrote to him that if he got it he wd. not be disappointed; whereas he is. I have not got it by me now and will not at present say more of it than this, that crowded as it is with beauties of the noblest sort, the deepest pathos and tragedy, besides a few touches of humour, finely conceived character, interest, romance, landscape, imagery, and unflagging music, still I am much of Mr. Patmore's mind: it either has not or else I have hitherto missed finding a leading thought to thread the beauties on—or almost worse, that I see one but it breaks and is unsatisfactory, namely that Mano is a kind of Adam and falls and also a kind of Second Adam and is crucified. I will write more hereafter.

I had not meant Mr. Patmore to know I wrote poetry, but since it has come naturally and unavoidably about there is no more to be said and you may therefore send me your book and I will point it and make a few corrections. You were right to leave out the marks: they were not consistent for one thing and are always offensive. Still there must be some. Either I must invent a notation applied throughout as in music or else I must only mark where the reader is likely to mistake, and for the present this is what I shall do.

I have a great deal more I could say, but must conclude.

I am your affectionate friend Gerard Hopkins S.J.

I may presently but will not just yet avail myself of your kind offer of the loose Purcells.

I have yet heard nothing particular about Grace. She will settle down and be happy: she is to simple-minded and too sweetnatured to let herself be soured or enfeebled by a grief.° She may even come to care for someone else, though no doubt she does not believe she ever could.

To Robert Bridges

University College, 85 & 86, Stephens Green, Dublin. | March 7 1884

My dearest Bridges,—

Remark the above address: it is a new departure or a new arrival and at all events a new abode. I dare say you know nothing of it, but the fact is that, though unworthy of and unfit for the post, I have been elected Fellow of the Royal University of Ireland° in the department of classics. I have a salary of £400 a year, but when I first contemplated the six examinations I have yearly to conduct, five of them running, and to the Matriculation there came up last year 750 candidates, I thought that Stephen's Green (the biggest square in Europe) paved with gold would not pay for it. It is an honour and an opening and has many bright sides, but at present it has also some dark ones and this in particular that I am not at all strong, not strong enough for the requirements, and do not see at all how I am to become so. But to talk of weather or health and especially to complain of them is poor work.

The house we are in, the College, is a sort of ruin and for purposes of study very nearly naked. And I have more money to buy books than room to put them in.

I have been warmly welcomed and most kindly treated. But Dublin itself is a joyless place and I think in my heart as smoky as London is: I had fancied it quite different. The Phoenix Park is fine, but inconveniently far off. There are a few fine buildings.

It is only a few days since I sent the MS book to Mr. Patmore (and in packing I mislaid, I hope not lost, your copy of the poem 'Wild air, world-mothering air',° so that I had to send that unfinished): he acknowledged it this morning.

I enclose a poem of Tennyson's° which you may not have seen. It has something in it like your Spring Odes and also some expressions like my sonnet on Spring.

I shall also enclose, if I can find, two triolets° I wrote for the Stonyhurst Magazine; for the third was not good, and they spoilt what point it had by changing the title. These two under correction I like, but have fears that you will suspend them from a hooked nose: if you do, still I should maintain they were as good as yours beginning 'All women born'.°

Believe me your affectionate friend Gerard Hopkins S.J.

There was an Irish row° over my election.

To Robert Bridges

Furbough House, near Galway. July 18 1884.

Dearest Bridges,—

I must let you have a line now, I see, and write more hereafter. I ought to have answered you before, but indeed I hardly thought you were in earnest in proposing I should be your best man,° pleasant and honourable as the position would be. But to show no other reasons why not, at the time you name I should be about beginning my examination work and it would be altogether impossible for me to be out of Ireland. However you do not want for friends better fitted to do the work than I.

I am here on holiday. I have been through Connemara, the fine scenery of which is less known than it should be. Yesterday I went to see the cliffs of Moher on the coast of Clare, which to describe would be long and difficult. In returning across the Bay we were in some considerable danger of our lives. Furbough House stands amidst beautiful woods, an Eden in a wilderness of rocks and treeless waste. The whole neighbourhood is most singular.

The weakness I am suffering from—it is that only, nervous weakness (or perhaps I ought not to say nervous at all, for I am not in any unusual way nervous in the common understanding of the word)—continues and I see no ground for thinking I can, for a long time to come, get notably better of it, but I may reasonably hope that this pleasant holiday may set me up a little for a while. Your enquiries are very kind: there is no reason to be disquieted about me, though weakness is a very painful trial in itself. If I could have regular hard exercise it would be better for me.

The reason of course why I like men to marry is that a single life is a difficult, not altogether a natural life; to make it easily manageable special provision, such as we have, is needed, and most people cannot have this.

I shall begin my annual eight days' retreat in a few days and then return to Dublin.

Coventry Patmore has kept your MS book° a long time, as though it were to give himself the opportunity of repentance for not admiring all the poems, and indeed appears to look on his condition as one of guilt and near to reprobation—which is very odd of him. And I believe it will be of no avail and that like Esau and Antiochus° he will not get the grace and is in a fair way to die in his sins.

I find that 2557 is divisible by nothing till you reach 20, beyond which I have not tried: what then can the length of the stanza be? And what is the subject of the poem?°

Believe me your affectionate friend

Gerard M. Hopkins S.J.

Write University *College*, Stephen's Green: the number is unnecessary.

To Robert Bridges

University College, 85 & 86, Stephen's Green, Dublin, |
Aug. 21 1884

Dearest Bridges,—

I must let you have a line to acknowledge, with many thanks, the receipt of the MS book° and two or three very kind letters. I guessed whose was the elegant and legible hand on two of the addresses. As for the piece of a new garment, I came to the conclusion it was put in to bigout the enclosure. I also concluded that that new garment was a pair of wedding trousers. Circumstances may drive me to use my piece as a penwiper.

It is so near your wedding that I do not know I ought to

write of anything else. I could not ask to be present at it; and indeed, much as I desire to see you and your wife and her mother and Yattendon itself, perhaps that would not be so good a day for this after all as some other. Only unhappily I do not see when that other is to be. However it is a fine buoyant saying, Non omnium rerum sol occidit, [nothing is certain except death].

I had an interesting letter from Mr. Patmore all in praise of you.

Several things in your letters call for reply, but not now. If you do not like 'I yield, you do come sometimes,'° (though I cannot myself feel the weakness you complain of it in it, and it has the advantage of being plain) will 'I yield, you foot me sometimes' do? 'Own my heart' is merely 'my own heart', transposed for rhythm's sake and then *tamquam exquisitius* [as if in a more recherché manner], as Hermann° would say. 'Reave' is for rob, plunder, carry off.

I find that in correcting 'Margaret' I wrote '*world* of wanwood' by mistake for 'worlds', as the sense requires.

Our society cannot be blamed for not valuing what it never knew of. The following are all the people I have let see my poems (not counting occasional pieces): some of them however, as you did, have shewn them to others. (1) The editor and subeditor of our *Month* had the *Deutschland* and later the *Eurydice* offered them—(2) my father and mother and two sisters saw these, one or both of them, and I have sent them a few things besides in letters—(3) You—(4) Cannon Dixon—(5) Mr. Patmore—(6) Something got out about the *Deutschland* and Fr. Cyprian Splaine, now of Stonyhurst, wrote to me to send it him and perhaps other poems of mine: I did so and he shewed it to others. They perhaps read it, but he afterwards acknowledged to me that in my handwriting he found it unreadable; I do not think he meant illegible—(7) On the other hand Fr. Francis Bacon, a fellownovice of mine, and an admirer of my sermons saw all and expressed a strong admiration for them which was certainly sincere. They are therefore, one may say, unknown. It always seems to me that poetry is unprofessional, but that is what I have said to myself, not others to me. No doubt if I kept producing I should have to ask myself what I meant to do with it all; but I have long been at a standstill, and so the things lie. It would be less tedious talking than writing: now at all events I must stop.

I must tell you a humorous touch of Irish Malvolio or Bully Bottom, so distinctively Irish that I cannot rank it: it amuses me in bed. A Tipperary lad, one of our people, lately from his noviceship, was at the wicket and another bowling to him. He thought there was no one within hearing, but from behind the wicket he was overheard after a good stroke to cry out 'Arrah,° sweet myself!'

I must write once more against the 3rd.

Believe me always your affectionate friend

Gerard M. Hopkins S.J.

Aug. 24 1884.

To Robert and Monica Bridges

University College, 85 & 86, Stephen's Green, Dublin. | Sept. 2 1884

My dearest Bridges and my dear Mrs. Bridges,—

This is to wish you the happiest of days tomorrow and all the blessings of heaven on that and all the days of your wedded life. I did not consider the mails; the consequence is that these wishes must, like the old shoe, be sent *after* you; but there is no harm in that if when they overtake you they ever after attend you.

More than this there is no need to write now.

I am affectionately yours both

Gerard Manley Hopkins S.J.

To Kate Hopkins, sen.

University College, 85, 86, Stephen's Green, Dublin | Nov. 26 1884

My dearest Mother,—

It is very long since I wrote and ought not to be and I am ashamed of it, but yet . . . however no matter about excuses. Also tell Kate I will write soon to her; I did to Grace, not that she had the first claim at all, but she made such a hullabaloo and said, what in her case was I believe unfounded, that it was like throwing letters to me into a well.

I do not seem to think it would be well for me to visit you at Christmas; better in the summer. You can easily understand reasons. If I came now I could not again so soon. Travelling long distances in winter is harder, more tiring, and the broken sleeps are a great trial to me. Then Grace is away. Then it is so soon after coming to Ireland; it does not look so well. Then the holidays are short and I have an examination at the end of them. Altogether I do not welcome it.

If I knew Milicent's° address I would write to her; I am sure I do not know what in the world, in which we scarcely ever meet, we gain by not writing. I might say the same of other people, but most of her. And I have never written to Lionel since he has been out: it seems a misery. And yet letter writing, so pleasant in doing, is a most harassing duty to set to with other work on hand.

We have enemies here—indeed what is Ireland but an open or secret war of fierce enmities of every sort?—and our College is really struggling for existence with difficulties within and without; which nevertheless I believe we shall weather, for no other reason than that Fr. Delany has such a buoyant and unshaken trust in God and wholly lives for the success of the place. He is as generous, cheering, and openhearted a man as I ever lived with. And the rest of the community give me almost as much happiness, but in particular Robert Curtis,° elected Fellow with me, whom I wish that by some means you could someday see, for he is my comfort beyond what I can say and a kind of godsend I never expected to have. His father Mr. Stephen Curtis Q.C. and mother live in town and I often see them and shd. more if I had time to go there. I lecture also and like it well enough, that is rather than not. But the College is poor, all unprovided to a degree that outsiders wd. scarcely believe, and of course—I cannot go into details—it cannot be comfortable. It is, this comes nearest it, like living at a temporary Junction and everybody knowing and shewing as much. No more time now. With best love to all believe me your loving son

Gerard M. Hopkins S.J.

To Kate Hopkins, jun.

University College, Stephen's Green, Dublin. Dec. 9 1884

Me dear Miss Hopkins,—

Im intoirely ashamed o meself. Sure its a wonder I could lave your iligant corspondance so long onanswered. But now Im just afther conthroiving a jewl of a convaniance be way of a standhen desk and tis a moighty incurgement towards the writin of letters intoirelee. Tis whoy ye hear from me this evenin.

It bates me where to commince, the way Id say anything yed be interistud to hear of. More be token yell be plased tintimate to me mother Im intirely obleeged to her for her genteel offers. But as titchin warm clothen tis undher a misapprehinsion shes labourin. Sure twas not the inclimunsee of the saysons I was complainin of at all at all. Twas the povertee of books and such like educational convaniences.

And now, Miss Hopkins darlin, yell chartably exkees me writin more in the rale Irish be raison I was never rared to ut and thats why I do be so slow with my pinmanship, bad luck to ut (savin your respects), but for ivery word I delineate I disremember two, and thats how ut is with me.

(The above very fair.)

The weather is wild and yet mild.

I have a kind of charge of a greenhouse.

I am hoping to hear Dvorak's Stabat Mater at Trinity College tomorrow. I think you heard it.

I have an invitation for Xmas to Lord Emly's.

A dear old French Father, very clever and learned and a great photographer, who at first wanted me to take to photography with him, which indeed in summer would be pleasant enough, finding that once I used to draw, got me to bring him the few remains I still have, cows and horses in chalk done in Wales too long ago to think of, and admired them to that degree that he is urgent with me to go on drawing at all hazards; but I do not see how that could be now, so late: if anybody had said the same 10 years ago it might have been different.

You spoke in your last of meeting Baillie. He was always the kindest and best of friends and I always look upon myself in the light of a blackguard when I think of my behaviour to him and of his to me. In this case however he has not written since you met him and I hope to be beforehand with him.

Tis a quare thing I didn't finish this letter yet. Ill shlip me kyard in betune the sheets the way yell know Im not desaivin ye.

Believe me your loving brother Gerard.

Dec. 13 1884

To Robert Bridges

University College, Stephen's Green, Dublin. | New Year's day 1885

Dearest Bridges,—

I wish you and your wife a very happy new year.

I believe it would have been better for me to have gone to Hampstead as they wanted me, since it seems I need a change; at all events I am jaded. It would have been the world of pleasant to have seen you.

What a pleasure must that music have been! 'Then what charm company' etc. Now talking of music I must tell you I have a great matter on hand. It is music to the Battle of the Baltic,° the tune made long ago and now I am harmonising it. My first attempt in harmony was the Crocus.° I got it sent to Sir Frederick Gore Ouseley a good time ago and he has not returned it. The reason must be that finding it will not do he cannot make up his mind to tell me so. Indeed the second and third verses were a kind of wilderness of unintelligible chords, but the first seemed to me very good. However this new thing will be intelligible, and in a few days I am going to send you the first two—or two first—verses (I hold it is all the same) and then I want you, please to get ——° as before to pass judgment on them—this one time more, as children go on. There is a bold thing in it: in the second verse a long ground bass, a chime of fourteen notes, repeated ten times running, with the treble moving freely above it. It is to illustrate 'It was ten of April morn by the chime'. If —— should approve it I am made, musically, and Sir Frederick may wallow and choke in his own Oozeley Gore. Then I have in the background Collins' Ode to Evening I mentioned to you before, which is a new departure and more like volcanic sunsets or sunrises in the musical hemisphere than anythin ye can conçave.

One word on Psyche and volcanic sunsets. The description of the one over the Cretan Sea° so closely agrees with an account I wrote in *Nature*,° even to details which were local only, that it is very extraordinary: you did not see my letter, did you? Swinburn[e], perhaps you know, has also tried his hand—without success. Either in fact he does not see nature at all or else he overlays the landscape with such phantasmata, secondary images, and what not of a delirium-tremendous imagination that the result is a kind of bloody broth: you know what I mean. At any rate there is no picture.

There is one stanza about Psyche's sister falling like a stone.° In suggestion it is one of the most brilliant in the poem but in execution very imperfect, and therefore I have been freer there than anywhere else.

I do not want to say more of Psyche now.

I shall be proud to send you the fragments, unhappily no more, of my St. Winefred. And I shd. independently be glad of your judgment of them.

I do not believe you will succeed in producing a 12 syll. or 6 foot line which shall not, as you say, be an Alexandrine.

There is, according to my experience, an insuperable tendency to the Alexandrine, so far, I mean, as this, that there is a break after the 3rd foot, cutting the line into equal halves. This is the first feature of the measure and will assert itself. It has some advantages, but it makes it monotonous; and to vary the division, the phrasing, successfully, and for long, is a most difficult matter. Common blank verse on the other hand is in this respect selfacting, for 2 ft. + 3 or 3 ft. + 2 or 2½ + 2½, one of which divisions almost every line you can without thinking make is sure to have, are all good and even without attention they will vary one another; whereas the equal division of the Alexandrine is first poor and then nearly invariable. Nevertheless I have grappled with this; how far successfully you will judge.

In such a case, the invention of a new vehicle, nothing wiser certainly can be done than to concert action as you propose to do: it is the best substitute for a past experience and a tradition.—But it is strange that you should select for comedy what I from its pathos chose for tragedy.°

I have found that this metre is smooth, natural, and easy to work in broken dialogue, so much so that it produces nearly the effect of 5 foot blank verse; but in continuous passages it is a very different thing. In passionate passages I employ sprung rhythm in it with good effect.

I am going, I am glad to say, for change to Clongowes Wood College, near Naas, tomorrow. I shall take Psyche with me and also try to copy out and send you the passages from *St. Winefred*. I wish it might act as a stimulus to go on with it. At times I have been very much pleased with some things in them.

You will perhaps say that besides the Alexandrine, which is a dimeter, there might be a trimeter, like the Greek. But the trimeter arises by taking the stresses of the odd feet stronger than those of the even and so coupling the feet in pairs of stronger and weaker. With quantity this subordination and coupling is easy, but in English it is hard and cannot be continuously done. Mr. Patmore has pointed out the smooth musical effect of it where it occurs, though better instances might, I believe, be quoted than the one he gives.° The impression of the Greek trimeter as a whole is very closely given by our 5 ft blank verse, though the metres are different. I do not think that taking a 6 foot line would bring us any nearer the Greek trimeter than we are now, rather the reverse; probably you think the same.

I hear that in a nocturn of Field's there is a chime as a ground bass. However I presume the treble is written to the bass; mine is not.

If —— will not do Stainer must: one of the two you must get for me. It is but a short little thing, two verses.

Believe me your affectionate friend

Gerard Hopkins S.J.

To Alexander William Mowbray Baillie

University College, Stephen's Green, Dublin. | April 24 1885

My dearest Baillie,—

I will this evening begin writing to you and God grant it may not be with this as it was with the last letter I wrote to an Oxford friend, that the should-be receiver was dead before it was ended. (There is no bad omen in this, as you will on reflexion— REMARK: *REFLEXION*: I USED TO WRITE *REFLECTION* TILL YOU POINTED OUT THE MISTAKE; YOU DID SO TWICE, FOR I HAD, THROUGH HUMAN FRAILTY AND INADVERTENCE, LAPSED— see.) I mean poor Geldart° whose death, as it was in Monday last's *Pall Mall*, you must have heard of. I suppose it was suicide, his mind, for he was a selftormentor, having been unhinged, as it had been once or twice before, by a struggle he had gone through. Poor Nash's° death, not long before, was certainly suicide and certainly too done in insanity, for he had been sleepless for ten nights: of this too you will have heard. It much comforts me and seems providential that I had renewed my friendship with Geldart some weeks before it was too late. I yesterday wrote to his widow. Three of my intimate friends at Oxford have thus drowned themselves, a good many more of my acquaintances and contemporaries have died by their own hands in other ways: it must be, and the fact brings it home to me, a dreadful feature of our days. I should say that Geldart had lent me his autobiography called (I wish it had another name) *A Son of Belial.*° It is an amusing and a sad book—but perhaps you have seen it. I am in it and Addis, Coles, Jeune, MacInnon, Nash, Jowett, Liddon, and lots more thinly disguised, though some I do not recognise. You are not there.

May 8—For one thing I was sorry when I got your late delightful letter. Since my sister told me of her meeting you I had been meaning to write and be first with you—but now I am slow even in answering. Some time since, I began to overhaul my old letters, accumulations of actually ever since I was at school, destroying all but a very few, and growing ever lother to destroy, but also to read, so that at last I left off reading; and there they lie and my old notebooks and beginnings of things, ever so many, which it seems to me might well have been done, ruins and wrecks; but on this theme I will not enlarge by pen and ink. However there were many of your letters among them and overflowing with kindness (but not towards Hannah° and MacFarlane; however you need not distress yourself so much about them; I agree with you in the main, and believe I used to remonstrate sometimes of old on their behalf, because they were good fellows and the persistency of their attentions was a most real compliment—a sort of compliment that as one gets older and writes the senile parenthetic style I am maundering in now one values a great deal higher—but still I can distinctly remember, though I shall not recall, real provocation they gave you; and you never did more than have a humourous fling at them; but to return) and for those letters I was deeply grateful and keep it constantly before me that I was undeserving of them; but still it was a cruel thing of you now to tell me that my own very first letter to you begins with 'Yes, you are a fool'. The context, I suppose, the sequel, I mean, does something to mitigate, but mitigate as you may I wish it were not said. But I have to regret so much! and what is it to withdraw a thing long after the event? Almost meaningless.

As I have told you before, the first thing not that you said to me but that I can remember your saying was some joke about a watering hose which lay on the grass plot in the Outer Quad: a small spray was scattering from it. I stood watching it and you, coming in from a walk, waving your stick at it quoted or parodied either 'Busy curious thirsting fly'° or the Dying Christian° to his Soul. You never could remember this after and IN FINE (an expression which, it has always appeared to me, could never take root in our garden and yet we could never make up our minds to throw back again over the wall into the French one where it came from) I am more sure that it was said than that you said it.

I think this is from a literary point of view (not from a moral) the worst letter I ever wrote to you, and it shall not run much longer. You will wonder I have been so long over it. This is part of my disease, so to call it. The melancholy I have all my life been subject to has become of late years not indeed more intense in its fits but rather more distributed, constant, and crippling. One, the lightest but a very inconvenient form of it, is daily anxiety about work to be done, which makes me break off or never finish all that lies outside that work. It is useless to write more on this: when I am at the worst, though my judgment is never affected, my state is much like madness. I see no ground for thinking I shall ever get over it or ever succeed in doing anything that is not forced on me to do of any consequence.

I forget what the verses were I shewed you and you 'did not criticise'. It is putting friendship unwisely to a strain to shew verses, neither did I do it much. Those verses were afterwards burnt and I wrote no more for seven years; then, it being suggested to write something I did so and have at intervals since, but the intervals are now long ones and the whole amount produced is small. And I make no attempt to publish.

You said, and it was profoundly true then, that Mr. Gladstone ought to be beheaded on Tower Hill and buried in Westminster Abbey. Ought he now to be buried in Westminster Abbey? As I am accustomed to speak too strongly of him I will not further commit myself in writing.

Much could be said about Ireland and my work and all, but it would be tedious; especially as I hope we may meet soon. I seem glad you keep up your Oriental studies.

Believe me always your affectionate friend

Gerard M. Hopkins S.J.

May 17 '85 and still winter.

To Robert Bridges

University College, Stephen's Green, Dublin. May 17 1885

Dearest Bridges,—

I must write something, though not so much as I have to say. The long delay was due to work, worry, and languishment of body and mind—which must be and will be; and indeed to diagnose my own case (for every man by forty is his own physician or a fool, they say; and yet again he who is his own physician has a fool for his patient—a form of epigram, by the bye, which, if you examine it, has a bad flaw), well then to judge of my case, I think that my fits of sadness, though they do not affect my judgment, resemble madness. Change is the only relief, and that I can seldom get.

I saw that *Ulysses* was a fine play, the action and interest well centred, the characters finely drawn and especially Penelope, the dialogue throughout good; nevertheless, perhaps from my mood of mind, I could not take to it, did not like it, beyond a dry admiration. Not however to remain in a bare Doctor Felldom on the matter, I did find one fault in it which seems indeed to me to be the worst fault a thing can have, unreality. I hope other people will think otherwise, but the introduction in earnest of Athene gave me a distaste I could not recover from. With *Prometheus* it was not the same. Three kinds of departure from truth I understand and agree to in a play—first in a History those changes and conventions without which, as in other works of art, the facts could not be presented at all; secondly a plot of fiction: though the facts never actually happened they are a picture of life and a sample of the sort of facts that do—those also subject to their own changes and conventions; lastly an allegory, where things that neither do nor could be mask and mean something that is. To this last class *Prometheus*, as I take it, belongs; moreover it was modelled on the Greek and scarcely meant for acting. But *Ulysses* is to act; and in earnest, not allegorically, you bring in a goddess among the characters: it revolts me. Then, not unnaturally, as it seemed to me, her speech is the worst in the play: being an unreality she must talk unreal. Believe me, the Greek gods are a totally unworkable material; the merest frigidity, which must chill and kill every living work of art they are brought into. Even if we put aside the hideous and, taken as they stand, unspeakable stories told of them, which stories nevertheless are as authentic as their names and personalities—both are equally imaginary; if you do not like that, both equally symbolical—putting these out of sight and looking only at their respectable side, they are poor ignoble conceptions ennobled bodily only (as if they had bodies) by the artists, but once in motion and action worthless—not gentlemen or ladies, cowards, loungers, without majesty, without awe, antiquity, foresight, character; old bucks, young bucks, and Biddy Buckskins. What did Athene do after leaving Ulysses? Lounged back to Olympus to afternoon nectar. Nothing can be made of it. May 21, 1885. The background of distance and darkness and doom which a tragedy should always have is shut out by an Olympian drop-scene; the characters from men become puppets, their blood-shed becomes a leakage of bran. (This, upon my word, is to ply the lash and to be unpardonable.) I see the nobility of the rest, but this one touch to my eye spoils all; it looks to me like fine relief all daubed and creamed over with heavy whitewash.

I do not wonder at those ladies reading *Nero* through at a sitting. It *is* very interesting and I feel quite the same. You offered to send me a correcter copy: I shd. be glad if you now would.

I must add there was another fault I had to find with *Ulysses* and it was to the same effect and same defect, of unreality; I mean the archaism of the language, which was to my mind overdone. I hold that by archaism a thing is sicklied o'er as by blight. Some little flavours, but much spoils, and always for the same reason—it destroys earnest: we do not speak that way; therefore if a man speaks that way he is not serious, he is at something else than the seeming matter in hand, *non hoc agit, aliud agit* [not doing that but something else]. I believe you agree with me in principle: if so I think that your practice in that play is beyond what your principle allows. But slight changes would satisfy me. The example of Shakspere (by a 'corrupt following', for it is an absurd fallacy—like a child having to repeat the substance of something it has been told and saying *you* and *I* wherever the speaker said *you* and *I*, whereas it should say *I* where he said *you* and so on) has done ever so much harm by his very genius, for poets reproduce the diction which in him was modern and in them is obsolete. But you know all this. . . .

It is too bad that I shd. so abuse *Ulysses* after your encouragement of *St. Winefred.* But how cd. you think such a thing of me as that I shd. in cold blood write 'fragments of a dramatic poem'?—I of all men in the world. To me a complete fragment, above all of a play, is the same unreality as a prepared impromptu. No, but we compose fragmentarily and what I had here and there done I finished up and sent as samples to see if I cd. be encouraged to go on—and I was encouraged; that is by your last, for before I thought you thought they wd. not do. There is a point with me in matters of any size when I must absolutely have encouragement as much as crops rain; afterwards I am independent. However I am in my ordinary circumstances unable, with whatever encouragement, to go on with *Winefred* or anything else. I have after long silence written two sonnets, which I am touching: if ever anything was written in blood° one of these was.

Of two metrical criticisms you made on the fragments° one I did not well understand, the other was a misunderstanding on your part.

About the music I shd. like to write at some length. But for the present I only say first, how could you think I shd. be offended at your criticism or remarks or wanted you to express yourself so modestly? May 28, 1885. Next I am much obliged for the quotations from Purcell, but could not get my household musician to play the one in open score nor have had time or opportunity of running after professionals, besides that for myself I have kept away some time now from the piano. Thirdly the bass solo you give me to shew the variety

Purcell could command by the modern system—well of that beautiful passage I have to say that it illustrates the well-known variety of the minor as we now understand it, a variety for which Purcell particularly prized it, but that that variety I did not need the illustrating of and, ahem, I can send you an illustration of my own which as it seems to me is happy in that way—made long ago. Then of course I admire and surely I could produce—it requires no more knowledge than I have already got for at least the simpler effects and in fact modulation even to remote keys and so on is not difficult to do; it may be to explain—could produce and have produced modulations, but in the two first verses of the *Battle of the Baltic*° (which has some eleven) I wanted to see what could be done (and for how long I could go on) without them. ——° of course thought they cd. not be done without even for that length and I do not dispute the judgment; I scarcely had myself heard my second verse—for that is the great difficulty in reality my only, and I fear my insuperable, one, that I cannot play. But nevertheless Palestrina and the old madrigal writers and others did produce masterpieces—and Hullah° says actually final in their kind, that is which you cannot develope by modern science; you can only change the school and kind—without modulations, but employing the modes; without even the authentic cadence: I wish I cd. study them. Then 'do I mean to rival Purcell and Mozart?' No. Even given the genius, a musician must be that and nothing else, as music now is; at least so it has been with all the great musicians. But I did aim at two things not in themselves unattainable, if to me far easier things were not now unattainable. But of these if ever, hereafter.

Believe me your affectionate friend

Gerard M. Hopkins S.J.

May 29 1885.

To Robert Bridges

University College, St Stephen's Green, Dublin. Sept. 1 1885.

Dearest Bridges,—

I have just returned from an absurd adventure, which when I resigned myself to it I could not help enjoying. A hair-brained fellow took me down to Kingstown and on board his yacht and, whereas I meant to return to town by six that evening, would not let me go either that night or this morning till past midday. I was afraid it would be compromising, but it was fun while it lasted.

I have been in England. I was with my people first at Hampstead, then at Midhurst in Sussex in a lovely landscape: they are there yet. And from there I went to Hastings to Mr. Patmore's for a few days. I managed to see several old friends and to make new ones, amongst which Mr. W. H. Cummings the tenor singer and composer, who wrote the Life of Purcell: he shewed me some of his Purcell treasures and others and is going to send me several things. I liked him very much but the time of my being with him was cut short. I did not attempt to see you: I did not know that visitors wd. at that time be very welcome and it wd. have been difficult to me in any case to come. I am very sorry to hear of Mrs. Bridges' disappointment:° somehow I had feared that would happen.

I shall shortly have some sonnets to send you, five or more. Four° of these came like inspirations unbidden and against my will.° And in the life I lead now, which is one of a continually jaded and harassed mind, if in any leisure I try to do anything I make no way—nor with my work, alas! but so it must be.

Mr. Patmore lent me Barnes' poems—3 volumes, not all, for indeed he is prolific. I hold your contemptuous opinion an unhappy mistake: he is a perfect artist and of a most spontaneous inspiration; it is as if Dorset life and Dorset landscape had taken flesh and tongue in the man. I feel the defect or limitation or whatever we are to call it that offended you: he lacks fire; but who is perfect all round? If one defect is fatal what writer could we read?

An old question of yours I have hitherto neglected to answer, am I thinking of writing on metre? I suppose thinking too much and doing too little. I do greatly desire to treat that subject; might perhaps get something together this year; but I can scarcely believe that on that or on anything else anything of mine will ever see the light—of publicity nor even of day. For it is widely true, the fine pleasure is not to do a thing but to feel that you could and the mortification that goes to the heart is to feel it is the power that fails you: *qui occidere nolunt Posse volunt*;° it is the refusal of a thing that we like to have. So with me, if I could but get on, if I could but produce work I should not mind its being buried, silenced, and going no further; but it kills me to be time's eunuch and never to beget. After all I do not despair, things might change, anything may be; only there is no great appearance of it. Now because I have had a holiday though not strong I have some buoyancy; soon I am afraid I shall be ground down to a state like this last spring's and summer's, when my spirits were so crushed that madness seemed to be making approaches—and nobody was to blame, except myself partly for not managing myself better and contriving a change.

Believe me, with kind wishes to Mrs Bridges,

your affectionate friend Gerard M. Hopkins S.J.

Sept. 8 '85.

This day 15 years ago I took my first vows.

I hope Mrs. Molesworth is well. Where is she now?

Is your brother John going to bring out a second volume?°

If I had not reread your letter I shd. have left it unanswered. The expression 'The Mass is good' is, I feel sure, never used in these islands. But the meaning in the circumstances is pretty plain and must be just what you take it to be. To satisfy the obligation of hearing mass on Sundays and the 'Festivals of Obligation' one must be present from at least the Offertory to the Priest's Communion. The question is well threshed out: for laxer and for stricter opinions see the Moral Theologians passim; whose name is Legion, but St. Alphonsus Liguori will do for all (Treatise *de Praeceptis Ecclesiae* or *De Decem Praeceptis Decalogi*). However the phrase would not easily be understood by your readers or hearers. I hope to see those plays.° Are the choral parts written strictly to the music? I never saw good poetry made to music unless that music itself had first been made to words.

To Everard Hopkins

Clongowes Wood College, | Naas | Nov. 5, 1885

Dear Everard,—

I am taking a short rest after deadly work.

I have with me here *Literature and Dogma* and *Ecce Homo* that you lent me (I almost thought you might forget). My long spell of work, which allowed of no other reading, interrupted my study of *L. and D.* and *Ecce Homo* I have read but a little of. Had I better send them back without more delay? or finish them? And by the by after *E. H.* I ought to read his later book called *Natural Religion*, on which I found an able review in Mallock's *Atheism* volume and I have another review of it by G. A. Simcox in the *Nineteenth* here in the room. These are very instructive books.

I have not read Drummond's book that you praise. My father has it, I think: I saw it in his hands.

While on books let me recommend you a masterly one I have just made the acquaintance of Moulton's *Shakespeare as a Dramatic Artist* (Clarendon Press, this year).

I have also *Diana*° by me. After all the difficult style, which can never never be simple, is very faulty.

I have seen your broadside in the *Graphic*. I can well fancy that the drawing, the draughtsmanship, has been injured in engraving and was finer than now appears (as my father led me to expect to find), but, to tell you the truth, I am disappointed in it for faults which are not the engraver's. You did not, I believe, realise that so large a design can by no means be treated as differing from one a half, a quarter, or an eig[h]th the size in its size only. As difficulties of perspective increase greatly with the scale so do those of composition. The composition will not come right of itself, it must be calculated. I see no signs of such calculation. I find it scattered and without unity, it does not look to me like a scene and one dramatic moment, the action of the persons is independent and not mutual, the groups do not seem aware of one another. The two wrestlers do not struggle hard enough and in general there is a want of liveliness. Small, no, Green, had a last-century election scene, better composed and livelier than yours, but defective in those respects too: the fighting figures seemed not to have been fighting when the drawing was made but before it, to have been 'struck so' (as children fear to be in making faces). And *then* drawn. I am glad therefore you got the commission but not satisfied with yr. discharge of it. I do not expect you are yourself, are you? (I need scarcely say that as my bent is for glowing colours so it is for violent action, but here at least violent action was in place.) The subject I expect was not congenial. The crowd being an essential element of it more of the crowd shd. have been seen and it shd. have been more crowded. Crowds have perhaps not been mastered in art yet. Doré (I do not like him, but we must admire his bucketfuls of talent) has good simultaneous-acting crowds, e.g. in Christ coming down the steps of the judgment hall. I have seen a fine crowd by Rembrandt. I think there [are] a good few (or a few good) crowds to be seen in well known pictures. What I have written appears discouraging—as I read it. But necessity the mother of invention has been in your case her stepmother and starved her: what I mean is that this drawing was made I suppose to order on an uncongenial subject. Naturally you would like repose and long flowing lines, low colours, and the conditions of grace and ease.

To touch on the *Eurydice* etc again. The run-over rhymes were experimental, perhaps a mistake; I do not know that I shd. repeat them. But rhyme, you understand, is like an indelible process: you cannot paint over it. Surely they *can* be recited but the effect must have been prepared, as many things must. I can only remember one, the rhyme to *electric*:° it must be read 'startingly and rash'. It *is* 'an effect'.

I am sweetly soothed by your saying that you cd. make any one understand my poem by reciting it well. That is what I always hoped, thought, and said; it is my precise aim. And thereby hangs so considerably a tale, in fact the very thing I was going to write about Sprung Rhy[th]m in general (by the bye rhythm, not metre: metre is a matter of arranging lines, rhythm is one of arranging feet; anapaests are a rhythm, the sonnet is a metre; and so you can write any metre in any rhythm and any rhythm to any metre supposing of course that usage has not tied the rhythm to the metre, as often or mostly it has), that I must for the present leave off, give o'er, as they say in Lancashire.

Every art then and every work of art has its own play or performance. The play or performance of a stageplay is the playing it on the boards, the stage: reading it, much more writing it, is not its performance. The performance of a symphony is not the scoring it however elaborately; it is in the concert room, by the orchestra, and then and there only. A picture is performed, or performs, when anyone looks at it in the proper and intended light. A house performs when it is now built and lived in. To come nearer: books play, perform, or are played and performed when they are read; and ordinarily by one reader, alone, to himself, with the eyes only. Now we are getting to it, George. Poetry was originally meant for either singing or reciting; a record was kept of it; the record could be, was, read, and that in time by one reader, alone, to himself, with the eyes only. This reacted on the art: what was to be performed under these conditions[,] for these conditions ought to be and was composed and calculated. Sound-effects were intended, wonderful combinations even; but they bear the marks of having been meant for the whispered, not even whispered, merely mental performance of the closet, the study, and so on. You follow, Edward Joseph? You do: then we are there. This is not the true nature of poetry, the darling child of speech, of lips and spoken utterance: it must be spoken; *till it is spoken it is not performed*, it does not perform, it is not itself. Sprung rhythm gives back to poetry its true soul and self. As poetry is emphatically speech, speech purged of dross like gold in the furnace, so it must have emphatically the essential elements of speech. Now emphasis itself, stress, is one of these: sprung rhythm makes verse stressy; it purges it to an emphasis as much brighter, livelier, more lustrous than the regular but commonplace emphasis of common rhythm as poetry in general is brighter than common speech. But this it does by a return from that regular emphasis towards, not up to the more picturesque irregular emphasis of talk—without however becoming itself lawlessly irregular; then it would not be art; but making up by regularity, equality, of a larger unit (the foot merely) for inequality in the less, the syllable. There it wd. be necessary to come down to mathematics and technicalities which time does not allow of, so I forbear. For I believe you now understand. Perform the *Eurydice*, then see. I must however add that to perform it quite satisfactorily is not at all easy, I do not say I could do it; but this is nothing against the truth of the principle maintained. A composer need not be able to play his violin music or sing his songs. Indeed the higher wrought the art, clearly the wider severance between the parts of the author and the performer.

Neither of course do I mean my verse to be recited only. True poetry must be studied. As Shakespere and all great dramatists have their maximum effect on the stage but bear to be or must be studied at home before or after or both, so I shd. wish it to be with my lyric poetry. And in practice that will be enough by itself alone to any one who has first realised the effect of reciting; for then, like a musician reading a score and supplying in thought the orchestra (as they can), no further performance is, substantially, needed. But you say you have not so realised it—or perhaps you have. Mr. Patmore never admired the *Eurydice* or any of my things, except some in common rhythm, for just this reason (I hope—and he himself suggested).

Much the same is the case with plain chant music. Many of those who do not admire it have never heard it performed (or, worse, have heard it murdered) and cannot conceive the performance; for to read and even play it, without the secret, is no good.

On the other hand there is verse, very good of its rhetorical kind (for that is what it is, rhetoric in verse), such as Macaulay's Lays, Aytoun's° ditto, and ever so much that the Irish produce, flowing, stirring, and pointed, which recited seems first rate but studied at leisure, by the daylight, does not indeed turn out worthless but loses the name of genuine poetry.

I asked you, did I? to try and find me Campion, Thomas Campion's 'Rose-cheeked Laura, come': I had almost forgotten. He was an Elisabethan, nothing, that I know of, to Edmund Campion the Jesuit his contemporary. The latter wd. have been, I shd. think, a great poet if he had chosen or chance had served, to judge by the noble eloquence of passages in his History of Ireland, read and made use of, as Simpson in his *Life of Campion* has shewn, by Shakespere. Thomas Campion's poem enquired for is an avowed experiment in rhythm and metre (rather metre) and bears the marks of so being; still it is beautiful and very striking. I *have* seen it in *some* handbook or collection of English poetry.

It seemed like death almost at first for us to leave Hampstead, but on the other hand Haslemere is a delightful thought. We shd. not be far from Midhurst either. It is artists' country. There is a capital paper on Surrey in the *Nineteenth* for August, worth having. The same number contains a paper by Fr. Ryder of the Oratory on 'A Jesuit Reformer and Poet,' to wit Fr. Spee, whose efforts and sufferings put down the witch mania and its hideous prosecution and persecutions.

By the bye, as prose, though commonly less beautiful than verse and debarred from its symmetrical beauties, has, at least possible to it, effects more beautiful than any verse can attain, so perhaps the inflections and intonations of the speaking voice may give effects more beautiful than any attainable by the fixed pitches of music. I look on this as an infinite field & very little worked. It has this great difficulty, that the art depends entirely on living tradition. The phonograph may give us one, but hitherto there could be no record of fine spoken utterance.

In drama the fine spoken utterance has been cultivated and a tradition established, but everything is most highly wrought and furthest developed where it is cultivated by itself; fine utterance then will not be best developed in the drama, where gesture and action generally are to play a great part too; it must be developed in recited lyric. Now hitherto this has not been done. The Greeks carried lyric to its highest perfection in Pindar and the tragic choruses, but what was this lyric? not a spoken lyric at all, but song; poetry written neither to be recited nor chanted even nor even sung to a transferable tune but each piece of itself a song. The same remark then as above recurs: the natural performance and delivery belonging properly to lyric poetry, which is speech, has not been enough cultivated, and should be. When performers were trained to do it (it needs the rarest gifts) and audiences to appreciate it it would be, I am persuaded, a lovely art. Incalculable effect could be produced by the delivery of Wordsworth's *Margaret* ('Where art thou, my beloved son?'—do you know it?). With the aid of the phonograph each phrase could be fixed and learnt by heart like a song.

I am now back at Stephen's Green and must lecture tomorrow and tonight conclude this long letter.

I am your loving brother Gerard.

I have seen none of those *St. Stephen's* (not Green) character sketches; cannot think what they can be like. I feel sure you have not found (at least for public purposes) your true vein yet, which I suppose to be something more refined than political drawing can allow of. | Nov. 8 1885.

To Everard Hopkins

University College. | St Stephen's Green. | Dublin. | Dec. 23 '85

Dear Everard,—

There are things in my last long letter that do not please me in the retrospect and I am afraid you are still less pleased with certain of them, the faults I found with your picture, nevertheless I did not want to discourage, and I knew that Arthur takes criticism very peaceably always. Indeed I seem to think this is not really the reason why you have not answered.

But have you not been dunned for those books you lent me? I must send them you back now, for even holidays bring no holiday to me and I do not want to keep them longer in hope of more leisure. Of course if I had not been a fool I could have had them read (Irish idiom and convenient) long since, in spare spells; but with the hope of making anything out of them, which at one time I entertained, vanished the desire of reading them.

Did not Seeley write *Ecce Homo*? and since that *Natural Religion*, in which the supernatural element, the miracles, taken for granted in the former book, has disappeared. He is the author of the *Expansion of England* and has an article in the last *Nineteenth* which is worth reading. I think you shd. read both: he will hit it off with you. Alas, all the men that in better days one might build on for England's good, like him and Matthew Arnold and, I do believe, Bradlaugh,° drift or ride or scud upon the tide of atheism, where all true guiding principle is lost. Unhappy country,—its morals ministered to by Booth and Stead° (you know no doubt, better than I do, from the English papers, that the crimes the *Pall Mall* was so zealous over have immensely increased); its foreign policy by Gladstone; its speculation by Matthew Arnold—not to speak of what is to befall from Ireland. The Pope has written the most beautiful letter to the English bishops, speaking in terms of such heartfelt affection for England that I kiss the words when I read them.

I enclose some Irish drawings (old ones). The National papers have a coloured cartoon every week and these pictures are a power. Is not Pat in the boat good? The artist is called O'Hea: he has a powerful chromo of an Irish peasant in the rebellion of 1798 at bay against an army of British redcoats, and this picture like everything said or done in Ireland will go to swell the gathering and insatiable flood of hatred.

Another thing you must read is Patmore's ode (in the *Unknown Eros*) 'O England, how hast thou forgot?' By the bye, how do you like Bridges' *Eros and Psyche*?

I take it for granted you will be tomorrow at Hampstead. My Christmas is much a clouded one, for I have suddenly to prepare papers for a supplementary matriculation examination to be held next month, as well as the scholarship, which I knew of before. But it was to be. Give all my best Christmas wishes, thank Grace for her pretty card, and believe me

your loving brother Gerard.

I have friends at Donnybrook, so hearty and kind that nothing can be more so and I think I shall go and see them tomorrow.

Christmas Eve, 1885
I think if I find I am not in yr. black books I shall soon send you a black ms book of my own containing nearly all my poems, and see if you quite come round to Sprung Rhythm.

To Alexander William Mowbray Baillie

University College, St. Stephen's Green, Dublin. | March 29 '86

Dearest Baillie,—

I am downcast about those ungentlemanly postcards,° the two last at all events, as I am afraid you must have thought them.

I have thought of some more etymologies from the Sanskrit given by Max Müller or others, viz. *Οὐρανός* | *varunas*, *varuna*, the nightly heaven (but what does this prove? only that two kindred languages had kindred words for heaven and divinised or deifed heaven, as where do men not?); *Προμηθεύς* | *pramanthas*, kindling-stick for the 'needfire' (not certain and, if certain, only shews that Prometheus *meant* as well as was the bestower of fire on man; besides that the Greek treatment of the myth due to the mistaken, if mistaken, etymology from *προμηθής*, which brings in *'Επιμηθεύς*,° is its most interesting, ethical, and religious part); *'Ερινύς* | *Saranyû* 'a mythical being in the Veda', as per M. M. (whom I have not got and therefore cannot say if the two mythical beings have anything in common beyond the name and the never having existed); *'Ερμείας, 'Ερμῆς* | *Sarameya* (spelling, especially dots, etc, not further known), a heavenly greyhound, hound of dawn (I have, in spite of Lang,° a considerable belief in the Solar myth and especially in these 'hounds of dawn', which are really very widespread and found in Greek, Irish, Egyptian—? the 'divine jackals'—as well as Indian mythology; but all that does not shew that Hermes, afterwards identified with Mercury, god of wages, was in Gk. religious history a hound of dawn: in fact he never was): I remember no more.

I do not dispute these etymologies nor deny they throw

light on the past history of Greek mythology, but I do say they do not throw much light and that what they throw is prehistoric, so to call it, and not part of the history proper of Greece and Greek religion, about which I believe Phoenicia and Egypt have more to say than India and the Pamir. And, though I do not maintain it, yet I believe it might be as easily maintained, that Ἀθήνη comes from *Aten* or *Athen* the disk of the sun as from *Ahana* the pretended dawn goddess. We do know the one was worshipped (furiously) and we do not the other. And I will risk it that Ῥαδάμανθυς is Ra-Ament or something like that, if *Ament* means *infernal*.

You will find about Ha-ka-phtah in 'Brugsch G. Insch., t. 1, p. 83'. It is then Brugsch's conjecture adopted by Maspero.

I am afraid the effect of all this will be to make you say 'A firm foot must be put down on this sort of thing AT ONCE', but if it makes you write so much the better. It is a great help to me to have someone interested in something (that will answer my letters), and it supplies some sort of intellectual stimulus. I sadly need that and a general stimulus to being, so dull and yet harassed is my life.

Believe me your affectionate friend

Gerard Hopkins S.J.

(If you dash Neprat I will 'run' Khepra, which please explain.)

I think proper names may have the article: e.g. T'ape | Thebes.

To Robert Bridges

University College, St. Stephen's Green, Dublin. June 1 '86

Dearest Bridges,—

I ought to have written 'hot foot' on my return from Yattendon, when the memory was quite fresh. It is however and will continue fragrant. That was a delightful day.

Mrs. Bridges was not as fancy painted her (indeed fancy

painted her very faintly, in watered sepia), but by no means the worse for that.

I was improved by my holiday. My anxiety mostly disappeared, though there is more reason than ever for it now, for I am terribly behindhand and cannot make up. But no more of that—nor now of anything further. (A lie: look on.)

By the bye the Paravicinis gave me Richard Crawley's *Venus and Psyche*, which I had long wanted to see. Did not like it. He is a true poet, but this poem is no success or at least it does not please. It is in the metre and manner markedly of *Don Juan*, mocking and discursive about modern life and so on. The verse very flowing and, where he took any pains, finely phrased. It is not serious; the scenes are scarcely realised; the story treated as a theme for trying style on. There is not the slightest symbolism.

This leads me to say that a kind of touchstone of the highest or most living art is seriousness; not gravity but the being in earnest with your subject—reality. It seems to me that some of the greatest and most famous works are not taken in earnest enough, are farce (where you ask the spectator to grant you something not only conventional but monstrous). I have this feeling about *Faust*° and even about the Divine Comedy, whereas *Paradise Lost* is most seriously taken. It is the weakness of the whole Roman literature.

Give my best love to Mrs. Bridges and Mrs. Molesworth and believe me your affectionate friend

Gerard Hopkins S.J.

I shd. add that Crawley is loose and makes his looseness much worse by quoting his original in the notes. And amazing to say, he is so when addressing *his sister*.

To Coventry Patmore

[University College, St. Stephen's Green, Dublin.] | June 4 1886

My dear Mr. Patmore,—

I have been meaning and meaning to write to you, to return the volumes of Barnes' poems you lent me and for other reasons, and partly my approaching examination work restrained me, when last night there reached me from Bell's the beautiful new edition of your works. I call it beautiful and think it is the best form upon the whole for poetry and works of pure literature that I know of and I thank you for your kindness in sending it. And I hope the bush or the bottle may do what little in a bush or bottle lies to recommend the liquor to the born and the unborn. But how slowly does the fame of excellence spread! And crooked eclipses and other obscure causes fight against its rise and progress.

Your poems are a good deed done for the Catholic Church and another for England, for the British Empire, which now trembles in the balance held in the hand of unwisdom. I remark that those Englishmen who wish prosperity to the Empire (which is not all Englishmen or Britons, strange to say) speak of the Empire's mission to extend freedom and civilisation in India and elsewhere. The greater the scale of politics the weightier the influence of a great name and a high ideal. It is a terrible element of weakness that now we are not well provided with the name and ideal which would recommend and justify our Empire. 'Freedom': it is perfectly true that British freedom is the best, the only successful freedom, but that is because, with whatever drawbacks, those who have developed that freedom have done so with the aid of law and obedience to law. The cry then shd. be Law and Freedom, Freedom and Law. But that does not please: it must be Freedom only. And to that cry there is the telling answer: No freedom you can give us is equal to the freedom of letting us alone: take yourselves out of India, let us first be free of you. Then there is civilisation. It shd. have been Catholic truth. That is the great end of Empires before God, to be Catholic and draw nations into their Catholicism. But our Empire is less and less Christian as it grows. There remains that part of civilisation which is outside Christianity or which is not essentially Christian. The best if gone, still something worth having is left. How far can the civilisation England offers be attractive and valuable and be offered and insisted on as an attraction and a thing of value to India for instance? Of course those who live in our civilisation and belong to it praise it: it is not hard, as Socrates said, among the Athenians to praise the Athenians; but how will it be represented by critics bent on making the worst of it or even not bent on making the best of it? It is good to be in Ireland to hear how enemies, and those rhetoricians, can treat the things that are unquestioned at home. I know that to mere injustice and slander innocence and excellence themselves stand condemned, but since there is always in mankind some love of truth and admiration for good (only that the truth must be striking and the good on a great scale) what marked and striking excellence has England to shew to make her civilisation attractive? Her literature is one of her excellences and attractions and I believe that criticism will tend to make this more and more felt; but there must be more of that literature, a continued supply and in quality excellent. This is why I hold that fine works of art, and especially if, like yours, that are not only ideal in form but deal with high matter as well, are really a great power in the world, an element of strength even to an empire. But now time and tediousness forbid me to write more on this.

It has struck me since I was at Hastings that, if it is not impertinent of me to say it, Miss Patmore might gain by taking some lessons from some painter.° It is true she does what no painter can either do or teach but it is also true there are other things she might with advantage learn. For in fact everyone is the better for teaching: it is universally true. It struck me that she was hampered by want of some mechanical knowledge, as in the use of washes for background, and she tends, I think, to use bodycolour in a way which would be considered vicious. This has naturally arisen from her circumstances; for in the delicate detail in which she so wonderfully excells the use of bodycolour is legitimate and even necessary and naturally she extended a practice with which she was familiar to a new field. I will send Barnes's poems back in a few days.

Believe me your sincere friend Gerard M. Hopkins S.J.

Please give my kindest remembrances to Mrs. Patmore and the Miss Patmores. I hope all are well and Piff° is not killing himself with his sensibilities.

June 6.

To Richard Watson Dixon

University College, St. Stephen's Green, Dublin. June 30 '86

My dear Friend,—

I am in the midst of my heaviest work of the year, the summer examinations, and not at all fit for them. This is why I delay writing and is some excuse for not earlier answering your former letter; which was however a fault.

There are first two points of what we may call business. The dedication:° this is a great honour, which on the one hand I do not like to decline but which nevertheless I have some dread of, for I do not want my name to be before the public. It is true your poems do not command a large public, unhappily; but then the small one might contain enemies, so to call people, of mine. So do which you think best: if you dedicate I am flattered, if you do not I am reassured.

I think there could be no objection to my lines appearing in the Birthday Book,° especially anonymously (as I should wish), but I ought to get a formal leave and will. However I should tell you that the poem in question is in three stanzas: did you know that? Nevertheless the first, the one you quote, might stand by itself. If so the text should be something about First-fruits:° there must be several that would do, but I think of none just now. The second line had better be 'Cheek and the wimpled lip' and the count made up to six. And the stopping 'This, all this, beauty' etc. is cumbrous: it is better 'This, all this beauty'.° I have nothing else to send, but something new might strike me. There is a 3-stanza piece made at a wedding° that possibly might do, but I rather think not: it is too personal and, I believe, too plainspoken.

I saw the Academy. There was one thing, not a picture, which I much preferred to everything else there—Hamo Thornycroft's statue of the *Sower*, a truly noble work and to me a new light. It was like Frederick Walker's° pictures put into stone and indeed was no doubt partly due to his influence. The genius of that man, poor Walker, was amazing: he was cut off by death like Keats and his promise and performance were in painting as brilliant as Keats's in poetry; in fact I doubt if a man with purer genius for painting ever lived. The sense of beauty was so exquisite; it was to other painters' work as poetry is to prose: his loss was irretrievable. Now no one admires more keenly than I do the gifts that go into Burne Jones's works, the fine genius, the spirituality, the invention; but they leave me deeply dissatisfied as well, where Walker's works more than satisfy. It is their technical imperfection I can not get over, the bad, the unmasterly drawing—as it appears to me to be. They are not masterly. Now this is the artist's most essential quality, masterly execution: it is a kind of male gift and especially marks off men from women, the begetting one's thought on paper, on verse, on whatever the matter is; the life must be conveyed into the work and be displayed there, not suggested as having been in the artist's mind: otherwise the product is one of those hen's-eggs that are good to eat and look just like live ones but never hatch (I think they are called wind eggs: I believe most eggs for breakfast *are* wind eggs and none the worse for it).—Now it is too bad of me to have compared Burne Jones's beautiful and original works to wind-eggs; moreover on better consideration it strikes me that the mastery I speak of is not so much the male quality in the mind as a puberty in the life of that quality. The male quality is the creative gift, which he markedly has. But plainly, while artists may differ indefinitely in the degree and kind or variety of their natural gifts, all shd., as artists, have come, at all events shd. in time come, to the puberty, the manhood of those gifts: that should be common to all, above it the gifts may differ.

It may be remarked that some men exercise a deep

influence on their own age in virtue of certain powers at that time original, new, and stimulating, which afterwards ceasing to stimulate their fame declines; because it was not supported by an execution, an achievement equal to the power. For nothing but fine execution survives long. This was something of Rossetti's case perhaps.

There is a Scotch painter Macbeth° whom I much admire. My brother Arthur, who is a painter too, took me to Macbeth's studio when I was last in town. There happened to be little of Macbeth's own there then, but he was employed on an etching of Walker's *Fisherman's Shop* for Messrs. Agnew and the original was of course with him. It is not a work that I care for very much except so far as I revere everything that Walker did (I remember the news of his death gave me a shock as if it had been a near friend's), though artists greatly admire the technic of it; but there were other etchings by Macbeth and other reproductions of Walker's pieces and most of them new to me, the *Ferry* I think it is called (an upper-Thames riverside scene), the *Plough* (a divine work), the *Mushroom Gatherers*, and others. If you have not yet studied Walker's work you have a new world of beauty to open and go in. You shd. also study where you can *North's*° things. It was my brother drew my attention to him. It seems Walker—I do not know that he studied under North but he learnt methods from him: 'North' said someone in vulgar phrase to my brother 'learnt', that is taught, 'Walker to paint'. He survived his pupil, if Walker was that. His landscapes are of a beautiful and poetical delicacy and truth at once. But I have seen very little of his.

I agree to Whistler's striking genius—feeling for what I call *inscape* (the very soul of art); but then his execution is so negligent, unpardonably so sometimes (that was, I suppose, what Ruskin particularly meant by 'throwing the pot of paint in the face of the public'): *his* genius certainly has not come to puberty.

Now something on music. A piece of mine, called, not by my wish, a madrigal in the programme, is to be performed at a school-conert in Dublin tomorrow. It is *Who is Sylvia?* set as a duet and chorus, the tune made very long ago, the harmonies lately set (and very great fears about their puberty entertained). I made it for a string orchestra. And I am very slowly but very elaborately working at 'Does the South Wind' for solos, chorus, and strings. Some years ago I went from Glasgow, where I was, one day to Loch Lomond and landed at Inversnaid (famous through Wordsworth and Matthew Arnold) for some hours. There I had an inspiration of a tune. The disproportion is wonderful between the momentary conception of an air and the long long gestation of its setting. I endeavour to make the under parts each a flowing and independent melody and they cannot be independently invented, they must be felt for along a few certain necessary lines enforced by the harmony. It is astonishing to see them come; but in reality they are in nature bound up (besides many others) with the tune of the principal part and there is, I am persuaded, a world of profound mathematics in this matter of music: indeed no one could doubt that.

I have written a few sonnets: that is all I have done in poetry for some years.

I have not seen Bridges' comedy.°

Swinburne has written for the *Times* an ode on the crisis. Somebody called it a rigmarole and I cd. not say it was not: on the contrary everything he writes is rigmarole. But I wonder how he finds it suits him to be clerical, as this ode with appeals to conscience and declaiming against assassination is. Moreover there was an earlier ode of his in honour of the 'Manchester Martyrs',° as the Irish call them: so then he has changed as much as Gladstone. As they neither of them have any principles it is no wonder. But the passage about Gordon and so on is to the point. It seems to me that 'bad is the best' that can happen now. With this sad thought I must conclude and am your affectionate friend

Gerard M. Hopkins S.J.

Some hindrance happened and the madrigal was not sung. If it had been I could not have heard it, for I was helping to save and damn the studious youth of Ireland.

July 3 1886.

You speak of 'powerful drawing' in Burne Jones's picture. I recognise it in the mermaid's face and in the treatment of her fishments and fishmanship, the tailfin turning short and flattening to save striking the ground—a stroke of truly artistic genius; but the drowned youth's knees and feet are very crude and unsatisfactory in drawing, as it seemed to me.

I have found your former letter, as old as December last, and must add a little more.

The sonnet of Gray's that you ask about is the wellknown one (the only one, I daresay) 'In vain to me': I remarked on its rhythmical beauty, due partly to the accent being rather trochaic than iambic. Wordsworth says somewhere of it that it is 'evident' the only valuable part of it is (I believe) 'For other notes' and the quatrain that follows.° Such a criticism is rude at best, since in a work of art having so strong a unity as a sonnet one part which singly is less beautiful than another part may be as necessary to the whole effect, like the plain shaft in a column and so on. But besides what he calls evident is not so, nor true.

You make a criticism on Handel. I have the very same feeling about him and you 'tell me my own dream', that 'one can never hear five bars of him without feeling that something great is beginning, something full of life'. A piece of his at a concert seems to flutter the dovecot of the rest of them, to be a hawk among poultry. The immediateness of the impression must be due, I suppose, to his power being conveyed into smaller sections of his work than other men's and not needing accumulation for its effect.

I was glad of an appreciative review° of your third volume in the *Academy* (I think) and much interested. Would I could read the work! but I cannot under present, which are permanent, circumstances do that.

I could wish you had been elected to that Chair.° But 'life is a short blanket'—profoundest of homely sayings: great gifts and great opportunities are more than life spares to one man. It is much if we get something, a spell, an innings at all. See how the great conquerors were cut short, Alexander, Caesar just seen. Above all Christ our Lord: his career was cut short and, whereas he would have wished to succeed by success—for it is insane to lay yourself out for failure, prudence is the first of the cardinal virtues, and he was the most prudent of men—nevertheless he was doomed to succeed by failure; his plans were baffled, his hopes dashed, and his work was done by being broken off undone. However much he understood all this he found it an intolerable grief to submit to it. He left the example: it is very strengthening, but except in that sense it is not consoling.

I passed a delightful day at Yattendon. Mrs. Bridges not as I had fancied her (which was but faintly), but none the worst for that.°

To Richard Watson Dixon

University College, Stephen's Green, Dublin. Aug. 7 '86.

My dear Friend,—

The note you speak of did not reach me and no doubt was never posted, for the post never misses (if there is a never in human things) and every alternative should be exhausted before we come to that. (And therefore I say that the number of the *Academy* which shd. have come to hand this morning was also not posted or, what is more likely, has gone astray in the house.)

If the poem° is printed it may rest, but I am going to see the Provincial tomorrow or next day and will ask him about it. I ought to have settled this before; but since I last wrote I have been altogether overwhelmed with examination-work, six or seven weeks of it without any break, Sundays and weekdays. Even now—but it is no use talking of it. . . .

It is not possible for me to do anything, unless a sonnet, and that rarely, in poetry with a fagged mind and a continual anxiety; but there are things at which I can, so far as time serves, work, if it were only by snatches. For instance I am writing (but I am almost sure I never shall have written) a sort of popular account of Light and the Ether. Popular is not quite the word; it is not meant to be easy reading, for such a difficult subject can only be made easy by a very summary and sketchy treatment; rather it is meant for the lay or unprofessional student who will read carefully so long as there are no mathematics and all technicalities are explained; and my hope is to explain things thoroughly and make the matter to such a reader, as far as I go in it, perfectly intelligible. No such account exists and scientific books, especially in English, are very unsatisfactory. The study of physical science has, unless corrected in some way, an effect the very opposite of what one would suppose. One would think it might materialise people (no doubt it does make them or, rather I shd. say, they become materialists; but that is not the same thing: they do not believe in Matter more but in God less); but in fact they seem to end in conceiving only of a world of formulas, with its being properly speaking in thought, towards which the outer world acts as a sort of feeder, supplying examples for literary purposes. And they go so far as to think the rest of mankind are in the same state of mind as themselves. I daresay I may gather together some illustrations of this: one will serve now. 'It is very remarkable' says Tait on *Light*° 'how slowly the human race has reached some even of the simplest, facts of optics [he rather means laws]. We can easily understand how constant experience must have forced on men the conviction [as if they were resisting it: the force would have been to make them think the contrary] that light usually moves in straight lines—i.e. that we see an object in the direction in which it really lies. [Where else shd. one expect to see it?] But' etc.

It will in any case be a pity for S. J. to have been added to my name in the book, for the letters act like italics, asterisks, or rubric.

Some learned lady having shewn by the flora that the season of the action in *Hamlet* is from March to May, a difficulty is raised about the glowworm's ineffectual fire in the first act, since glowworms glow chiefly from May to September. Mr. Furnival having consulted an authority learns that the grub, though not so easily found, shines nearly as bright as the fullgrown worm, that is beetle, and begins in March, and so all is saved. Does not this strike you as great trifling? Shakspere had the finest faculty of observation of all men that ever breathed, but it is ordinary untechnical observation, neither scientific nor even, like a farmer's professional, and he might overlook that point of season. But if he knew it he would likely enough neglect it. There are some errors you must not make, as an eclipse at the halfmoon or a lobster 'the

Cardinal of the seas', but others do not matter and convention varies with regard to them. If I am not mistaken, there are notorious and insoluble inconsistencies in *Hamlet*, due to Shakspere's having recast the play expressly for Burbage, who was elderly, 'short, stout, and scant of breath' (or something of the sort), without taking the trouble to correct throughout accordingly—not even wishing I dare say; for no one can so conceive of Hamlet's person. Besides there are inconsistencies in the Iliad, Aeneid, Don Quixote, Three Musketeers, and so on; it is a frailty of literature. And indeed on reflection the defence makes the matter worse. For few of the audience could know that glowworms do shine, if you look well for them, in March. So that Shakspere would have been breaking Aristotle's rule that in art likely seeming fiction is better than unlikely seeming fact.

By the by, why should Worsworth-worship be 'a difficult thing'? It is a common one now, is it not? Not *the* common, but like soldiers in a crowd, not a numerous but a notable fact. Did you see what Lord Selborne° lately said? What I suppose grows on people is that Wordsworth's particular grace, his *charisma*, as theologians say, has been granted in equal measure to so very few men since times was—to Plato and who else? I mean his spiritual insight into nature; and this they perhaps think is above all the poet's gift? It is true, if we sort things, so that art is art and philosophy philosophy, it seems rather the philosopher's than the poet's: at any rate he had it in a sovereign degree. He had a 'divine philosophy' and a lovely gift of verse; but in his work there is nevertheless *beaucoup à redire* [much that needs rewriting]: is due to the universal fault of our literature, its weakness is rhetoric. The strictly poetical insight and inspiration of our poetry seems to me to be the very finest, finer perhaps than the Greek; but its rhetoric is inadequate—seldom firstrate, mostly only just sufficient, sometimes even below par. By rhetoric I mean all the common and teachable element in literature, what grammar is to speech, what thoroughbass is to music, what theatrical experience gives to playwrights. If you leave out the embroidery (to be sure the principal thing) of for instance the *Excursion* and look only at the groundwork and stuff of the web is it not fairly true to say 'This will never do'? There does seem to be a great deal of dulness, superfluity, aimlessness, poverty of plan. I remember noticing as a boy, it was the discovery of a trade secret, how our poets treat *spirit* and its compounds as one syllable: it is, though founded really on a mistake, the mere change of pronunciation, a beautiful tradition of the poets. Wordsworth had told himself or been told this trifle: why did he not learn or someone tell him that sonnets have a natural *charpente* and structure never, or at least seldom, to be broken through? For want of knowing this his inspired sonnets, εὔμορφοι κολοσσοί° [beautiful statues], suffer from 'hernia', and combine the tiro's blunder with the master's perfection.

Believe me your affectionate friend Gerard Hopkins

Aug. 9.

To Robert Bridges

University College, Stephen's Green, Dublin. Oct. 13 1886

Dearest Bridges,—

Fr. Mat Russell of ours (he is Sir Charles Russell's brother), who edits a little half-religious publication the *Irish Monthly*, wrote to me lately for an opinion of some Latin verses furnished him; and this led to two things. The first was my suddenly turning a lot of Shakspere's songs° into elegiacs and hendecasyllables (my Latin muse having been wholly mum for years) and sending him one copy (and the rest I believe I can and shall get published in the Trinity *Hermathena* by means of Mr. Tyrrell). The other was that he proposed to me to introduce your poems to the fewish but not despicable readers of his little periodical. Now this I must do, as soon as it shall become possible; but you must therefore send me (not for this purpose *Prometheus*, which I have, but) those pamphlets copies of which I think I left at Stonyhurst. It is no doubt wasteful work giving me presentation copies; but the above is my most permanent abode and the nest likely to be best feathered.

Yours Gerard M. Hopkins S.J.

By the bye, I say it deliberately and before God, I would have you and Canon Dixon and all true poets remember that fame, the being known, though in itself one of the most dangerous things to man, is nevertheless the true° and appointed air, element, and setting of genius and its works. What are works of art for? to educate, to be standards. Education is meant for the many, standards are for public use. To produce then is of little use unless what we produce is known, if known widely known, the wider known the better, for it is by being known it works, it influences, it does its duty, it does good. We must then try to be known, aim at it, take means to it. And this without puffing in the process or pride in the success. But still. Besides, we are Englishmen. A great work by an Englishman is like a great battle won by England. It is an unfading bay tree. It will even be admired by and praised by and do good to those who hate England (as England is most perilously hated), who do not wish even to be benefited by her. It is then even a patriotic duty *τῇ ποιήσει ἐνεργεῖν* [to be active in producing poetry] and to secure the fame and permanence of the work. Art and its fame do not really matter, spiritually they are nothing, virtue is the only good; but it is only by bringing in the infinite that to a just judgment they can be made to look infinitestimal or small or less than vastly great; and in this ordinary view of them I apply to them, and it is the true rule for dealing with them, what Christ our Lord said of virtue, Let your light shine before men that they may see your good works (say, of art) and glorify yr. Father in heaven° (that is, acknowledge that they have an absolute excellence in them and are steps in a scale of infinite and inexhaustible excellence).

Let me hear that you got all my letters. One, begun I think in Wales and sent from here, was addressed to Judge Fry's° at Bristol, the next to Yattendon and had (I believe it was that one) a torn drawing in it. Well of course you must have got that one, but the one to Bristol with the long address you may not. Earlier ones are I think accounted for.

Did I ever send you St. Patrick's 'Breastplate' or prayer? I do now at all events. Read it and say if it is not one of the most remarkable compositions of man.

To Richard Watson Dixon

University College, St. Stephen's Green, Dublin. Oct. 23 1886

My dear Friend,—

There are some points in your letter I have to reply to. First of the Greek mythology. Of course I agree with the rest of the world in admiring its beauty. Above everything else the Greeks excelled in art: now their mythology was the earliest of their arts that have in any way survived, older in the main than Homer's poems, and is I daresay as much more beautiful than other mythologies as Homer's epic is than other epics; speaking of epic proper. It is free from that cumber of meaningless and childish rubbish which interrupts and annoys one even in the midst of fine invention in for instance the Irish legends.

This however is to speak of it as stories, as fairytales, well invented well told fairytales. But mythology is something else besides fairytale: it is religion, the historical part of religion. It must have been this side of the Greek mythology I was speaking of in that letter; and could I speak too severely of it? First it is as history untrue. What is untrue history? Nothing and worse than nothing. And that history religion? Still worse. I cannot enter on this consideration without being brought face to face with the great fact of heathenism. Now we mostly pass heathenism by as a thing utterly departed, which indeed it is not but in India rank and flourishing; but if for once we face it what are we to say of it? For myself literally words would fail me to express the loathing and horror with which I think of it and of man setting up the work of his own hands, of that hand within the mind the imagination, for God Almighty who made heaven and earth. Still he might set up beings perfect in their kind. But the Greek gods are rakes, and unnatural rakes. Put that aside too; put yourself in the position of a man who like Homer first believes in them, next forgets or passes over their wickedness: even so are the Greek gods majestic, awe inspiring, as Homer that great Greek genius represents them? They are not. The Indian gods are imposing, the Greek are not. Indeed they are not brave, not self controlled, they have no manners, they are not gentlemen and ladies. They clout one another's ears and blubber and bellow. You will say this is Homer's fun, like the miracle-plays of Christendom. Then where is his earnest about them? At their best they remind me of some company of beaux and fashionable world at Bath in its palmy days or Tunbridge Wells or what not. Zeus is like the Major in *Pendennis* handsomer and better preserved sitting on Olympus as behind a club-window and watching Danae and other pretty seamstresses cross the street—not to go farther. You will think this is very Philistine and vulgar and be pained. But I am pained: this is the light in which the matter strikes me, the only one in which it will; and I do think it is the true light.

But I grant that the Greek mythology is very susceptible of fine treatment, allegorical treatment for instance, and so treated gives rise to the most beautiful results. No wonder: the moral evil is got rid of and the pure art, morally neutral and artistically so rich, remains and can be even turned to moral uses.

The letter you saw must have been in criticism of Bridges' *Ulysses*. I was set against that play by the appearance of Athene in the prologue or opening. Bridges took her almost seriously: so then did I, and was disgusted. But I hold it was a false step of his: the heathen gods cannot be taken seriously on our stage; nowadays they cannot even be taken humorously; and it would tell against the play's success. I know that was a noble play; but I had another objection besides to it, the great severity, the aridity even the joylessness of the lyrics. So I damped and damned and must have hurt Bridges.

I feel now I am warm and my hand is in for my greater task, Wordsworth's ode;° and here, my dear friend, I must earnestly remonstrate with you; must have it out with you. Is it possible that—but it is in black and white: you say the ode is not, for Wordsworth, good; and much less great.

To say it was the second ode in the language was after all only a comparative remark: one might maintain, though I daresay you will not, that English is not rich in odes. The remark therefore is not of itself extravagant. But if the speaker had said that it was one of the dozen or of the half dozen finest odes of the world I must own that to me there would have seemed no extravagance. There have been in all history a few, a very few men, whom common repute, even where it did not trust them, has treated as having had something happen to them that does not happen to other men, as having *seen something*, whatever that really was. Plato is the most famous of these. Or to put it as it seems to me I must somewhere have written to you or to somebody, human nature in these men saw something, got a shock; wavers in opinion, looking back, whether there was anything in it or no; but is in a tremble ever since. Now what Wordsworthians mean is, what would seem to be the growing mind of the English speaking world and may perhaps come to be that of the world at large / is that in Wordsworth when he wrote that ode human nature got another of those shocks, and the tremble from it is spreading. This opinion I do strongly share; I am, ever since I knew the ode, in that tremble. You know what happened to crazy Blake, himself a most poetically electrical subject both active and passive, at his first hearing: when the reader came to 'The pansy at my feet' he fell into a hysterical excitement. Now commonsense forbid we should take on like these unstrung hysterical creatures: still it was a proof of the power of the shock.

The ode itself seems to me better than anything else I know of Wordsworth's, so much as to equal or outweigh everything else he wrote: to me it appears so. For Wordsworth was an imperfect artist, as you say: as his matter varied in importance and as he varied in insight (for he had a profound insight of some things and little of others) so does the value of his work vary. Now the interest and importance of the matter were here of the highest, his insight was at its very deepest, and hence to my mind the extreme value of the poem.

His powers rose, I hold, with the subject: the execution is so fine. The rhymes are so musically interlaced, the rhythms so happily succeed (surely it is a magical change 'O joy that in our embers'), the diction throughout is so charged and steeped in beauty and yearning (what a stroke 'The moon doth with delight'!). It is not a bit of good my going on if, which is to me so strange in you and disconcerting, you do not feel anything of this. But I do hope you will reconsider it. For my part I shd. think St. George and St. Thomas of Canterbury wore roses in heaven for England's sake on the day that ode, not without their intercession, was penned; for, to better a little the good humoured old cynical proverb, 'When grace of God is gone and spent Then learning is most excellent' and goes to make the greatness of a nation—which is what I urge on Bridges and now on you, to get yourselves known and be up betimes on our Parnassus.

Now no more. I will copy you soon some odd ends, sonnets. Have you my song for my play of *St. Winefred* called *The Leaden Echo and the Golden Echo*? If not I will try and copy it as time serves: I never did anything more musical.

May the Muses bring you to a better mind. May God Almighty, and this without reserve.

I am your affectionate friend Gerard M. Hopkins S. J.

Oct. 24. Examinations over and I begin lecturing tomorrow.

To Robert Bridges

University College, Stephen's Green, Dublin. Oct. 28 '86.

Dearest Bridges,—

To't again; for though my last was long and tedious and the one before that, if I remember, a literary budget, I have not yet dealt with your last.

My examinations are over till the next attack of the plague. My lectures, to call them that grand name, are begun: vae unum abiit et vae alterum venit [alas, though one has gone another comes]. I was I cannot tell when in such health and spirits as on my return from Cadwalader and all his goats but 331 accounts of the First Punic War with trimmings, have sweated me down to nearer my lees and usual alluvial low water mudflats, groans[2], despair[4], and[3] yearnings[1].

Now I have at much length remonstrated with Canon Dixon for slighting Wordsworth's Ode on the Intimations, at which he might have taken offence but on the contrary he took it with his usual sweetness; and I beg you will my remonstrances with you about Barnes and Stephenson; of both of whom, but especially S., you speak with a sourness which tinges your judgment.

It is commonly thought of Barnes that 'local colour' is just what he excells in and this is my own opinion. A fine and remarkable instance (a case of colour proper) was quoted by the *Saturday* in the article on him which followed the news of his death.° But of him another time or never; no more now. (The expression 'the supposed emotions of peasants' grates on me, but let it pass.)

I have not read *Treasure Island*.° When I do, as I hope to, I will bear your criticisms in mind. (By the bye, I am sorry those poor boys lost the book because you found consecutive fifths somewhere. However give 'em Rider Haggard's *King Solomon's Mines*.° They certainly will enjoy it; anyone would; and the author is not a highflier.) Nevertheless I mean to deal with two of these criticisms now, for it is easy to do so on the face of them.

One is that a boy capable of a brave deed would be incapable of writing it down—well *that* boy. Granting this, still to make him tell it is no fault or a trifling one.° And the criticism, which ignores a common convention of romance or literature in general, is surely then some ἀγροικία [rusticity, boorishness] on your part. Autobiography in fiction is commonly held a hazardous thing and few are thought to have succeeded in it on any great scale: Thackeray in *Edmond* is I believe held for one of the exceptions. It is one of the things which 'O Lord, sir, we must connive at'. The reader is somehow to be informed of the facts. And in any case the fault is removeable without convulsing the structure of the whole: like a bellglass or glass frame over cucumbers or flowers it may be taken off, cleansed, and replaced without touching them. So this criticism I look on as trifling.

The other criticism is the discovery of a fault of plot about the whereabouts of some schooner:° I take your word for it. One blot is no great matter, I mean not a damning matter.° One blot may be found in the works of very learned clerks indeed. *Measure for Measure* is a lovely piece of work, but it was a blot, as Swinburne raving was overheard for hours to say, to make Isabella marry the old Duke. *Volpone* is one of the richest and most powerful plays ever written, but a writer in a late *Academy*° points out a fault of construction (want of motive, I think, for Bonario's being at Volpone's house when Celia was brought there): it will stand that one fault. True you say that in Stevenson's book there are many such: but I do not altogether believe there are.

This sour severity blinds you to his great genius. *Jekyll and Hyde*° I have read. You speak of 'the gross absurdity' of the interchange.° Enough that it is impossible and might perhaps have been a little better masked: it must be connived at, and it gives rise to a fine situation. It is not more impossible than fairies, giants, heathen gods, and lots of things that literature teems with—and none more than yours.° You are certainly wrong about Hyde being overdrawn: my Hyde is worse. The trampling scene is perhaps a convention: he was thinking of something unsuitable for fiction.

I can by no means grant that the characters are not characterised, though how deep the springs of their surface action are I am not yet clear. But the superficial touches of character are admirable: how can you be so blind as not to see them? e.g. Utterson frowning, biting the end of his finger, and saying to the butler 'This is a strange tale you tell me, my man, a very strange tale'. And Dr Lanyon: 'I used to like it, sir [life]; yes, sir, I liked it. Sometimes I think if we knew all' etc. These are worthy of Shakespeare. Have you read the *Pavilion on the Links* in the volume of *Arabian Nights* (not one of them)? The absconding banker is admirably characterised, the horror is nature itself, and the whole piece is genius from beginning to end.

In my judgment the amount of gift and genius which goes into novels in the English literature of this generation is perhaps not much inferior to what made the Elizabethan drama, and unhappily it is in great part wasted. How admirable are Blackmore and Hardy! Their merits are much eclipsed by the overdone reputation of the Evans—Eliot—Lewis—Cross woman (poor creature! one ought not to speak slightingly, I know), half real power, half imposition. Do you know the bonfire scenes in the *Return of the Native* and still better the sword-exercise scene in the *Madding Crowd*, breathing epic? or the wife-sale in the *Mayor of Casterbridge* (read by chance)? But these writers only rise to their great strokes; they do not write continuously well: now Stevenson is master of a consummate style and each phrase is finished as in poetry. It will not do at all, your treatment of him. (Today is Degree-day at the R.U. and a holiday.) . . .

To Coventry Patmore

University College, Stephen's Green, Dublin. | Nov. 7. 1886.

My dear Mr. Patmore,—

Your pamphlet must, I think, have miscarried: the name *How I managed my Estate* or to that effect is familiar but I believe from a review in the *Academy*. It is like a dream to me that I saw such a pamphlet lying about, but at any rate I did not recognise it as belonging to me, much less read it. And therefore I shd. be glad if you wd. be so kind as to send another copy.

The long letter I spoke of was cancelled, as it often happens to me to cancel letters and it would be better if it happened oftener still; best of all would be never to write anything that could need cancelling.

I seem to have been among odds and ends of poets and poetesses of late. One poetess was Miss Kate Tynan,° who lately published a volume of chiefly devotional poems, highly spoken of by reviews. She is a simple brightlooking Biddy with glossy very pretty red hair, a farmer's daughter in the County Dublin. She knows and deeply admires your Muse and said this, which appears in some way noteworthy—complaining that you are sometimes austere or bare or something like that: '*How* is it, Fr. Hopkins, that however bare it is it is always poetry?' I am at present Bridges' Muse-broker and had to send Miss Tynan an invoice of him. I am to read Miss Tynan herself when she comes, that is, as many pages as she has walked to and fro over—to say of her what one might say of any writer. Then there is a young Mr. Yeats° who has written in a Trinity College publication some striking verses and who has been perhaps unduly pushed by the late Sir Samuel Ferguson° (I do not know if you have read or heard of him: he was a learned antiquary, a Protestant but once an ally of Thomas Davis and the Young Ireland Party, but he withdrew from them and even suppressed some of his best poems for fear they, or he, shd. be claimed by the Nationalists of later days; for he was a poet; the *Forging of the Anchor* is, I believe, his most famous poem; he was a poet as the Irish are—to judge by the little of his I have seen—full of feeling, high thoughts, flow of verse, point, often fine imagery and other virtues, but the essential and only lasting thing left out—what I call *inscape*, that is species or individually-distinctive beauty of style: on this point I believe we quite agree, as on most: but this is a serious parenthesis). I called on his, young Yeats's, father by desire lately; he is a painter; and with some emphasis of manner he presented me with *Mosada: a Dramatic Poem* by W. B. Yeats, with a portrait of the author by J. B. Yeats, himself; the young man having finely cut intellectual features and his father being a fine draughtsman. For a young man's pamphlet this was something too much; but you will understand a father's feeling. Now this *Mosada* I cannot think highly of, but I was happily not required then to praise what presumably I had not then read, and I had read and could praise another piece. It was a strained and unworkable allegory about a young man and a sphinx on a rock in the sea (how did they get there? what did they eat? and so on: people think such criticisms very prosaic; but commonsense is never out of place anywhere, neither on Parnassus nor on Tabor nor on the Mount where our Lord preached; and, not to quote Christ's parables all taken from real life but in the frankly impossible, as in the *Tempest*, with what consummate and penetrating imagination is Ariel's 'spiriting' put before us! all that led up and that must follow the scenes in the play is realised and suggested and you cannot lay your finger on the point where it breaks down), but still containing fine lines and vivid imagery.

I find that Miss Tynan has a great admirer in Lord Lytton who writes to her at length and has invited her to visit him.

By the bye I saw a letter of yours to the *Times* written as a rally against Mr. Gladstone, not however proposing any alternative policy.

This is a foolish letter of gossip, I must bring it to an end. Since I returned from Wales I have been in better health than usual, fitter for work; and very much better spirits. And I am hoping to write (if not this year a book, yet) this year a paper for the *Society of Hellenic Studies*, to which I belong, (or some other quarter) on the Dorian Measure,° the true scansion of perhaps half or more than half of the Greek and Latin lyric verse: I do believe it is a great and it is an unsuspected discovery. Give my kind regards to your circle and believe me

your sincere friend Gerard Hopkins, S.J.

To Richard Watson Dixon

University College, St. Stephen's Green, Dublin. Jan. 27 '87

My dear Friend,—

It is long since I heard from you. You sent me no more of your proofs; of which, if I could be of any use, I am sorry on the one hand and yet I own that in school time I can scarcely undertake anything.

The winter, though much less severe in Ireland than in England, tried me more than any yet; half killed me; and leaves me languishing. Especially it has attacked my eyes, but perhaps this effect will pass off. The weather is now of a summer mildness.

I have done some part of a book on Pindar's metres and Greek metres in general and metre in general and almost on art in general and wider still, but that I shall ever get far on with it or, if I do, sail through all the rocks and shoals that lie before me I scarcely dare to hope and yet I do greatly desire, since the thoughts are well worth preserving: they are a solid foundation for criticism. What becomes of my verses I care little, but about things like this, what I write or could write on philosophical matters, I do; and the reason of the difference is that the verses stand or fall by their simple selves and, though by being read they might do good, by being unread they do no harm; but if the other things are unsaid right they will be said by somebody else wrong, and that is what will not let me rest.

I was at Xmas and New Year down with some kind people in Co. Kildare,° where I happened to see the portrait of two beautiful young persons, a brother and sister, living in the neighbourhood. It so much struck me that I began an elegy in Gray's metre,° but being back here I cannot go on with it. However I must see if I can enclose you a copy of the part done.

Have you heard of any great admirers of *Mano* or your other poems since *Mano* came out, by letter or otherwise? I set up a little Propaganda for Bridges' muse here lately, distributing, with commendations, the copies he sent me; also I have got a lady to compose her Doctorate-of-Music diploma work to his *Elegy on a Lady whom Grief* etc; and I tell people of you when I can put in a word. But it seems one can do little in this distracted globe and one is inclined to let things alone.

I have made the acquaintance of the young and ingenuous poetess Miss Kate Tynan, a good creature and very graceful writer, highly and indeed somewhat too highly praised by a wonderful, perhaps alarming, unanimity of the critics; for the truth is she is not exactly an original 'fountain in a shady grove' (the critics would not be standing all round her so soon if she were), but rather a sparkling townfountain in public gardens and draws her water from other sources. She half knows this herself and lately wrote me a letter which for various reasons I am slow to answer and as long as I do not I cannot help telling myself very barbarously that I have stopped *her* jaw at any rate.

Jan. 29—Bridges says he has three works on hand. Like 'Young Copperfield' (according to Steerforth), he is going it.

Believe me your affectionate friend

Gerard M. Hopkins S.J.

To Robert Bridges

University College, St. Stephen's Green, Dublin. Feb. 17 '87

Dearest Bridges,—

I am joyed to see your hand again and delighted to hear your praise of the Canon's book.° I too have thought there is in him a vein of truly matchless beauty: it is not always the whole texture but a thread in it and sometimes the whole web is of that. But till you spoke I had almost despaired of my judgment and quite of publishing it. The pathetic imagination of *Sky that rollest ever*° seems to me to have nothing like it but some of Coleridge in our literature.

Mrs. Waterhouse has not written: it never indeed entered my head that she would, the piece° being a fragment too. But I wanted to pay her a compliment and conceived she would like this particular poem. It is in a commoner and smoother style than I mostly write in, but that is no harm: I am sure I have gone far enough in oddities and running rhymes (as even in some late sonnets you have not seen) into the next line. I sent a later and longer version to C. D., who much admired and urged me to write lots of it. It should run to about twice the present length and when complete I daresay you will like it. I am amused and pleased at Maurice W.° expounding it: it is not at all what I wanted to happen, but after all if I send verse to Mrs. Waterhouse I cannot suppose no one else in the house will see it.

Tomorrow morning I shall have been three years in Ireland, three hard wearying wasting wasted years. (I met the blooming Miss Tynan again this afternoon. She told me that when she first saw me she took me for 20 and some friend of hers for 15; but it won't do: they should see my heart and vitals, all shaggy with the whitest hair.) In those I have done God's will (in the main) and many many examination papers. I am in a position which makes it befitting and almost a duty to write anything (bearing on classical study) which I may feel that I could treat well and advance learning by: there is such a subject; I do try to write at it; but I see that I cannot get on, that I shall be even less able hereafter than now. And of course if I cannot do what even my appliances make best and easiest, far less can I anything else. Still I could throw myself cheerfully into my day's work? I cannot, I am in prostration. Wales set me up for a while, but the effect is now past. But out of Ireland I shd. be no better, rather worse probably. I only need one thing—a working health, a working strength: with that, any employment is tolerable or pleasant, enough for human nature; without it, things are liable to go very hardly with it.

Now come on Mrs. Gaskell. What ails poor Mrs. Gaskell? One book of hers I have read through, *Wives and Daughters*: if that is not a good book I do not know what a good book is. Perhaps you are so barbarous as not to admire Thomas Hardy—as you do not Stevenson; both, I must maintain, men of pure and direct genius.

Have you followed the course of late Homeric criticism? The pendulum is swinging heavily towards the old view of a whole original Iliad. In the track of the recent dialectic investigations I have made out, I think, a small but (as a style-test) important point; but my induction is not yet complete.

I will bear in mind to send for the *Feast of Bacchus* at an early opportunity, if (but that is not certain) one should occur.

I am almost afraid I have offended, not offended but not pleased, Mr. Patmore by a late letter: I hope it is not so bad. I hope you will enjoy yourselves there: let me see, do you know Mrs. Patmore? If you do you cannot help liking her. With best love to Mrs. Bridges I am your affectionate friend

Gerard.

Yesterday Archbishop Walsh° had a letter in the *Freeman* enclosing a subscription to the defence of Dillon and the other traversers on trial for preaching the Plan of Campaign and saying that the jury was packed and a fair trial impossible. The latter was his contribution to the cause of concord and civil order. Today Archbp. Croke° had one proposing to pay no taxes. One archbishop backs robbery, the other rebellion; the people in good faith believe and will follow them. You will see, it is the beginning of the end: Home Rule or separation is near. Let them come: anything is better than the attempt to rule a people who own no principle of civil obedience at all, not only to the existing government but to none at all. I shd. be glad to see Ireland happy, even though it involved the fall of England, if that could come about without shame and guilt. But Ireland will not be happy: a people without a principle of allegiance cannot be; moreover this movement has throughout been promoted by crime. Something like what happened in the last century between '82 and 1800 will happen in this: now as then one class has passed off its class-interests as the interests of the nation and so got itself upheld by the support of the nation; now as then it will legislate in its own interest and the rest will languish; distress will bring on some fresh convulsion; beyond that I cannot guess.

The ship I am sailing in may perhaps go down in the approaching gale: if so I shall probably be cast up on the English coast.

After all I have written above my trouble is not the not being able to write a book; it is the not being fit for my work and the struggling vainly to make myself fitter.

Feb. 18 1887.

To Alexander William Mowbray Baillie

St Stephen's Green, Dublin. |
20 February 1887

Dearest Baillie,

. . . *Ferrule*—I have heard this pronounced (by an Irishman) *furl*. This wd. be a fresh accommodation, for a ferrule, (on a stick) does furl the wood.

Jaunty—But *jaunty* now *means* 'on the jaunt'. Either then Skeat is mistaken or it is an interesting case of a word passing from one root to another.

Lapwing, which I do not dispute, is another and striking case. It appears that it now has come to mean in another and ininverted shape much the same as it did in the beginning and to express its meaning not less happily.

So also *stark naked*: we certainly understand and convey the same thought as in 'stark mad'—stiffly, uncompromisingly so and so.

In like manner *touchy*, *uproar*, *upside down* now mean what they seem to mean.

Wiseacre I cannot understand. Does Skeat mean it is really *derived* from the German *Weissager*?

Counterpane is perhaps a complicated matter. If I am not mistaken old writers call pieces of cloth (and not only of glass) *panes*. *Counterpane* wd. then be perfectly regular. Still it may be like *lapwing* above.

. . . There remains a word about Home Rule and so on. In general I am sure we agree on this as on most matters, but particular conclusions vary with particular facts. Home Rule of itself is a blow for England and will do no good to Ireland. But it is better than worse things. You would understand that if you lived in Ireland. My position is not at all a favourable one for observing the country, still it is much better than people in England can have and they in fact do not at all realise the situation. People think that Ireland was always a 'distressful country', troubled and hard to rule at the best, and they do not see that things are worse than or so bad as they have read of their being before. I do not say things are as bad as they were during the horrors of Irish rebellions or the greater horrors of their putting down. I only say that we are approaching a state of things which must be put an end to either by the sword or by Home Rule. It is, if people would see it, high praise of our constitution that it should enable us to pass through a crisis of which the natural end is war / without war; for now for the first time the Irish are using the constitution against England. But the country is in a peaceful rebellion, if you can understand what that is, and the rebellion is becoming more serious. Every step which has been taken since, say, the Land Act of 1881 (I cd. go much further back, but that is enough), to satisfy—satisfy it could not, but let us say to better the condition of Ireland, has made things worse. The Irish had and have deep wrongs to complain of in the past and wrongs and abuses to amend which are still felt in the present. But the strange and alarming thing is that the removal of and the wish to remove these has not conciliated them, it has inflamed them. For these steps have done nothing to give them, but have nevertheless done much to bring them nearer getting, the object of their undying desire and now of their flaming passion. This is what they called Nationhood. The passion for it is of its nature insatiable and Home Rule will not satisfy it; it will be a disappointment too like the rest; but it will have some good effects and it will deliver England from the strain of an odious and impossible task, the task of attempting to govern a people who own no principle of civil allegiance (only religious, and that one is now strained), not only not to the existing government, in which they share, but to none at all; and of enforcing a law which the people wish to set at nought and to defeat. For such a complexion of things no constitution was made: absolute monarchy with strong forces at command alone could deal with it, and that miserably. Things will not mend: if they would mend now they would have mended before. Consider. There was a feud between the two most prominent classes in the country, landlords and tenants. The position of the landlords was superior; they oppressed the tenants. The position of the tenants was bettered till it became more favourable than that of any other tenant farmers. And the feud increased. Agriculture happened then to suffer, the prosperity of England and Ireland declined, all classes were strained; the tenants combined to ask reductions of rent: the landlords mostly gave those reductions. And the feud increased. The landlords, once able to evict at will, try to evict for non-payment of three, four, five, six, seven years' rent: sometimes they cannot, at other times three kingdoms and two continents are set on fire by it. The feud fills the world. Not content with a court for reducing the rents of the unwilling landlord, not appeased by the willing reductions of others, the Plan of Campaign is invented. Mostly it succeeds, and with it the feud increases. The judges with one mouth pronounce it against the law: members of parliament all the more boldly promote it and the feud, now a struggle with the law, increases. I have said nothing of the sieges and battles, a miniature war, which has meanwhile gone on. The traversers are put on their trial: an Archbishop, the people's nominee, who has already approved of the Plan of Campaign, now attacks the justice of the court which is to try its promoters. Another Archbishop° proposes to refuse taxes. The trial will end, I suppose, today either in some miscarriage, which will be a victory for the traversers, or perhaps in a verdict which the people will with indignation disregard. For they allow neither the justice of the law nor the honesty of its administrators. Be assured of this, that the mass of the Irish people own no allegiance to any existing law or government. And yet they are not a worthless people; they have many true and winning virtues. But their virtues do not promote civil order and it has become impossible to govern them. Cost what it may, what wise man would try or wish to govern a people that own no duty to any law he can enforce? It is a hopeless task: they must have Home Rule with all that it may cost both them and us. You would say so if you lived here. Gladstone is a traitor. But still they must have Home Rule.

Do not believe this is only a struggle for land. I will explain that point (if I may speak so boldly) another time. This is really an old story, an *altes stück* [ancient play]: everything, if we look in the right quarter, is known. What is happening now happened in the last century and so, I suppose, what happened then will happen now. Proportions and features no doubt differ, but the main thing is the same. Hullabaloo, long letter!

Your affectionate friend Gerard M. Hopkins S.J.

To Michael F. Cox°

Monasterevan, | Ireland. | Lady Day 1887

My dear Dr. Cox,

—I have had a book of yours° too long and ought to have returned it. This was brought to my mind in setting my things to rights yesterday. I will bring it you on getting back.

I am led to make some remarks on the matter. Irish writers on their own history are naturally led to dwell on what in history is most honourable to Ireland: every patriotic spirit would feel itself so led. They are also led to dwell on what in history is most dishonourable to England: this also is natural, and there is plenty of room for doing it. Still it is the way with passion to exceed; and the passion here in question is often said, by Irishmen themselves, to be the deepest feeling of an Irish heart. Now since the object of history is truth and truth is likely to suffer from the play of passion, it is desirable that Irish writers on Irish history should be on their guard especially on this matter, and, failing that, it is left for Englishmen like myself to do what we can (which is almost, under the circumstances, nothing at all) to point out untruths and overstatements and understatements due to passion and correct them. The devil is not so black, the saying is, as he is painted.

There are in perhaps all the heaviest charges of accusation by Ireland against England certain circumstances not justifying indeed but mitigating and essentially modifying the nature of the wrong done. These circumstances are always unknown to or forgotten or wilfully suppressed by popular writers and speakers. Even those that lie on the surface of history are so treated; how much more then those that appear on research. And this my position has brought me to feel not only with sorrow but with the deepest indignation and bitterness. The late Mr. Maguire M.P. in his book on the Irish in America, the purpose of which was to warn English statesmen of the danger of not listening to the claims of Ireland, mentions that he once had to set right an Irish American who supposed there to be duties imposed by England on Irish exports: when he informed him that all such duties had long since been removed the man's countenance fell and betrayed his disappointment. This man did not care that Ireland should prosper; he cared only for the food of his hatred against England. This no doubt is not the mind of the lady who writes on Irish Woollens; still I should like her to have known and knowing to have mentioned certain points, one of which at least is very material. I learnt them from a paper in last April's number of the *English Historical Review* by the Rev. W. Cunningham,° and perhaps it might have been expected that a lady of so much research as that pamphlet shows her to be and who was only restrained by insuperable difficulties from verifying a single mention of

Irish goods in the old poet Fazio degli Uberti should have found out this important fact.

This is that the most extensive (and in the 17th century seemingly the only) Irish woollen industry was frieze, that this was never checked by English legislation (but on the contrary expressly excepted in the acts), and nevertheless that it is now not far from dead.

And indeed I gather from her own paper some such process with regard to the Irish woollen industries in general. In the 14th century we hear from Dante's contemporary Fazio degli Uberti of certain fine Irish serges as being exported as far as Florence; one or two centuries later we hear of certain coarse stuffs as selling at Antwerp (if I remember); and later than that, though my authority for this is Cunningham's paper, quoting Sir Wm. Pettie,° it seems that nothing but frieze was exported and little of that and that little mostly to England. The reason I presume is that Ireland was early in the field with woollen goods, but other nations learnt to make as good or better or at all events goods which what with the cost of freight and, maybe, import duties, foreign goods could not compete with. This then was not England's doing.

And in fact why do at least the plainer people not wear more frieze? The reasons, whatever they are, are to be sought in some principle of wider reach than acts of parliament.

In Cunningham's paper you will find other points which deserve to be borne in mind (I might more sadly say, which deserve suppression); as that the party injured by the legislation of 1699 and thereafter was the Protestant party (though of course in the end the prosperity of the whole country was affected); that this party themselves wanted to keep the cloth manufacture out of Catholic hands; that the outcry from England was made only by the west-country weavers and clothiers and not from anticipation only of rivalry but from serious and actual loss by emigration to Ireland of their workpeople (a selfish spirit no doubt but one scarcely to be got rid of in commerce and the same by which Swift and those who thought with him were actuated in the way of retaliation); that parliament did not do all that these people wanted nor from their self-interested motives but from political ones; that they meant to save the English manufacturers from serious loss and no more, not to ruin the Irish one, though it is true the measures they took had that effect, being excessive and, to a rising trade, ruinous; and lastly that the actual evil done was small and rather the prevention of wealth that might have come than the destruction of what was.

I am yours very truly Gerard M. Hopkins.

March 26.

To Robert Bridges

University College, St. Stephen's Green, Dublin. March 29 '87

Dear Bridges,—

I found your letter on coming back to town last night from Monasterevan, quite too late for return of post. However for the curiosity of the thing I answer your queries.

The irises of the present writer's eyes are small and dull, of a greenish brown; hazel I suppose; slightly darker at the outer rims.

His hair (see enclosed sample, carriage paid) is lightish brown, but not equable nor the same in all lights; being quite fair near the roots and upon the temples, elsewhere darker (the very short bits are from the temple next the ear, the longer snip from the forehead), and shewing quite fair in the sun and even a little tawny. It has a gloss. On the temples it sometimes appears to me white. I have a few white hairs, but not there.

It is a very pleasant and flattering thought that Wooldridge is painting my portrait, but is it (and was yours) wholly from memory? I am of late become much wrinkled round the eyes and generally haggard-looking, and if my counterfeit presentment is to be I shd. be glad it were of my youth.

And if Wooldridge is still with you tell him not to trouble to answer that letter at all nor to make the enquiries, which I have made elsewhere (besides which I feel pretty sure the matter never struck Rockstro nor perhaps anyone else and that I have the key to the history of modern music in what my enquiry points to, viz. that modern harmony could not arise till the old system and its tuning was got rid of and that it was goodness, not dulness, of ear which delayed its growth). Presently I hope to write to him again, not lengthily, and may enclose something.

I shd. have felt better for the delicious bog air of Monasterevan were it not that I had a sleepless night of it last night.

The young lady of my Elegy° was tossed in the earthquake. She and her mother ran down lightly clad and spent the next day under an umbrella (against sun, not rain). She was greatly terrified and begged and prayed her father to fetch her home, which I fancy he has not yet done.

I am yours affectionately Gerard M. Hopkins S.J.

If I can manage to read the Feast of Bacchus it must be in the ensuing Easter holidays. You shall hear in a day or two.

To Robert Bridges

[Incomplete letter]

University College, St. Stephen's Green, Dublin. July 30 1887

. . . The drama ought to grow up with its audience; but now the audience is, so to say, jaded and senile and an excellence it knows of already cannot move it. Where a real novelty is presented to it, like Gilbert's and Sullivan's operas, which are a genuine creation of a type, it responds. However I cannot write more now and I have not the proper knowledge of the subject.

I have been reading the Choephoroi carefully and believe I have restored the text and sense almost completely in the corrupted choral odes. Much has been done in this way by dint of successive effort; the recovery, from the 'pie' of the MSS, of for instance the last antistrophe of the last ode is a beautiful thing to see and almost certain; but both in this and the others much mere pie remains and it seems to me I have recovered nearly all. Perhaps I might get a paper on it into the *Classical Review* or *Hermathena*: otherwise they must wait to be put into a book; but when will that book or any book of mine be? Though I have written a good deal of my book on Metre. But it is a great pity for Aeschylus' choruses to remain misunderstood, for it is his own interpretation of the play and his own moral to the story.

What a noble genius Aeschylus had! Besides the swell and pomp of words for which he is famous there is in him a touching consideration and manly tenderness; also an earnestness of spirit and would-be piety by which the man makes himself felt through the playwright. This is not so with Sophocles, who is only the learned and sympathetic dramatist; and much less Euripides.

On Irish politics I had something to say, but there is little time. 'It only needs the will,' you say: it is an unwise word. It is true, it (that is, to govern Ireland) does 'only need the will'; but Douglas Jerrold's joke is in place, about Wordsworth (or whoever it was) that could write plays as good as Shakespeare's 'if he had the mind', and 'only needed the mind'. It is a just reproach to any man not to do what lies in his own power and he could do if he would: to such a man you may well say that the task in question only needs the will. But where a decision does *not* depend on us and we cannot even influence it, then it is only wisdom to recognize the facts—the will or want of will in those, not us, who have control of the question; and that is the case now. The will of the nation is divided and distracted. Its judgment is uninformed and misinformed, divided and distracted, and its action must be corresponding to its knowledge. It has always been the fault of the mass of Englishmen to know and care nothing about Ireland, to let be what would there (which, as it happened, was persecution, avarice, and oppression): and now, as fast as these people wake up and hear what wrong England has done (and has long ceased doing) to Ireland, they, like that woman in Mark Twain, 'burst into tears and rushing upstairs send a pink silk parasol and a box of hairpins to the seat of war'. If you in your limited but appreciable sphere of influence can bring people to a just mind and a proper resolution about Ireland (as you did, you told me, take part in your local elections) do so: you will then be contributing to that will which 'only is wanting'; but do not reproach me, who on this matter have perhaps both more knowledge and more will than most men. If however you think you could do but little and are unwilling even to do that (for I suppose while you are writing plays you cannot be canvassing electors), then recognise with me that with an unwavering will, or at least a flood of passion, on one, the Irish, side and a wavering one or indifference on the other, the English, and the Grand Old Mischiefmaker° loose, like the Devil, for a little while and meddling and marring all the fiercer for his hurry, Home Rule is in fact likely to come and even, in spite of the crime, slander, and folly with which its advance is attended, may perhaps in itself be a measure of a sort of equity and, considering that worse might be, of a kind of prudence.

I am not a judge of the best way to publish. Though double columns are generally and with reason objected to yet I thought *Nero* looked and read well with them. (I am convinced it is one of the finest plays ever written.) I have not seen Miss Taylor° for long: I half fear she has given up the Elegy.

I know scarcely anything of American literature and if I knew much I could not now write about it.

I hope soon to write to Canon Dixon. Give him my best love I am happy to think of your being together.

I daresay I shall be at Haslemere within the week. Court's Hill Lodge is the name of the house and is probably now not necessary.

Monsignor Persico° is going about. His coming will certainly do good. I should like to talk to him, perhaps may. I have met him at a great dinner.

Your affectionate friend Gerard.

Aug. 1 1887. 'Getting old'—you should never say it. But I was fortythree on the 28th of last month and already half a week has gone.

To Coventry Patmore

20 Oct. 1887

My dear Mr. Patmore,

. . . when I read yr. prose and when I read Newman's and some other modern writers' the same impression is borne in on me: no matter how beautiful the thought, nor, taken singly, with what happiness expressed, you do not know what *writing prose* is. At bottom what you do and what Cardinal Newman does is to think aloud, to think with pen to paper. In this process there are certain advantages; they may outweigh those of a perfect technic; but at any rate they exclude that; they exclude the belonging technic, the belonging rhetoric, the own proper eloquence of written prose. Each thought is told off singly and there follows a pause and this breaks the continuity, the *contentio*, the strain of address, which writing should usually have.

The beauty, the eloquence, of good prose cannot come wholly from the thought. With Burke it does and varies with the thought; when therefore the thought is sublime so does the style appear to be. But in fact Burke had no style properly so called: his style was colourlessly to transmit his thought. Still he was an orator in form and followed the common oratorical tradition, so that his writing has the strain of address I speak of above.

But Newman does not follow the common tradition—of writing. His tradition is that of cultured, the most highly educated, conversation; it is the flower of the best Oxford life. Perhaps this gives it a charm of unaffected and personal sincerity that nothing else could. Still he shirks the technic of written prose and shuns the tradition of written English. He seems to be thinking 'Gibbon is the last great master of traditional English prose; he is its perfection: I do not propose to emulate him; I begin all over again from the language of conversation, of common life'.

You too seem to me to be saying to yourself 'I am writing prose, not poetry; it is bad taste and a confusion of kinds to employ the style of poetry in prose: the style of prose is to shun the style of poetry and to express one's thoughts with point'. But the style of prose is a positive thing and not the absence of verse-forms and pointedly expressed thoughts are single hits and give no continuity of style.

After all the very Paper which leads me to make these remarks is entitled 'Thoughts on Knowledge' etc, so that I am blaming you for not doing what you do not attempt to do. Perhaps then I ought to blame you for not attempting and doing. However I have said my say and feel inclined to burn it. . . .

During the summer examinations one of my colleagues brought in one day a *St. James's Gazette*° with a piece of criticism he said it was a rare pleasure to read. It proved to be a review by you of Colvin's book on Keats. Still, enlightening as the review was, I did not think it really just. You classed Keats with the feminine geniuses among men and you would have it that he was not the likest but rather the unlikest of our poets to Shakspere. His poems, I know, are very sensuous and indeed they are sensual. This sensuality is their fault, but I do not see that it makes them feminine. But at any rate (and the second point includes the first) in this fault he resembles, not differs from Shakspere. For Keats died very young and we have only the work of his first youth. Now if we compare that with Shakspere's early work, written at an age considerably more than Keats's, was it not? such as *Venus and Adonis* and *Lucrece*, it is, as far as the work of two very original minds ever can be, greatly like in its virtues and its vices; more like, I do think, than that of any writer you could quote after the Elizabethan age; which is what the common opinion asserts. It may be that Keats was no dramatist (his *Otho* I have not seen); but it is not for that, I think, that people have made the comparison. The *Cap and Bells* is an unhappy performance, so bad that I could not get through it; senselessly planned to have no plan and doomed to fail: but Keats would have found out that. He was young; his genius intense in its quality; his feeling for beauty, for perfection intense; he had found his way right in his Odes; he would find his way right at last to the true functions of his mind. And he was at a great disadvantage in point of education compared with Shakspere. Their classical attainments may have been much of a muchness, but Shakespere had the school of his age. It was the Renaissance: the ancient Classics were deeply and enthusiastically studied and influenced directly or indirectly all, and the new learning had entered into a fleeting but brilliant combination with the medieval tradition. All then used the same forms and keepings. But in Keat's time, and worst in England, there was no one school; but experiment, division, and uncertainty. He was one of the beginners of the Romantic movement, with the extravagance and ignorance of his youth. After all is there anything in *Endymion* worse than the passage in *Romeo and Juliet* about the County Paris as a book of love that must be bound and I can't tell what? It has some kind of fantastic beauty, like an arabesque; but in the main it is nonsense. And about the true masculine fibre in Keats's mind Matthew Arnold has written something good° lately.

My brother also sent me a paper of yours on Women's Rights,° very, perhaps cruelly, plainspoken.

The night, I think, before I began this letter I had a dream touching you which raises a point of interest. I thought I was at a station where cheap trips were advertised. I went to the bookingoffice and pulling out what I had in my purse, about three and sixpence, said 'I don't care where I go: put me down as near the sea as you can'. The clerk gave me a ticket for Lewes. I rejoiced and said to myself that I should now be able to get over to you at Hastings for a night. I think I have never been near Lewes these twenty years but in passing it to and from Hastings on my visit to you. So then, though I felt surprised at the Lewes ticket, it would seem that in my dream it was really Hastings suggested Lewes, not Lewes Hastings, and that I was really constructing the plot which should bring Hastings about, unknown to myself, all the time.

Believe me very sincerely yours Gerard M. Hopkins

Oct. 24, 1887.

In reality I was in August in England at Haslemere, where my family now live, and had thoughts of trying to get over to see you, but time (principally) did not serve. Remember me kindly to all.

After rereading your letter—I can by no means remember,

when I was enjoying your hospitality,° that it was give on my part and take on yours; and if it was, it seems to me I must have babbled greatly.

To Robert Bridges

University College, St. Stephen's Green, Dublin. Nov. 6 1887

Dearest Bridges,—

I must write at once, to save you the trouble of copying that music:° I reproduced it by a jelly-process at Stonyhurst on purpose and only wanted the copy back in case you had one already. I do not remember anything about the harmony: it is the tune I think so good, and this I revived my memory of before I sent it you. I cannot at all make out the meaning of 'If your sister has learnt harmony I can't understand what the moderns mean'. Grace did learn harmony, but girls are apt not to study things thoroughly and perhaps she has not kept it up as she should. I remember years ago that the organist at Liverpool found fault with a hymn of hers, in four parts, very regular, for hidden fifths in the inner parts. But he was an ignoramus: I did not know then but I know now that hidden fifths must be and are freely used in the inner parts and are only faintly kept out of the outer ones. And see what became of him: he got drunk at the organ (I have now twice had this experience: it is distressing, alarming, agitating, but above all delicately comic; it brings together the bestial and the angelic elements in such a quaint entanglement as nothing else can; for musicians never play such clever descants as under those circumstances and in an instant everybody is thrilled with the insight of the situation) and was dismissed. He was a clever young fellow and thoroughly understood the properties of narrow-necked tubes.

I am thankful to you for the account of the Coda, over which you gave yourself even unnecessary trouble. You say the subject is treated in many books. That was just it. I had not got those books and the readiest source of information was you. It seems they are formed on an invariable plan and that Milton's sonnet° gives an example. Of course one example was enough if there is but one type; but you should have said so.

I want Harry Ploughman to be a vivid figure before the mind's eye; if he is not that the sonnet fails. The difficulties are of syntax no doubt. Dividing a compound word by a clause sandwiched into it was a desperate deed, I feel, and I do not feel that it was an unquestionable success.° But which is the line you do not understand? I do myself think, I may say, that it would be an immense advance in notation (so to call it) in writing as the record of speech, to distinguish the subject, verb, object, and in general to express the construction to the eye; as is done already partly in punctuation by everybody, partly in capitals by the Germans, more fully in accentuation by the Hebrews. And I daresay it will come. But it would, I think, not do for me: it seems a confession of unintelligbility. And yet I don't know. At all events there is a difference. My meaning surely *ought* to appear of itself; but in a language like English, and in an age of it like the present, written words are really matter open and indifferent to the receiving of different and alternative verse-forms, some of which the reader cannot possibly be sure are meant unless they are marked for him. Besides metrical marks are for the performer and such marks are proper in every art. Though indeed one might say syntactical marks are for the performer too. But however that reminds me that one thing I am now resolved on, it is to prefix short prose *arguments* to some of my pieces. These too will expose me to carping, but I do not mind. Epic and drama and ballad and many, most, things should be at once intelligible; but everything need not and cannot be. Plainly if it is possible to express a sub[t]le and recondite thought on a subtle and recondite subject in a subtle and recondite way and with great felicity and perfection, in the end, something must be sacrificed, with so trying a task, in the process, and this may be the being at once, nay perhaps even the being without explanation at all, intelligible. Neither, in the same light, does it seem to be to me a real objection (though this one I hope not to lay myself open to) that the argument should be even longer than the piece; for the merit of the work may lie for one thing in its terseness. It is like a mate which may be given, one way only, in three moves; otherwise, various ways, in many.

There is some kind of instinct in these things. I wanted the coda for a sonnet which is in some sort 'nello stilo satirico o bernesco'.° It has a kind of rollic at all events. The coda is an immense resource to have. This sonnet, I hope, very shortly. . . .

Your affectionate friend Gerard M. Hopkins S.J.

No, I do not ask 'enthusiastic praise'. But is it not the case that the day when you could give enthusiastic praise to anything is passing or past? As for modern novels I will only say one thing now. It is in modern novels that wordpainting most abounds and now the fashion is to be so very subtle and advanced as to despise wordpainting and to say that old masters were not wordpainters. Just so. Wordpainting is, in the verbal arts, the great success of our day. Every age in art has its secret and its success, where even second rate men are masters. Second rate, third rate men are fine designers in Japan; second rate men were masters of painting in Raphael's time; second rate men were masters of sculpture in Phidias' time; second rate men of oratory in Cicero's; and so of many things. These successes are due to steady practice, to the continued action of a school: one man cannot compass them. And wordpainting is in our age a real mastery and the second rate men of this age often beat at it the first rate of past ages. And this I shall not be bullied out of.

For my case I shd. also remark that we turned up a difference of taste and judgment, if you remember, about Dryden. I can scarcely think of you not admiring Dryden without, I may say, exasperation. And my style tends always more towards Dryden. What is there in Dryden? Much, but above all this: he is the most masculine of our poets; his style and his rhythms lay the strongest stress of all our literature on the naked thew and sinew of the English language, the praise that with certain qualifications one would give in Greek to Demosthenes, to be the greatest master of bare Greek. I am driven to the backguard device of a palimpsest envelope.

To Richard Watson Dixon

University College, St. Stephen's Green, Dublin. Dec. 22 1887

My dear Friend,—

It is long since I wrote to you, and I wonder why I should stint myself in one of the best pleasures of life. Bridges has a little daughter,° I dare say you have heard; born on the 6th, I think. The weather, which has been wild but not dark or cold with us, has now turned to a sharp bright frost: I hope you do not find this, as you used to do at Carlisle, too searching. Tomorrow I am going down to my friends at Monasterevan° in Co. Kildare, the scene of many misadventures (not to me) and now of the poisoning of the hounds, which threatens to put an end altogether to hunting in all that neighbourhood and with it to Punchestown races—what would mean on the whole the withdrawal of a great deal of money from the country. But that is how we live now and with fervour cut off our nose to revenge ourselves on our face.

I enclose two sonnets,° works of infinite, of over great contrivance, I am afraid, to the annulling in the end of the right effect. They have also too much resemblance to each other; but they were conceived at the same time. They are of a 'robustious' sort and perhaps 'Tom's Garland' approaches bluster and will remind you of Mr. Podsnap with his back to the fire. They are meant for, and cannot properly be taken in without, emphatic recitation; which nevertheless is not an easy performance.

I have Blake's poems by me. Some of them much remind me of yours. The best are of an exquisite freshness and lyrical inspiration, but there is mingled with the good work a great deal of rubbish, want of sense, and some touches of ribaldry and wickedness.

I cannot find your last letter, in which I think you spoke of shewing me some new poems. I should greatly like to read them; but I could not do so, I am afraid, with the closeness which is needed for serviceable criticism. I ought to have written about this before.

I thought I might copy some more sonnets, but they seem not quite ready and time runs. I cannot get my Elegy° finished, but I hope in a few days to see the hero and heroine of it, which may enable me (or quite the reverse; perhaps that: it is not well to come too near things).

Believe me your affectionate friend Gerard M. Hopkins

Dec. 23 1887. The post is gone. I wish you a very happy Christmas and new year.

I am at work on a great choral fugue! I can hardly believe it.

To Kate Hopkins, sen.

Monasterevan [25 December 1887]

My dearest Mother,—

I wish you a very merry Christmas season and happy new year and thank you for your kind gift, which I found waiting for me. Thank the girls for their letters. I hope Grace duly got the music: she does not mention its arrival, but I think she should have had it before the date of her letter.

You will see that I am staying with my kind friend Miss Cassidy and her sister Mrs. Wheble, and three younger Whebles are also in the house, cousins.

I assisted the parish priest, who is recovering from a dangerous sickness, in giving communion this morning. Many hundreds came to the rail, with the unfailing devotion of the Irish; whose religion hangs suspended over their politics as the blue sky over the earth, both in our landscape but immeasurably remote and without contact or interference. This phenomenon happens to be particularly marked at Monasterevan.

With best love to all, I am your loving son Gerard.

Christmas Day 1887.

These three young Whebles° rejoice in the names of Tristram, Ursula, and Leo. They are half English, half Irish, and their nationality is thus divided: outwardly or in the body they are almost pure Paddy and Biddy, inwardly and in the mind mainly John Bull. The youngest boy Leo is a remarkably winning sweetmannered young fellow.

To Robert Bridges

University College, St. Stephen's Green, Dublin. Jan 12 1888

My dear Bridges,—

. . . At Monasterevan I tried to get some outstanding and accumulated sonnets ready for hanging on the line, that is in my book of MS, the one you wrote most of, and so for sending to you. All however are not ready yet, but they will soon be. I could send one tonight if time served, but if possible I should like to despatch this letter. It is now years that I have had no inspiration of longer jet than makes a sonnet, except only in that fortnight in Wales: it is what, far more than direct want of time, I find most against poetry and production in the life I lead. Unhappily I cannot produce anything at all, not only the luxuries like poetry, but the duties almost of my position, its natural outcome—like scientific works. I am now writing a quasi-philosophical paper on the Greek Negatives: but when shall I finish it? or if finished will it pass censors? or if it does will the *Classical Review* or any magazine take it? All impulse fails me: I can give myself no sufficient reason for going on. Nothing comes: I am a eunuch—but it is for the kingdom of heaven's sake.

Did you see Wooldridge in town? No doubt. And how is he getting on? painting, music, and all. I am sure he is right in the advice he gave me, to be very contrapuntal, to learn that well. I want to do so if I can; it is the only way. I have fooled at it too much. I have found a thing that, if I had my counterpoint well at my fingers' ends, wd. be most valuable: it is that the tunes I make are very apt to fall into fugues and canons, the second strain being easy counterpoint to the first or to its fugal answer. E.g. my Crocus, which you once expressed an admiration for, makes a canon with itself at the octave two bars off and, as far as I have found, at one bar off too. This is a splendid opening for choral treatment. And I have a fine fugue on hand to 'Orpheus with his lute';° but I shall not hurry with it, but keep the counterpoint correct. There seems to be, I may remark, no book that bridges the gap between double counterpoint and fugue. For instance, I have Ouseley° on both and Higgs° on Fugue and neither breathes a word on so simple a point as this, that the answer in Bach and Handel enters, that is that the counterpoint begins, freely on an unprepared discord. But this is contrary to the elements of counterpoint proper. What I ought to do, or somebody else rather to have done, is to tabulate Bach's practice and principles.

We are suffering from the region-fog, as it seems to be. I have been a little ill and am still a little pulled down; however I am in good spirits. Term has begun.

There, I have copied one—*Tom's Garland*. It has many resemblances to *Harry Ploughman*, a fault in me the sonnetteer, but not a fault that can be traced home to either of the sonnets. They were conceived at the same time: that is how it is. But I have too much tendency to do it, I find. 'There is authority for it'—not the lady of the strachey,° but Aeschylus: he is always forgetting he said a thing before. Indeed he never did, but tried to say it two or three times—something rich and profound but not by him distinctly apprehended; so he goes at it again and again like a canary trying to learn the Bluebells of Scotland. To bed, to bed: my eyes are almost bleeding.

With best wishes to Mrs. Bridges,

I am your affectionate friend Gerard M. Hopkins

By saying you are going to register your little daughter as an Elizabeth I take you to signify that you reserve her for Mr. Beeching to christen at Yattendon.°

Jan. 13 1888. What, by the bye, is that new departure in yr. poetry which 'it was high time' you made?—Talking of this, Hall Caine, that poor Deiphobus of yours, said in some review lately that whether a good book shall be a hit and live, or no, appears to him, from literary history, to be as purely a matter of chance as anything he knows of. And if, as I suppose, he is speaking with consideration, what he says sounds to me sense and I daresay he is right.

To Robert Bridges

University College, St. Stephen's Green, Dublin. Feb. 10 1888

Dearest Bridges,—

Know that the copy of your Paper° never came, so that I have none at all, and you said I might have several: I am content with one and please send one; if two, I can do better still.

I laughed outright and often, but very sardonically, to think you and the Canon could not construe my last sonnet;° that he had to write to you for a crib. It is plain I must go no farther on this road: if you and he cannot understand me who will? Yet, declaimed, the strange constructions would be dramatic and effective. Must I interpret it? It means then that, as St. Paul and Plato and Hobbes and everybody says, the commonwealth or well ordered human society is like one man; a body with many members and each its function; some higher, some lower, but all honourable, from the honour which belongs to the whole. The head is the sovereign, who has no superior but God and from heaven receives his or her authority: we must then imagine this head as bare (see St. Paul much on this) and covered, so to say, only with the sun and stars, of which the crown is a symbol, which is an ornament but not a covering; it has an enormous hat or skull cap, the vault of heaven. The foot is the daylabourer, and this is armed with hobnail boots, because it has to wear and be worn by the ground; which again is symbolical; for it is navvies or daylabourers who, on the great scale or in gangs and millions, mainly trench, tunnel, blast, and in others ways disfigure, 'mammock' the earth and, on a small scale, singly, and superficially stamp it with their footprints. And the 'garlands' of nails they wear are therefore the visible badge of the place they fill, the lowest in the commonwealth. But this place still shares the common honour, and if it wants one advantage, glory or public fame, makes up for it by another, ease of mind, absence of care; and these things are symbolized by the gold and the iron garlands. (O, once explained, how clear it all is!) Therefore the scene of the poem is laid at evening, when they are giving over work and one after another pile their picks, with which they earn their living, and swing off home, knocking sparks out of mother earth not now by labour and of choice but by the mere footing, being strong-shod and making no hardship of hardness, taking all easy. And so to supper and bed. Here comes a violent but effective hyperbaton or suspension, in which the action of the mind mimics that of the labourer—surveys his lot, low but free from care; then by a sudden strong act throws it over the shoulder or tosses it away as a light matter. The witnessing of which lightheartedness makes me indignant with the fools of Radical Levellers. But presently I remember that this is all very well for those who are in, however low in, the Commonwealth and share in any way the Common weal; but that the curse of our times is that many do not share it, that they are outcasts from it and have neither security nor splendour; that they share care with the high and obscurity with the low, but wealth or comfort with neither. And this state of things, I say, is the origin of Loafers, Tramps, Cornerboys, Roughs, Socialists and other pests of society. And I think it is a very pregnant sonnet and in point of execution very highly wrought. Too much so, I am afraid.

I have more, not so hard and done before, but I am not prepared . . . [the rest is missing.]

On referring° to yr. letter I see you speak of modern music, not music of this century. It is, I suppose, as you say. I hope your rheumatism is abated, is gone: why not gone? But I have a poor, very charming friend on his back with spinal disease: when he complains of rheumatic pains his doctor rubs his hands with joy and says nothing cd. be better.

To Coventry Patmore

Milltown Park, Milltown, Dublin | May 6 1888

My dear Mr. Patmore,—

I have greatly to beg your pardon for leaving you so long unanswered. This however is the second letter begun, and the other ran some length, but is cancelled.

Your news was that you had burnt the book called *Sponsa Dei*, and that on reflexion upon remarks of mine. I wish I had been more guarded in making them. When we take a step like this we are forced to condemn ourselves: either our work shd. never have been done or never undone, and either way our time and toil are wasted—a sad thought; though the intention may at both times have been good. My objections were not final, they were but considerations (I forget now, with one exception, what they were); even if they were valid, still if you had kept to yr. custom of consulting your director, as you said you should, the book might have appeared with no change or with slight ones. But now regret is useless.

Since I last wrote I have reread Keats a little and the force of your criticism on him has struck me more than it did. It is impossible not to feel with weariness how his verse is at every turn abandoning itself to an unmanly and enervating luxury. It appears too that he said something like 'O for a life of impressions instead of thoughts!'° It was, I suppose, the life he tried to lead. The impressions are not likely to have been all innocent and they soon ceased in death. His contemporaries, as Wordsworth, Byron, Shelley, and even Leigh Hunt, right or wrong, still concerned themselves with great causes, as liberty and religion; but he lived in mythology and fairyland the life of a dreamer. Nevertheless I feel and see in him the beginnings of something opposite to this, of an interest in higher things and of powerful and active thought. On this point you shd. if possible read what Matthew Arnold wrote.° His mind had, as it seems to me, the distinctively masculine powers in abundance, his character the manly virtues, but while he gave himself up to dreaming and self indulgence of course they were in abeyance. Nor do I mean that he wd. have turned to a life of virtue—only God can know that—, but that his genius wd. have taken to an austerer utterance in art. Reason, thought, what he did not want to live by, would have asserted itself presently and perhaps have been as much more powerful than that of his contemporaries as his sensibility or impressionableness, by which he did want to live, was keener and richer than theirs. His defects were due to youth—the self indulgence of his youth; its ill-education; and also, as it seems to me, to its breadth and pregnancy, which, by virtue of a fine judgment already able to restrain but unable to direct, kept him from flinging himself blindly on the specious Liberal stuff that crazed Shelley and indeed, in their youth, Wordsworth and Coleridge. His mind played over life as a whole, so far as he a boy, without (seemingly) a dramatic but still with a deeply observant turn and also without any noble motive, felt at first hand, impelling him to look below its surface, cd. at that time see it. He was, in my opinion, made to be a thinker, a critic, as much as a singer or artist of words. This can be seen in certain reflective passages, as the opening to *Endymion* and others in his poems. These passages are the thoughts of a mind very ill instructed and in opposition; keenly sensible of wrongness in things established but unprovided with the principles to correct that by. Both his principles of art and his practice were in many things vicious, but he was correcting them, even eagerly; for *Lamia* one of his last works shews a deliberate change in manner from the style of *Endymion* and in fact goes too far in change and sacrifices things that had better have been kept. Of construction he knew nothing to the last: in this same *Lamia* he has a long introduction about Mercury, who is only brought in to disenchant Lamia and ought not to have been employed or else ought to be employed again. The story has a moral element or interest; Keats was aware of this and touches on it at times, but could make nothing of it; in fact the situation at the end is that the sage Apollonius does more harm than the witch herself had done—kills the hero; and Keats does not see that this implies one of two things, either some lesson of the terrible malice of evil which when it is checked drags down innocence in its own ruin or else the exposure of Pharisaic pretence in the wouldbe moralist. But then if I could have said this to Keats I feel sure he wd. have seen it. In due time he wd. have seen these things himself. Even when he is misconstructing one can remark certain instinctive turns of construction in his style, shewing his latent power—for instance the way the vision is introduced in *Isabella*. Far too much now of Keats.

You sent me also a paper of yours in the *St. James's*.° But I did not like the text of it, from Newman,°and so I could not like the discourse founded on that. This was a paradox, that man is not a rational or reasoning animal. The use of a paradox is to awake the hearer's attention; then, when it has served that end, if, as mostly happens, it is not only unexpected but properly speaking untrue, it can be, expressly or silently, waived or dropped. But this you do not do with the paradox in question; you appear to take it in earnest. I always felt that Newman made too much of that text; it is still worse that you should build upon it. In what sense is man contemplative, or active, and not rational? In what sense may man be said not to be rational and it might not as truly be said he was not active or was not contemplative? He does not always reason; neither does he always contemplate or always act—of course human action, not merely so through animal or vegetable functions. Everyone sometimes reasons; for everyone, arrived at the age of reason, sometimes asks Why and sometimes says Because or Although. Now whenever we use one of these three words we reason. Longer trains of reasoning are rarer, because common life does not present the need or opportunity for them; but as soon as the matter requires them they are forthcoming. Nor are blunders in reasoning any proof that man is not a rational or reasoning being, rather the contrary: we are rational and reasoners by our false reasoning as we are moral agents by our sins.—I cannot follow you in your passion for paradox: more than a little of it tortures.

Now, since writing the above, I have read the paper again, but indeed I cannot like it at all. The comment makes the text worse: for you say contemplation is in this age very rare indeed: is then reasoning in this age very rare indeed or none? Other paradoxes follow; as that 'persons like General Gordon or Sir Thomas More would stare if you called anything they did or suffered by the name of sacrifice'. Did they then make no sacrifices? And if their modesty shrank from that word (I do not feel sure that it would) is the word not true? And do we not speak of Christ's sacrifice? and they were following him.

Also the 'truly sensible man never opines', though 'many things may be dubious to him'. But the definition of opinion is belief accompanied by doubt, by fear of the opposite being true; for, since many things are likely only but not certain, he who feels them to be most likely true knows also that they may possibly be untrue, and that is to opine them—though in English the word *opine* is little used except jocularly. Here no doubt you did not want to speak with philosophic precision (and in the same way say that 'to see rightly is the first of human qualities': I suppose it is the rightness or clearness or clearsightedness of the seeing that is the quality, for surely seeing is an act); but then the matter is philosophical, the title is so, the reference is to a philosophical work, and therefore philosophical precision would be in place and I in reading crave for it. But you know best what comes home to the readers you are aiming at. Yet after all there is nothing like the plain truth: paradox persisted in is not the plain truth and ought not to satisfy a reader. The conclusion, about the unpardonable sin, is on dangerous ground: but I do not understand it and few readers, I think, will. You see, dear Mr. Patmore, that I am altogether discontented with this paper and can do nothing but find fault.

I saw somewhere (I do not think you told me) that the Second Part of the *Angel*° is to appear or has appeared in the same cheap form as the First and I am glad. Also having been asked to write a paper for a review I said I would write on your poems, but I am not sure I shall be able to carry this out, for work presses and I am in a languishing state of body.

And now, with kind regards to all your circle, I am, my dear Mr. Patmore, yours very sincerely Gerard M. Hopkins.

May 7 1888. Yesterday was the anniversary of the Phoenix Park murders. The present also is a crisis, owing to the Pope's late action.° I have not time now to speak of matters political, but they must engross the mind of people living where I do and would do so even if I were in England. . . .

To Kate Hopkins, sen.

University College, St. Stephen's Green, Dublin. | July 5 1888

My dearest Mother,—

I am now working at examination-papers all day and this work began last month and will outlast this one. It is great, very great drudgery. I can not of course say it is wholly useless, but I believe that most of it is and that I bear a burden which crushes me and does little to help any good end. It is impossible to say what a mess Ireland is and how everything enters into that mess. The Royal University is in the main, like the London University, an examining board. It does the work of examining well; but the work is not worth much. This is the first end I labour for and see little good in. Next my salary helps to support this college. The college is very moderately successful, rather a failure than a success, and there is less prospect of success now than before. Here too, unless things are to change, I labour for what is worth little. And in doing this almost fruitless work I use up all opportunity of doing any other.

About my holiday I have no plan and know nothing.

We no longer take the *Times* now, so whenever you like to post a number it will be welcome.

The weather has been wet and cold, so that yesterday, after leaving off winter clothing for less than a week, I returned to it again.

I spent a few days lately at Judge O'Hagan's at Howth—the kindest people; and their house is beautifully but somewhat bleakly situated, overlooking the Bay of Dublin southwards.

I owe my father a letter, but it is no time to write now.

I am your loving son Gerard.

To Robert Bridges

Monzie Villa, Fort William, North Britain. Aug. 18 1888

Dearest Bridges,—

I am much in your debt for a letter, but at this time of the year you must not be surprised at that. Six weeks of examination are lately over and I am now bringing a fortnight's holiday to an end. I have leave to prolong it, but it is not very convenient to do so and I scarcely care. It appears I want not scenery but friends. My companion° is not quite himself or he verges towards his duller self and so no doubt do I too, and we have met few people to be pleasant with. We are in Lochaber (and are happily pestered with no sentiment) and have been to the top of Ben Nevis and up Glencoe on the most brilliant days, but in spite of the exertions or because of them I cannot sleep (which is the very mischief) and we have got no bathing (it is close at hand but close also to the highroad) nor boating and I am feeling very old and looking very wrinkled and altogether. . . . Besides we have no books except the farce of the fellow reading Minchin's *Kinematics*:° he is doing so now and dozing and shd. be in bed; this book I leave to him entirely, you may suppose, and have bought Dana's° *Two Years Before the Mast*, a thoroughly good one and all true, but bristling with technicality—seamanship—which I most carefully go over and even enjoy but cannot understand: there are other things though, as a flogging, which is terrible and instructive *and it happened*—ah, that is the charm and the main point. With the other half of the same shilling I bought *The Old Curiosity Shop*; never read it before, am not going to give in to any nonsense about Little Nell (like, I believe, Lang I cannot stand Dickens's pathos; or rather I can stand it, keep a thoroughly dry eye and unwavering waistcoat), but admire Dick Swiveller and Kit and Quilp and that old couple with the pony.

But business first. Your last little letter to me I never read. I never got it. I think perhaps Mrs. Bambury did and hope there was nothing in it which shd. call a blush onto her cheek as, I will say, there was nothing in Mrs. Bridges's beautifully written note of acceptance to Mrs. Bambury to cause a pang to me except of course that it was not what the envelope purported. This note I enclose.

I greatly admired the hand in which you wrote from Seaford and hope you will continue to employ it.

I will now go to bed, the more so as I am going to preach tomorrow and put plainly to a Highland congregation of MacDonalds, MacIntoshes, MacKillops, and the rest what I am putting not at all so plainly to the rest of the world, or rather to you and Canon Dixon, in a sonnet in sprung rhythm with two codas.°

Aug. 19. That is done—I am unfortunate in the time of my letters reaching you. The last contained mockery at the Rondeliers, of whom Lang is ringleader, is he not? and you read it seated next him on your trap in the extreme confidence of a country drive; so that, too probably, you let him know what I said and he will never forgive me. You should be very discreet about such matters.

Canon Dixon sent me his *Eudocia*. I admired it, but found it not particularly interesting as a story. It was all over genius not remarkably well employed. I did not agree with some metrical peculiarities.

I think you were not quite correct in your paraphrase of the passage in Galatians. I will say what I think it means, but perhaps not in this letter.

I was asked to my friends at Howth to meet Aubrey de Vere.° However he was called away to London and when I came was gone. I was disappointed, till it was mentioned that he did not think Dryden a poet. Then, I thought and perhaps said, I have not missed much. And yet you share this opinion or something like it with him. Such are the loutish falls and hideous vagaries of the human mind.

Of Handel, by the bye. If it was only recitative of his you did not like and 'wavered in your allegiance' never mind. The recitative which arose in the Renaissance at Florence, artificially and by a sort of pedantry, was to begin with bad, and Handel's employment of it always appeared to me to be his poorest part: the thing is so spiritless and mean, with vulgar falls and floundering to and from the dominant and leading note. The only good and truly beautiful recitative is that of plain chant; which indeed culminates in that. It is a natural development of the speaking, reading, or declaiming voice, and has the richness of nature; the other is a confinement of the voice to certain prominent intervals and has the poverty of an artifice. But Handel is Handel. I was at the Glasgow Exhibition (a very fine one) and heard a piece of an organ-recital ending with a chorus by Handel: it was as if a mighty besom swept away so much dust and chaff. . .

I agree about cricket and Darwinism and that 'everything is Darwinism'. But especially a ship. However the honeycomb is not quite so plain a matter as you think. The learned, I believe, are divided on the question whether the shape of the cells is really to be called a matter of mechanics. For observe: the cell can only be symmetrical, with a true hexagonal section and so on, by the bees being stationed at equal distances, working equally, and so on; in fact there is a considerable table of *caetera paria* [the other things that are equal]. But this implies something more than mechanical to begin with. Otherwise the hexagonal etc cell wd. be the type *tended to* only and seldom or never arrived at; the comb wd. be like the irregular figures of bubbles in the froth of beer or in soapsuds. Wild bees do, I believe, build something like that. But grant in the honey bee some principle of symmetry and uniformity and you have passed beyond mechanical necessity; and it is not clear that there may not be some special instinct determined to that shape of cell after all and which has at the present stage of the bee's condition, nothing to do with mechanics, but is like the specific songs of cuckoo and thrush. Now to bed or rather to pack. I will therefore conclude, though there must have been more to say. With kindest remembrances to Mrs. Bridges and Mrs. Molesworth, believe me your affectionate friend Gerard M. Hopkins.

To Robert Bridges

University College, Stephen's Green, Dublin. Sept. 7 1888

Dearest Bridges,—

I believe I wrote to you last from Fort William. I went thence to Whitby, to be with my brothers, and returned here after being 3 weeks away. Since, I have been trying to set a discursive MA. Examination Paper, in a distress of mind difficult both to understand and to explain. It seems to me I can not always last like this: in mind or body or both I shall give way—and all I really need is a certain degree of relief and change; but I do not think that what I need I shall get in time to save me. This reminds me of a shocking thing that has just happened to a young man well known to some of our community. He put his eyes out. He was a medical student and probably understood how to proceed, which was nevertheless barbarously done with a stick and some wire. The eyes were found among nettles in a field. After the deed he made his way to a cottage and said 'I am blind: please let me rest for an hour'. He was taken to hospital and lay in some danger—from shock, I suppose, or inflammation—, but is recovering. He will not say what was the reason, and this and other circumstances wear the look of sanity; but it is said he was lately subject to delusions. I mention the case because it is extraordinary: suicide is common.

It is not good to be a medical man in the making. It is a fire in which clay splits. There was a young man in this house in my first year, an Englishman, manly and winning too, the sweetest mannered boy. After he left us he went astray. I tried to call on him, but after many trials, finding he shunned me, I gave up trying. I hear he has made a mess of it and is going to make a new beginning in Australia.

There are as many doctors as patients at Dublin, a'most.

Feeling the need of something I spent the afternoon in the Phoenix Park, which is large[2], beautiful[1], and lonely. It did me good, but my eyes are very, very sore. Also there goes ten. Goodnight. Sept. 8 (it is now 20 years to a day since I began my noviceship). Well and I had a great light. I had in my mind the first verse of a patriotic song° for soldiers, the words I mean: heaven knows it is needed. I hope to make some 5 verses, but 3 would do for singing: perhaps you will contribute a verse. In the Park I hit on a tune, very flowing and spirited. I enclose the present form of this, just the tune, for I cannot set a bass till I have an instrument. I believe however that you can make nothing of a bare tune; at which I am surprised.—I find I have made 4 verses, rough at present, but I send them: do you like them and could you add one? I hope you may approve what I have done, for it is worth doing and yet it is a task of great delicacy and hazard to write a patriotic song that shall breathe true feeling without spoon or brag. How I hate both! and yet feel myself half blundering or sinking into them in several of my pieces, a thought that makes me not greatly regret their likelihood of perishing.

By the bye you misquote the same modern author in writing 'airy between towers': what is not so? it should be 'branchy between towers'.°

I enclose by the same hand a sonnet of some standing which Canon Dixon has had and you have not. I have also several more, done at long intervals. Also another.°

You asked if you might use a thought of mine about the work (it was said of a canon in music) finding the man and not the man the work: by all means; you will execute it in chryselephantine.

Can there be gout or rheumatism in the eyes? If there can I have it. I am a gouty piece now.

Gouty rhymes to Doughty. Since you speak so highly of his book I must try to see it: to read 1200 pages° I do not promise. But I have read several reviews° of it, with extracts. You say it is free from the taint of Victorian English. H'm. Is it free from the taint of Elizabethan English? Does it not stink of that? for the sweetest flesh turns to corruption. Is not Elizabethan English a corpse these centuries? No one admires, regrets, despairs over the death of the style, the living masculine native rhetoric of that age, more than I do; but ''tis gone, 'tis gone, 'tis gone'. He writes in it, I understand, because it is manly. At any rate affectation is not manly, and to write in an obsolete style is affectation. As for the extracts I saw they were not good even as that—wrong as English, for instance calling a *man* a jade; and crammed with Latin words, a fault, let do it who will.

But it is true this Victorian English is a bad business. They say 'It goes without saying' (and I wish it did) and instead of 'There is no such thing' they say a thing 'is non-existent' and *in* for *at* and *altruistic* and a lot more.

Here is the tune:°

This is not final of course. Perhaps the name of England is too exclusive. I am

Your affectionate friend Gerard M. Hopkins

Where is the letter than went to Mrs. Bambury?°

By the bye, Doughty wd. not after all be grateful to you; for this is what you say: 'Monica . . . suspects that I must be drivelling and *reminds me to tell you of* a very remarkable book' etc

To Robert Bridges

University College, St. Stephen's Green, Dublin. Sept. 25 1888

Dearest Bridges,—

I am sorry to hear of our differing so much in taste: I was hardly aware of it. (It is not nearly so sad as differing in religion). I feel how great the loss is of not reading, as you say; but if I did read I do not much think the effect of it would be what you seem to expect, on either my compositions or my judgments.

I *must* read something of Greek and Latin letters and lately I sent you a sonnet, on the Heraclitean Fire,° in which a great deal of early Greek philosophical thought was distilled; but the liquor of the distillation did not taste very Greek, did it? The effect of studying masterpieces is to make me admire and do otherwise. So it must be on every original artist to some degree, on me to a marked degree. Perhaps then more reading would only *refine my singularity*, which is not what you want.

(While I remember it, in the other sonnet° that went with

that was a false rhyme you overlooked—*thronged* instead of *swarmed*: please make the correction.)

But not on my criticisms either, I suspect. Wide reading does two things—it extends knowledge and it adjusts the judgment. Now it is mostly found that a learned judgment is less singular than an unlearned one and oftener agrees with the common and popular judgment, with which it coincides as a fine balance or other measure does with the rule of thumb. But, so far as I see, where we differ in judgment, my jugdments are less singular than yours; I agree more than you do with the mob and with the *communis criticorum*. Presumably I shd. agree with these still more if I read more and so differ still more from you than now. Who for instance is singular about Dryden, you or I? These considerations are very general, but so far as they go they appear to be reasonable.

To return to composition for a moment: what I want there, to be more intelligble, smoother, and less singular, is an audience. I think the fragments I wrote of *St. Winefred*, which was meant to be played, were not hard to understand. My prose I am sure is clear and even flowing. This reminds me that I have written a paper for an Irish magazine the *Lyceum*, organ of this College, one may say. I was asked and I rewrote something I had by me and it is to appear next month.° And yet I bet you it will not: my luck will not allow it. But if it does, I then bet you it is intelligible, though on an obstruse subject, Statistics and Free Will—and I mean very intelligible. (This, by the bye, is a badly made logical bed; for I can only win one wager by losing the other. But never mind.)

I send an improved version of my war-song,° less open to the objections made, and am your affectionate friend

Gerard Hopkins.

To Robert Bridges

Univ. Coll., Stephen's Green, Dublin. Oct. 3 1888.

Dearest Bridges,—

In spite of matter in your last for which presently, when time allows (for I shall tomorrow being examining), you will, I assure you, 'be handled without gloves' I ask your opinion of a sonnet° written to order on the occasion of the first feast since his canonisation proper of St Alphonsus Rodriguez, a laybrother of our Order, who for 40 years acted as hall-porter to the College of Palma in Majorca: he was, it is believed, much favoured by God with heavenly lights and much persecuted by evil spirits. The sonnet (I say it snorting) aims at being intelligible.

Honour should flash from exploit, so we say;
Strokes once that gashed the flesh, that galled the shield,
Should tongue that time now, trumpet now that field

And, on the fighter, forge his glorious day.
On Christ they do; on martyr well they may:
But, be that war within, the sword we wield
Unseen, the heroic breast not outward-steeled,
Earth hears no hurtle then from fiercest fray.
Yet God the mountain-mason, continent—
Quarrier, earthwright; who, with trickling increment,
Veins violets and tall trees makes more and more,
Could crowd career with conquest while there went
Those years on years by of world without event
That in Majorca Alfonso watched the door.

Or, against singularity, we may try this:

Yet God that mountain, and that continent,
Earth, all, builds; or, with trickling increment,
Veins violets, etc.

No, this:

Yet God that hews mountain and continent,
Earth, all; that else, with trickling increment
Veins violets etc.

And I am your affectionate friend Gerard M. Hopkins

And please do not put it aside 'for further neglect' but answer smart. It has to go to Majorca.

Call in the Canon, have a consultation, sit, and send result by return—or soon.

Tell him I lately passed Warkworth on my way from Glasgow to Whitby, but there was no stopping. I looked out at the station.

To Robert Bridges

Univ. Coll., Stephen's Green, Dublin. Oct. 19 '88

Dearest Bridges,—

You remark, I am glad to find, a 'lambness' in my last letter: now in the present I shall have somewhat as schoolboys say, to 'lamb in'. But first of various matters.

My little Paper on *Statistics and Free Will* obeyed the general law and did not appear; so I win that wager, if you remember. The editor made some objections which involved recasting it: I have partly done so, and when it is all recast he will no doubt find others. But meantime I get into print in a way I would not. My father wrote a little book on Numbers, the numbers one to ten, a sketchy thing, raising points of interest in a vast, an infinite subject: the *Saturday* lately had a paper on this book, making great game of it from end to end (of it and the article), including something I had contributed to it; however I was not named. . . .

Next, music. I am glad to find it is only there we are so far apart. But the contrary is true: there we agree well enough and the rift is elsewhere. I agree to your musical strictures and almost invite your rebukes and if I do not do so heartily it is because a perfect organisation for crippling me exists and the one for 'encouragemental purposes' (modern English) is not laid down yet. I agree that for contrapuntal writing we shd. read the great masters and study the rules, both. The great masters unhappily I cannot read (unless very little), but the rules I do carefully study, and just on account of the great formality of the art of music it happens that mere adherence to them, without study of examples from the masters, produces—given faculty—results of some interest and value. (I like not that last sentence: it is too much in the manner of the magazines I read and too far entirely from Doughty and the Mighty Dead.) And my madrigal in canon, so far as it has gone, is strict and Sir Robert Stewart (a demon for rule) says it is correct and that it might even have been freer. But, as you say, you have not seen it and now that I have no piano I cannot go on with it. This morning I gave in what I believe is the last batch of examination-work for this autumn (and if all were seen, fallen leaves of my poor life between all the leaves of it), and but for that want I might prance on ivory this very afternoon. I have had to get glasses, by the bye: just now I cannot be happy either with or without them. The oculist says my sight is very good and my eye perfectly healthy but that like Jane Nightwork I am old. And, strange to say, I have taken to drawing again. Perverse Fortune or something perverse (try me): why did I not take to it before? And now enough, for I must whet myself, strop myself, be very bitter, and will secrete and distil a good deal beforehand.

However with no more stropping than the palm of my hand and chopping at a hair, no but at the 'broth of goldish flue'° (how well now does the pleasing modern author come in in his own illustration and support!), I can deal with one matter, the sonnet on St. Alphonsus. I am obliged for your criticisms, 'contents of which noted', indeed acted on. I have improved the sestet (in itself I do not call the first version 'cheeky', the imagery as applied to God Almighty being so familiar in the Scripture and the Fathers: however I have not kept it). But now I cannot quite understand nor so far as I understand agree with the difficulty you raise about the continents and so on. It is true continents are partly made by 'trickling increment'; but what is on the whole truest and most strikes us about them and mountains is that they are made what now we see them by trickling *de*crements, by detrition, weathering, and the like.* And at any rate whatever is markedly featured in stone or what is like stone is most naturally said to be hewn, and to *shape*, itself, means in old English to hew and Hebrew *bara* / to create, even, properly means to hew. But life and living things are not naturally said to be hewn: they grow, and their growth is by trickling increment.

I will not now interpret the thought of the sestet. It is however, so far as I can see, both exact[2] and pregnant[1].

I am altogether at a loss to see your objection to *exploit* and to *so we say*. You will allow—would, I shd. think urge on

* By the bye, some geologists say the last end of all continents and dry land altogether is to be washed into the sea and that when all are gone 'water will be the world', as in the Flood, and will still be deep and have to spare.

me—that where the ὄνομα κύριον° [the correct name for a thing] has nothing flat or poor about it it is the best word to use in poetry as in prose, better I mean than its paraphrase. Now *exploit* is the right word, it is κύριον, there is no other for the thing meant but *achievement*, which is not better, and it is a handsome word in itself: why then should I not say it? Surely I should. By 'regular indoors work' I understand you to mean a drawing finished at home with the eye no longer on the object, something poorly thrown in to fill up a blank the right filling of which is forgotten. But 'so we say' is just what I have to say and want to say (it was made out of doors in the Phoenix Park with my mind's eye on the first presentment of the thought): I mean 'This is what we commonly say, but we are wrong'. The line now stands 'Glory is a flame off exploit, so we say' and I think it must so stand.

I am warming myself at the flame of a little exploit of my own done last night. I could not have believed in such a success nor that life had this pleasure to bestow. Somebody had tried to take me in and I warned him I wd. take him in at our next meeting. Accordingly I wrote him a letter from 'the son of a respected livery and bait stables in Parteen° oftentimes employed by your Honoured Father' asking for an introduction to one of the Dublin newspapers 'as Reporter, occasional paregraphs or sporting inteligence'. The sentence I think best of was one in which I said I (or he) could 'give any color which may be desired to reports of speeches or Proceedings subject to the Interests of truth which must always be the paremount consideration'. It succeeded beyond my wildest hopes and action is going to be taken. The letter is even to be printed in the *Nation* as a warning to those who are continually applying in the like strain; but before this takes place I must step in.

It is as you say about Addis.° But why should you be glad? Why at any rate should you burst upon me that you are glad, when you know that I cannot be glad?

It seems there is something in you interposed between what shall we say? the Christian and the man of the world which hurts, which is to me like biting on a cinder in bread. Take the simplest view of this matter: he has made shipwreck, I am afraid he must even be in straits: he cannot support himself by his learned writings; I suppose he will have to teach. But this is the least. I hope at all events he will not pretend to marry, and especially no one he has known in his priestly life. Marriage is honourable and so is the courtship that leads to marriage, but the philanderings of men vowed to God are not honourable nor the marriages they end in. I feel the same deep affection for him as ever, but the respect is gone. I would write to him if I had his address, which, I am sorry to say, is still or was lately somewhere at Sydenham; for after bidding farewell to his flock he had not the grace to go away.

This is enough for the time and I will put off the lambing to another season. With kindest remembrances to Mrs. Bridges and Mrs. Molesworth, I am your affectionate friend

Gerard M. Hopkins.

Oct. 20 '88.

To Robert Bridges

Univ. Coll., Stephen's Green, Dublin. April 29 1889.

Dearest Bridges,—

I am ill to-day, but no matter for that as my spirits are good. And I want you too to 'buck up', as we used to say at school, about those jokes° over which you write in so dudgeonous a spirit. I have it now down in my tablets that a man may joke and joke and be offensive; I have had several warnings lately leading me to make the entry, tho' goodness knows the joke that gave most offence was harmless enough and even kind. You I treated to the same sort of irony as I do myself; but it is true it makes all the world of difference whose hand administers. About Daniel° I see I was mistaken: if he pays you more than and sells you as much as other publishers (which however is saddening to think of: how many copies is it? five and twenty?) my objections do not apply. Then you ought to remember that I did try to make you known in Dublin and had some little success. (Dowden I will never forgive:° could you not kill Mrs. Bridges? then he might take an interest in you). Nay I had great success and placed you on the pinnacle of fame; for it is the pinnacle of fame to become educational and be set for translation into Gk. iambics, as you are at Trinity: this is to be a classic; 'this', as Lord Beaconsfield said to a friend who told him he found his young daughter reading *Lothair*, 'O this is fame indeed'. And Horace and Juvenal say the same thing. And here I stop, for fear of it ripening into some kind of joke.

I believe I enclose a new sonnet.° But we greatly differ in feeling about copying one's verses out: I find it repulsive, and let them lie months and years in rough copy untransferred to my book. Still I hope soon to send you my accumulation. This one is addressed to you.

Swinburne has a new volume out,°which is reviewed in its own style: 'The rush and the rampage, the pause and the pullup of these lustrous and lumpophorous lines'. It is all now a 'self-drawing web'; a perpetual functioning of genius without truth, feeling, or any adequate matter to be at function on. There is some heavydom, in long waterlogged lines (he has no real understanding of rhythm, and though he sometimes hits brilliantly at other times he misses badly) about the *Armada*, that pitfall of the patriotic muse; and *rot* about babies, a blethery bathos into which Hugo and he from opposite coasts have long driven Channel-tunnels. I am afraid I am going too far with the poor fellow. Enough now, but his babies make a Herodian of me.

My song° will be a very highly wrought work and I do hope a fine one. Do you think canon wd. spoil the tune? I hope not, but the contrary. But if the worst came to the worst, I could, since a solo voice holds its own against instruments, give the canon-following to a violin. I shall hear what Sir Robert Stewart says about it. This is how it now stands. I tried at first to make the air such that it shd. be rigidly the same in every note and rhythm (always excepting the alterations to save the tritone) in all its shifts; but I found that impracticable and that I had reached the point where art calls for loosing, not for lacing. I now make the canon strict in each verse, but allow a change, which indeed is besides called for by the change of words, from verse to verse. Indeed the air becomes a generic form which is specified newly in each verse, with excellent effect. It is like a new art this. I allow no modulation: the result is that the tune is shifted into modes, viz. those of

La, Mi, and Sol (this is the only way I can speak of them, and they have a character of their own which is neither that of modern major and minor music nor yet of the plain chant modes, so far as I can make out). The first shift is into the mode of La: this shd. be minor, but the effect is not exactly that; rather the feeling is that Do is still the keynote, but has shifted its place in the scale. This impression is helped by the harmony, for as the Third is not flattened the chords appear major. The chord at the beginning of every bar is the common chord or first inversion; the $\frac{6}{4}$ may appear in course of the bar and discords are in passing or prepared. Perhaps the harmony may be heavy, but I work according to the only rules I know. I can only get on slowly with it and must hope to be rewarded in the end. Now I must lie down.

Who is Miss Cassidy? She is an elderly lady who by often asking me down to Monasterevan and by the change and holiday her kind hospitality provides is become one of the props and struts of my existence. St. Ernin founded the monastery: a singular story is told of him. Henry VIII confiscated it and it became the property of Lord Drogheda. The usual curse on abbey lands attends it and it never passes down in the direct line. The present Lord and Lady Drogheda have no issue. Outside Moore Abbey, which is a beautiful park, the country is flat, bogs and river and canals. The river is the Barrow, which the old Irish poets call the dumb Barrow. I call it the burling Barrow Brown.° Both descriptions are true. The country has nevertheless a charm. The two beautiful young people live within an easy drive.

With kind love to Mrs. Bridges and Mrs. Molesworth, I am
your affectionate friend Gerard.

To Kate Hopkins, sen.

University College, Dublin. May 5. 1889

My dearest Mother,—

I am grieved that you should be in such anxiety about me and I am afraid my letter to my father, which you must now have seen and ought, it seems to me, to have had before this morning's letter was sent, can not much have relieved you. I am now in careful hands. The doctor thoroughly examined me yesterday. I have some fever; what, has not declared itself. I am to have perfect rest and to take only liquid food. My pains and sleeplessness were due to suspended digestion, which has now been almost cured, but with much distress. There is no hesitation or difficulty about the nurses, with which Dublin is provided, I dare say, better than any place, but Dr. Redmond this morning said he must wait further to see the need; for today there is no real difference; only that I feel better.

You do not mention how Mary° is.

I am and I long have been sad about Lionel, feeling that his visits must be few and far between and that I had so little good of this one, though he and I have so many interests in common and shd. find many more in company. I cd. not send him my Paper,° for it had to be put aside.

It is an ill wind that blows nobody good. My sickness falling at the most pressing time of the University work, there will be the devil to pay. Only there is no harm in saying, that gives *me* no trouble but an unlooked for relief. At many such a time I have been in a sort of extremity of mind, now I am the placidest soul in the world. And you will see, when I come round, I shall be the better for this.

I am writing uncomfortably and this is enough for a sick man. I am your loving son | Best love to all.

Gerard.

NOTES

1 *Dr. Müncke.* Müncke taught 'guttural French to many and good, sound German to a few' pupils at Highgate School 1857–64. GMH learned his French from another master, M. Prosper Puyo.

Elgin House. One of two boarders' houses of Highgate School, leased by the school. The other was Grove Bank. John Nesfield was in charge of Elgin in 1862.

Lewis. A mistake for George Henry Lewes, whose *Life and Works of Goethe* was published in two volumes in 1855.

2 *Oak Hill.* The Hopkins family home from 1852–86. See letter of 5 Nov. 1885.

Karslake. Lewis Karslake *1844–1912) attended Highgate from Sept. 1857 to Dec. 1860

3 *Dyne.* The Revd. John Bradley Dyne (1809–98). After being a fellow of Wadham College, Oxford, dean, and lecturer in Divinity, he became in 1838 headmaster of Highgate. Despite his tyrannical manner, the school grew steadily, and the peak of the academic success achieved while he was headmaster occurred during the time Hopkins was there (1854–63), when 20 of the 286 boys won scholarships or exhibitions to Oxford or Cambridge.

Nesfield. John C. Nesfield (1836–1919) was at Highgate 1852–5, when he left with the Governors' Gold Medal and a School Exhibition. After reading classics at Oxford, he returned to Highgate as an assistant master for five years before becoming Director of Public Instruction in Northern India, where he wrote several popular textbooks.

Bord's. Richard T. Bord was at Highgate from Sept. 1858 to Dec. 1862.

4 *Alexander Strachey.* Strachey (1845–1900) attended Highgate briefly Jan. 1861–Dec. 1862, when he went to Trinity College, Cambridge.

5 *The Lanes of Thurloe Square.* Richard J. Lane (1800–72) was a line-engraver and prolific lithographer who frequently had pictures in the Royal Academy. Two of his daughters were artistic; the eldest, Clara, exhibited water-colours of fruit and flowers annually at the Society of Female Artists from its inception in 1857 and at the Royal Academy. She was also an illustrator. GMH took one of her coloured sketches with him to Oxford.

6 *Sir Rogers.* Sir Roger Cholmeley's or Highgate School.

Sherborne. King's School, Sherborne.

ἀνήριθμον γέλασμα. Aeschylus, *Prometheus Bound*, 90.

specimen. See OAH, p. 6, from which it differs slightly.

7 '*the Vision of Sin*'. Published 1842. By Tennyson, who commented, 'This describes the soul of a youth who has given himself up to pleasure and

Epicureanism. He at length is worn out and wrapt in the mists of satiety. Afterwards he grows into a cynical old man . . . joining in the Feast of Death. Then we see the landscape which symbolizes God, Law and the future life.'

8 *Lord Dundreary.* A memorable character in Tom Taylor's play *Our American Cousin*, which was being performed at the time at the Theatre Royal, Haymarket.

St. Simeon Stylites. By Tennyson (published 1842). Hopkins did later draw the picture. See LIII, p. 210.

Il Mystico. See OAH, p. 7.

write back whether you approve. See OAH pp. 7–10.

Contemplation. 'A windy day in summer' and 'A fragment of anything you like' (OAH p. 11) follow.

Corinthian capital . . . old style. These are not extant.

9 *Tennyson's Eagle.* 'The Eagle' (published 1851), ll. 2–3: 'Close to the sun in lonely lands, | Ringed with the azure world, he stands'.

congratulations. On his Balliol exhibition.

Mr Frodsham. Probably a watchmaker. Coleridge had mixed up his correspondence so that Mr Frodsham received the note for GMH, and GMH the receipt for Mr Frodsham acknowledging the return of a watch.

C.C.C. or Ch. Ch. Corpus Christi College or Christ Church.

Long. The summer vacation.

Patriarch. Dyne.

Palmer. The Revd. Edwin Palmer, who had been a scholar of Balliol, was a fellow there 1845–67. He became Corpus Professor of Latin. Elected a fellow of Corpus in 1873, he resigned in 1878 to become archdeacon of Oxford and a canon of Christ Church.

Once a Week . . . Stream. Issue of 14 Feb. 1863. This version differed from the final one of 1871. It is reproduced in LIII, pp. 437–8.

Clarke. See Biographical Register. He was going to join his uncle in Australia.

10 *Union.* The Oxford Union, where a debate was held each Thursday evening and where students could read newspapers and journals and write letters.

oak to sport. An outer door to his set of rooms which he could shut if he were out or did not want to be disturbed.

Southby. Arthur Southby (1844–1925) had been a schoolfellow of GMH's at Highgate School, which he attended Jan. 1858–Dec. 1862. He was a member of Wadham College.

Darent Harrison. William A. Darent Harrison had an exhibition at Corpus in 1861. He got a 2nd in Greats in 1864.

Cresswell. Oswald E. Creswell (1843–1908) was a scholar of Trinity in 1863, then again a member of Balliol till 1867, when he obtained a 2nd in Greats.

Nash. Thomas Nash (1845–85) was at Balliol 1863–7. He took a 2nd in Maths in 1866 and a 1st in Greats in 1867 and became a barrister. See letter of 24 Apr. 1885.

Secker. Augustus M. Secker (1844–92) took a 3rd in Greats in 1864 and a 4th in Law and History in 1866. He became vicar of Bozeat 1883–92.

11 *Oxford Rifle Corps*. During the 1860s and 1870s dozens of volunteer rifle corps were formed all over the country. Muirhead and Bridges had belonged to one at Eton, where over half the senior boys were enrolled.

Bethell. Hon. Walter J. Bethell (1842–1907) had been at Balliol since 1860. He became a barrister.

Geldart. See Biographical Register.

Barrett. Alfred Barratt (1844–81) took a 1st in Greats in 1865 and a 1st in Law and History in 1866. He became a fellow of Brasenose and secretary to the Oxford University Commission in 1880.

Ilbert. [Sir] Courtenay P. Ilbert (1841–1924) was a member of Balliol 1860–6. He won several scholarships and took a 1st in greats in 1864. He was a fellow of Balliol 1864–74 then became a lawyer and parliamentary draftsman, serving on the council of the Governor-General of India and as assistant counsel to the Treasury before becoming clerk of the House of Commons.

Aunt Katie's. See Biographical Register (Katherine Beechey).

Bagley Wood. Hopkins walked out to Bagley Wood a number of times while he was an undergraduate and noted in his Diaries and Journal subjects for sketches near it.

Grandmamma's. See Biographical Register (Ann Hopkins).

Owen. Revd. Donald M. Owen (1829–1904) had been a scholar at Balliol 1847–52 and became rector of Mark's Tey, of Ideford, and of Calverleigh, Devon.

12 *Browne*. Charles G. Browne (1845–1920) was a member of Balliol 1864–8, took a 3rd in Greats in 1867, and was ordained in 1871.

Strachan Davidson. James Leigh Strachan-Davidson (1843–1916) was an exhibitioner at Balliol in 1862 and obtained a 1st in Greats in 1866. He became a fellow of Balliol 1866–1907 and Master of the college 1907–16. He edited a number of classical texts and published *Problems of the Roman Criminal Law* (1912).

13 *Riddell*. The Revd. James Riddell (1822–66) was a scholar of Balliol in 1841, took a 1st in Greats in 1845, and was a fellow of the college for the rest of his life. See letter to Urquhart of 24 Sept. 1866.

Woolcomb. The Revd. Edward C. Woollcombe (1816–80) had been a member of Oriel 1833–7, when he was made a fellow of Balliol. He was a tutor 1840–69 and dean 1841–74.

Oily Smith. Henry J. Smith (1826–83) took a 1st in Maths in 1848 and was a fellow of Balliol 1850–74. He was a tutor in Maths and, from 1860, Savilian Professor of Geometry.

14 *the Revd. H. Wall.* Henry Wall (1810–75) was also Wykham Professor of Logic 1849–73.

Jebb. Arthur T. Jebb (1840–94) was at Balliol 1860–4, took a 3rd in Greats, and became a barrister.

Warman's. John Warman (1841–1918) had been at Highgate before becoming a member of Balliol in 1860. He became a fellow of Radley College and was then rector of Boxford 1884–1915.

Reiss. Frederick A. Reiss (1843–1935) took a 3rd in Law and History in 1866, was ordained in 1868, and became rector of Donnington in 1904.

Hannah, whose son is at this coll. The Ven. Archdeacon John Hannah was Warden of Glenalmond. His son was John Julius Hannah (1844–1931), who was at Balliol 1862–6. After serving as vicar and rector in Brighton, he became dean of Chichester 1902–29.

15 *Amcotts.* Vincent A. Cracroft-Amcotts (1845–81) took a 3rd in Law and History in 1866 and became a barrister. GMH described him to his mother as the 'Genteel Skeleton . . . He plays the piano brilliantly, and is the greatest *dilettante* in the college. He also writes very good poetry. For the rest, as the French say, he is said to have delivered his conscience in an envelope to the keeping of the Church, and raves against Handel' (LIII. p. 77).

Jenkyns. John Jenkyns (1843–1915) took a 2nd in Greats in 1866 and was ordained in 1871.

16 *Smalls.* Responsions, the first of the three main examinations.

17 *—forgot the clouded Forth.* Tennyson, 'The Daisy'. GMH later told Bridges that the metre of the poem had influenced his poem 'The Loss of the Eurydice' (LI, p. 48).

Pöpehenic. C. C. Abbott suggests this may refer to Pope's reputation as 'the wasp of Twickenham'.

Fragment from an unpublished. 'A Vision of the Mermaids' (OAH, pp. 11–15).

three pictures by Millais. The Wolf's Den, *My First Sermon*, and *The Eve of St Agnes* were hung.

Eddis. Eden U. Eddis was a portrait painter who occasionally painted landscapes or biblical subjects. Between 1834 and 1883 he exhibited over 100 pictures at the British Academy.

19 *Catholicism.* In the sense of High Anglican or Anglo-Catholic belief.

Alfred Erskine. Hardy; see Biographical Register.

20 *Mrs Cunliffe*. Baillie's cousin, to whom GMH was introduced by family friends and whom he called a 'charming person'.

21 *Miss Storys*. See GMH's poem 'Miss Story's character' (OAH, p. 15 and note).

Pilate. Incomplete (OAH, pp. 18–20).

Judas. Unknown to me.

Floris in Italy. OAH, pp. 36–9, 40.

A voice from the world. OAH, pp. 42–6.

three religious poems. Possibly 'Barnfloor and Winepress' (OAH, pp. 25–6), 'New Readings' (OAH, pp. 26–7), and 'He hath abolished the old drouth' (OAH, p. 27).

The Lover's Stars. OAH, pp. 23–4.

a soliloquy of one of the spies left in the wilderness. OAH, pp. 21–3.

Richard. OAH, pp. 21, 49–51.

nobility of the subject. 'Dantis Exsilium' (Dante's Exile). Richard Brooke Michell (Balliol) won the prize.

Mods. Moderations, the second of the major examinations.

22 *Miss . . . Rossetti*. Maria Francesca Rossetti (1827–76); see note to p. 202.

George Macdonald. Macdonald (1824–1905) was a minor novelist and writer of children's stories.

Peter Cun[n]ingham. Cunningham (1816–69) edited texts and was an author and critic. His father, Allan Cunningham (1784–1842), had written numerous popular ballads and *Lives of the Most Eminent British Painters, Sculptors and Architects* (1829–33).

'*Nothing . . . let fall*'. Pope's 'Epistle II To a Lady [Martha Blount]'.

> Nothing so true as what you once let fall:
> 'Most women have no characters at all.'

23 *Enoch Arden*. Published 1864.

Hexameron. An essay society founded by Liddon in 1864 which met six times a term 'to promote discussions upon subjects of interest so far as may be consistent with adherence to the doctrines of the Catholic Faith [i.e. High Anglicanism]'. 'On the Origin of Beauty: A Platonic Dialogue' may have been written for this although it would have been uncomfortably long to read aloud. See J, p. xxiii.

26 *In Memoriam*. st. cxxi begins 'Sad Hesper . . .'.

27 *Wordsworth*. 'Composed near Calais, on the Road Leading to Ardres, August 7, 1802'.

Stanley. Arthur P. Stanley (1815–81) was a scholar at Balliol. He wrote a *Life of Dr Arnold*, a book on *Sinai and Palestine*, where he travelled in

1852–3, and several ecclesiastical works. He became Oxford Professor of Ecclesiastical History, secretary of the Oxford University Commission, and dean of Westminster.

28 *The ethics of friendship*. Unsigned, vol. 10, pp. 299–310.

Floris in Italy. OAH, pp. 36–9.

Io. OAH, p. 34.

30 *The author of Romola*. George Eliot (1863).

Villari. Pasquale Villari. At this time GMH had probably read only the first volume; in Feb.–Mar. 1865 he noted vol. ii of the *History of Girolamo Savonarola and of his Times* (translated by Leonard Horner, 1863) among his list of books to read. It is possible that the facts GMH mentions about Villari and Rio were gathered from a review rather than from the books cited.

Rio's History of Christian Art. Alexis F. Rio, *De l'art chrétien* (new edn., 4 vols., 1861–7).

Colenso's trial. John W. Colenso (1814–83) was from a poor Cornish family, became second wrangler at Cambridge in 1836, a master at Harrow, and tutor of St John's College, Cambridge, and published several books on mathematics. He was also vicar of Forncett St Mary's, Norfolk, and became bishop of Natal in 1853, where he became concerned about the treatment of the natives by officials. He wrote a Zulu dictionary and grammar, translated several books of the Old Testament and the New Testament into Zulu. He then suggested that the Pentateuch was a forgery. For this, opposition to the doctrine of eternal punishment, and his toleration of the Zulus' custom of polygamy, he was convicted in 1864 of heresy. The Royal Courts were powerless to uphold the conviction but in 1869 the English bishops succeeded in deposing him. He stayed on in the see ministering to his supporters.

31 *Coles*. Vincent Stuckey Coles (1845–1929) had been a friend of Bridges's and Dolben's at Eton, where he was the nominal leader of the High Church group. He was secretary of Hexameron in 1867 and a close friend of Liddon's. He later became Principal of Pusey House, Oxford. 'Cole's humility deceived many into taking him at his own valuation; actually his spiritual power influenced not Oxford only but penetrated the whole Anglican Communion' (DNB).

Mr Geldart. Thomas Geldart was the father of GMH's friend, Edmund Geldart (1844–85). He moved from Reigate to take on the Manchester City Mission in 1856.

33 *Street the architect*. George E. Street (1824–81) was a devout High Anglican who had been apprenticed to Gilbert Scott and, like him, did much cathedral restoration, including Salisbury, Carlisle and York Minster. GMH knew a number of his churches (see J, pp. 256, 351, 397). The information about Lavington had probably been given to GMH at a dinner on 4 July held by Mr and Mrs William Holland,

one of whose daughters had been Street's second wife. GMH sought him from Sept. to the end of the year with a request from Bridges to design a communion flagon for the church at Thornton, where his brother-in-law, the Revd. William Glover, was rector (see letters of 22 and 24 Sept. 1866).

34 *almuces. OED*: early form of 'amices'.

35 *Rochdale.* The Anglican rectory at Rochdale became Bridges's home when his mother married the Revd Dr Molesworth in 1854.

36 *business.* See next letter.

37 *Mr Oakley.* Frederick Oakley (1802–80) had been a fellow of Balliol 1827–45, when he left the Tractarians and became a Roman Catholic. He was canon of the Westminster diocese from 1852. He wrote many theological treatises, including a critical review of Pusey's 'Eirenicon', which GMH noted in his diary in 1865/6 at a time when his enthusiasm for Catholicism was becoming evident in his conversation.

minimising Catholicism. Undogmatic Catholicism possibly compatible with High Anglicanism.

39 *Morris.* Described by GMH as 'Urquhart's Brittany friend', who had two sisters and lived at King's Kerswell, Devon (LIII, pp. 102–3). Urquhart seems to have acted as private tutor to him (see letter of 22 Sept. 1866).

Mr. Street. See letter of 10 July 1866.

40 *Fili hominis, putasne vivent ossa ista? Domine Deus, tu nosti.* Ezek. 37: 3 "Son of man, dost thou think these bones shall live?' [And I answered:] 'O Lord God, Thou knowest." The chapter describes God's resurrection of the house of Israel from dead bones and mentions the promise of Christ's kingdom.

John Walford. Walford (1839–94) had been a master at Eton but was converted to Catholicism in Mar. 1866 and, after a short time at the Oratory, became a Jesuit in 1867. He looked after GMH when he first entered the novitiate. See letter of 10 Sept. 1868.

42 *Mr. Street.* See letters of 10 July and 22 Sept. 1866.

45 *Challis had written a pamphlet.* H. W. Challis, *A Letter to John Stuart Mill . . . on the Necessity of Geometry and the Association of Ideas* (1867).

Magnificavit . . . laetantes. Ps. 125: 3: 'The Lord hath done great things for us; whereof we are glad'.

46 *communicatio in sacris.* See letter of 16 Oct. 1866. 'The Church strictly forbids all communion in sacred things with non-Catholics'. Failing to attend church in the university was punished with fines.

47 *Monsignor Eyre.* Perhaps Charles Eyre (1817–1902), the archbishop for the Western District and Delegate Apostolic for Scotland in 1868 and archbishop of Glasgow in 1879.

Master. The Revd. Robert Scott (1811–87), who edited the Greek-English Lexicon with Dean Liddell. While GMH was an undergraduate he occasionally wrote essays for him.

49 *place*. Originally 'shape', cancelled.

only in a few instances. Originally 'not at all', cancelled.

Dr. Pusey. The copy of Pusey's letter in LIII is dated 10 Oct. and C. C. Abbott notes as curious GMH's apparent disregard of Pusey's refusal in it to see him 'to satisfy relations'. The most likely explanation of GMH's allusions to Pusey in this and the two following letters is if Pusey's letter (LIII, p. 400) actually dates from the 20th, not the 10th. Only a typed copy is now extant.

51 *I cd. not go to see him*. See previous note.

53 *Todmorden*. Where Bridges's brother-in-law, the Revd. Antony Plow, was vicar. This would have been in Aug. while GMH was staying with Bridges and his family.

55 *a Church*. 'true' cancelled before 'Church'.

57 *Barnfloor and Winepress*. OAH, pp. 25–6.

Beyond the Cloister. Probably 'A Voice from the World', GMH's 'answer to Miss Rossetti's "Convent Threshold"' (OAH, pp. 42–6).

Isabel.

> Why would he for the momentary trick
> Be perdurably fined?—O Isabel!
>
> (*Measure for Measure*, III. i 111–12)

Oratory. In Birmingham. The Institute of the Oratory of St Philip Neri was founded at Rome in 1575. Subsequent religious communities modelled on this lived together without vows. The Oratory at Birmingham was established by John Henry Newman in 1847 when he returned from Rome. As well as a religious community, the Oratory included a boys' school founded in 1858.

58 *Dolben's death*. He drowned on 28 June 1867 while swimming in the Welland River.

Paris. GMH spent 10–18 July in Paris with Basil Poutiatine, the admiral's eldest son and a contemporary of his at Oxford. For GMH's notes on the trip, see J, pp. 147–8.

Edgell. Alfred T. Wyatt-Edgell (1849–1928) had been a close friend of Dolben's at Eton. He had similar religious inclinations and was converted to Catholicism in 1868.

beauty. MS originally 'promise' cancelled, then 'beauty (in body . . .)'.

printing, his poetry. Although Dolben's father was proud of his son's ability, the poems were not printed until 1911, when Bridges edited a selection with an affectionate introduction (rev. edn. 1915).

Finedon. The large family estate of the Mackworth Dolbens. Dolben was buried beneath the altar in the family chapel.

59 *Mr. Oxenham.* Henry Oxenham (1829–88) had been ordained in the Church of England but was a convert to Catholicism in 1857 although retaining belief in his Anglican orders. He maintained close ties with young men at Oxford and sent GMH congratulations when he obtained his 1st in 1867, notes which, Hopkins joked, were 'harder to answer than the Greats papers' (J, p. 320).

bucculae. Visor, pieces covering the cheeks.

Wharton. Perhaps Edward Wharton, who, having taken a 1st in Greats in 1867, was a fellow of Jesus College, Oxford.

61 *O'Hanlon's death.* O'Hanlon (1843–67) had been a fellow of Lincoln and died on 8 Nov.

62 *cruet.* A communion flagon for the church at Thorndon (Sussex) where William Henry Glover, husband of Bridges's elder sister Caroline, was rector. See letters of 10 July, 22 and 24 Sept. 1866.

schools. Greats. Bridges did get a 2nd.

Ecce Homo. By John Seeley (1865). See letter of 5 Nov. 1885.

B.N.C. Brasenose College, Oxford.

63 *Ruskin's new book. Time and Tide, by Weare and Tyne: Twenty-Five Letters to a Working Man of Sunderland on the Laws of Work* (2nd edn., 1868).

damned, shepherd'. As You Like It, III. ii. 30 ff.

64 *minor orders.* See letter of 20 Sept. 1874.

Rogers. James Edwin Rogers, Professor of Political Economy 1862–8 and 1888–91.

a transl. of Horace . . . Mathews. Odes, Epodes and the Secular Song, trans. Charles S. Mathews (1867).

Pervigilium Veneris. An anonymous hymn to love and the spring.

66 *We.* Hopkins was travelling with Edward Bond (see Biographical Register). GMH made notes of the trip in his journal: see J, pp. 168–84.

68 *my Summa.* OAH. p. 85. See J, p. 165 (11 May 1868). Humphry House argues convincingly that the 'Slaughter of the Innocents' noted on this day refers to the destruction of the copies Hopkins possessed of his poems. He did not try to retrieve copies of them held by others since the 'slaughter' was symbolic of his dedicating himself to a religious rather than artistic life.

St. Dorothea' Perhaps close to the version in OAH, pp. 84–5, which is considered the earliest extant example of GMH's use of sprung rhythm.

Whý should thís desert be? As You Like It, III. ii. 133.

Thoú for whóm Jóve would swear. Love's Labours Lost, IV. iii. 117.

69 *Grandmamma . . . Aunt Annie*. See Biographical Register (Ann Hopkins, Ann Eleanor Hopkins).

70 *such dreadful grief*. Mrs Plow was Bridges's sister Harriett. On 2 Mar. 1868 the Plows were attacked by the lover of a 16-year-old servant-girl whom they had dismissed and sent home to get her away from the liaison, for which they considered her too young. Mr Plow was savagely attacked with a hatchet, a servant was shot dead and partially dismembered, and Harriett, who had recently given birth, was shot at and attacked in bed with a poker. Mr Plow died ten days later. Harriett never fully recovered and died a year later.

71 *your lodgings*. Bridges had become a medical student at St Bartholomew's Hospital, London, in Oct. 1869 (see LIII, p. 107).

to say. In MS followed by 'If this should reach you', cancelled.

73 *secretary to the International*. The International Working Men's Association was formed in Sept. 1864. It was divided in its policies because it brought together people of incompatible political opinion. The International was blamed for the rising of the Paris Commune, although that exploded largely out of the state of French politics of the time. There were fears that the Assembly was about to restore the monarchy and widespread discontent at the refusal to pay the National Guard, who had defended France against the Germans. Among the social reforms called for were wider educational opportunities, a reduction in the working day, the abolition of night shifts for bakers, and, as with the French Revolution, an end to the power of the Church. However, although the revolutionaries held Paris from 18 Mar. to 28 May, they were not well organized and government troops were able to enter the city through an undefended gate. During the following week some 20,000 citizens were killed and some 750 soldiers. The revolutionaries built barracades and burnt a number of historic public buildings. It is most unfortunate that we do not know when in May Bridges's letter was written. His comment may have arisen from his work during his medical training at the charity hospital St Bartholomew's in London. His exceptional concern for his patients there sometimes led him into conflict with the authorities.

long. In MS followed by 'warned us of the country of'; 'us of' cancelled before the rest.

any. In MS followed by 'public', cancelled.

74 *mostly*. MS originally read 'partly', cancelled.

75 *his new book. Literature and Dogma* (1873).

Grammar of Assent. Published 1870.

De Morgan's Budget of Paradoxes. Published 1872.

Snae Fell. See J, pp. 232–6, for GMH's notes on this holiday.

76 *the writer*. Andrew Lang reviewed Bridges' *Poems* (1873) in the *Academy* (17 Jan. 1874), 53–4.

Next they that . . . double row. from 'Elegy: On a Lady, whom grief for the death of her Betrothed killed', which Lang singled out as the 'best poem' in the volume.

so much offended about that red letter. While Bridges would not have approved of Hopkins's views there (the most revolutionary he ever expressed), they are unlikely to have caused him to drop the correspondence. The 'unkindness' at Roehampton (letter of 2 Apr. 1871)—probably a blunt attempt to convert RB—and the increasing loss of common interests are likely to have been far more important.

One of my sisters. Grace: see Biographical Register.

'O earlier shall the rose[bud]s blow'. By William Johnson, later Cory, in his volume *Ionica*. Johnson had been at Eton.

78 *Provincial.* Fr Peter Gallwey (1820–1906) was appointed Provincial in 1873. He said kind and encouraging things to Hopkins on a number of occasions (see e.g. J, p. 227 (27 Oct. 1872); p. 236 (27 Aug. 1873); p. 249 (31 July 1874)). He became Superior of St Beuno's in 1876 while GMH was studying theology there.

79 *Tyndall's address.* Tyndall's address as President of the British Association to a meeting in Belfast on 19 Aug. 1874 was reported in the *Academy* (22 Aug. 1874), 209–17. John Tyndall (1820–93) was born in county Carlow. After working as a railway engineer and teacher of mathematics and surveying, he studied at Marburg, receiving his PhD in 1850. He began publishing papers on aspects of magnetism and, on his return to England in 1851, became Professor of Natural Philosophy at the Royal Institution; FRS 1852. He was friendly with T. H. Huxley, with whom he lectured, and with Michael Faraday, whom he succeeded as superintendent of the Royal Institution in 1867. His publications included work on glaciers in the Alps, heat, light, and sound. His papers were widely known and translated into many languages.

Matterhorn. GMH and Edward Bond had met Tyndall at Breil, Switzerland, where Tyndall was preparing to climb the Matterhorn. He prescribed medicine for Bond, who had fallen sick (see J, p. 182).

died. Br. Richard O'Neil, who probably died of typhus contracted at Roehampton (J, p. 260).

80 *Wallace.* William Wallace, *The Logic of Hegel*, trans. with prolegomena (1874).

Duns Scotus. Duns Scotus (*c.* 1266–1308), known as the 'subtle doctor', was not a popular thinker at this time although some of the beliefs he defended—such as Mary's Immaculate Conception—were accepted by the Catholic Church during the 19th century. The book GMH found was Scotus's *Oxford Commentary* on the *Sentences* of Peter Lombard, which contains a passage defending man's ability to encounter reality through his senses: 'By grasping just what things are of themselves, a person separates the essences from the many additional incidental features associated with them in the sense image . . . and sees what is true . . . as a more universal truth' (tr. A. B. Wolter). This notion resembles GMH's idea of 'inscape'.

81 *Mr Nicholas Breakspear*. Probably Eustace John Breakspeare, who later contributed a book on Mozart to the Musical Masters series.

the account of the actual shipwreck. Excerpts from the newspaper accounts of the wreck of the *Deutschland* are reprinted in LIII, pp. 439–43.

82 *comet*. It turned out to be Praesepe, a nebula in Cancer.

Aunt Anne . . . Aunt Kate. See Biographical Register (Ann Eleanor Hopkins, Katherine Beechey).

my poem. 'The Wreck of the Deutschland'. GMH had written to his mother on 26–8 June, 'I have asked Fr. Coleridge the editor [of the *Month*], who is besides my oldest friend in the Society, to take it, but I had to tell him that I felt sure he wd. personally dislike it very much, only that he was to consider not his tastes but those of the *Month*'s readers. He replied that there was in America a new sort of poetry which did not rhyme or scan or construe; if mine rhymed and scanned and construed and did not make nonsense or bad morality he did not see why it shd. not do. So I sent it . . . The poem was too late for July but will appear in the August number. He wants me however to do away with the accents which mark the scanning. I would gladly have done without them if I had thought my readers would scan right unaided but I am afraid they will not, and if the lines are not rightly scanned they are ruined. Still I am afraid I must humour an editor, but some lines at all events will have to be marked.' At this time the *Month* did not publish much poetry. In May and June there were a couple of simple poems by Lady Catharine Petre and three other poems. There was no poetry in the July number and only 'A Rhythm of St Hildebert of Tours' in August.

83 *Fr Morris's*. Fr. John Morris (1826–93) was converted to Catholicism in 1846 and joined the Jesuits in 1867. He was a historian and lectured on history at St Beuno's. He later became Master of Novices. See letter of 12 Oct. 1881.

Silver Jubilee. See OAH, pp. 119–21, for these three poems.

Joseph and his Brethren. By Charles Wells (1824), repr. with an introd. by Swinburne in 1876.

84 *see me*. In MS 'or, as your present . . . see you' interlineated after sentence was complete.

a very serious examination. Examination in moral theology 'to see', GMH told his mother, 'whether I am fit to hear confessions' (LIII, p. 143).

pamphlets. *The Growth of Love* (1876) published anonymously and *Carmen Elegiacum . . . de Nosocomio Sti Bartholomaei Londinensi*, a farewell to Dr Patrick Black for whom he had been a house physician.

85 *consulting physician*. Bridges saw some 30,000 patients that year and worked long hours in the wards.

Donec . . . solus eris. Ovid, *Tristia*, i. 9, ll. 5–6. The second line should read: 'tempora si fuerint nubila solus eris', which GMH began to write before altering it. ('While you continue lucky you will have many friends, if sad times come you will be alone.')

no interest. After sketching the Hospital's long history (it was founded in 1325), Bridges gives brief descriptions of the current members of staff.

Quale . . . etc.

Quale animal nunquam peperit bona terra, ut haberet
Spina duas alas bis totidemque pedes:

'An animal such as the good earth never produced, the spine having two wings and twice as many feet.' GMH was evidently working out a translation as he wrote: 'way' originally read 'sort'; 'drops' was originally 'dies' and 'goes to bed' originally 'sleeps'; 'the knowledge' was an interlineated addition, as was 'but it cannot mean . . . the sleeper'.

Hoc . . . etc.

Hoc genus infidum studii perit ante cubantes,
Haec doctrina parum sufficit arte suis:
(ll. 447–8)

This treacherous type of study perishes before [its students] go to bed; this doctrine is hardly sufficient in art for its own [adherents].' Medical knowledge was expanding very rapidly at the time and Bridges found it a constant struggle to remember the large amount of information he was expected to know.

86 *like the 5th best*. 'In all things beautiful', *Poetical Works*, no. 31, revised. GMH commented on this poem a number of times and began a Latin translation of it (OAH, p. 174).

weak third line. ''Tis joy the foldings of her dress to view', revised to ''Tis joy to watch the folds fall as they do'.

prow . . . show. Bridges retained this: '. . . her launchèd passion, when she sings, | Wins on the hearing like a shapen prow | Borne by the mastery of its urgent wings: | Or if she deign her wisdom, she doth show . . .' (ll. 9–12).

personification is wrong. 'Timidity':

A thousand times has, in my heart's behoof,
My tongue been set his passion to impart:
A thousand times has my too coward heart
My mouth reclosed, and fixed her to the roof.

Bridges changed 'her' to 'it'.

III. 'First Love', *Poetical Works*, no. 59, ''Twas on the very day Winter took leave'.

XIII. From 'Poetry': 'The lower animals have this defence', not in *Poetical Works*.

87 *By the waters . . . returned. Paradise Lost*, xi. 79; *Paradise Regained*, iv. 289, i. 175, iv. 639.

written a paper on Milton's verse. 'The Blank Verse of Milton' in the *Fortnightly Review* (Dec. 1874), 767–81.

two sonnets. 'God's Grandeur' and 'The Starlight Night'.

Tennysonian touch. VI is 'This world is unto God a work of art' *Poetical Works*, no. 16 heavily revised); VII 'O weary pilgrims' (*Poetical Works*, no. 23; with altered sestet). They express views on religious questions with which GMH would not have agreed.

88 *Our Father . . . XXII*. 'Eternal Father who didst all create' (*Poetical Works*, no. 69); 'Tears of love . . .' (*Poetical Works*, no. 40); Since not the enamour'd sun' (*Poetical Works*, no. 54).

89 *William Butterfield*. An earlier letter containing Hopkins's request for a list of the buildings Butterfield had designed has not been found. In his diary GMH noted a number of the buildings, often churches, designed or restored by Butterfield (1814–1900), who had been responsible for the chapel at Balliol (1856–7) and new buildings at Merton and Keble. GMH's most extensive notes are on 'Butterfield's Church at Babbicombe' about which he had mixed feelings. His most revealing statement is about All Saints', Margaret Street (designed 1859), which he visited after the Royal Academy on 12 June 1874: 'I wanted to see if my old enthusiasm was a mistake, I recognised certainly more than before Butterfield's want of rhetoric and telling, almost to dullness, and even of enthusiasm and zest in his work—thought the wall-mosaic rather tiresome for instance. Still the rich nobility of the tracery in the open arches of the sanctuary and the touching and passionate curves of the lilyings in the ironwork under the baptistery arch marked his genius to me as before' (J, p. 248).

90 *Bremen stanza*. 'The Wreck of the Deutschland', st. 12.

Fĭftȳtwō Bĕdfŏrd Squāre. Bridges's address in London.

'why should this : desert be? As You Like It, III. ii. 115.

There to meet with Mac : beth'. Macbeth, I i. 7.

Grongar Hill. By John Dyer (1699–1758); it describes the River Towy. GMH may have had in mind the line 'Along with Peace close ally'd'.

counterpointed verse. See letters of 5 Oct. 1878, 22 Dec. 1880.

91 *some of my sonnets*. 'Walking by the Sea' (rev. and retitled 'The Sea and the Skylark'), marked 'standard rhythm, sprung and counterpointed', and 'In the Valley of the Elwy', marked 'standard rhythm, in parts sprung and in others counterpointed'.

'lashed : rod'. 'The Wreck of the Deutschland', l. 10.

92 *grandfather's end.* His maternal grandfather Dr John S. Smith (1792–1877).

Lepanto. A sea battle of 7 Oct. 1571 in which the allied Christian forces defeated the Ottoman Turks, capturing 117 galleys and thousands of men. Although it only temporarily kept Cyprus from Turkish control, it was hailed as one of the great victories of Christian Europe and was the subject of countless paintings.

94 *the other day.* 24 Mar. 1878.

Tennyson's Violet. Not 'The Violet' but 'The Daisy'.

95 *ode*: MS: 'a lyric' amended to 'an ode'.

1878. GMH wrote 1877 by mistake.

If it were done . . . sqq. Macbeth, I. vii. 1 ff.

96 *critic in the Athenaeum.* C. C. Abbott identifies him as Theodore Watts-Dunton (1832–1914), who had been a solicitor but gave up law to become a literary critic. He wrote a successful novel, *Alwyn* (1898), as well as critical essays.

grandfather. His maternal grandfather, Dr John S. Smith (1792–1877) had been a student at St Thomas's and Guy's Hospital with Keats.

97 *hearts of oak furled . . . 'grimstones'.* The remarks are explanations of lines in 'The Loss of the Eurydice'. (i) ll. 5–6, '. . . One stroke | Felled and furled them, the hearts of oak'. (ii) ll. 15–16 '. . . Must it, worst weather, | Blast bole and bloom together?' (iii) l. 37. (iv) l. 41 'Then a lurch forward, frigate and men. (v) *a trochee.* MS: 'two trochees' amended to 'a trochee, a dactyl'. ll. 46–7, '. . . care-drowned and wrapped in Cheer's death . . .'. (vi). ll. 53–6, 'It is even seen, time's something server, | In mankind's medley a duty-swerver, | At downright "No or yes?" | Doffs all, drives full for righteousness'.

98 (vii) 'mortholes' Not in any extant MS but presumably once used in ll. 39 or 40. (viii) ll. 76–80, 'Look, foot to forelock', etc. (ix) ll. 101–2, 'That a starlight-wender of ours would say | The marvellous Milk was Walsingham Way (x) l. 105, 'O well wept, mother have lost son'.

99 (xi) l. 37, MS *A* 'grimstones' mended to 'Heavengravel'.

Vale of Clwyd . . . Eurydice. Neither the 'Vale of Clwyd' nor RB's 'Ode on the Eurydice' seem to be extant.

Highgate School. Dixon had been a master there for some months in 1861.

Christ's Company. Published 1861.

Mr. Law. Actually Samuel Lobb, who was an assistant master for mathematics 1857–62. He died in 1876.

other volume. Historical Odes and Other Poems (1864).

Prize Essay too. 'The Close of the Tenth Century of the Christian Era' (1858) (Arnold Prize Essay).

100 *historical work. The History of the Church of England from the Abolition of the Roman Jurisdiction* was reviewed in the *Athenaeum* (9 Feb. 1878). Dixon's history was eventually to extend to 6 vols. Bridges found them very readable and considered them Dixon's best work.

Joseph. Charles Wells, *Joseph and his Brethren*; see note to p. 83.

'*wolfsbane' and other passages. Christ's Company*, pp. 90–1.

Mark and Rosalys. 'La Faerie or Lovers' World' (*Christ's Company*).

101 *Mother and Daughter.* 'Concealment: The Story of a Gentleman of Dauphiny', in *Historical Odes.*

It is the time to tell of fatal love'. 'Perversity: The Story of Ermolae', in *Historical Odes.*

the Feathers of the Willow. 'Song', in *Historical Odes.*

'Her eyes like lilies . . . the bees'. 'St John' in *Christ's Company*, st. 30.

my metres. Although Bridges did not like Hopkins's handling of sprung rhythm in 'The Wreck of the Deutschland', he was excited by Hopkins's rhythmic experiments in his sonnets and asked Hopkins whether he could try using them himself. Hopkins overlooked the request in answering the letter and, prompted no doubt by Bridges, sent an encouraging reply on a postcard nine days later. Bridges's poems in sprung rhythm are among his most successful.

102 *so kind an answer.* Dixon had replied, '. . . You cannot but know that I must be deeply moved, nay shaken to the very centre, by such a letter as that which you have sent me: for which I thank you from my inmost heart' (LII, p. 4).

a prize for an English poem. 'The Escorial' dated Easter 1860 (OAH, pp. 1–5).

Philip Worsley the poet. Worsley (1835–66) wrote *Poems and Translations* (1863). Matthew Arnold had praised his translations of *The Odyssey* and part of *The Iliad.* He died of consumption.

Fame . . . laborious days'. 'Lycidas', ll. 70–2.

ode . . . 'on Departing Youth'. 'What has been lost save beating ears | That sought for praise in all the tides of air . . .', *Historical Odes.*

103 *Unmarked from the horizon-shore.* 'Sympathy: An Ode', *Historical Odes.*

> What, if the sea far off
> Do make its endless moan;
> What, if the forest free
> Do wail alone;
> And the white clouds soar
> Untraced in heaven from the horizon shore? . . .

Burne Jones . . . cut off. Dixon had written, 'I was talking to my friend Burne-Jones the painter a while ago . . . who said among other things, "One only works in reality for the one man who may rise to understand one, it may be ages hence"'. Dixon and Edward Burne-Jones had been friends at King Edward's School, Birmingham, and as undergraduates at Oxford (LII, p. 4).

Rossetti. Dixon had said, '... I received a letter of warm and high approbation and criticism from Rossetti (whom you mention in your letter) about three years ago, when he read my poems, which he had not seen before' (LII, p. 5).

roundels and so forth. Poems (1873).

104 *'Yes, one time ... bitterness he had'.* These lines are from 'La Faerie, or Lovers' World', st. 36 and st. 31.

Pickering. No, Edward Bumpus.

105 *Hurrahing Sonnet* 'Hurrahing in Harvest' (OAH, p. 134).

Falcon sonnet. 'The Windhover' (OAH, p. 132).

Curtal Sonnet. 'Pied Beauty' (OAH, pp. 132–3).

Faded Flower song. 'I have loved flowers that fade'. Of GMH's suggestions, Bridges may have accepted the third, since 'exquisite' does not appear in the first stanza of the published version.

106 *'proper hue'.* Dixon had written, 'I remember Burne-Jones once saying that he thought one line of Milton's the worst that was ever written. It was—'Celestial rosy red, love's proper hue' ' (*Paradise Lost*, vii. 619).

Masson. David Masson, *The Life of John Milton* (1881).

107 *Scherer.* Edmond Henri A. Scherer. Arnold's review was printed in the *Quarterly Review* (Jan. 1877), 186–204, repr. *Mixed Essays.*

Thalaba. Robert Southey, *Thalaba the Destroyer* (1801).

little understood. In 1887 Bridges wrote an essay on Milton's metre at the request of Henry Beeching, who wanted it for a sixth-form text of *Paradise Lost* that he was preparing. Bridges sent a draft of his essay to GMH for comment. Hopkins wrote: 'I cannot but hope that in your metrical Paper you will somewhere distinctly state the principle of Equivalence and that it was quite unrecognised in Milton's and still more in Shakespere's time. All, but especially young students, need to [be] made clearly to understand what metrical Equivalence is, that it is in use in English now, and that it was not then—and that it was Milton's artifices, as you explain them, that helped to introduce it ...' (LI, p. 259). See letter of 27 Feb. 1879.

108 *'Hóme ... wíles'. Paradise Regained,* iv. 639; i. 175.

110 *be.* MS 'me'.

112 *Preface.* Originally probably intended for *Poems* (1879) but modified and published in *Poems* (1880). It drew attention to the poems written in sprung rhythm, cautioning the reader to pay 'attention to the natural quantity and accent of the syllables' rather than imposing alternate stress and urging the articulation of unstressed syllables when 2 or 3 of these occur together. Bridges ends by saying, 'The author

disavows any claim to originality for the novelty: this is almost entirely due to a friend, whose poems remain, he regrets to say, in manuscript.'

Academy. Issue of 25 Jan. 1879, p. 76.

113 *Nabuchodonosor*. Dan. 4: 24.

Pharisees. Luke 11: 41.

114 *26th year of episcopate*. 'The Silver Jubilee'.

a May piece. 'The May Magnificat' (OAH, pp. 139–40).

Paters. Walter Pater had been one of GMH's tutors at Oxford and during his time there in 1879 Hopkins said, 'Pater was one of the men I saw most of'.

115 *Keble College*. See letter of 26 Apr. 1877.

Bridges' new book. *Poems* (1879) 'by the author of "The Growth of Love"'.

Mr. Green. T. H. Green (1836–82) was appointed Whyte's Professor of Moral Philosophy in 1878. He was known for analyses of the philosophy of Kant, Hegel, and Hume. An agnostic himself, he urged undergraduates who had lost their faith to maintain contact with those who had not. When he died GMH wrote to Baillie, 'I always liked and admired poor Green. He seemed to me upright in mind and life. I wish I had made more of the opportunities I had of seeing him in my 10 months at Oxford, for he lived close by' (LIII, p. 249).

Mr Alsager Hill. Hill (1839–1906) was a barrister who drew attention to the problems of unemployment and advocated the establishing of labour exchanges. From 1869 he worked for the Charity Organisation Society.

Thorold Rogers. James E. Rogers (1823–90), who had been Drummond Professor of Political Economy at Oxford while GMH was an undergraduate.

'Silver Spooner'. The Revd. W. A. Spooner (1844–1930), who was a fellow of New College and eventually became Master. His name derived from his pale appearance, the result of albinism. GMH had noted in his diary in 1865 that he was to 'dine with A. Spooner on Monday'. Spooner later became a friend of Bridges's.

Sir Gore Ouseley. The Revd. Sir Frederick A. Gore Ouseley (1825–89) had been Professor of Music at Oxford since 1855. He was a prolific composer of church music and wrote three books on musical theory. GMH used his book on *Counterpoint, Cannon and Fugue* (LI, p. 271) and sent his fugal arrangement of Patmore's poem 'The crocus, while the days are dark' to him for comment, but does not appear to have received a response (LI, pp. 199, 201–2, 207). John Stainer said that he had been immeasurably helped by Ouseley during the two years he had been organist at St Michael's, Tenbury, before going up to Oxford.

116 *a book of Mallock's.* William H. Mallock (1849–1923), who had been at Balliol. His popular satire *The New Republic: Culture, Faith and Philosophy in an English Country House* was published serially in *Belgravia* in 1871 and in book form in 1877. In it Jowett appeared as Dr Jenkinson, T. H. Huxley was Mr Storks, and John Tyndall was Mr Stockton.

trees are saved. See letter of 19 Jan. 1879.

not today . . . Jubilee. OAH, p. 120, reads, 'Your wealth of life is some way spent' and omits the comma after 'Silver'.

do not ask Gosse anything of the sort. Edmund Gosse liked Bridges's poetry. Bridges, wanting to help GMH, was anxious to persuade Gosse to write about Hopkins's poetry as well as his own. See letter of 22 Apr. 1879. At this time Gosse and Bridges were both just beginning to establish their literary reputations.

117 *'winding the eyes'.* 'The Lantern out of Doors', ll. 9–11.

121 *not so long ago. Henry [not Thomas] Vaughan*, ed. Revd H. F. Lyte (1847).

'primrosed and hung with shade'. 'Silex Scintillans, Regeneration', st. 1, l. 4.

And here in dust . . . appear. 'Thalia Rediviva, The Revival'.

123 *aspens . . . felled.* GMH wrote 'Binsey Poplars' (OAH, pp. 142–3) about this.

two pieces . . . last finish. Presumably 'Duns Scotus's Oxford', dated 'Oxford, March 1879', although Dixon's copy is not extant, and 'Binsey Poplars', dated 'March 13 1879'.

124 *'hero' stanza.* ll. 109–12:

> But to Christ lord of thunder
> Crouch; lay knee by earth low under:
> 'Holiest, loveliest, bravest,
> Save my hero, O Hero savest.

The obscurity lies in the omission in the last line of the relative pronoun 'that' before 'savest'. Bridges singled out this fault in his Preface to the Notes in his edition of Hopkins's *Poems* (1918).

Lang's. Andrew Lang, who had helped Bridges by writing a largely favourable review of *Poems* (1873). Bridges showed him Hopkins's poems, hoping that he would like and promote them, but Lang found them too eccentric.

125 *preface.* See letter of 19 Jan. 1879.

'Hail is hurling'. 'A Passer By', l. 6, reads, 'When skies are cold and misty, and hail is hurling'. cf. 'The Wreck of the Deutschland', l. 98, 'Hurling the haven behind'.

'Father fond'. 'Morning Hymn', st. 3, reads: '. . . and near | As father fond art found'. cf. 'In the Valley of the Elwy'; l. 4 reads: '. . . being a father and fond'.

Alexandrines. 'Henry Purcell' (OAH, p. 143).

126 *forthcoming volume*. GMH had written to Bridges, 'since my last postcard the good Canon has sent me a "note of admiration" and makes the characteristic proposal to introduce me to the public by "an abrupt footnote" under the year 1540 . . .' (9 Apr. 1879; LI, p. 77).

sach. In his explanation of l. 10 of the sonnet, 'Henry Purcell', GMH had written, '*Sake* is a word I find it convenient to use: I did not know when I did so first that it is common in German, in the form *sach*. It is the *sake* of "for the sake of", *forsake, namesake, keepsake*. I mean by it the being a thing has outside itself, as a voice by its echo, a face by its reflection, a body by its shadow, a man by his name, fame, or memory, *and also* that in the thing by virtue of which especially it has this being abroad, and that is something distinctive, marked, specifically or individually speaking, as for a voice and echo clearness; for a reflected image light, brightness; for a shadow-casting body bulk; for a man genius, great achievements, amiability, and so on. In this case it is, as the sonnet says, distinctive quality in genius.'

'Anything more delicious'. C. C. Abbott asked Mrs Bridges about this unpublished poem and she replied, 'RB used occasionally to write comic verses with ingenious rhymes to amuse his friends. I know there was one on a river picnic. I have no copy of it, but seem to remember hearing this line quoted, among others' (LI, p. 85).

Muirhead. Lionel Muirhead (1845–1925), one of Bridges's closest friends from their schooldays at Eton. Muirhead had to leave Oxford without taking a degree because of eye trouble. He was known there for his talent as an artist, a reputation which had prompted GMH to try to become friends with him. In 1868 he travelled in Egypt and Syria with Bridges and, when Bridges returned to England, continued travelling in Mesopotamia until mid-1870. He made a number of beautiful sketches on the trip. Letters telling of his adventures in the Middle East are published in *Selected Letters of Robert Bridges*, ed. Donald Stanford, vol. i (1983). Muirhead subsequently settled in Oxfordshire, inheriting Hasely Court in 1898.

all the music you have. Bridges later edited *The Yattendon Hymnal* with H. E. Woolridge, a collection of 100 hymns, to some 40 of which he contributed words, often translations of old Latin hymns. He also pointed chants.

127 *'O earlier'*. 'O earlier shall the rosebuds blow', a song whose words were written by William Johnson, later Cory, and published in *Ionica* (1858). See letter of 22 Jan. 1874.

Candle sonnet. 'The Candle Indoors', dated 'Oxford '79' (OAH, p. 144).

recast. MS reads 'improved copy', cancelled.

offence of the rhymes. Bridges objected to 'plied/reply' in ll. 3–4:

> With the sweetest air that said, still plied and pressed,
> He swung to his first poised purport of reply.

Fr. Parkinson . . . country. Fr. Parkinson (1819–1904) joined the Society of Jesus in 1851 and was headmaster and the Superior at St Aloysius's 1875–87. GMH wrote to Bridges on 8 Apr. 1879, 'the reason you have not heard from me sooner is that my chief Rev. T. B. P. has thought well to break his collarbone and be laid up in a charming country house commanding the White Horse Vale, throwing the whole of the work at the hardest time of the year on his underling' (LI, p. 75).

at Mount St. Mary's 'The Brothers', (OAH, pp. 151–2).

like the Eurydice. 'The Bugler's First Communion' (OAH, pp. 146–8).

little song. 'Morning, Midday, and Evening Sacrifice' (OAH, pp. 148–9). A note by Bridges suggests that GMH wrote a musical setting for the poem but it is not extant.

Vale of Clwyd. Unknown. See letter of 30 May 1878.

128 *sonnet*. 'Andromeda' (OAH, p. 148).

birthday lines. 'A Complaint' (OAH, pp. 76–7). Probably written for his sister, Milicent.

Barnes' Dorset . . . poems. A collected edition of Barnes's earlier volumes was published in 1879 entitled *Poems of Rural Life in the Dorset Dialect*. GMH later wrote musical settings for two of Barnes's poems.

Gosse's paper. Edmund Gosse reviewed *Poems of Rural Life* . . . in the *Academy* (26 July 1879), 60–1.

129 *Linden Ore*. Actually 'Lindenore'.

'Alive in the Spring'. C. C. Abbott suggests 'In the Spring'.

V. S. S. Coles. See letter of 28 Aug. 1865.

Michelangelo's sonnets . . . verse. For *The Growth of Love* Bridges wrote a prose précis of the ideas he wanted to express before setting them in verse.

Non ha l'ottimo . . . concetto. Michelangelo. In J. A. Symonds's edition, he titled it 'The Lover and the Sculptor'.

' 'Tis joy . . . to view'. *The Growth of Love*, final version in *Poetical Works*, no. 31, 'In all things beautiful, I cannot see'. GMH was to begin a Latin translation of this poem, 'Nempe ea formosa est' (OAH, pp. 174–5).

130 *Hector*. 'I heard great Hector sounding war's alarms', *The Growth of Love*, no. 53, in *Poetical Works*, but modified from the version GMH saw.

The other. 'Regret'. 'If I coud but forget and not recall', no. 41 in *The Growth of Love*, greatly modified in *Poetical Works*.

131 *'I have loved flowers'*. 'I have loved flowers that fade', *Shorter Poems*, Book II, no. 13, in *Poetical Works*.

'one irrevocable day'. From 'If I coud but forget and not recall'. Although Bridges initially adopted GMH's revision, he later dropped the line, which does not appear in *Poetical Works*, 'The Growth of Love', no. 41.

Marzials. Hopkins's letter of 13 May 1878 suggests that Bridges had received a note praising his poems from Theophilus Marzials, who had published a Rondel in the *Athenaeum* in Apr. 1877. Bridges had experimented with this and other elaborate poetic forms in his first volume of poems (1873), a book much admired by Edmund Gosse although Bridges himself later tried to suppress it.

beauty. GMH wrote a number of poems in which he expressed distinctions between the different kinds of beauty, among them 'The Handsome Heart', 'Morning, Midday, and Evening Sacrifice', 'The Leaden Echo and the Golden Echo', and 'To what serves Mortal Beauty'.

132 *St. Paul, aemulor te Dei aemulatione.* 'I am jealous of you with the jealousy of God', 2 Cor. 11: 2.

133 *The Ship. The Growth of Love.* In *Poetical Works*, no. 15, 'Who builds a ship must first lay down the keel'. Bridges followed Hopkins's suggestion.

The other. 'When I see childhood'. Perhaps *The Growth of Love*, no. 42, in *Poetical Works.*

'The careless . . . May'. l. 7 of 'If I coud but forget', *The Growth of Love*; *Poetical Works*, no. 41, which reads, 'The Flowers and leafy ecstasy of May'.

Ride o'er the seas'. From 'The Ship'. RB changed it to 'O'erride the seas . . .'.

kind offer. Probably Bridges's attempt to persuade his friend, Philip Rathbone, to show GMH his collection of pictures. Bridges had travelled in Italy with the Rathbones in 1874. Philip was active in politics and a benefactor of local art galleries.

Bugler. In the Preface to the Notes (*Poems*, 1st edn.) Bridges wrote, 'The rhyme to *communion* in "The Bugler" is hideous, and the suspicion that the poet thought it ingenious is appalling'.

134 *Sacrifice.* 'Morning, Midday, and Evening Sacrifice'.

In silk-ash . . . cooling'. The line read 'Silk-ashed but core not cooling'.

Weber . . . another sphere. Carl M. Weber (1786–1826). An interesting comment. Weber, whose greatest interest was in opera, has been praised for the dramatic quality of his music. It is slightly showy, and highly individual, with what has been called 'consciously cultivated "exaggeration"'. In his lesser pieces this has been criticized as a straining after effect. The vivid freshness with which Weber evoked scenes from nature has won considerable praise. Some of his work is highly patriotic in tone and in a number of pieces he incorporated national folk tunes. Hopkins would probably have approved of the clear Catholicism evident in Weber's masterpiece *Der Freischütz.*

135 *they are sent.* Dixon had written, 'Should you be angry that I sent your Loss of the Eurydice, or part of it, to one of the Carlisle Papers, giving

your name, and a line or two of introduction from myself?' (LII, p. 29; 19 Oct. 1879.) See next letter.

Fr. Joseph Stevenson. Stevenson (1806–95) was a well-known archivist and editor, one of the first appointed to the Public Record Office. He joined the Jesuits in 1877, some five years after the death of his wife.

137 *St. Winefred's Martyrdom.* GMH was to work at this play for some seven years. He did not finish it and only fragments are extant, most of these are transcriptions of parts written between Oct. 1884 and Apr. 1885. For details of the story and the composition see OAH, pp. 371–2.

another on Margaret Clitheroe. Incomplete; see OAH, pp. 125–7.

140 *comforting praises . . . overrate your poems.*' Bridges had taken his first collection of Hopkins's poems (MS *A*) to show Dixon, who had not previously seen some of them. Dixon wrote to GMH about them, 'I can only say that they confirm, not increase, the admiration which I feel: and which is so great as to convince me that you must from pure sympathy have much over-rated my own writings: which are very imperfect in comparison with yours or his' (i.e. Bridges's) (LII, p. 35; 15 Nov. 1880).

'Rightly be swift'. 'Romance', st. 3, *Christ's Company.*

141 *Ode to Summer.* See letter of 4 June 1878.

Bridges . . . his visit. for an account of this, see Bridges's Memoir of Dixon reprinted in his *Three Friends*, pp. 120–4.

epic on . . . northern mythology. A confusion; Bridges noted: 'R. W. D. had reams of Northern epics. I did not praise them: but praised 'Mano', in the revision of which I worked hard, tho' I cd not persuade D to mitigate the historical diversions as much as I wished . . .' J. Sambrook suggests in *A Poet Hidden* (London, 1962, p. 51) that they may have been based on the Twilight of the Gods and that Dixon may have been dissuaded from publishing them when William Morris produced his Northern tales in verse.

sorrows of sympathy. 'Ode on Conflicting Claims', in *Odes and Eclogues* (1884).

143 *'She had cóme from a crúise, tráining séamen.* 'The Loss of the Eurydice', l. 13.

145 *a little piece.* 'Spring and Fall' (OAH, p. 152).

Brothers. GMH revised this poem a number of times. The final version is in OAH, pp. 151–2.

146 *Oozy Gore.* Sir F. A. Ouseley Gore. See note to p. 115.

the instance Pat gives. Coventry Patmore, 'Prefatory Study on English Metrical Law', bound with *Amelia*. See letter of 1 Jan. 1885.

147 *Márgarét . . . unléaving?* 'Spring and Fall'; see letter of 22 Dec. 1880.

suggested another. In a letter of 5–10 Sept. 1880 GMH suggested that Wyatt was using a line with a central caesura and 'thinks himself at liberty to give each wing of the line two or three stresses at pleasure, as in doggrel, but not, as I have said, more than two syllables, a stress and a slack, to each foot'.

148 *The Dead Child.* 'On a Dead Child', in *Poems* (1880). One of the few poems to be written directly out of Bridges's experience as a doctor.

perfect. Most critics have disagreed with GMH's suggestions, which would disturb the tranquil tone of the poem.

149 *Mr. Hall Caine.* Dixon had written to GMH, 'A Mr Hall Caine, a stranger to me but friend of Rossetti's, has written for my consent to reprint a couple of my Sonnets in a large collection of Sonnets . . . which he is publishing . . . In my reply I mentioned you . . . & have received . . . a request to send him an example of your work. I send him today the two sonnets "Starlight Night" & "Skylark": not of course for publication without your consent: but for inspection; to gratify him. I now write to ask if you will consent that some sonnet of yours s[d]. be published with your name by him. If so, will you, send him one—I think it had better be one in ordinary rhythm: or at most a counterpointed one: but of that you will judge . . .' (LII, pp. 46–7; 28 Mar. 1881). However, the collection was designed to 'demonstrate the impossibility of improving upon the acknowledged structure whether as to rhyme-scheme or measure' and, faced with Hopkins's many innovations, Hall Caine refused to include his work. Bridges was infuriated and withdrew his own sonnet from the collection in protest. See LI, pp. 128, 132–3.

'Rise . . . woods'. The first line of 'The Fall of the Leaf', from *Odes and Eclogues* (1884).

Love's Casuistry'. Selected Poems.

150 *'Margaret, are you grieving'.* 'Spring and Fall'; see letter of 22 Dec. 1880.

151 *Bishop of Liverpool.* The bishop of Liverpool 1873–94 was the Rt. Revd. Bernard O'Reilly (1824–94).

152 *improve.* Bridges had contracted pneumonia complicated by empyema. He was dangerously ill and took nearly six months to recover.

you did run . . . Galatians. Gal. 5: 7. 'Ye did run well; who did hinder you that ye should not obey the truth?'

153 *ode on Edmund Campion S.J.* Unknown.

154 *Lothair.* By Disraeli (1870).

156 *Of the sonnets themselves.* Most of these are unpublished; 'The World and its Workers' appeared in *Selected Poems.*

Ode on the Death of Dickens. In *Last Poems.*

Nature and Man. In *Lyrical Poems.*

'frigid fancy'. In his letter of 16–18 Sept. 1881, GMH had suggested that Browning had been guilty of 'false perspective' in a passage in 'Instans Tyrannus', vii. 1–8, in which he describes the sky forming a

shield to protect one man from another. Hopkins protested, 'the vault of heaven is a vault, hollow, concave towards us, convex upwards; it therefore could only defend man on earth against enemies above it, an angry Olympus for instance. And the tyrant himself is inside it, under it, just as much as his victim . . . This comes of frigid fancy with no imagination' (LII, pp. 56–7).

157 *'carried away . . . dissimulation'*. Gal. 2: 13.

158 *Tu verba vitae aeterna habes*. John 6: 68. 'Thou has the words of eternal life.'

God. MS 'holy th' cancelled.

Fr. Morris. See letter of 6 Aug. 1876. Hopkins commented to his mother that while the group of novices to which he had belonged would roar with laughter whenever anything went wrong, those of Fr. Morris bore his 'impress', were 'staid', and never laughed (LIII, p. 161; Christmas Eve 1881).

159 *Non ha l'ottimo . . . circonscriva*. The sonnet should run:

> Non ha l'ottimo artista alcun concetto,
> ch' un marmo solo in sè non circonscriva
> col suo soverchio.

'The best of artists hath no thought to show | which the rough stone in its superfluous shell | doth not include.' See letter of 14 Aug. 1879.

160 *Earth has not anything to shew more fair*. Wordsworth, 'Composed Upon Westminster Bridge'.

Captain or colonel or knight-at-arms. Milton, 'When the Assault was Intended to the City', l. 1.

Both them I serve and of their train am I. Milton, 'O nightingale that on yon bloomy spray', l. 14.

'In vain to me the smiling mornings shine'. A sonnet quoted by Wordsworth in the Preface to the *Lyrical Ballads*, where he placed ll. 6–8, 13–14 in italics, remarking that these were the only lines of any value.

161 *Spencer*. Spenser.

162 *I have*. MS 'may' before 'have', cancelled.

write no more. See letter of 7 Aug. 1868.

marriage. In Feb. 1882 Dixon, who had been widowed, married a Miss Routledge, the daughter of George Routledge, High Sheriff and Deputy Lieutenant of the County, to whom Dixon was chaplain.

164 *Fr. Beschi*. Fr. Constanzo G. Beschi, *Tem-bav-ani* (3 vols., 1851–3).

Fr. Southwell. Robert Southwell (?1561–95). Educated at Douai and Rome, he came to England in 1586, becoming domestic chaplain to the countess of Arundel. He was captured celebrating mass in 1592, repeatedly tortured, imprisoned for three years (during which he wrote most of his poetry), and executed. 'The Burning Babe' is probably his best-known poem today.

Campion. Edmund Campion (1540–81) was a fellow of St John's College, Oxford. He was a novice at Brno in Moravia and was ordained in Prague, where he was sent to teach. In 1580 he entered England secretly on a mission to promote Catholicism in the country. He was captured, tortured, and executed at Tyburn with Ralph Sherwin and Alexander Briant on 1 Dec. 1581.

Mr. Simpson in his Life. Richard Simpson, *Edmund Campion: A Biography* (1867).

flower pieces. Daniel Zeghers (or Seghers) (1590–1661). A pupil of Jan Breughel's, he became the leading Flemish flower painter of his generation. He joined the Society of Jesus in 1614 and from 1627, when he settled in Antwerp, monastery records show that his fame was such that a number of the distinguished people of the day visited him.

165 *St. Stanislaus*. St Stanislaus Kostka (1550–68) was a Jesuit only during the last year of his life. He was canonized in 1726.

Bourdaloue. Louis Bourdaloue (1632–1704), a French Jesuit who preached in Paris for 34 years and whose command of oratorical technique was much admired.

Suarez. Francisco Suarez (1548–1617). It was the thought of Aquinas as commented on by Suarez that GMH would have been taught at Mount St Mary's.

Molina. Louis de Molina (1535–1600), a Spanish theologian considered one of the pre-eminent moral theologians of the 16th century, whose reconciliation of the ideas of man's free will and God's omniscience is still accepted today.

St. Ignatius. St Ignatius Loyola (1491/5–1556) came from an aristocratic family and initially followed a military career. A wound brought him a prolonged period of inactivity during which he found his religious vocation. At Manresa in 1522–3 he wrote the *Spiritual Exercises*, which form an integral part of the life of members of the Society of Jesus, an order which he later founded. He was canonized in 1622.

your book. Canon Dixon's book was his *History of the Church of England from the Abolition of the Roman Jurisdiction* (1878). In ii., 230–2 he comments that, although the Society of Jesus has encouraged its many talented and cultured members, '. . . it has been remarked with truth that the Jesuits, with all their culture, cannot boast the greatest names in any department. Their system consumed them: and after all, the end of their system was active and political, not intellectual.' Except in England it has in this area been more influential than any other order, but the later Benedictines have contributed more to literature than the Jesuits and the Franciscans given more to theology. Dixon was worried in case GMH was hurt by these comments and hoped that he would have an opportunity of altering them. Hopkins's response must have been reassuring.

166 *Cobbett's Reformation*. William Cobbett (1763–1835) was largely self-educated. After serving as a soldier in America, he became a journalist and eventually an MP. His *History of the Protestant 'Reformation' in England and Ireland* was published in 1824. It criticizes Protestant attitudes to Catholicism and blames the Reformation for causing pauperism.

up to date. It was re-edited by Cardinal F. Gasquet in 1898.

pauperism. Letter XVI in the *History* contains the main discussion of pauperism.

Song. Probably 'Sky that rollest ever'. Part of GMH's tune and Grace's setting is extant; see LII, p. 169.

Mr Metcalf's. William Metcalfe. Dixon had described him as 'for years the only person in Carlisle with whom I could exchange a word about art of any sort. He is highly held by a few who know: among them the late Dr. Wesley, who wrote to him that he "reverenced every note that he had written"' (LII, p. 91).

167 *Morris*. William Morris (1834–96), poet, artist, and designer. Extremely productive, he wrote a number of long poems and romances, made translations from Greek and Icelandic, as well as designing patterns for wallpaper and textiles and founding the Kelmscott Press. He had strong socialist sympathies evident not only in his numerous lectures but also in such romances as *News from Nowhere* and *The Dream of John Ball*. Dixon had known many of the Pre-Raphaelites at Oxford and his poetry has, as GMH remarked, a Pre-Raphaelite flavour.

168 *Muirhead*. See notes to p. 126.

169 *drudge the music*. Music written to an occasional poem by Thomas Flatman, a welcome 'On the King's Return to White-hall after his Summer's Progress', printed LI, p. 311.

strange and unpleasant. Bridges took this rebuke seriously and evidently apologized for causing GMH pain. On 26 Nov. 1882 Hopkins wrote to him, 'When I reproached you for treating me as if I were not in earnest I meant, and I mean now, to open up no further question; it was only of the injustice to myself I was thinking then. But "pain" is not the word: it was a mild rebuke to you for being so unreasonable towards me. However a man who is deeply in earnest is not very eager to assert his earnestness, as they say when a man is really certain he no longer disputes but is indifferent. And that is all I say now, that to think a man in my position is not in earnest is unreasonable and is to make difficulties' (LI, p. 163).

170 *'Pete'* . . . *Academy*. 'Pete' is 'Come up From the Fields Father', in *Leaves of Grass*; 'To the Man-of-War-Bird' and 'Spirit that form'd this Scene'

(*Academy* (24 Sept. 1881), 239) are also from *Leaves of Grass*. Saintsbury's review of the new edition of *Leaves of Grass* was in the *Academy* (10 Oct. 1874), 398–400.

Salon. John Constable's paintings *The Hay Wain*, *A View near London* (Hampstead Heath), and *The Lock on the Stour* were shown at the Paris Salon of 1824.

171 *this piece.* 'The Leaden Echo and the Golden Echo'.

'or . . . dropped'. 'It is the handkerchief of the Lord; | A scented gift and remembrance designedly dropt.'

become. MS 'becoming'.

172 *Greene.* Robert Greene (?1560–92), a writer of pamphlets, romances (including *Pandosto*), and five plays, among them *The Honorable Historie of Friar Bacon and Friar Bungay*. His plays and poems had been edited by Dyce in 1831 and an edition of the complete works was currently being prepared by Grosart (1881–6).

174 *play's acting. Prometheus the Firegiver* was a masque so its decorative qualities were of prime importance, but Bridges intended to write drama and was interested in learning convincing characterization. *Nero*, Part I, was the first of his plays.

English compounds. GMH had written, 'It makes one weep to think what English might have been; for in spite of all that Shakspere and Milton have done with the compound I cannot doubt that no beauty in a language can make up for want of purity. In fact I am learning Anglosaxon and it is a vastly superior thing to what we have now' (LI, pp. 162–3; 26 Nov. 1882).

175 *at all.* MS reads 'or at'.

Prometheus. Prometheus the Firegiver; see letter of 4 Nov. 1882.

sonnet. Bridges changed the rhymes to which GMH objected. The octave in the 1889 edition reads:

> Sweet sleep / dear unadorned bride of toil /
> Whom in the dusk of night mens bodies low
> Lie to receive / and thy loved coming know /
> Closing the cloudy gate on days turmoil:
> Thou through the lost ways entereth to despoil
> The ready spirit and on worn flesh bestow
> Such comfort as through trembling souls will flow
> When Gods Welldone doth all their sins assail.

176 *image's sake.* 'God's Grandeur', l. 2, reads: 'It will flame out, like shining from shook foil'.

judge's sentence. One of several legal cases in which GMH took an interest. *Belt* v. *Lawes* was a libel suit in which Belt won damages of £5,000 for Lawes's statement that he had not made certain sculptures he had claimed. Lord Chief Justice Coleridge expressed the view that there had been a gross miscarriage of justice. In Mar. 1884, 14 months after Hopkins's letter, the Court of Appeal confirmed the original verdict.

Noel Paton. Joseph Noel Paton (1821–1901), a popular Scottish artist, who frequently chose subjects from fairy-tales or history. He exhibited a number of pictures at the Royal Academy.

178 *Vernon Lee . . . Contemp*. 'Vernon Lee', [Violet Paget], 'Impersonality and Evolution in Music', *Contemporary Review* (Dec. 1882), 840–58. Hopkins's account is very different from those conclusions of Guerney's that Lee praises and even further from her position. Lee praises Guerney for suggesting in his *Power of Sound* (1880) that music is 'the most formal and ideal of all arts, unique in the fact that the form it creates resembles and signifies nothing beyond itself,' (p. 846). She suggests that the argument should be taken further, that, as the Russian Formalists were to argue for literary forms, musical form evolves; 'art is affected by civilization; it absorbs from it and is constrained by it; but it has physico-mental necessities of its own, which determine what it may absorb and by what it may be constrained' (p. 858).

roking. see *English Dialect Dictionary*: 'rauk', to stir, poke about; search.

Swedenborg. Emanuel Swedenborg (1688–1772). Trained as a scientist, he tried to find a scientific explanation of the universe. In middle age, he began working on mystical subjects. Hopkins objected to his appointing himself interpreter of Scripture, which he did after a series of visions. The first of these GMH describes, omitting in his account that the reptiles or worms were considered by Swedenborg to be a purging of his overeating.

181 *Mr. Rae's pictures*. GMH sent Bridges an account of his visit: Mr Rae, he said, 'has built himself a handsome house and it is full of beautiful objects wherever your eye can rest. Mrs Rae was at home and spent hours in taking me about and shewing me everything, then gave me lunch, and asked me to come again. She was simple and homely and at the same time lively, with a real enthusiasm for art and understanding of it and had nothing whatever of the "cultshah" manner: I suppose she dates from before it came in. She was very kind, I liked her very much. The pictures were beautiful of course. They still buy: there was that queer landscape of the Beloved in the Canticles by Spencer Stanhope which I saw at the Grosvenor last year. She said by the by that he too had nothing of the modern nonsense, was a gentleman and nothing else. I might run on all about these pictures . . .' (LI, p. 130; 15 May 1881).

édition de luxe of a new book. *Prometheus the Firegiver* (Oxford: Daniel Press, 1883).

sonnet. 'Henry Purcell'. See letter of 4 Jan. 1883.

182 *St. Paul gives us*. Phil. 2: 5–11.

183 *vehemently*. MS adds 'with you', cancelled.

'the good . . . scarce is. Coventry Patmore, 'The Wedding Sermon' from *Victories of Love*.

184 *Jacob*. A type of the eternally blessed. Although a second son, he was materially far more successful than his elder brother.

more trouble than it is worth. On 19 Apr. GMH had told Bridges that he would shortly have 'finished an exercise in the second species in two parts on "Pray, Goody, please to moderate", pretty elaborate, and I want to know on authority if it is correct and if not where.'

Stainer. John Stainer (1840–1901). Despite losing the sight in one eye as a child, he was a prolific composer, writer of books on theory and history, and an organist. As a youth, his beautiful voice won him a place as a chorister at St Paul's; he spent two years under the guidance of Sir Frederick Gore Ouseley as organist at St Michael's, Tenbury, and then went up to Oxford, where he became organist at Magdalen College in 1860, and of the University in 1861. He was one of a group of artists and musicians with whom Bridges was friendly while he was a medical student in London. GMH obtained Stainer's *Theory of Harmony* (1871), which he called 'a capital treatise . . . though his theory is not final, it is great step forward . . . I am sure that Stainer must be very nice to know and meet' (LI, p. 199; 11 Nov. 1884). In 1889 Stainer succeeded Sir Frederick Gore Ouseley as Professor of Music at Oxford.

one . . . in three-foot couplets. 'The Blessed Virgin compared to the Air we Breathe', OAH, pp. 158–61.

friend. Bridges cut out the name wherever it occurred. The musical friend may have been Hubert Parry.

185 *drew her . . . endured*. 'The Wreck of the Deutschland', ll. 107, 112.

And. The rest of the letter is missing.

Simcox. George A. Simcox (1841–1905) had been at Corpus 1858–62, took a 1st in Greats, and became a fellow of Queen's College, lecturer, and librarian. His best-known work is a *History of Latin Literature from Ennius to Boethius* (2 vols., 1883), but he also wrote a *Prometheus Unbound, a Tragedy* (1867), various shorter poems and romances, and edited classical texts with his younger brother. GMH told his mother that 'besides being amiable [he] is the most eccentric and witty men I ever met' (LIII, p. 108; 20 Oct. 1869).

186 *one sonnet*. 'Ribblesdale', (OAH, pp. 156–7).

'I remember a house'. 'In the Valley of the Elwy' (OAH, pp. 131–2).

'Earth, sad Earth'. 'Mercy' in *Historical Odes*.

piece. 'The Blessed Virgin compared to the Air we Breathe'.

'Blue in the mists all day'. 'Nature and Man' in *Lyrical Poems*. See letter of 12 Oct. 1881.

linger. Dixon's poem was *Mano*, RB's was *Prometheus the Firegiver*. Both were lengthy.

187 *'louchéd'*. '. . . sweet landscape with leaves throng | And louchéd low grass' ('Ribblesdale').

your book. Mano.

'unity of action'. Dixon had asked GMH, 'what do you understand by "unity of action"? The phrase is used by Hall Caine in a good article on Shakespeare in The Contemporary [June 1883, pp. 883–900] in a way that I do not understand of it. I forget his exact words, something like the end being harmonious with the inception. I thought it meant having a single plot. Greek dramas have a single plot' (LII, p. 110; 12 Aug. 1883).

188 *New Arabian Nights*. By Robert Louis Stevenson (1882).

story by him in Longman's . . . Romance. For story see next note; 'A Gossip on Romance', *Longman's Magazine* (Nov. 1882).

189 *Fourvières*. 'The Treasure of Franchard', in *Longman's Magazine* (Apr.–May 1883).

190 *'Her virtue . . . endears'*. From Book II of *The Angel in the House*, Canto IX, 'The Friends'. Among the 32 emendations GMH sent Patmore in a previous letter was the statement that 'Her virtue all virtue so endears' 'is only endurable by slurring "all"; but that wants emphasis. Would not "Her virtue virtue" do?'. This change Patmore made in 1885. GMH's most serious objection, a moral one, is in the letter of 24 Sept.

'Beauty'. *The Angel in the House*, Book II, 'Preludes', no. 2.

Ugliness does. MS replaces 'Good disguises'.

191 *'Women should be vain'*. *The Angel in the House*, Book II, Canto VI, 'The Love-Letters'.

'The Koh-i-noor'. Ibid., Canto VIII, 'In Love'.

'Because . . . desert'. Ibid., 'Husband and Wife', 'The Married Lover'.

schoolboy. MS 'schoolday'.

192 *carelessness . . . vanity*.

Her virtues please my virtuous mood,
  But what at all times I admire
Is, not that she is wise and good,
  But just the thing which I desire.
With versatility to sing
  The theme of love to any strain,
If oft'nest she is anything,
  Be it careless, talkative, and vain.

'The low sun . . . colour'. *The Idylls of the King*, 'Elaine', l. 134.

193 *courtesy*.

Because, although in act and word
  As lowly as a wife can be,

Her manners, when they call me lord,
Remind me 'tis by courtesy;

Canto XII, 'The Married Lover'.

Mrs. Graham. From *The Victories of Love.*

194 *'Blessed Virgin'.* See letter of 7 Mar. 1884. GMH had lost his copy of the poem. Bridges made a transcription from MS *A* and sent this. Hopkins began to copy it into MS *B* but did not have time to complete it before moving to Dublin. In the move, he mislaid Bridges's transcription and sent the album to Coventry Patmore. Discouragingly, it was this poem, of which only one-third had been copied, that Patmore singled out for praise.

195 *Francis Newman.* The younger brother (1805–97) of John Henry Newman. Like his brother he thought deeply about his religious convictions, but resigned his fellowship at Balliol in 1830 on finding that he could not give the assent to Anglican doctrine required of Oxford dons. He later became Professor of Latin at University College, London (1846–63).

196 *a grief.* In a letter of 5–6 Aug. 1883 Hopkins wrote to Bridges, 'When my people were abroad last year they met at Montreux . . . a young man Henry Weber son to a doctor at Sensburg in East Prussia. He was attracted by Grace's playing and, the weather keeping them in, was constantly at her piano: when they parted, though they had known each other for less than a fortnight, they were both deeply in love. In spite of his frail health, his uncertain prospects, and the obvious reasons against such a match my father and mother could not refuse to let it be an engagement. After some illusory rallies, just when Grace and he had persuaded themselves that he was to recover and all would be well, suddenly at the last, he died. The news reached Grace on the very eve of Magdalen's wedding. It was an overwhelming blow. Magdalen wished the wedding to be put off, but that was neither possible nor desirable; but a gloom was cast over the day and Grace kept her room. She then set her heart on seeing her lover's grave. An escort was found for her as far as Berlin and at the station nearest Sensburg Mrs Weber met her. Now she is with them and they treat her like one of themselves . . . My father and mother are going to fetch her home and that is how I am to go to Holland.' Magdalen was GMH's cousin, the daughter of Mrs Marsland Hopkins. She married Archibald Commelin.

197 *the Royal University of Ireland.* In the 1850s Newman had suggested the establishing of a Catholic university in Ireland but, moving from Dublin, he withdrew from the scheme in 1858. Very little progress was made until 1879 when a charter was granted for a royal university. There were several different proposals each with its Irish advocates but in 1882 it was decided that the university should be composed of several colleges. The Jesuit University College, to which Hopkins was attached, was opened in 1883. Like the University of London, it was

primarily an examining body, only teaching a small proportion of the students who sat its papers.

'Wild air . . .'. 'The Blessed Virgin compared to the Air we Breathe'.

poem of Tennyson's. 'Early Spring'.

two triolets. GMH seems to have sent 'λέγεταί τι καινόν' [Is there any news today?] and 'The Child is Father to the Man'. The one 'spoilt' by the *Stonyhurst Magazine* began 'When you ask for Cockle's Pills' (OAH, pp. 157–8).

198 *'All women born'*. 'All women born are so perverse', from *Poems* (1873). It was set to music by Frank Bridge in 1916.

Irish row. Fr. Reffé, who was Dean of Studies at Blackrock, another of the University's colleges, had also been a candidate but Fr. Delaney, President of University College, objected to a cross appointment. Delaney was anxious to secure GMH not only because he was known to be a good classicist but also for financial reasons; as he was a Jesuit, Hopkins's salary of £400 was paid not to him but to the College, which needed the money. Hopkins was elected by a vote of 21 to 3 but was resented by members of the other colleges, who considered that University College was gaining too many new posts. He was also disliked simply because he was English.

best man. Bridges married Mary Monica Waterhouse, elder daughter of the architect, Alfred Waterhouse, on 3 Sept. 1884.

199 *MS book*. MS *B* (see OAH, p. xl). In 1883, Bridges, fearing that in MS *A* he possessed the only copy of some of Hopkins's best poems, began to transcribe them into a second album (MS *B*). Hopkins worked on it several times, amending poems and transcribing new ones into it. These copies provide the 'text' for most of Hopkins's mature poetry.

Esau and Antiochus. Gen. 27: 34–5; 1 Macc. 2: 48, 63. The Douai Bible has a note calling Antiochus 'that man of sin'.

poem. *Eros and Psyche* (1884; rev. and enlarged, 1894).

MS book. MS *B*; see letter of 18 July 1884.

200 *'I yield . . . sometimes'*. 'Peace' (OAH, p. 149).

Hermann. Gottfried Hermann (1772–1848) was an influential Greek scholar who emphasized the importance of linguistic research in classical philology. He wrote books on Greek grammar and the teaching of metrics.

201 *Arrah*. This was one of 89 contributions GMH made to the *English Dialect Dictionary*. For discussions of Hopkins's work on etymology, see James Milroy, *The Language of Gerard Manley Hopkins* (1977), N. H. MacKenzie, 'Hopkins, Yeats and Dublin in the Eighties', in *Myth and Reality in Irish Literature*, ed. J. Ronsley (1977), 88–90, and N. White, ' G. M. Hopkins's Contributions to the EDD', in *English Studies* (Aug. 1987), 325–35.

202 *Milicent's*. GMH's eldest sister (1849–1946). Like Grace, she was interested in music. In 1878 she became a nun in a High Anglican order centred on All Saints' Home, London, where Maria Francesca Rossetti had been a sister 1873–6.

Robert Curtis. Professor of Natural Philosophy. He was an Irish Jesuit, who was not ordained because he suffered from epilepsy. An excellent mathematician, he had been a scholar of Trinity College, Dublin.

204 *music to the Battle of the Baltic*. 'The Battle of the Baltic' by Thomas Campbell. See the view of John Stevens (J, pp. 477–8) and Michael Dunham, 'Hopkins's Musical Setting of "The Battle of the Baltic"', in *Hopkins Quarterly* (Fall 1982), 87–90.

the Crocus. Coventry Patmore, 'The Year': 'The crocus while the days are dark'.

205 *to get*—. Bridges cut out the name wherever it appeared in GMH's letters.

Cretan Sea. *Eros and Psyche*, 'March', sts. 24–6.

Nature. GMH's letters are reprinted in LII, Appendix II. A further letter (30 Oct. 1884) was printed in *Hopkins Research Bulletin* (1971, no. 2) and in Patricia M. Ball's *Science of Aspects* (1971), pp. 148–50.

like a stone. *Eros and Psyche*, 'August', st. 27.

206 *tragedy*. 'St Winefred's Well'. Bridges used the metre for *The Feast of Bacchus*.

he gives. Patmore's *Essay on Metrical Law* was bound with his poem *Amelia* and prompted correspondence with both GMH and Bridges. See Derek Patmore, 'Three Poets discuss New Verse Forms', in the *Month* (Aug. 1951), 68–78.

207 *Geldart*. See Biographical Register.

Nash's. Thomas Nash. See letter of 22 Apr. 1863.

208 *A Son of Belial*. By [Nitram Tradleg] Martin Geldart (1882).

Hannah. John J. Hannah. See letter of 4 May 1863.

209 *'Busy curious thirsting fly'*. 'Busy, curious, thirsty fly', William Oldys, (anacreontic).

Dying Christian. 'Animula, vagula, blandula', put into English by Pope.

212 *written in blood*. Probably one of the sonnets to which W. H. Gardner gave the name 'the sonnets of desolation'. Bridges thought it might have been 'Carrion Comfort'. More recently, N. H. MacKenzie has suggested 'I wake and feel the fell of dark not day'.

fragments. 'St Winefred's Well', see letter of 1 Jan. 1885.

213 *'the Battle of the Baltic'*. See note to p. 204.

—Name cut out by Bridges.

Hullah. John P. Hullah (1812–84). A conductor, teacher, and composer, he wrote the music for three operas (including Dickens's *The*

Village Coquettes (1836)), many songs, and several treatises on singing and vocal music.

214 *Mrs. Bridges' disappointment.* A miscarriage.

Four. GMH originally wrote 'three'.

against my will. This is generally thought to refer to some of the sonnets of desolation. The most likely poems are 'To seem the stranger', 'I wake and feel', 'No worst', 'Patience, hard thing', and 'My own heart'. GMH was still working on 'Carrion Comfort' in 1887.

215 *qui occidere nolunt Posse volunt.* Actually 'qui nolunt occidere quemquam | posse volunt.' 'Even those who do not want to kill anybody would like to have the power to do it,' (Juvenal, *Satires*, x. 96–7).

second volume. John Affleck Bridges, RB's eldest brother, had published *Wet Days* in 1879. He later produced two further volumes of verse and several books of reminiscences.

216 *plays. The Return of Ulysses* (1884) and *The Feast of Bacchus.*

Literature . . . Diana. Matthew Arnold, *Literature and Dogma* (1873); John Seeley's *Ecce Homo* (1865) (see letter of 12 Feb. 1868) and *Natural Religion* (1882); William Mallock, *Atheism and the Value of Life* (1884); Henry Drummond, *Natural Law in the Spiritual World* (1883); George Meredith, *Diana of the Crossways* (1885).

217 *electric.* 'The Loss of the Eurydice', ll. 23–4 rhyme 'he | Came . . . deadly-electric'.

219 *Macaulay's . . . Aytoun's.* Thomas Babington Macaulay (1800–59), *Lays of Ancient Rome* (1842); William Aytoun (1813–65), *Lays of the Scottish Cavaliers* (1849).

222 *Bradlaugh.* Charles Bradlaugh (1833–91) was a well-known advocate of free thought. Elected MP for Northampton in 1880, he had not been allowed to take his seat because he refused to swear on the Bible. Re-elected in 1881, the same argument started again and continued until 1886, when he finally received permission to join the House of Commons. GMH heard him speak with Mrs Annie Besant in 1879 and remarked to Baillie, 'To think I could ever have called myself a Liberal! "The Devil was the first Whig". These two are at large (I mean Bradlaugh and Besant) and the Government is arresting Irish agitators, that will do far more harm in prison than on the stump.'

Booth and Stead. Probably William Booth (1829–1912), the outspoken founder of the Salvation Army, who was an enthusiast with little knowledge of theology. William Thomas Stead (1849–1912) had become the editor of the *Pall Mall Gazette* in 1883 and used his position to advocate social and political change.

223 *ungentlemanly postcards.* They contained enthusiastic theories and questions about the influence of Egypt on Greek etymology and can be read in LIII, pp. 258–62. The last and shortest read, 'I have it.' | Information, lore, earnestly requested on "Neprat, divinité des grains",

[rise up, especially from the sea | shrink back] of course from the inundations. G. | My last card.' See letter of 3 Feb. 1883 for GMH's idea of what constituted gentlemanliness.

'Επιμηθεύς. Afterthought, brother of Prometheus (forethought).

Lang. Andrew Lang, *Custom and Myth* (1884).

225 *Faust*. See letter of 8 May [1861].

227 *Miss Patmore . . . painter*. Bertha Patmore. Ruskin, who gave her lessons in drawing, praised her for having an exquisite sense of beauty.

228 *Piff*. Francis Joseph Mary Epiphanius, born in 1883. He was the child of old age and, according to Gosse, Coventry Patmore was much preoccupied with him. GMH told his mother that 'Piffy' was 'of such a strange sensibility and imagination that it beats anything I ever saw or heard of. He treats flowers as animated things, animals as human, and cries—howls—if he thinks they are hurt or even hears of their being hurt: I witnessed some cases. I should not like it in a brother of mine' (LIII, p. 172; 20 Aug. 1885).

The dedication. *Lyrical Poems* (1887) printed by H. Daniel (at Bridges's suggestion). It was 'Dedicated to the Reverend Gerard Hopkins by the Author'.

Birthday Book. The first verse of 'Morning, Midday, and Evening Sacrifice' was printed, attributed at the bottom to 'Hopkins'. Dixon had been given the stanza by Bridges. The only known copy of the Birthday Book, in the British Library, has been mislaid.

First-fruits. Lev. 2: 12 was chosen. 'As for the oblation of the first-fruits, ye shall offer them unto the Lord'.

'Cheek . . . all this beauty'. Dixon ignored the suggestion for l. 2 but followed that for l. 5.

229 *at a wedding*. 'At the Wedding March' (OAH, p. 150).

Frederick Walker's. Walker (1840–75) was largely self-trained, and worked as an illustrator before exhibiting his first oil painting at the Academy in 1863. GMH saw his *Harbour of Refuge* in 1874 (see J, p. 240).

230 *Macbeth*. Robert Walker Macbeth (1848–1910). A painter and later etcher of others' works. GMH saw his *Phillis on the New-Mown Hay* at the Academy in 1874 (see J, p. 244).

North's. John William North (1842–1924) was a painter of genre and landscape, an illustrator, and wood-engraver. He was friendly with R. W. Macbeth and Frederick Walker, with whom he travelled in Algiers and who sometimes added the figures to his landscape paintings.

231 *Bridges' comedy. The Feast of Bacchus*.

Swinburne . . . 'Manchester Martyrs'. Swinburne, 'The Commonweal, a Song for Unionists' in *The Times* (1 July 1886); 'An Appeal to England' (20 Nov. 1867).

232 *follows*. Inaccurate; see note to p. 160.

review. By Mandell Creighton (1843–1901), a friend of Bridges's from Oxford whom Dixon had met a few times (27 Feb. 1886). He was made honorary canon of Newcastle in 1883, fellow of Emmanuel College, Cambridge, in 1884, and bishop of London in 1896. Like Dixon, he was a historian and edited the *English Historical Review* 1886–91 and wrote, among others, *Simon de Montfort* (1876), a *History of the Papacy* (1882, 1894), and *Cardinal Wolsey* (1888).

elected to that Chair. The Chair of Poetry at Oxford. Dixon had withdrawn before the election, as Bridges was to do 10 years later.

233 *I have found . . . worse for that*. These 6 paragraphs may not belong to this letter.

poem. See letter of 30 June 1886.

234 *Tait on Light*. Peter G. Tait, *Light* (1884).

235 *Lord Selborne*. Lord Selborne had delivered the final Presidential Address of the Wordsworth Society on 9 July 1886.

236 εὔμορφοι κολοσσοί. Aeschylus, *Agamemnon*, 416.

Shakspere's songs. GMH wrote Latin versions of 'Come unto these yellow sands', 'Full fathom five', 'While you here do snoring lie', 'Tell me where is Fancy bred?' 'Orpheus with his lute made trees', and part of 'When icicles hang by the wall'; Greek versions of 'Tell me where is Fancy bred?' and 'Orpheus with his lute'. See OAH, pp. 171–4.

237 *true*. MS originally read 'necessary'.

Let your light . . . heaven. Matt. 5: 16.

Judge Fry's. Monica Bridges and Roger Fry were cousins.

239 *Wordsworth's ode*. 'Intimations of Immortality'.

242 *article . . . death*. *Saturday* (16 Oct. 1886).

Treasure Island. Published 1882.

King Solomon's Mines. Published 1886.

trifling one. Bridges's writes, 'My objection was not to his telling, but to his narration being sometimes in a vein untrue to his character as required by his actions, the two being incompatible and bad as art. RB'

schooner. Bridges: 'This I gave as an instance of the author's art [wh. is not disguised] breaking down'.

damning matter. Bridges: 'There are others in plenty'.

243 *writer in a late Academy*. H. C. Beeching (16 Oct. 1886) quoting from J. A. Symonds's *Ben Jonson*.

Jekyll and Hyde. Published 1886.

interchange. Bridges: 'No—of the means employed, wh. is physical & sh[d] have been magical.

yours. Bridges: '[but does not make chemistry of]'

244 *Miss Kate Tynan.* Katherine Tynan (Mrs Hinkson) (1861–1931). A prolific Irish writer, she wrote over 100 novels, several volumes of poems, and an autobiography in 5 vols. She was a close friend of W. B. Yeats in his youth. Some of her letters to GMH are printed in LIII, pp. 430–1.

245 *Mr. Yeats.* William Butler Yeats (1865–1939). Most of what was published in the *Dublin Review* was printed in *The Wanderings of Oisin* (1889).

Sir Samuel Ferguson. Ferguson (1810–86) took his degree at Trinity College, Dublin, and became keeper of the records of Ireland. His most important historical work was *Ogham Inscriptions in Ireland, Wales, and Scotland* (published posthumously 1887). He also wrote poems on Irish mythological and historical characters.

246 *Dorian Measure.* Neither the paper nor the book was published. GMH wrote quite a bit of the book but does not seem to have completed it.

247 *Co. Kildare.* The family were the Cassidys. See letters of 25 Dec. 1887 and 29 Apr. 1889.

elegy in Gray's metre. 'On the Portrait of Two Beautiful Young Peopole' (OAH, pp. 176–7).

248 *Canon's book. Lyrical Poems* (1887); see letter of 30 June 1886.

Sky that rollest ever. Later titled 'Wayward Water'.

the piece. 'On the Portrait of Two Beautiful Young People'. See letter of 27 Jan. 1887.

Maurice W. Monica's younger brother (1868–90), who died from pneumonia. His death was a considerable blow to the family. Bridges's poem, 'I never shall love the snow again' is about it.

249 *Archbishop Walsh.* William Walsh (1841–1921). The first Primate of Ireland to have been educated there and a fierce nationalist. He had used Hopkins's appointment as a test case to oppose the concentration of so many teaching fellowships in University College. See letters of 7 Mar. 1884, 20 Feb. 1887.

Archbp. Croke. William Croke (1824–1902), an ardent advocate of Home Rule. See letter of 20 Feb. 1887).

253 *an Archbishop . . . Another Archbishop.* William Walsh; William Croke. See notes above.

Michael F. Cox. Cox (b. 1852) was a distinguished physician in Dublin. He was a lecturer in the Medical School of the Catholic University of Dublin and, as an examiner of the Royal University of Ireland, a colleague of GMH's.

book of yours. Arts and Industries in Ireland by S[arah] A[tkinson] (1882), identified by N. H. MacKenzie. It is the second of the book's two essays, 'Irish Wool and Woollens: Passages from the History of the Staple Trade', that GMH discusses.

254 *the Rev. W. Cunningham.* William Cunningham (1849–1919) was a distinguished economic historian.

255 *Sir Wm. Pettie.* Sir William Petty (1623–1687) was Surveyor-General of Ireland. His *Maps of Ireland* (1685) and *Political Anatomy of Ireland* (1691) give very detailed accounts of the country.

257 *Elegy.* 'On the Portrait of Two Beautiful Young People'; see letters of 27 Jan., 17 Feb. 1887.

259 *Mischiefmaker.* W. E. Gladstone.

Miss Taylor. GMH wrote to Bridges (26 Nov. 1886): 'Miss Taylor of 1 Sandford Parade, Ranelagh, Dublin, last year took her degree of Bachelor of Music at the Royal University: her diploma piece, a Magnificat, was then performed and sounded learned and melodious. I was introduced to her and call on her; she lends me Blow and I lend her Purcell. She is a nice unassuming girl. She is now going to take her Doctor's degree and consulted me on the subject matter of the diploma work. On consideration I saw I cd. kill two birds, a dove and an eagle, with one stone. I have advised the *Elegy on one whom grief for the loss of her beloved killed.* I added what could interest her, and she warmly welcomed the proposal. . . . I want you to send her the text; if necessary, even copied in MS: it is not too much to ask, the circumstances considered. You will appear to full orchestral accompaniment.' (LI, p. 244.)

Monsignor Persico. Ignatius Persico (1823–96). In Mar. 1887 he had been appointed archbishop of Tamiatha, commissioned to report on the involvement of the clergy in Irish politics. However, the Holy See condemned the Plan of Campaign, nullifying his report before it could be published. By the Plan of Campaign (1886–7), tenants whose landlords refused to reduce their rents were to pay what they considered fair rent to a political leader who was to act as intermediary, retaining the money till the landlord agreed to the new rent.

261 *St. James's Gazette.* Issue of 28 June 1887, p. 7.

262 *Matthew Arnold . . . something good.* Arnold wrote the preface to *Keats* (1880), repr. *Essays in Criticism*, second series.

a paper . . . Women's Rights. Perhaps 'Why Women are Dissatisfied', in *St James's Gazette* (19 Sept. 1887), 6–7.

263 *hospitality.* GMH stayed with the Patmores in Aug. 1885.

music. A previous letter suggests that this was a song but not one written by GMH (LI, p. 263).

264 *Coda . . . Milton's sonnet.* 'Tom's Garland' has two codas of a half line and a couplet as does Milton's sonnet 'On the New Forces of Conscience under the Long Parliament'.

unquestionable success. Perhaps l. 17, 'broad in bluff hide his frowning feet lashed'.

265 *nello stilo . . . bernesco?* In a satiric or burlesque style. The Italian satirists, especially the followers of Francesco Berni (1496–1535), had often used the caudated sonnet.

266 *daughter*. Elizabeth.

friends at Monasterevan. The Cassidys.

two sonnets. 'Harry Ploughman' and 'Tom's Garland' (OAH, pp. 177, 178).

267 *Elegy*. 'On a Portrait of Two Beautiful Young People'; see letters of 27 Jan., 17 Feb., and 29 Mar. 1887.

Whebles. Ursula and Leo were probably the children whose portrait prompted Hopkins's poem 'On the Portrait of Two Beautiful Young People'. See N. White in *English Language Notes*, 8 no. 3 (Mar. 1971), 206–8.

269 *'Orpheus with his lute'. Henry VIII*, III. i. The fugue is not extant.

Ouseley. Sir Frederick A. Gore Ouseley (see letter of 12 Feb. 1879). His three books on musical theory were: *A Treatise on Harmony* (1868), *A Treatise on Counterpoint, Canon and Fugue: Based upon that of Cherubini* (1869), and *A Treatise on Musical Form and General Composition* (1875). It is presumably to the second of these that GMH was referring.

Higgs. James Higgs, *Fugue* (1878).

lady of the strachey. Twelfth Night, II. v. 38–9. Malvolio, a steward, contemplating the possibility of marrying the Lady Olivia, says, 'There is example for 't: the lady of the strachey married the yeoman of the wardrobe'.

Yattendon. She was christened at Yattendon on 29 Jan. 1888.

270 *Paper. Milton's Prosody*. See notes to p. 107.

last sonnet. 'Tom's Garland'. See letters of 6 Nov., 22 Dec. 1887.

271 *On referring*. A postscript written at the head of the first page.

272 *'O . . . of thoughts'*. 'O for a life of Sensations rather than of Thought!', letter to Benjamin Bailey (22 Nov. 1817).

what Matthew Arnold wrote. See note to p. 262.

274 *a paper . . . St. James's*. 'Real Apprehension', *St James's Gazette* (20 Jan. 1888), 6–7.

text . . . from Newman. 'Man is not a reasoning animal; he is a seeing, feeling, contemplating, acting animal.'

275 *Second Part of the Angel*. Titled *The Victories of Love and Other Poems*, Cassell's National Library (1888).

the Pope's late action. On 28 Apr. the Pope had sent a telegram to the Irish bishops condemning the Plan of Campaign and boycotting. This was seen by many Irish as acquiescent with English wishes and there were a number of angry meetings of protest. Shortly afterwards the Pope issued an encyclical on liberty which was politically far more ambiguous, as can be seen from a lengthy article on it by R.F.C. in the *Month* (Aug. 1888).

277 *companion*. The Revd. Robert Curtis; see letter of 26 Nov. 1884.

Minchin's Kinematics. George Minchin Minchin, *Uniplanar Kinematics of Solids and Fluids* (1882).

Dana's. Richard Dana (1815–82) was an American lawyer and politician who served aboard a ship in the Pacific in 1834–6 and published his experience in the book *Two Years Before the Mast* (1840).

278 *sonnet . . . with two codas*. 'That Nature is a Heraclitean Fire and of the Comfort of the Resurrection' (OAH, pp. 180–1).

Aubrey de Vere. A poet and critic (1814–1902). He had been converted to Catholicism in 1851 and was Professor of English Literature in the Catholic University. In 1864 he had urged Coventry Patmore, who needed a change of scene, to go on holiday with him to Rome.

281 *patriotic song*. 'What shall I do for the land that bred me?' For tune see p. 284.

branchy between towers. 'Duns Scotus's Oxford' (OAH, p. 142).

sonnet . . . Also another. 'That Nature is a Heraclitean Fire . . .' and 'To what serves Mortal Beauty'.

1200 pages. Charles Doughty, *Travels in Arabia Deserta* (2 vols., 1888).

several reviews. Among them one in the *Athenaeum* (17 Mar. 1888), 334, and one by Sir Richard Burton in the *Academy* (28 July 1888), 47–8. He mentioned the archaism of Doughty's style. GMH seems to have been drawing on the article in the *Saturday Review* (31 Mar. 1888), 391–2, which included, as an example of the book's 'extraordinary' style, 'it seemed the jade might have been, if great had been his chance, another Tiberius Senex'.

282 *tune*. Reproduced LI, p. 284, and J, pp. 491–2 (letter of 25 Sept. 1888).

Mrs. Bambury. See previous letter.

Heraclitean Fire. 'That Nature is a Heraclitean Fire and of the Comfort of the Resurrection'.

other sonnet. 'To what serves Mortal Beauty'.

283 *next month*. Nothing by GMH appeared. See letter of 19 Oct. 1888.

war-song. See previous letter.

284 *sonnet*. 'In Honour of St Alphonsus Rodriguez' (OAH, pp. 182, 387).

287 *'broth of goldish flue'*. 'Harry Ploughman', l. 1.

ὄνομα κύριον. Aristotle, *Poetics*.

288 *Parteen*. Suburb of Limerick.

Addis. Addis had left the Roman Catholic communion and married one of his parishioners. See Biographical Register.

289 *those jokes*. Bridges destroyed the letters in which they appeared.

Daniel. Henry Daniel, whose printing press at Worcester College, Oxford, was used for a number of Bridges's volumes. GMH had joked to Bridges that he was aiming at oblivion by descending into Daniel's Den, an allusion to the fact that Daniel often printed about twenty copies of his works (LI, p. 302).

Dowden . . . never forgive. Edward Dowden (1843–1913). BA Trinity College, Dublin; Professor of English Literature, Trinity College from 1867. His publications included *Shakspere: His Mind and Art* (1875), *A Shakspere Primer* (1877), and a *Life of Shelley* (1886). In July 1894, in an article on 'The Poetry of Robert Bridges' (*Fortnightly Review*), 44–60, Dowden wrote, 'Fr. Hopkins . . . left . . . at my door two volumes by Mr Bridges, and with them a note begging that I would make no acknowledgement of the gift. I did not acknowledge it then; but, with sorrow for a fine spirit lost, I acknowledge it now.'

290 *new sonnet*. 'To R. B.' (OAH, p. 184).

Swinburne has a new volume out. *Poems and Ballads*, third series (1889).

My song. Presumably 'What shall I do for the land that bred me?' but only the melody is extant.

291 *burling Barrow Brown*. 'On the Portrait of Two Beautiful Young People'.

292 *Mary*. Perhaps a relative of his father's living with the family. In Aug. 1877 GMH had written to his father, 'Mary's photographs are of Snowdon, Cadair Idris, and Valle Crucis Abbey . . .'. In 1885 he had sent advice for her about using leeches to ease toothache and in the letter to his father of 3 May 1889 (the letter referred to in the opening sentence) GMH had asked after her and sent his 'best love and wishes'.

Paper. On the Argei, reed dolls thrown into the Tiber by the Vestal Virgins, Pontiffs, and other officials. The significance of the ceremony was disputed. Hopkins's paper is unknown.

INDEX